PRACTICAL TOURISM RESEARCH

CABI TOURISM TEXTS are an essential resource for students of academic tourism, leisure studies, hospitality, entertainment and events management. The series reflects the growth of tourism-related studies at an academic level and responds to the changes and developments in these rapidly evolving industries, providing up-to-date practical guidance, discussion of the latest theories and concepts, and analysis by world experts. The series is intended to guide students through their academic programmes and remain an essential reference throughout their careers in the tourism sector.

Readers will find the books within the CABI TOURISM TEXTS series to have a uniquely wide scope, covering important elements in leisure and tourism, including management-led topics, practical subject matter and development of conceptual themes and debates. Useful textbook features are employed throughout the series, such as case studies, bullet point summaries and helpful diagrams to aid study and encourage understanding of the subject.

Students at all levels of study, workers within tourism and leisure industries, researchers, academics, policy makers and others interested in the field of academic and practical tourism will find these books an invaluable and authoritative resource, useful for academic reference and real world tourism applications.

Titles available

Ecotourism: Principles and Practices
Ralph Buckley

Contemporary Tourist Behaviour: Yourself and Others as Tourists
David Bowen and Jackie Clarke

The Entertainment Industry: An Introduction
Edited by Stuart Moss

Practical Tourism Research
Stephen L.J. Smith

PRACTICAL TOURISM RESEARCH

Stephen L.J. Smith

Department of Recreation and Leisure Studies
University of Waterloo, Ontario,
Canada

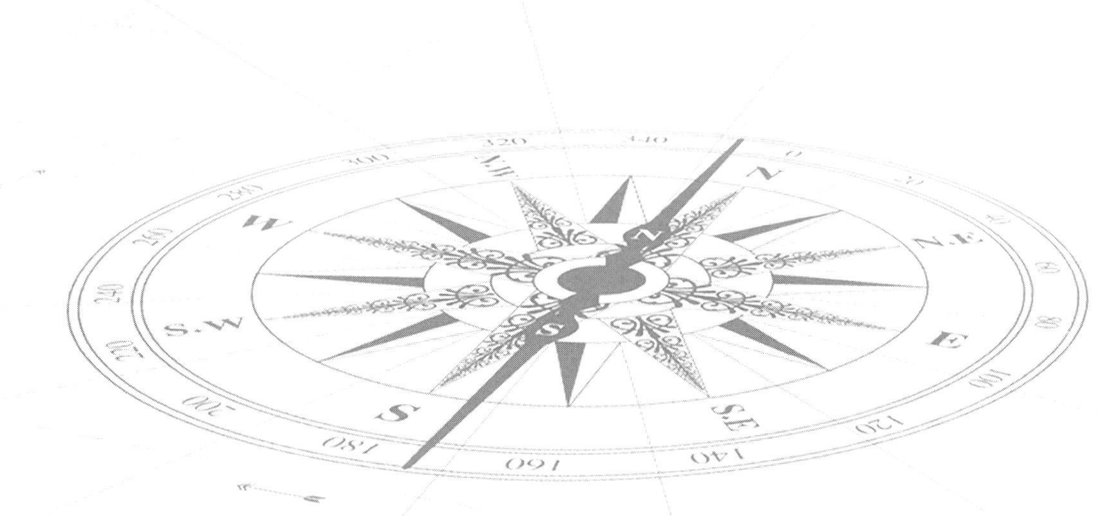

CABI is a trading name of CAB International

CABI Head Office
Nosworthy Way
Wallingford
Oxfordshire OX10 8DE
UK

Tel: +44 (0)1491 832111
Fax: +44 (0)1491 833508
E-mail: cabi@cabi.org
Website: www.cabi.org

CABI North American Office
875 Massachusetts Avenue
7th Floor
Cambridge, MA 02139
USA

Tel: +1 617 395 4056
Fax: +1 617 354 6875
E-mail: cabi-nao@cabi.org

A catalogue record for this book is available from the British Library, London, UK.

Library of Congress Cataloging-in-Publication Data

Smith, Stephen L. J., 1946-
Practical tourism research / Stephen L.J. Smith.
p. cm.
Includes bibliographical references and index.
ISBN 978-1-84593-632-7 (alk. paper)
1. Tourism--Research--Methodology. I. Title.

G155.A1S5697 2010
338.4'791072--dc22

2009041232

ISBN: 978 1 84593 632 7

Commissioning editor: Sarah Hulbert
Production editor: Kate Hill

Typeset by SPi, Pondicherry, India.
Printed and bound in the UK by Cambridge University Press, Cambridge.

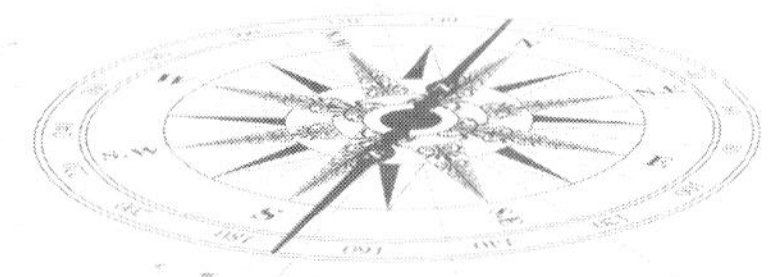

CONTENTS

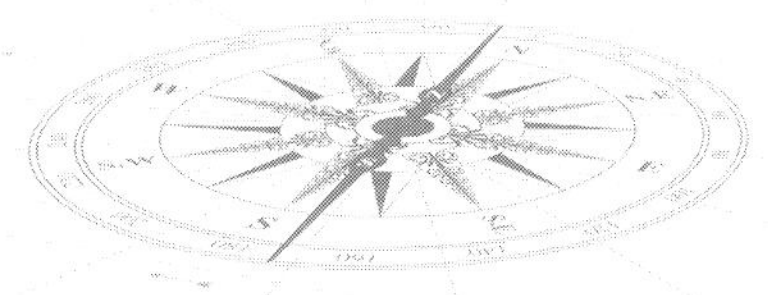

PREFACE

Why should you read this book? In a nutshell: the book will help you do and report tourism research, offer advice on avoiding mistakes and provide practical tips for the new (and more experienced) tourism researcher.

Tourism research is done by many different people for many different reasons. Some do it because it is a requirement to earn a degree from their college or university. Others, such as consultants or government officials, do it because it is part of their job. Some do it because they need to answer questions to assist the making of informed decisions related to policy, planning, marketing or product development. A few, such as your author, do it because we love to do it. Regardless of your motivation, this book is intended to provide you with advice about how to not just survive a tourism research project, but to create something of which you can be proud. I hope you enjoy and learn from the time we will spend together in this book.

This book is based on solid social-science thinking, practice and principles, leavened with three decades of personal experience in conducting research in academic, industry, not-for-profit and governmental environments. Furthermore, the book is written in a style that reflects my personality and voice. What you read reflects how I converse with my students and colleagues. What you are getting here is the authentic Steve Smith personality.

Some of the topics we'll cover are:

- **The nature of research**: we'll begin our journey with some thoughts on the nature of tourism research. Much of the progress in the world – from developing new pharmaceuticals to the marketing of television programmes – is grounded in research. Research can be done well or done badly. This is not just a matter of understanding the technical aspects, but of whether the researcher understands the nature of the research enterprise (itself). We will, in this book, consider the nature of research and what makes it special. We will look at the different ways and contexts in which research can be done. Tourism research, like other research, begins with asking questions. This should be obvious, but some scholars believe that research begins with a world view, an epistemology or a political philosophy. Perhaps for them, this is true. But for me and the majority of 'real world' tourism researchers, research is about discovering new and useful knowledge – answering questions to help decision makers understand social trends, make a destination more competitive, visitors happier, employees more fulfilled and productive, communities better places in which to live, businesses more successful, environments healthier, crises resolved (or avoided) and so on. As is usually the case, the devil (or genius) is in the details. In this vein, here are some of the questions this book attempts to answer:

- What sorts of questions are legitimate or important for you to ask?
- What data are appropriate to answer different questions and how do you access and interpret those data?
- How do you use research by people who have also studied your topic?
- What logic can you use to answer your questions?
- What tools are available to help you interpret the data or evidence you collect?
- How do you avoid bias or error in your conclusions?
- How do you best present the results of your research to an audience or a client?

- **Planning the research project**: after some reflections on the nature of tourism in the first chapter, we turn our attention in the second to how to plan a research project. Although there are many different purposes and styles of doing research, most involve the same tasks:
  - specifying the purpose of research;
  - identifying objectives;
  - reviewing relevant research; and
  - developing a work plan, especially data collection, analysis and communication or reporting strategy.

  This book will give you practical advice about each of these tasks, as well as about different types of research. The chapter will also discuss how to do a literature review, an essential step in most research.
- **Survey design and sampling**: in chapters 3–5 we'll move into the nitty-gritty of designing questionnaires and sampling, and how to conduct and code transcripts from personal interviews and focus groups. The next set of chapters (6–7) looks at the construction and use of indices and scales, other metrics used for assessing tourism marketing performance, and selected business management research tools.
- **Case study and content analysis**: chapters 8–9 describe the logic and procedures used in case studies and content analyses. Case study is a popular technique, but one that is sometimes misunderstood. We'll look in detail at what constitutes a case study research design. The chapter on content analysis considers not only traditional (text-based) content, but also graphic images (including web-based content).
- **Presenting results**: the book concludes with a discussion on presenting your results. The production of a written report is described, of course, as are suggestions for making an oral presentation (somewhat ironically because the medium of communication here is still print). Special attention is paid to how to use that now-standard visual aid, PowerPoint. We will also look at how to prepare posters for presentation at conferences. Poster presentations are becoming more common at tourism research conferences, and guidelines for producing them are included here.
- **Appendix**: the book offers one appendix, an introduction to common statistical tests for tourism research. The appendix will not tell you *how* to do a certain test, but it will provide you with a quick and easy description of what a test is intended to do and generally when to use it. If your professor or supervisor suggests you do a chi square test or you read a reference to ANOVA in a research paper, and you are not certain what the method is, the appendix in this book will help you get a clue or two.

Each of the chapters also offers a variety of focus boxes – short but detailed comments about some topic relevant to the chapter. These focus boxes provide you with 'real world' or practical commentary that will illuminate some aspects of the topics discussed in each chapter.

A few words about what this book is *not* might be helpful. As I alluded to above, this is not a statistics text. There are many excellent texts and websites that will tell you how to conduct various statistical tests. Use them if you need to 'do statistics'. Statistics are certainly useful for tourism researchers, but this book was written in response to a more fundamental and pressing need: basic research design relevant to tourism.

The book does not address forecasting methods. This is a technical issue whose treatment would have greatly increased its length. Moreover, there are several excellent tourism forecasting books already in print. For similar reasons, segmentation is not explored. That topic, too, is the subject of entire books. Moreover, the important issues associated with segmentation go far beyond just research design, and move into marketing strategy and tactics. Forecasting, marketing and segmentation are important enough not to 'diminish' them through offering only a cursory discussion.

In preparation for writing this book, I spoke with numerous colleagues about texts being used in their tourism research courses, and learned that most were dissatisfied. They were all supplementing selected texts with their own materials. I knew the feeling. I had grown dissatisfied with my own *Tourism Analysis* (1995, Longman) as a text and had begun to supplement it with other readings, including material reproduced (with permission of the publisher, Butterworth-Heinemann) from Paul Brunt's excellent *Market Research in Travel and Tourism* (1977).

These comments reassured me that there was room in the market for a new book on research design. And so began a 2-year labour of love. Besides drawing on my own experience and knowledge, I drew from the insights and experiences of colleagues and friends. I identify the people who were influential in the creation of this book in the 'Acknowledgements'.

In addition to Paul Brunt, I want to mention Doug Frechtling, an accomplished tourism economist. I unashamedly used the title of his *Practical Tourism Forecasting* (1996, Butterworth-Heinemann) as the inspiration for this book's title.

Many of the people I mention in the acknowledgements will not know they are listed there until they read the acknowledgements, or even that they were influential in my writing this book. But I know, I honour them and, by reading the acknowledgements, you will know of them, too.

Happy reading and researching!

ACKNOWLEDGEMENTS

Many people have contributed to the writing of this book, some knowingly, others unknowingly. At the risk of missing some – to whom I apologize for any failure of my memory – I'd like to acknowledge the following (in alphabetical order).

From CABI: Nigel Farrar, Publisher, who was the catalyst that started this whole project. Sarah Hulbert was my gracious and professional editor throughout the writing process. I thank both of them.

Research colleagues in academe, government and industry: Conrad Barber-Dueck (Statistics Canada), Paul Brunt (University of Plymouth), Dave Bryanton (Atlantic Canada Opportunities Agency), Heather Clark (Niagara College), Rod Cunningham (McKellar, Cunningham, and Associates), Doug Frechtling (George Washington University), Denisa Georgescu (Parks Canada), Chris Jackson (Statistics Canada), Sarah Khalid (who did the graphics), Jocelyn Lapierre (Statistics Canada), Rob McCloskey (Atlantic Canada Opportunities Agency), Peter McFadden (Waterloo Regional Immigrant Employment Network), Scott Meis (Scott M. Meis and Associates), Laurel Reid (Tourism Synergies Ltd), Wayne Smith (Charleston College) and, especially, Elena Venkova (see the dedication).

I also want to thank my students in Rec 380, 'Tourism Analysis' and my graduate students who helped generate many ideas and questions during our lively discussions of research philosophy and practices. They are too numerous to mention individually, with the exception of Honggen Xiao (now at Hong Kong Polytechnic University). He has become a valued friend and colleague, and a continuing source of intellectual stimulation.

Any errors of omission or commission or any perspectives on research with which you might disagree are my responsibility alone.

This book is dedicated to
Elena Venkova,
my personal muse and cherished wife.

chapter 1

The Nature of Tourism Research

WHY THIS IS IMPORTANT

Tourism is complex, perhaps among the most complex topics in social science. It is a form of human behaviour; a social phenomenon; an economic sector; a policy field; and a source of social, environmental, and economic change. It can create jobs or destroy them. It displaces traditional cultures as well as reinvigorates them. It brings people together as well as divides them.

Researchers who study tourism look at it from many different perspectives, from anthropology to economics. They use many different tools, from participant observation to statistical analysis, to collect and analyse data. They ask many different types of questions, and use the answers for many different types of purposes.

This chapter will introduce you to some of the ways that social scientists think about tourism and how they ask questions about it. A core message of this chapter is that there is no single 'right' way of doing tourism research. However, research can be done well or not so well. Understanding some of the key perspectives – what social scientists call 'paradigms' – is important to help you pose questions that can be answered by research and to design a research plan to provide those answers. Tourism research requires both knowledge you learn through study (which is the purpose of this book) and skills you develop with practice. That is something you have to learn on your own, with guidance from your advisor or teacher.

To begin our journey, we will start with a typically academic question: what is tourism?

WHAT IS TOURISM?

Definitions are something academics like to discuss and debate, not just because of the intellectual fun of debate but because definitions have profound relevance for research. All tourism research is fundamentally shaped by how the researcher defines tourism. The definition may be explicit or implicit, but there is always a definition of tourism somewhere behind every research project. There are many different definitions because the definitions are used for many different purposes. A few of these purposes include monitoring trends in the volume of visitors coming to a destination; identifying markets; planning product development; formulating policy; or outlining the scope of a book or journal.

Researchers sometimes suggest there are two basic ways of defining tourism. One might be called 'supply-side', the other, 'demand-side'. A supply-side definition emphasizes the businesses and other organizations that provide tourism services. A demand-side definition focuses on the people engaged in tourism as consumers. While the supply-side and demand-side distinctions are useful, they miss the full diversity of tourism definitions. Other approaches emphasize tourism as a system (combining supply and demand) or even as a field of study or set of beliefs. Most definitions include, in some form, the notions of demand and supply – the temporary movement of people and sources of services for those people. However, the relative emphasis on these varies and, as you will see in Table 1.1, definitions may include other concepts.

An important definition not included in Table 1.1 is the definition by the World Tourism Organization (UNWTO) (2007). This definition is significant enough to merit separate attention. The World Tourism Organization, a United Nations organization with 157 member

Table 1.1. Examples of tourism definitions.

Definition	Comments
Tourism is a sum of relations and phenomena resulting from the travel and stay of non-residents in as much as this stay does not create a permanent residence (Sessa, 1971, p. 5)	This is an early demand-side definition, emphasizing the concepts of residency and non-residency. It does not address motives of travel beyond the explicit exclusion of travel to change residence. The phrase 'sum of relations and phenomena' is vague
Tourism is the study of man away from his usual habitat, of the industry which responds to his needs, and of the impacts that both he and the industry have on the hosts' socio-cultural economic and physical environments (Jafari, 1977, p. 5)	Jafari developed this definition to explain the scope of a journal he founded, *Annals of Tourism Research*. It expresses a broad conception of tourism – supply, demand and impacts. Note that the definition describes tourism as a field of study
Tourism can be defined as the science, art, and business of attracting and transporting visitors, accommodating them, and graciously catering to their needs and wants (McIntosh and Goeldner, 1977, p. ix)	McIntosh wrote this supply-side definition in a textbook to emphasize tourism as an industry and career choice. Note that it specifies attractions, transport, and accommodation as well as other needs
The tourist industry consists of all those firms, organizations, and facilities which are intended to serve the specific needs and wants of tourists (Leiper, 1979, p. 390)	This is an early supply-side definition emphasizing the sources of services for tourists, whom Leiper defines as 'a person making a discretionary, temporary tourism which involves at least one overnight stay' and excluding any activities to earn money while on the trip

(Continued)

Table 1.1. Continued.

Definition	Comments
Tourism is the amalgam of industries that directly supply goods and services to facilitate business, pleasure, and leisure activities away from the home environment (Canadian National Task Force on Tourism Data, 1989, p. 31)	This Task Force definition was developed to provide a framework to support the collection of tourism statistics, and to emphasize tourism as a form of economic activity to permit comparisons between tourism and other industries. It proposes that tourism be viewed as a 'synthetic' industry – a combination of other industries
Tourism is the set of ideas, the theories, or ideologies for being a tourist, and it is the behaviour of people in touristic roles, when the ideas are put into place (Leiper, 1990, p. 17)	Compare this later definition by Leiper with his earlier one. In this later definition, he has moved away from a supply-side view and describes tourism more abstractly – as a set of ideas. Leiper is now focusing on tourism as an '-ism' (such as 'capitalism' or 'socialism'). Note, he frames tourism in terms of touristic roles
Tourism may be defined as the sum of the phenomena and relationships arising from the interaction of tourists, business suppliers, host governments and host communities in the process of attracting and hosting these tourists and other visitors (McIntosh and Goeldner, 1990, p. 4)	McIntosh has moved from his earlier supply-side definition to this more systemic view of tourism. He implicitly includes not just the provision of services but also activities such as marketing, planning and information services. 'Tourists' refers to temporary visitors staying overnight; 'other visitors' refers to same-day visitors
Tourism itself is an abstraction. It doesn't exist…it is not even a discipline…it is a field made up of many physical, programme and action parts (Gunn and Var, 2002, p. 4)	Gunn and Var offer a provocative view of tourism – that it does not exist in a discrete or tangible way. This view is presented as background to their ideas about tourism planning, noting that such planning must be for specific entities such as attractions or destination regions

nations, has been mandated by the United Nations to collect, analyse, publish, standardize and improve tourism statistics serving the general purposes of international organizations. Its definition thus enjoys official status for the purpose of tourism statistics. UNWTO's definition has been accepted by most national statistical offices as the guide for collecting and reporting on the number of international visitors and the value of their spending. It defines tourism as the activity of people temporarily away from their usual environment for a period not exceeding 1 year, and for virtually any purpose of travel, with the following exceptions: persons visiting a place for the purpose of earning money during their visit and students in long-term programmes (1 year or more, even though they may periodically return home) are not considered to be engaged in tourism. Similarly, members of diplomatic corps and members of the military while travelling in their official capacity are not considered to be engaged in tourism. Also, refugees and nomads are not counted as visitors.

Beyond these exceptions, virtually anyone making a temporary trip away from her or his usual place of residence may be considered to be engaged in tourism. This includes not just people on vacation, but people travelling to see family or friends, travelling for medical purposes, religious purposes, study visits, business meetings or conventions. Those who take tourism trips are called **visitors**; those who stay overnight are called **tourists**; those who return home without spending the night away are called **same-day visitors** (sometimes they are also called excursionists, but this term can be confusing because it is also applied to people taking side-trips during the course of a vacation).

The concept of usual place of residence – sometimes referred to as usual environment – is central to this definition. It means that tourism is something you do when you travel away from where you normally live. So how does a researcher determine when someone has travelled outside their usual environment? The UNWTO notes that each country will develop its own operational definition. There are at least four ways operationally to define usual environment.

The first is to allow travellers to self-define themselves. For example, a researcher might simply ask, 'How many trips did you take out of town last month?' There is some appeal in allowing respondents to decide themselves whether they took a trip to outside their usual environment, but this approach has a couple of disadvantages. Respondents may ask, 'What do you mean by "out of town"?' This will often be the case when the respondent lives in a place where two or more different municipalities are immediately contiguous to each other. In other words, should a person walking only 100 m from one city into its neighbouring city and who thus technically has left town (with respect to the city where she lives) be considered to have taken a tourism trip? Not likely. Then there is the problem of people who live in rural areas, not 'towns'. Moreover, it is impossible to make reliable comparisons of tourism behaviour among individuals or populations because there is no assurance that respondents are defining the concept in comparable ways.

Another approach is to use trip frequency. You might argue that any destination you visit at least once per month over the course of a year is part of your usual environment. This approach, too, is logical. If you visit a place frequently, regardless of how far away it is, it could reasonably be considered to be part of your usual environment. However, this approach also has inherent limitations. In particular, it does not address the question of how a destination should be defined – that is, is it a business, a neighbourhood, a city, a province or state, or even a nation? On the other hand, if you visited a museum only once that is only 5 km from your home in a part of town you normally never visit, is it outside your usual environment?

You might use a legal boundary such as a national border (this is conceptually similar to the notion of 'going out of town'). Indeed, the boundary approach defines international visitors. However, the boundary approach may not work well when applied to domestic tourism. City boundaries are often just a political construction rather than a behavioural or social reality. Adjacent counties or regions often do not represent truly different environments and you might not even notice the border when you cross it. Provincial or state borders are more likely to represent different environments, but there is still much intra-provincial travel that does not match what researchers (or marketers) would consider to be truly tourism. Intra-provincial travel can also be an important form of tourism on which many businesses depend, so excluding intra-provincial travel is not wise.

Finally, you can use a distance threshold, defining any trip beyond a specified distance to be tourism. While the choice of a distance threshold is arbitrary, the use of distance has some advantages. The choice of an appropriate threshold could represent what you consider to be a reasonable approximation of your usual environment. The use of distance ensures statistical consistency across populations and jurisdictions, and over time. Distance thresholds also avoid the debate about the nature and scale of destinations.

However defined, tourism may be classified into six forms: three that are basic and three that are combinations of the basic forms. **Domestic** tourism refers to trips taken by a person in the country where he or she lives. If you take a trip in the country where you live, you are

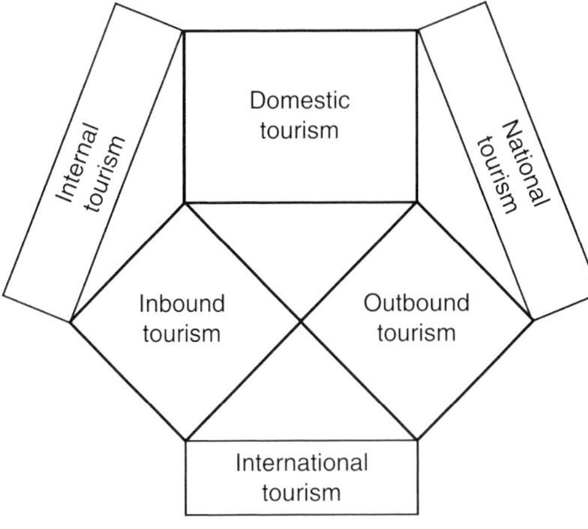

Fig. 1.1. Forms of tourism.

engaged in domestic tourism. If you leave the country where you live to visit another country, you are engaged in **outbound** tourism (from the perspective of your country). The country you are visiting will consider you to be an **inbound** tourist. The process of crossing borders – both inbound and outbound – represents **international** tourism. A key concept in each definition is the country of residence. Your citizenship is not an issue in determining what form of tourism you are engaged in; the issue is where you live. Thus, a person who is a citizen of the USA but living in Canada would be considered by the USA to be an international visitor when he travels to the USA. He would not be a domestic visitor in the USA, because he does not live there even though he is a citizen of the USA.

Two other forms of tourism are recognized by the UNWTO, although these terms are not widely used. **National** tourism refers to all the tourism trips made by the residents of a given country, whether domestically or to other countries. **Internal** tourism refers to all the tourism trips made in a given country, whether by visitors coming from another country or by residents of that county. Figure 1.1 describes these combinations.

Case Study 1.1, which is included at the end of this chapter, describes the evolution of Canada's operational definition of tourism.

IS TOURISM AN INDUSTRY?

The UNWTO definition views tourism from the demand-side. Tourism is something people do; it is not something businesses produce. Because an industry is a set of businesses that produce essentially the same product using essentially the same technology, tourism cannot be considered to be an industry. Industries are identified by their core product, and are officially identified in Systems of National Accounts when their output is sufficiently large to merit monitoring by the government. Industries in any nation are categorized by Standard Industrial Classification systems that are a hierarchical listing of industries at various levels of generality. Here is a simple example of the hierarchical structure of an industry classification system (this one is based on a small part of the manufacturing sector as classified in the North American Industrial Classification System (NAICS), the system used by Canada, Mexico and the USA). The numbers preceding each category are the NAICS codes for that industry:

3 Manufacturing.
- 311 Food manufacturing.
  - 3114 Fruit and vegetable preserving and specialty food manufacturing.
    - 311410 Frozen food manufacturing.

The concept of an industry is like a telescope in that it can be extended, to view a large set of economic activities, or contracted, to examine more precisely a short list, depending on your interests. It should be noted that industries are born and they may die. Just over a century ago, there was no motor vehicle manufacturing industry (although, to be pedantic, there were no

Standard Industrial Classification systems 100 years ago, either). On the other hand, there was a buggy manufacturing industry but, over time, it was replaced by motor vehicle industry.

Returning to the question of whether tourism is an industry, the goods and services used by visitors in the course of their making tourism trips are so diverse they cannot be meaningfully thought of as being produced by a single industry. There is no logical way to think of, for example, accommodation services and air travel as being products of the same industry. However, while there is no single tourism industry, there are numerous **tourism industries**. These are industries that would cease to exist or whose output would be substantially reduced if there were no tourism. These services include accommodation, transportation, food services, recreation and entertainment (especially attractions), travel trade services (such as tour operators and travel agencies) and convention services. Collectively, these goods and services are referred to as **tourism commodities**. Thus, tourism commodities are those goods and services that would be produced only at substantially reduced levels in the absence of tourism.

In principle, one can estimate the size of a synthetic or 'statistical tourism industry' by combining the outputs of all individual tourism industries. However, there are some dilemmas if you try to do that. First, not all tourism commodities (the goods and services produced by tourism industries) are consumed by visitors. Some are consumed by people engaged in non-tourism activities. For example, restaurants are a tourism industry, but many people eating in restaurants are local residents. Visitors also spend on non-tourism commodities, such as books or sunscreen. Further, tourism commodities can be produced by different tourism industries as well as by non-tourism industries. Meals are prepared and sold by airlines and hotels, not just restaurants. Furthermore, department stores might also offer tourism commodities such as a restaurant, car rental services or a travel agency as part of their services. Table 1.2 illustrates this complex pattern. The columns represent tourism and non-tourism industries; the rows are tourism and non-tourism commodities. The examples in each cell illustrate types of commodities consumed by visitors. Remember, each of these could also be purchased by a non-visitor.

In order to estimate the contribution of tourism to an economy, you need to identify how much of the revenues in each tourism industry is due to visitors and how much to non-visitors. You also need to estimate how much visitors spend on goods and services produced by non-tourism industries. This is not easy. A method that has been developed to do this is known as the **Tourism satellite account** or TSA (see Focus Box 1.1). The term 'satellite' has nothing to do with outer space. It refers to the fact that these accounts are a satellite of (or an annex to) a country's System of National Accounts – the accounts that describe the input and output of all economic activity in a country. The ratio between the total value of the output of an industry and the output consumed by people engaged in tourism is known as the tourism ratio.

Table 1.2. Commodity and industry patterns in tourism.

	Tourism industries	**Non-tourism industries**
Tourism commodities	Hotel rooms Motor coach transportation Restaurant meals	Department store restaurants Department store travel agencies University field trips
Non-tourism commodities	Long-distance telephone services in hotels Branded T-shirts sold by theme restaurants Duty-free shopping on board aircraft	Travel insurance sold by insurance companies Sunscreen sold by drug stores Travel books sold by book stores

Focus Box 1.1. Tourism satellite accounts (TSAs).

Traditionally, tourism statistics focused on the profiles and numbers of visitors. While some estimates of the economic magnitude of tourism were occasionally made, these estimates were often unreliable and not comparable to statistics on the economic magnitude of traditional industries. Although tourism is fundamentally a consumption phenomenon, governments need to understand not only the magnitude of tourism as an economic sector but also how tourism demand and supply are linked (in the context of a TSA, 'supply' refers to the total output of a tourism industry). Moreover, tourism consumption is not limited to a set of predefined goods and services. What makes tourism consumption distinct is that it is defined by the context in which the consumption occurs – it is made in support of temporary trips outside a person's usual environment. A key task, then, in measuring tourism is to be able to track the portion – and only the portion – of the supply and demand of consumer goods and services associated with tourism trips.

The concept of satellite accounts was introduced in 1991 to the tourism field at the UNWTO International Conference on Travel and Tourism Statistics in Ottawa, Canada. French statisticians had developed the original concept of satellite accounts as a way of measuring aspects of a national economy not captured in traditional Systems of National Accounts, such as volunteer work and education. Canadian statisticians built on this work, extending the concept to tourism. Statistics Canada published the world's first TSA in 1994.

TSAs are basically a set of definitions and tables that are formulated in a logical way that is consistent with Systems of National Accounts (large matrices that report the economic activity in a nation's industries). When fully developed, TSA tables describe:

- expenditures on tourism commodities by consumers, reported by domestic, inbound and outbound tourism trips by type of commodity;
- the value of the production of tourism commodities by type of industry and type of commodity;
- net value added by tourism activity (contributions to national Gross Domestic Product);
- jobs created;
- gross fixed capital formation (the value of investment in assets such as improvements to land, buildings (including second homes), machinery and equipment (including aircraft, cruise vessels, motor coaches, railway coaches and passenger watercraft);
- expenditures on collective consumption, such as visitor information bureaux, collection of tourism statistics, control and regulation of tourism businesses, visa and passport controls and special civil defence services provided to protect visitors; remember, though, that such spending is not considered as being *tourism* expenditures; and
- other visitor measures, such as numbers of arrivals and departures, length of stay, visitors' choices of accommodation and modes of transportation, and numbers of firms providing tourism services.

Some examples of tourism ratios for selected tourism commodities may be seen in Table 1.3. The table shows revenues from visitors (labelled 'Tourism Demand') as well as total revenues (labelled 'Total Demand'). The **tourism ratio** is simply tourism demand divided by total demand.

The magnitudes of tourism ratios vary, reflecting different degrees of importance of visitors to the businesses in each industry. These ratios are national averages, based on total annual output. The portion of any individual business's income from visitors can differ greatly from these averages. A locally owned coffee shop located in a predominantly residential section of

Table 1.3. Tourism ratios: Canada, 2006 (from Statistics Canada, 2007).

Commodity	Tourism demand (million CA$)	Total demand (million CA$)	Tourism ratio (%)
Passenger air transport	12,806	13,486	95.0
Vehicle rental	1,592	2,334	68.2
Vehicle fuel	6,793	31,642	21.5
Accommodation	10,631	11,691	90.9
Food and beverage	9,895	49,657	19.9
Recreation and entertainment	4,816	21,668	22.2
Travel agency services	3,257	3,277	99.4
Convention fees	222	243	91.4

a town may earn nothing from visitors, while an internationally branded restaurant located in a resort town might earn virtually 100% of its revenues from visitors. None the less, the ratios provide an indication of the extent to which each industry depends on tourism. As you can see, passenger air travel, accommodation services, travel agency services and convention fees are almost 'pure' tourism, whereas tourism is less important as a source of revenue for food services, vehicle fuel and recreation and entertainment services.

An important implication of UNWTO's definition of tourism is that certain types of expenditures someone might think are tourism are, in fact, not tourism. As, we have seen, the UNWTO definition defines tourism as activities by people on a trip (and certain activities undertaken prior to making a trip, such as buying a tour package). Spending by businesses, governments and other organizations in support of tourism, while very important in making tourism trips possible, is not considered to be tourism spending. Thus, spending by airlines to buy or lease aircraft; governments to collect tourism statistics or to operate national parks; airport authorities to build or expand airports; development companies to build hotels; or destination marketing organizations to market tourism are not tourism expenditures. The scope of tourism, as an economic sector, is limited to the activities of visitors. It does not include spending by businesses or agencies in support of tourism.

A LOOK AT TOURISM RESEARCH

Some general perspectives

Tourism research – as all research – is about asking and answering questions. There are many different types of questions and many ways of answering them. Our focus in this book is on research questions, not on questions generally. A research question is characterized by three qualities:

- Research questions involve the creation of new knowledge. If your question can be answered by looking through a book or doing an Internet search, it is not a research question.

- Research questions should be answerable. The answer may be tentative or incomplete, but it should be possible at least to begin to answer it. Questions arising in philosophy, metaphysics, ethics or religion, such as 'why was I born?' are usually not research questions. These can be important questions but they cannot be answered by research. Questions that start with 'why...?' often are not research questions. Research questions more typically start with 'how', 'how many', 'where' or 'what'.
- Research questions are answered through collecting and analysing data. The answers many people have to questions about the meaning of life and other philosophical issues are not based on the collection and analysis of data. Ideally, the collection and analysis of data should be done and reported in such a way that an independent researcher could replicate your findings – or at least, he or she could follow the logic of how you answered the question.

Research questions may also be contrasted with management questions or problems. Questions that managers often face have very different qualities to research questions. These include the following:

- Management problems tend to be complex, broad issues with multiple facets. As a result, they may not have simple answers.
- Management problems often are not expressed in a way that immediately suggests researchable questions. Indeed, many management problems are not answerable by research. They require other tactics or strategies.
- Management problems are often sparked by a crisis, either internally generated or externally imposed. As a result, managers usually look for solutions that are quick to develop and implement; they are also concerned about the costs of acquiring or implementing the answer to the problem.
- Some solutions to management problems may be financially, socially or politically problematic. Moreover, the implementation of a solution may require moral courage, political connections or a strong base of support within the organization.

For those management questions that can be answered by research, you, as a researcher, need to consider several things. The nature of the management problem must be well understood by both the manager and you, the researcher. You need to be able to reframe the problem as a question you, as a researcher, can answer. A valuable skill for any researcher is to be able to help a manager reformulate a general sense of a problem into something that can be addressed in a practical way. The quality of data on which the answer will be developed is essential, but the data and subsequent analysis must be affordable and produced in a timely way. You will find practical guidelines for planning and conducting research projects elsewhere in this book.

Beyond the immediate benefit of answering questions, research can help managers and decision makers in tourism agencies, organizations and businesses base their decisions on empirical information. If seen as credible, research can help a decision maker overcome dysfunctional personal biases, and resist political pressure. For example, political officials, especially in smaller jurisdictions, may have personal agendas related to remaining in office or returning political favours that could lead to marketing decisions that do not adequately meet market demands. For example, sometimes managers are pressured by elected officials to use tourism marketing budgets to reward advertising firms for political support, regardless of the merit of the firms as tourism marketers. Politicians sometimes do not want to cooperate with adjacent jurisdictions either as a matter of ego or out of a misplaced sense of competition, even if visitors do not see the two different jurisdictions as distinct destinations. In other words, market realities may dictate cooperation in tourism marketing – a conclusion that can be gleaned from properly conducted research – but such cooperation has to overcome personal and political biases. Unfortunately, having research data alone does not always allow you to convince someone to change his or her mind if his or her decisions are based on non-empirical criteria. Making bad managerial decisions based on emotions is ultimately not a research question.

A few other challenges faced by some tourism researchers include the following. Some industry practitioners automatically dismiss research as 'ivory tower' or not practical for decisions in the real world. This can be true of some academic research, but it is not an accurate characterization of all research. At other times, research will be dismissed as being 'too general'. In other words, the level of data collection and analysis is done at a high level, such as at a national perspective, and does not reflect local conditions. This is a common problem with research conducted by government agencies. Unfortunately, the only solution to making research more specific or precise is to increase significantly the budget available for larger samples and more detailed analyses. This is rarely an option.

Research is also sometimes criticized as being 'historic' or backward-looking. This refers to the fact that much data collection focuses on past behaviour or business experiences. Examining what happened in the past is needed to understand the impacts of tourism, but businesses usually want forward-looking information. They would like answers to questions such as what are the forces that will affect their business success in the coming season. Or, what changes are coming in air capacity to a destination? Or, what is the competition planning for next year? Such questions can sometimes be answered through the use of tools known as **leading indicators**, which we will look at later in this book.

Types of tourism research

Research can be classified several different ways. Brunt (1997, p. 2), for example, suggests the following classification based on who initiates a project and how the project is managed:

Pure research: research undertaken for academic interest or in the pursuit of a university degree. Its emphasis is on generating knowledge, not solving practical problems. The researcher is in control of the research project, and usually selects the topic solely on the basis of their curiosity. The researcher is normally free to publish the results in a journal or present them at a conference.

Action research: research undertaken to solve practical problems. The research is usually conducted as a partnership between the researcher and a client concerned with the problem. Control of the research project typically is shared between the researcher and the party who will use the results. The subject of research is usually defined by the client; the client also often has control over the release of any results. The project may be initiated by either the researcher or the client.

Consultancy: research commissioned by a client or organization. The researcher may have to compete with other researchers for the project by submitting a formal proposal, and works with the client under terms specified by a legally binding contract. The results are usually never published because such research is often commercially valuable or politically sensitive. There are two other types of research that can be added to Brunt's list:

Workplace research: research conducted internally by employees of an organization. In this situation, you may be assigned a specific research task, and might work as part of a team. More senior analysts in an organization may identify potential research projects that would be of benefit to their employer and then either do the research themselves or assign it to one of their staff. While some tourism organizations, especially government agencies and larger destination-marketing organizations, might have job positions labelled as 'researcher' or 'analyst', employees who have other job titles will often be assigned research projects to complete. In other words, 'tourism research' is more likely to be one of many responsibilities you will have on a job rather than have as part of your job title.

'Delay research': this type of research may sound like a sarcastic classification, but it can be a reality. Delay research occurs when a manager is hesitant about making a decision because of the potential consequences or when someone in authority needs to be seen taking action but is uncertain about what to do. In such circumstance, he might say, 'We need more research'. Certainly, more research is sometimes needed before making a decision, but at other times the decision maker 'just' requires courage and wisdom – not research. If you are employed as a researcher and you find yourself being directed to undertake research that appears to have the sole purpose of delaying a decision, you have the delicate challenge of discussing the matter with your supervisor and suggesting, if possible, that more time and money spent on research may not be an appropriate action. Research can provide information, but it cannot provide wisdom and courage. However, it can, regrettably, be a delaying tactic.

A different way of classifying research is to look at its functions – the fundamental purposes of research. In this context, 'function' refers to basic perspectives of research rather than the intended application of or motivation for doing research. These basic functions are description, explanation and prediction.

Description: description refers to research that seeks better to identify or measure what exists. The questions asked in descriptive research often use phrases such as 'how many' and 'where'. Although 'descriptive research' is sometimes used as a pejorative phrase, accurate, timely and relevant description is fundamental to most research. Moreover, descriptive research in tourism is not necessarily simple. Even a question as basic as how many people visited your city last year can be difficult to answer accurately.

Explanation: explanatory research is undertaken to understand how a pattern or phenomenon you have described has developed. For example, once you have been able to estimate how many people visited your city, you may want to understand the forces that influence the number of people who come to your city, and the reasons the number increased or decreased from the year before.

Although the distinction between description and explanation appears clear, it can be fuzzy in practice. For example, if the number of visitors to your city decreased from one year to the next, and you observed that the city's tourism marketing budget had been cut, you might conclude that the budget cuts were the cause of the decline. On the other hand, your attempt to explain some observation can run deeper than an immediately obvious answer. In other words, you might observe that the tourism marketing budget was cut and the number of visitors to the city dropped. However, you have yet to explain why reduced spending on marketing caused a decline in visitor numbers.

A deeper explanation of the reason for the drop in visitor numbers would address more fully the connection between the marketing budget and the number of visitor arrivals, and whether there are other factors that influence visitor numbers. You might also want address the reasons for the marketing budget cutback. Perhaps the budget was cut after the election of city councillors who were hostile to tourism. If so, then the 'real' reason visitors numbers fell was because of a change in municipal politics. But then you might want to look at the reasons for anti-tourism councillors being elected.

The questions about causes could continue in a very long chain. The point here is that an explanation may be viewed simply as a more elaborate form of description. One could spend a long time exploring the links of causes and effects, with each level of explanation viewed as a description.

Prediction: predictive research is the attempt to forecast what will happen in the future (forecasting and prediction can be treated as synonymous, although some researchers use 'prediction' as a general term and limit 'forecasting' to the use of statistical models). Forecasting is a complex task and is largely beyond the scope of this book. However, a few words about basic forecasting approaches will be useful. Forecasting methods may be classified as either empirical (sometimes called quantitative) or subjective (sometimes called qualitative). Frechtling (1996) notes that forecasting tools in empirical forecasting models range from simple extrapolations of past trends (which ignore explanations of the causes of change) to more sophisticated statistical modelling that attempts to express the reasons for change as one or more equations, using historical data to calibrate the equations.

The two important subjective forecasting tools in tourism are the **Delphi method** and the **consumer intentions survey**. These are described as subjective or qualitative methods because they use opinions rather than mathematics to generate forecasts. The Delphi method is a formal, structured process for soliciting the opinions of a panel of experts and working with them to reach a consensus about some aspect of the future. The consumer intentions survey asks a sample of people in some origin market (such as another province or state) about their intentions to visit your destination. The results of a consumer intentions survey are actually statistical tabulations of the opinions of consumers, so they represent a combination of both empirical (quantitative) and subjective (qualitative) approaches. Consumer intentions can be a useful leading indicator of future levels of visitation, although travel intentions are not a very precise predictor of actual visitor levels.

Coming back to the functions of research, some researchers identify a fourth function, **prescription**, also called **action research**. As we have already noted, action research is research undertaken in partnership with a client to solve a specific problem. It can also be referred to as 'prescriptive research' because the objective is to prescribe a solution for some problem. However, it is not truly a function of research in the same sense as description, explanation and prediction. Instead, action research employs one or more of these functions. The primary distinction of action research is that it concludes with a set of recommendations for actions, policies or other things that will solve the problem being studied. Action research is better thought of as a context for doing research than a distinct function of research.

Still another classification of tourism research reflects basic value perspectives on tourism. This classification system was first proposed by Jafari (1992). He describes his classifications as four platforms for doing research. These platforms represent a form of intellectual history of perspectives on tourism. As such, the emergence of these different perspectives can also be envisioned as a type of intellectual debate about how to study tourism.

Advocacy platform: this type of research is done by researchers who fundamentally value tourism as a positive force, particularly as a contributor to the economy of a destination, and undertake research to help further the benefits of tourism. This work focuses on questions related to measuring the economic benefits of tourism, or at identifying new product opportunities or markets for a destination to pursue. This type of research usually involves description, explanation and some forecasting.

Cautionary platform: eventually, researchers began to be aware of the negative effects of tourism. Their work raises cautions or questions about the costs of tourism. These costs are not necessarily financial (although they can be); rather, they refer to environmental or social problems created by tourism in a destination or, more generally, as a form of international trade. This type of research, too, usually involves description, explanation and some forecasting.

Adaptancy platform: the debates between the proposition (or thesis) that tourism is a 'passport' to growth (advocacy platform) and its antithesis of tourism as a source of social and environmental problems (cautionary platform) led to the development of a 'synthesis' – the third platform, adaptancy. Researchers working from the viewpoint of this platform acknowledge that tourism offers both benefits and imposes costs. Their work concentrates on how to optimize benefits while either avoiding or ameliorating the costs. This type of research typically is action research, prescribing strategies to achieve the goals desired by the client or seen as important by the researcher.

Science platform: the most recent platform to have emerged is the 'science' platform. This type of research is usually empirical (a term we will discuss later in this chapter) and politically neutral. Tourism is looked at as a phenomenon worthy of study in its own right, and not necessarily as a force to be promoted, thwarted or controlled. Examples of this type of work include efforts to develop more precise measures of the magnitude of tourism – visitors, jobs and so on – in a destination without the judgement of whether the number is too high or too low.

THINKING ABOUT THINKING: SOME BASIC DEFINITIONS

The previous section described different ways of classifying research and different contexts in which research is done. We will now look, in more detail, at how researchers think – how they look at the world, frame their questions and organize their thoughts. Let us start with a few definitions. Our look at the following terms will be brief, just to introduce you to some key ideas about each term. Entire books have been written about each of these, exploring the concepts in great detail.

Induction and deduction

Researchers generally use two broad types of logic in their work. Induction (or inductive reasoning) is arguably the most common. It refers to the collection of specific pieces of information or the observation of specific events, from which general conclusions are derived. Induction tends to be open-ended in that it is exploratory, with the conclusions emerging only as the research unfolds.

Deduction begins with a set of concepts or models that suggest testable hypotheses or predictions. The hypotheses are then tested or the predictions made, and the results assessed to confirm or reject the hypotheses or the accuracy of the forecast.

Induction and deduction appear to be opposites; indeed, the 'feel' of the logic of each is quite different. However, induction and deduction are part of a cycle of research. You might begin collecting specific information on some tourism phenomenon that eventually allows you to create a model or to make a statement about some general processes regarding the phenomenon (inductive reasoning). These statements can then be formulated as hypotheses for further testing (deductive reasoning). The results of the deductive process might then lead you into further inductive research to further refine your ideas, which can then be retested. Induction and deduction thus become part of a cycle that, you hope, will lead to greater and more accurate insights into some tourism phenomenon.

Models

Tourism researchers frequently use models to describe how they believe some aspect of tourism operates or functions. These models may be mathematical in the form of a set of interrelated equations, but more commonly they are graphic – often a drawing with boxes and lines connecting the boxes, although other types of graphic presentations are possible. Models have a number of characteristics that affect their usefulness in tourism research.

Models simplify. They are a way of representing some tourism entity, function or phenomenon in a way that the essential features can be easily grasped. However, this simplification means that models are incomplete. Including every detail and permutation of a real-world tourism phenomenon would make the model impossible to use for research. The value of simplification can be seen in, for example, Butler's (1980) resort life cycle model (see Fig. 1.2) that describes how resort areas rise and decline. The model is basically a classic growth curve such as that originally developed in biology – an S-shaped curve on a standard *X–Y* graph, where the *Y*-axis represents the number of visitors and the *X*-axis represents time. Different stretches along the curve are associated with different types of tourist, from explorers to mass market. The model does not include many other variables that could be important in understanding the evolution of destinations, such as total revenues, visitor satisfaction, resort profitability and various impact measures.

The model has been used by many researchers who have found it a useful conceptual tool because the model is simple and permits modification or adaptation. This is another characteristic of models – they can be easily modified. In the case of the resort life cycle model, researchers are free to use whatever time frame (the *X*-axis) makes sense to them. Similarly, researchers can use whatever scale of visitor numbers on the *Y*-axis they choose, or even change the *Y*-axis to profitability or some other characteristic. The precise shape of the curve is also not specified, permitting further experimentation and modification.

In brief, models allow you to describe some aspect of tourism clearly, and to play with ways of changing your description to explore alternative structures or relationships.

Hypotheses

The word hypothesis sometimes is used casually to mean speculation, but in research it has a more formal meaning. It refers to a statement of a possible relationship between variables that is formulated for testing. This proposed relationship is based on previous research findings or on a relationship suggested by a model. When hypotheses are subject to statistical testing, they are often (but not

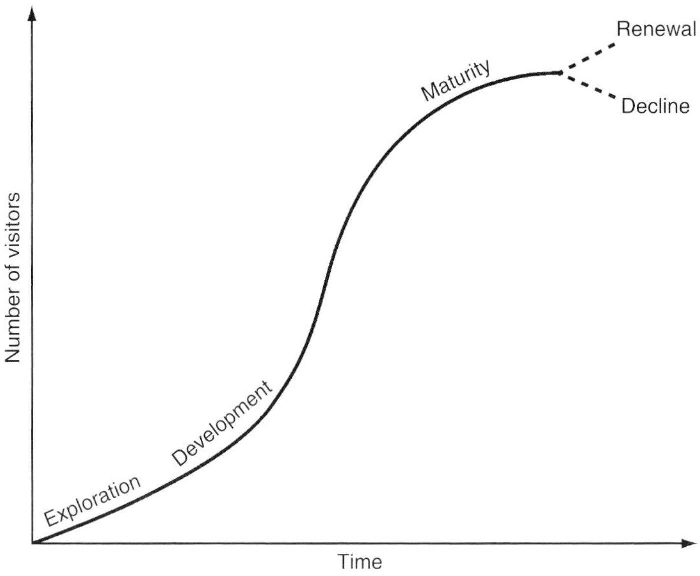

Fig. 1.2. The resort life cycle model.

always) worded as a 'null hypothesis'; that is, they are worded to state the suggestion that there is no relationship between the two variables. This may sound perverse, but there is a logic here, based on the concept of error. In the case of hypothesis testing, there are two types of error: Type I and Type II. These are not very descriptive names, so they are better described in the following way.

A **Type I error** is a false positive. In other words, you conclude something is true when, in fact, it is not. For example, if a woman takes a home pregnancy test and the test indicates she is pregnant, but she really is not – that's a false positive. A **Type II error** is a false negative – the conclusion that something is not true when, in fact, it is. If a man goes in for a paternity test and the test reveals he is not the father, but in fact, he is – that's a false negative.

Researchers generally want to avoid a Type I error more than a Type II error. If you are going to make an error in testing a hypothesis, it is usually safer if you conclude there is no relationship even when there is one, than to conclude a relationship exists when, in fact, it does not. Stating your hypotheses as null hypotheses minimizes your chances of making a Type I error. In other words, you are more likely to conclude there is no particular pattern or relationship in the data you are studying when there is one, than to conclude that a relationship exists when one does not exist. (You may need to read this paragraph a couple of times to think that point through!)

Statistical tests for null hypotheses are given thresholds of **probability** to minimize the chances that what we conclude from the test is due to accident. Tourism researchers traditionally work with a probability of 0.05 (or one chance in 20). There is nothing special about using 0.05 – it is just tradition. Some researchers choose to be more conservative and use a threshold of 0.01 – one chance in 100. The choice depends on how serious the results of any errors would be. For tourism marketing, for example, the chance of one-in-20 error is probably quite acceptable. However, in the case of testing a new drug, a one-in-20 error that a new drug causes cancer is unacceptably high.

Let's consider the value of 0.05. If you set the threshold for your null hypothesis test at 0.05, it means that if the results of your statistical tests have a probability of 0.05 or lower, there is only one chance in 20 (or lower) that the pattern you are seeing is due to chance. You thus reject the null hypothesis of no relationship, which means you have evidence that a relationship exists. Remember, though, there is still one chance in 20 that your conclusion of a relationship existing is wrong. Another way of thinking about this is that if you are testing 20 different hypotheses and the statistical tests all have a probability of 0.05, on average you could expect that at least one of those tests is wrong.

Theory

Theory is a word with many different definitions. In academe, the term usually has the connotation of something of broad importance. However, in practice, the word is often used vaguely or loosely by tourism researchers. In fact, it is used in so many different ways, that – unless a writer/speaker carefully defines the term – you may not be certain how the word is being used or whether the word means anything at all.

In the natural sciences, a theory is a formal, explicit description of some aspect of reality that has been determined to provide repeatable and falsifiable (testable) predictions. The purposes of a theory are both to explain how a phenomenon functions and to make predictions about unknown aspects of that phenomenon. Scientific theories are subject to revisions as new data become available or when a prediction logically based on the theory repeatedly fails.

Calling something a theory in the scientific tradition does not mean that the set of propositions are only hypothetical or speculative. Rather, a theory has been rigorously tested and provides accurate predictions. The propositions may continue to be called a theory for years because scientists understand that they can never be 100% certain about the accuracy of their propositions. However, it is incorrect to think that if something is 'only' a theory, it has questionable accuracy. A theory typically builds on pre-existing theories, although it may replace those earlier theories; it is supported by many lines of interconnected evidence, often incorporating other theories. Scientists developing theories try to keep the theory as parsimonious – simple – as possible while still explaining the phenomenon being studied. This latter point is known as '**Occam's razor**' test. Occam was a 14th century logician who proposed that any explanation of a phenomenon should make as few assumptions and be as simple as possible. This is sometimes expressed as the notion that if several explanations of a phenomenon are possible, the simplest one is probably the correct one.

The word 'theory', as noted, though, is used in many other ways. In mathematics, it refers to a set of definitions, axioms (self-evident truths or assumptions), theorems (propositions that have been proved true through deductive logic) and techniques that are related to each other such as game theory or network theory. In the arts, it refers to a set of accepted principles guiding how the arts should be created or expressed, such as music theory. Social scientists often use the term to refer to thinking that reflects a systematic logic that includes a set of principles and a conceptual model describing how various phenomena relate to each other, regardless of whether these relationships are supported by empirical evidence. The term is sometimes used to mean what might be better described as ideology in the sense of a set of beliefs and values, as in 'feminist theory'. Grounded theory, a term that first appeared in psychology, is not a theory in any of these senses discussed here, but refers to a research method (more about this later).

'Theory' is also used to refer to a set of beliefs based on experience that someone believes to represent a valid interpretation of past events, such as 'I'm offering lower prices in the shoulder season on the theory that visitors like a bargain'. Or, even more casually, 'theory' refers to a conjecture made without adequate evidence, which is virtually the opposite of how scientists use the term. Table 1.4 summarizes a typology of the uses of the term 'theory' in tourism research, based on my review of articles referring to theory in the three leading tourism journals: *Annals of Tourism Research*, *Journal of Travel Research* and *Tourism Management*.

Table 1.4. A typology of 'theory' in tourism.

Category	Brief description	Additional comments
Theory of the first type	'Traditional' theory of the form found in economics or the natural sciences	Type 1 theory is based on substantial empirical evidence and integrated with other theories that address connected phenomena. It is based on falsifiable hypotheses. Generally, only one theory can exist at any one time. The repeated failure of hypotheses derived from a theory indicates the theory is probably false and needs to be refined or replaced. However, this type of theory has significantly declined in tourism research
Theory of the second type	Theory is synonymous with an a priori, usually empirical, model	Type 2 theory is also based on substantial empirical evidence, but may or may not be integrated with other theories that address connected phenomena. It, too, is based on falsifiable hypotheses. Multiple theories describing the same phenomena may exist simultaneously

(Continued)

Table 1.4. Continued.

Category	Brief description	Additional comments
Theory of the third type	Theory is equated with statistical analysis	Type 3 theory is a statistical model used for description, explanation or prediction. However, the model is ad hoc – not tied to or based on an explicit, formal conceptual foundation or theory – nor is it integrated with a larger conceptual framework. These theories typically produce falsifiable hypotheses. This type of theory would be better labelled 'model'
Theory of the fourth type	Theory is an untested/ untestable verbal or graphic model	Type 4 theory is similar to Type 2 theory in that it represents a conceptual model used for description or explanation. It differs from Type 2 theory, however, in that the models are not or cannot be expressed in ways that are falsifiable. They tend to be verbal, but may also be supported by graphic representations. This type of theory, too, would be better labelled 'model' or 'concept'
Theory of the fifth type	Epistemology as theory	Type 5 theory is a formally articulated way of looking at the world that lacks falsifiable hypotheses. It presents propositions that shape the type of questions asked, information collected and how observations are interpreted. However, such research is ultimately subjective and cannot be independently verified. This type of theory should be labelled 'epistemology', 'paradigm' or 'research design', not 'theory'
Theory of the sixth type	Grounded theory	Type 6 theory involves the derivation of themes arising from a structured, sequential, subjective coding of interview transcripts. Findings of this grounded theory cannot be generalized beyond the specific context of the research. Different researchers observing the same phenomena may come to very different conclusions, based on their personal world views. This approach should be referred to as sequential or iterative coding, not as theory
Theory of the seventh type	Theory as an ungrounded label or adjective	Type 7 theory represents the invocation of the word 'theory' without any further development, articulation or linkage to existing theory. No falsifiable statements, propositions or hypotheses are developed, nor is an a priori model used to guide data collection or analysis. Empirical results may be presented, although these usually are descriptive only and do not reflect any deeper model or insights. This use of 'theory' is the fastest growing usage in tourism research, perhaps because of the increasing pressure on researchers to position their work as contributing to 'theory'

It may be tempting to conclude that the word 'theory' has no meaning. As you can see, however, the problem is that the word has too many meanings. Whenever you hear or read someone using the word 'theory', try to get a sense of how the user is defining the term. This book will generally avoid the use of 'theory' because of the lack of precision in its denotation. If you want to use the word, I suggest limiting it to theories of either Type 1 or Type 2. Words like model, concept, paradigm, research design, method or epistemology are clearer and more precise terms that should be used for the five other types of 'theory'.

THINKING ABOUT THINKING: RESEARCH PARADIGMS

Researchers approach their work from a number of different perspectives, which they call paradigms. Different paradigms reflect different assumptions about the nature of reality and the processes of how people comprehend reality. 'Paradigm' has been defined as 'a loose collection of logically held together assumptions, concepts, and propositions that orientates thinking and research' (Bogdan and Biklen, 1982, p. 30). The following discussion provides only a very brief overview of some of the more important paradigms used in tourism research. There is a very large body of literature on each that explores their strengths and weaknesses, nuances, applications, competing conceptualizations and historical evolution. Indeed, some scholars' primary activity is critiquing and debating paradigms rather than actually collecting and analysing data.

Three notions are central to any research paradigm. The first is **epistemology**. Epistemology is derived from the Greek word '*episteme*', or 'knowing'. In other words, epistemology is the philosophical inquiry into how we come to know things. The second notion is **ontology**. It is derived from the Greek '*onto*' (philosophers and social scientists like to create words based on Greek origins because it makes the concepts sound more scholarly), which means 'being'. Ontology is the philosophy of the nature of reality. Epistemology and ontology are distinct concepts but clearly related. Together, they describe how we come to know something as well as the nature of that 'something'. The third notion is **methodology**, which – not surprisingly – comes from the Greek '*methodus*', or 'pursuit'. Methodology refers to the *study* of the procedures used to collect and interpret information on some subject. It also is used to refer directly to the tools or procedures – the methods – a researcher uses. (Some authors appear to prefer 'methodology' as a word over 'method' because it is a bigger word – a phenomenon I call syllabic inflation.)

Perhaps the most common way of classifying research paradigms is by labelling them as either quantitative or qualitative. The distinction is often viewed as one emphasizing methods. An example of a quantitative method is a closed-ended survey – a survey that presents respondents with printed questions accompanied by boxes representing possible answers to be ticked. The data would then be analysed using statistical tests. An example of a qualitative method is an in-depth personal interview – a conversation between a researcher and a subject during which the researcher poses questions, probes answers and explores for meanings and deeper insights into what the subject is saying. The analysis of the meaning of the interview is done through mental processes shaped by a systematic look at the content of the transcript of the interview.

The terms quantitative and qualitative, however, can be misleading. Quantitative methods are used to study qualities such as a subject's attitudes through the use of Likert scaling (which we will look at later in this book). Qualitative methods may be used to collect quantitative data such as the number of times a person used a given word in an interview. Not only is the distinction between qualitative and quantitative research often imprecise, but many researchers who identify themselves as belonging to one school or the other see the nature of the distinction differently. Many qualitative researchers – although not all – view the distinction as being more about epistemology and ontology than methodology. They see the distinction as being about how researchers believe they can come to know something and about how they perceive the nature of reality rather than about the technical details of the methods they use. Some colleagues describe themselves as 'qualitative researchers' and see the most fundamental concern in doing research as selecting and being able to defend a particular epistemological paradigm, rather than selecting an important question to be answered.

On the other hand, many quantitative researchers – although not all – view the differences as simply being about methods. Their focus tends to be more on technical details of methods and tools used to answer questions than on philosophical musings of the deeper roots of the various paradigms. They (as I do) view the fundamental concern in research as the identification of and effort used to answer an important question.

These distinctions are often not that critical for actually conducting practical research, although they can be interesting if you want to understand more about the philosophy of science. In this book, we will be more concerned with choosing appropriate methods to answer different types of questions. Moreover, we will use the terms '**empiricism**' (or '**empirical**') and '**subjective**', instead of 'quantitative' and 'qualitative'.

Empiricism

The word empiricism is, as you might have anticipated, derived from the Greek. In this case, the word is '*empeiria*', or experience. Philosophers have written extensively on different types, nuances and assumptions of empiricism; simply put, empiricism refers to the use of observation or experience to gain knowledge. It is based on the belief that there is an objective, knowable reality that exists outside the researcher's mind. Empirical research involves the systematic observation and recording of data that are then studied to form conclusions.

These conclusions can be descriptions of some pattern, the development of explanations about the forces creating that pattern (recall our discussion earlier about the fuzzy distinction between description and explanation) or the making and testing of predictions about how the pattern will change in the future. Inductive reasoning is a common logic in empirical research. You begin by collecting data; you then analyse it and reach some conclusions. However, deduction can be used, too. For example, you might have a restaurant location model that predicts fast-food restaurants will cluster near busy intersections in cities and near busy exits/entrances along limited-access expressways. You collect data on restaurant locations from a number of cities to test whether your model is accurate. In this case, you began with a belief or hypothesis and then test it by collecting data – which is the essence of deductive logic.

There are many empirical methods. Surveys are one of the most common. Other empirical methods include field research (such as observing the locations of restaurants), the analysis of secondary data (such as analysing hotel registration records) or conducting experiments (such as testing alternative landscape designs to minimize fertilizer runoff into water bodies. An important characteristic of empirical methods is that the data, analysis and results are, in principle, available for anyone to verify independently or replicate. They are also 'self-correcting' in the sense that, if you have an expectation about the results of a research project, empirical methods will indicate whether your expectations or predictions were wrong. Empirical research, though, cannot prove you are right. An example may make this clearer.

Assume you have developed a model that predicts the relationship between expenditures on marketing by a destination and the number of visitors who will come to that destination. You observe that a destination-marketing organization decreases its marketing budget by 20% and your model predicts visitation will fall by 15% a year later. You collect data on the number of visitors a year after the budget cut. If you find that the number of visitors remained stable or even rose, you have to conclude there is something wrong about your model. On the other hand, if the number of visitors fell by 15%, you may feel gratified your prediction was accurate. However, you cannot be certain that it was because the model is accurate or whether it is due to a coincidence. If you continue to test your model with subsequent years of data, and your predictions continue to be borne out, you have growing confidence that the model is correct, but there is no guarantee that you might not simply be observing a series of fortunate coincidences.

In many circumstances, the results of a test will not be clear-cut. In this example, we assumed your model predicted a drop of 15%, but what if you observed a drop of 8%? Is that difference enough to conclude that the model is not accurate? In a field as complex and volatile as tourism marketing, there must be tolerance for a degree of error in forecasting; the magnitude of acceptable error is a matter of professional judgement. However, repeated attempts to make a prediction that turns out to be dramatically wrong must lead you to conclude that there is a problem with your model.

On the other hand, researchers are sometimes tempted to make too much of insignificant but suggestive differences in data, especially when working with relatively small samples. For example, you might have a hypothesis that proposes a relationship between two variables such as: the size of a destination's planning budget will be positively correlated with the profitability of tourism firms operating in the destination. You collect data from 12 destinations and compare the average level of profitability of tourism firms in the destination with the largest planning budgets against the combined average of profitability and the average planning budget of the 11 other destinations. You find a positive correlation whose statistical significance is 0.10 (compared with the usual criterion of 0.05). You really believe that the more money spent on planning, the greater the profitability of tourism firms. You might be tempted to change the level of significance to 0.10 to be able to claim your hypothesis is supported. Some researches will do just that, on the grounds that their sample is so small that an 'overly stringent' statistical test is 'unfair' for a small sample.

Lowering your standards in a case like this is ultimately an ethical judgement in an ambiguous situation. At least in this case, you might try other tests, such a regression where you plot budgets against profits in a graph so you can see a trend line across all ten destinations. Or you compare the means of budget and profit across the quartiles (the average profitability of the three destinations with the highest levels of profitability versus the second best performing set of destinations, then the third, and so on). If some of the other tests confirm your hypothesis, you might be justified in arguing the support of your hypothesis. Otherwise, perhaps you should be more conservative and modest and conclude there is no evidence.

The fact that different statistical tests can yield conflicting results is well known to statisticians. This fact is behind the cynical suggestions that 'there are liars, damn liars and then there are statisticians'. When I hear this sentiment voiced, I point out that I believe these three categories are mutually exclusive and that I am a statistician – so I ask the person making the assertion, 'Which are you?'.

Taleb (2007) offers some deeper and more pointed commentary on the wisdom of empiricism and the risk of doing research that cannot be tested. In his book, *The Black Swan*, he tells the story about how prior to about AD 1600, European ornithologists believed all swans were white. Every swan they saw was white, so they had no reason to doubt their belief that all swans are white. Then, when Australia was discovered, the early explorers saw black swans. For those people who cared about bird plumage, this was a shock. It took only one black swan to prove the belief that all swans are white to be wrong.

The point of this story is that knowledge you reach through empirical research is fundamentally asymmetrical. It can prove you are wrong; it cannot prove you are correct. Any positive result might be a matter of luck, and future evidence will reveal that your model or conclusions are incorrect. It may not sound like it, but this ability to prove yourself wrong is a key advantage of empirical research. Being able to learn whether your ideas, conclusions or models are wrong protects you and others from acting on erroneous ideas. In other words, it helps keep you from making a Type 1 – false positive – error. This is a particular advantage of empirical approaches over subjective approaches. In an age of increasing accountability as well as of growing demands for evidence-based practice (Gambrill, 2003), tourism researchers need to be sure their findings can be properly evaluated and not lead their clients or supervisors into making bad decisions.

It must be acknowledged that empirical paradigms do not provide answers to all the questions that policy makers and decision makers might seek. Questions about the history of some aspect of tourism require data drawn from personal recollections, interpretations and selected evidence – all of which are subjective. Understanding the story of how a concept evolved, whether it concerns definitions of tourism, a policy or proposed legislation, cannot be told using purely empirical evidence. Understanding how someone emotionally responds to an advertisement or interprets a tourism experience ultimately involves subjective interpretation by both the subject and the researcher. Assessing social impacts of tourism also depends heavily on subjective methods, in that personal experiences of residents as well as visitors should be considered.

Thus, empiricism has its limits, and those limits not only include the possibility of ambiguous results or inconclusive data drawn from small samples but, more importantly, the inability to provide answers to some questions marketers, policy makers, planners and other decision makers would like to have. This is why subjective paradigms are important in tourism research. You will often find, in practice, that many research problems require a combination of empirical and subjective methods. Rather than positioning oneself as an empiricist or as a follower of one of the subjective paradigms, many researchers are pragmatists, using whatever combination of methods helps answer their questions.

Subjective paradigms

Subjective paradigms are based on the notion that reality is personally defined by the subject and/or the researcher, rather than on an objective reality that can be perceived by different observers who would agree on the nature of that reality. These paradigms reflect the personal values of the researcher and employ data collection methods and, especially, analytical processes that are not necessarily observable by someone other than the researcher. A key difference between empirical and subjective paradigms is in the types of questions that are asked. Putting it somewhat too simply, empiricists typically ask questions about how, where, when and how many; subjective researchers often ask questions about why or what it means.

The terms and classifications used to describe different types of subjective paradigms are diverse, sometimes to the point of being contradictory. You can often find, within any given paradigm, philosophical debates about assumptions, definitions, processes and terminology. Thus, the following description is only one possible description of these paradigms.

Grounded theory: as noted previously, grounded theory is not 'theory', but a systematic method designed to lead a researcher into concluding some general patterns based on the collection and systematic coding of subjective data. The method is still evolving, being first articulated by Glaser and Strauss in 1967. It is sometimes known as the 'constant comparative method', reflecting the role of continual comparison of observations with previous observations by the researcher.

The basic idea behind the grounded theory method is that the researcher systematically collects data, primarily but not necessarily just through interviews. Observations are compared and coded as the researcher collects more and more data, eventually 'revealing' patterns that make sense to the researcher. These patterns are ultimately stated as 'theory', which may be either a general statement of patterns and processes (which could then be subjected to testing by someone else) or a statement specific to the situation being studied. The patterns or processes that are identified by the researcher are described as 'emergent', meaning that they gradually form in the mind of the researcher and evolve with increasing data and study.

Although Glaser and Strauss jointly created the grounded theory approach, they eventually split over details of the method. The split continues to generate debate among practitioners of the method. The gist of the debate concerns whether the categories into which observations are placed are well defined at the outset, perhaps based on existing literature on a topic (Strauss's approach), or whether they emerge through constant comparison and examination of the data being collected (Glaser's approach).

One of the central principles of Glaser's approach is that 'all is data' (Glaser, 2001). A researcher should use whatever information that becomes available relevant to their subject. Thus, you might use not only interviews, but articles, books, conference presentations, comments by experts, Internet sources, newspaper articles, even television shows or radio talk programmes. Indeed, even empirical data sources might be useful. In this view, the grounded theory approach is not limited to just qualitative data. However, it is still fundamentally a subjective paradigm in that the analysis and emergence of patterns, general processes and other findings is based on your intuition. Properly done, a grounded theory approach should help ensure your interpretations are shaped by data, and the emerging patterns are tested against new information. Still, because so much of the method is based on interpretation rather than empirical analysis, grounded theory is subject to the narrative fallacy (see Focus Box 1.2).

Focus Box 1.2. Narrative fallacies and confirmation errors.

Nassim Taleb (2007), in his book, *The Black Swan,* describes two risks for researchers working in what he calls 'the narrative disciplines' – what we describe in this book as subjective paradigms: the narrative fallacy and the confirmation error.

The **narrative fallacy** refers to the tendency of people to impose a story on a series of observations to make sense out of them. The story need not be true, nor do the facts need to be related to each other. People like a story to help them remember or understand what they are seeing or hearing. This tendency has been demonstrated by psychologists, and is sometimes referred to as post hoc rationalization. This phenomenon refers to the tendency for people to look for an explanation for some experience, even though the explanation they may offer is not correct. For example, Nisbett and Wilson (1977) presented a group of female subjects with 12 pairs of stockings, asking which they preferred and why. Texture and colour were among the most common reasons given by the women to explain their preferences. In fact, all the stockings were identical. The subjects apparently felt, in response to the researchers' questions, the need to: (i) express preferences; and (ii) justify those preferences. The subjects provided 'explanations', even though those explanations were false.

Stories simplify; they help us make sense of myriad facts so that those facts are easier recall and to form into a pattern we can understand. Consider the following two statements: 'My boyfriend and I went on vacation last summer. We got engaged last summer'. Now consider the single statement: 'My boyfriend and I went on vacation last summer and got engaged'. There is no additional information in the second statement but it adds a narrative element, a story that links the two statements. The second statement seems much more meaningful, more informative, even though it adds no additional empirical information.

(Continued)

Focus Box 1.2. Continued.

It suggests a story that is easier to remember than two independent facts. This is the origin of the narrative fallacy. We create stories to make sense of a series of observations, whether or not those observations are logically linked.

Confirmation error is the tendency for a researcher to see only evidence that confirms his or her beliefs or models, and to ignore evidence that disproves them. It also refers to the belief that the absence of contrary evidence proves the conclusions. To illustrate this point, Taleb uses the example of a turkey being fattened for dinner on the American holiday, Thanksgiving (turkey is the traditional protein served on that holiday). For the first 1000 days of the turkey's life, the turkey is nurtured and fed by a farmer raising it for the dinner table. The turkey comes to believe the farmer raising her has only her happiness and well-being in his heart. Every day that goes along only confirms the turkey's belief in the goodness of her care-giver. However, on the day before Thanksgiving, 'something *unexpected* will happen to the turkey: it will incur a revision of belief' (Taleb, 2007, p. 40). Thus, despite 1000 observations 'proving' that the farmer had the turkey's best interests at heart, it took only one contrary example to prove the turkey's belief in the kindness of the farmer being wrong.

Here's another example of a different form the confirmation error may take. I had a graduate student who was interested in understanding how seniors (the student was a senior) differed from younger people in their motivations and experiences associated with cruise vacations. He interviewed seniors and analysed their answers in great detail, developing a story that illustrated all the ways in which he felt seniors acted differently and had different reactions to cruising than other passengers. These differences were based on personal observations the student had made in his own life. Although he concluded seniors had distinctive motives, expectations and experiences with cruising, he never interviewed non-seniors to determine their motivations, expectations and experiences. He had approached his research with a preconceived set of expectations about how his conclusions would turn out and never bothered to look for data that might negate his beliefs. As a result, he ultimately had to rewrite his conclusions so that they addressed only his subjects and not extend them to making inferences about people he had never interviewed.

The style of data interpretation that interprets findings to support a predetermined set of conclusions – a temptation found in both empirical as well as subjective research, although it is more prevalent in subjective research – has been cynically described by Gelman and Weakliem (2009, p. 315) as analysis that is 'more 'vampirical' than 'empirical' – [conclusions] unable to be killed by mere evidence'.

A couple of important principles in *all* research are: (i) keep an open mind – avoid pre-forming conclusions that may bias your results; and (ii) actively look for counter-examples to your findings – try to find evidence that suggests your preliminary conclusions are incorrect. Being open to having your ideas proved wrong may be uncomfortable, but it is essential in any credible research.

Interpretism: this paradigm emphasizes the belief that 'reality', at least in the sense of meaning and understanding, is constructed in the mind of individuals. This paradigm is sometimes called **constructivism** or **constructionism** (we'll briefly look at the differences between these terms shortly). At one level, the idea that each of us may have our own interpretation of events is common-sense understanding. Most of us understand that different people probably have different interpretations of the same event, and that the meanings we invest in some experiences are our own interpretations. Interpretists sometimes describe this as 'multiple realities'.

Interpretists are interested in asking questions about how other people create meaning of events and what those meanings are. The questions may focus on the individual, such as exploring the meanings of a vacation trip to each member of a family. Or the researcher may be interested in how society constructs shared meanings of some phenomenon. For example, a researcher might explore how different groups interpret 'tourism' as a concept and what forces gave rise to different interpretations. The term 'constructionism' is sometimes used to refer to this broader, more social perspective while 'constructivism' is sometimes used to refer to the focus on the individual. Other researchers use the two terms synonymously.

Interpretists believe they must get to know their subjects well and be emotionally immersed in their research. They generally do not accept the desirability of keeping themselves, their values or their perceptions distinct from the subject they are studying. Interpretists usually make their values and perspectives explicit as part of their research. Because they view (to varying degrees of literalness) that there is no objective reality, interpretists emphasize written or spoken words – discourse – as the source of knowledge. Language is seen not just as a communication tool for conveying information about reality, but as reality itself.

At the most radical level, some interpretists even deny objective reality. Examples of this perspective can be found in writers such as Foucault (1972), who asserted that discourse (language) 'constructs' the very objects it considers, or Derrida (1976, p. 158), who claims that 'there is nothing outside of the text'. This is an extreme position that leads to absurd assertions if accepted literally. Even radical interpretists go to conferences or go on vacation. When doing so, they do not deny the existence of the audience to whom they are speaking or the materiality of the aircraft on which they fly. Bradley (1998, p. 68) describes the position of the radical interpretists (a position he rejects) in the following way: 'Talk about the mind is viewed as an artefact of cultural forces, an epiphenomenon shaped by the conventions of discourse. Discourse is real. Everything else is relative to discourse'. These radical interpretists are sometimes known as 'subjectivists'.

A more reasonable position is to view interpretism not as a statement about reality (ontology), but about how we come to understand the world (epistemology). In other words, a moderate interpretist would emphasize that much of what we understand about the world occurs through language. Language allows us to comprehend and communicate meaning, but there is still an objective reality beyond language. For example, that many people take temporary trips away from home is an objective reality; which of those trips we label as 'tourism' is a socially constructed concept. Furthermore, the reasons for those trips and their meaning to the traveller are personally constructed concepts. The distinction between meaning (sometimes called 'truth') and reality ('facts') was explained to me by my doctoral supervisor during an intense philosophical discussion over a pint in this way: 'Steve, whatever is still there after you stop believing in it, is reality'.

One of the weaknesses of the interpretist approach is that much of the data and analysis cannot be reliably tested by an independent researcher. Indeed, it is difficult even for the original researcher to avoid being influenced by their own beliefs and assumptions, to ensure that the conclusions are accurate and not shaped by subconscious assumptions or beliefs. Interpretists, perhaps even more than grounded theorists, are vulnerable to both the narrative fallacy and confirmation error (see Focus Box 1.2).

On a practical level, interpretist research is time consuming and typically based on small samples. This means that it is not easy to apply to or to generalize to larger populations. The insights from an interpretist approach may be quite revelatory or provocative, but there is no guarantee that they apply to anyone other than the individuals interviewed. Interpretist research, with its focus on individual interpretations, may miss the impact of larger social forces, especially if the subject is not conscious of the impact of those forces on themselves.

Critical theory: this paradigm is not really a theory, either, but a view of the world that sees society in terms of conflict, inequity and power struggles. This belief in the primacy of oppression in social relations is an example of a broader social force that an interpretist might miss if the subject accepts his oppression as 'that's just the way life is'. Critical theorists also believe that people are capable, creative and have substantial potential but that some people oppress others, blocking them from achieving their potential. Critical theory research seeks to uncover examples, and the causes, of oppression or social injustice. More than that, critical theory is a form of action research that is intended to empower people to promote what the critical theorist interprets as a more egalitarian society. Critical theory that focuses on gender relations from a woman's perspective is known as feminist research.

While an interpretist sees that personal values influence how she will interpret what she hears from her subjects and thus will make their values explicit, a critical theorist will be driven by these values. Those values will shape the researcher's motivations and direct her research activities as well as her conclusions. Evidence will be selected and interpreted by the researcher to reveal 'the truth' of oppression. Once 'the truth' is known, the critical theorist then moves her findings into action to help individuals change their situation.

Because critical theory research presumes that social relations are driven by power struggles and inequalities, all observations are interpreted in light of this viewpoint. In other words, even more than with interpretism, critical theory research is not only subjective but biased towards a predetermined conclusion. Either only evidence that supports the conclusion of social inequality (or the proposed actions to redress inequality) will be reported, or it will be reinterpreted to support a foregone conclusion. Critical theorists thus are especially vulnerable to confirmation error, seeing only evidence that supports their beliefs and ignoring or reinterpreting evidence that contradicts those beliefs.

Critical theory research may be driven more by the researcher's personal agenda for political action than a desire truly to better understand social patterns. Because a key feature of critical theory research is to plot out an action agenda, research will be conducted to guide and support a plan of action to implement social change. A risk in critical theory is that the direction of social change and the strategy to implement it will be determined not so much by objective, fact-based research (the existence of which critical theorists deny is possible) as by a personal, subjective political agenda.

CONCLUSIONS

The study of tourism is fascinating and challenging. Tourism is a topic with many different faces, and that can be studied from many different perspectives. Tourism research is virtually always based on a definition of tourism, which may be spelled out or left implicit. Regardless, it is important for you to understand how an author defines tourism when you read someone else's work and to be conscious of your own definition when you do research.

Similarly, it is important to understand that tourism can be studied from a number of disciplines (economics, geography, planning, sociology, to name a few) as well as with different paradigms. Each paradigm has its own set of values, assumptions and ways of viewing the world. These can be broadly categorized as either empirical or subjective. Empirical paradigms focus on observable data and the findings can generally be tested to determine whether or not they are erroneous. There are two key limitations in empirical research. First, empiricism can not prove you are right – only that you are wrong (hence the use of the term 'falsifiable' rather than 'verifiable' when referring to testing empirical findings). Positive findings may be overturned with the collection of additional data at some time in the future. Second, empirical research generally does not allow probing into meanings, values and the deeper nature of tourism experiences. Questions about meanings, symbolism and values require subjective approaches. These approaches, though, also have limitations, such as susceptibility to the narrative fallacy and confirmation error.

Tourism research is a social phenomenon. The collection of data often involves talking with other people, and perhaps working with other researchers. Even when a researcher works alone and uses secondary data sources, they will eventually share the results with other people. Tourism researchers typically develop extensive networks, often internationally, as we collaborate with and communicate with other researchers. In addition to personal communications, we communicate through journals and books, and attend conferences where we share ideas. Our professional networks are important to us for our work and sometimes even as a basis for forming friendships.

One of the most useful strategy tools for building a professional network is to join one or more tourism research associations (see Focus Box 1.3). Associations function as virtual scientific communities (Xiao, 2007) that link researchers with each other and promote research. All have annual conferences at which researchers present and hear about the latest research, and some associations have regional chapters, hold workshops and provide other opportunities for researchers to network. Many have student membership categories with reduced membership rates. Joining an association as a student can help you develop contacts that might facilitate job-searching as well as give you an opportunity to make presentations that help build your CV.

Tourism research is a rewarding and enjoyable activity, whether in a business, government or non-governmental agency, consultancy or university. The following chapters will provide you with valuable skills to help you conduct useful and high-quality tourism research.

Focus Box 1.3. Tourism research associations.

tourism, as other research fields, has a number of associations around the world that promote networking among members and the sharing of tourism research. The following are brief profiles of some of the better-known associations. The information was accurate at the time of writing, but no guarantee can be made about whether all details, especially contact information, are current.

Asia Pacific Tourism Association (APTA) http://apta.donga.ac.kr/

APTA promotes tourism research in the Asia–Pacific area, and encourages members to share the results of their research through the *Asia Pacific Journal of Tourism Research* and an annual conference. There are more than 300 members from over 20 nations, primarily Asia–Pacific countries, but membership is open to researchers in other parts of the world, too.

Association for Tourism and Leisure Education (ATLAS) http://www.atlas-euro.org/
ATLAS works to develop transnational educational initiatives in tourism and leisure. It provides a forum to promote faculty and student exchanges and transnational research, and to facilitate curriculum and professional development. ATLAS currently has members in more than 70 countries. It organizes international conferences on tourism and leisure topics as well as regional meetings in Africa and the Asia–Pacific. ATLAS also publishes a series of research monographs.

(Continued)

Focus Box 1.3. Continued.

Association Internationale d'Experts Scientifique du Tourisme (AIEST) http://www.aiest.org/
The objectives of AIEST are to promote networking among members, to promote and facilitate tourism research by its members, to promote the creation and networking of tourism research centres and to organize meetings and courses on tourism as a 'scientific subject'. The association has a strongly European focus, but has more than 400 members in over 50 countries on all continents (except Antarctica). AIEST has created several working groups to deepen scientific activities between its annual congresses.

Council for Australian University Tourism and Hospitality Education (CAUTHE) http://www.cauthe.com.au/
CAUTHE's goal is to promote the development of tourism and hospitality education and research in Australia. It has 24 university members as well as about 200 individual members. Although the association positions itself as serving Australian universities, individual members come from many other parts of the world, including other parts of the Asia–Pacific, Europe and North America. Its signature activity is an annual conference that includes not just research but tourism, hospitality, and leisure education and practice. Although the conference is positioned as a national conference, it draws delegates from many nations.

International Council on Hotel, Restaurant and Institutional Education (CHRIE) http://www.chrie.org
Primarily an association emphasizing education in hospitality and tourism, CHRIE links faculty and students in high schools, colleges and universities offering programmes in hotel and restaurant management, food service management and culinary arts. It also has corporate partners who help advance the mission of CHRIE. The mission is to facilitate information exchange, promote research and provide educators with products and services related to education, training and resource development in hospitality and tourism. CHRIE has approximately 2000 members and chapters in the USA, Canada, Europe and the Asia–Pacific.

International Society of Travel and Tourism Educators (ISTTE) http://www.istte.org/
ISTTE seeks to improve the quality of education and research in travel, tourism and hospitality industries by promoting the exchange of information through an annual conference and a journal, *Journal of Teaching in Travel and Tourism*. The association also has a scholarship programme and job-listing service. Approximately 150 members are from North America, Europe and the Asia–Pacific

Travel and Tourism Research Association (TTRA) http://www.ttra.com/
TTRA's goals are to facilitate members' access to information to support research; to educate members in research, marketing and planning skills through publications, conferences and networking; to encourage professional development and recognize research and marketing excellence through award programmes; to promote networking among members; to foster development of tourism research and related curricula in institutes of higher education; and to promote the development and application of professional research in the travel and tourism industry. With over 700 members, TTRA is organized into a number of US-based chapters, a Canadian chapter and a European chapter.

Case Study 1.1. The Evolution of an operational definition of tourism.

tourism, like many social phenomena, is both real and 'constructed'. Tourism trips are a real phenomenon, but which trips we decide to label as 'tourism' is a matter of convention and, to a degree, arbitrary. For example, the World Tourism Organization defines tourism in terms of trips 'outside the usual environment'. While this phrase may sound reasonable, there is no consensus on what constitutes 'outside the usual environment'. Operational definitions of 'usual environment' often are the result of historical accident or convenience rather than of any objective process. This case study describes the evolution of Canada's concept of 'usual environment' as an illustration of how the definition of tourism is ultimately a 'constructed' concept rather than one that has an independent, objective existence.

Canada debuted as a major international destination in 1967 with the success of Expo'67, one of the most heavily attended World's Fairs in history. Following the success of that event, the federal government realized that: (i) tourism offered significant economic opportunities for the nation; and (ii) there was very little information on Canadians' travel patterns. This recognition led, in 1971, to the first national survey of domestic travel patterns. The survey was conducted by the Canadian Government Office of Tourism (CGOT) in consultation with the ten provincial governments. At the request of seven of the ten provinces, CGOT used 25 miles (40 km) as the minimum travel distance; for the other three (following the practice of the contemporaneous US Travel Survey) CGOT used 100 miles (160 km). While the individual provinces could use their results for their own purposes, the lack of a consistent definition prevented meaningful comparisons across the country. The survey was repeated in 1977 with a standard threshold for all provinces of 100 miles. After another lapse of 3 years, Transport Canada, who had been conducting a 'Travel-to-Work Survey' since 1973, conducted a national survey of tourism patterns using a threshold of 50 miles (80 km).

The 50-mile threshold was selected because the 'travel-to-work' survey examined all travel less than 50 miles 'including travel to work, automobile usage, and other aspects of the trip' (Statistics Canada, 1977, p. 8). In 1977, discussions were conducted between Transport Canada and CGOT to determine what distance threshold should be used to separate the scope of the 'travel to work' survey and the tourism survey. Transport Canada suggested that a maximum of 50 miles for its travel-to-work survey would pick up virtually all commuters and that anyone making a longer trip was probably engaged in tourism. CGOT was 'not sure what definition [was] the best since some provinces [were] using definitions such as 'overnight stay' [while others were using] 25 miles'. CGOT concluded that it did 'not have any specific objection to the 50 miles definition' (Statistics Canada, 1977, p. 9). Both sponsors ultimately agreed that 'the 50 mile limit was acceptable because, at this distance, comparisons with other surveys and existing sets of data could be done' (Statistics Canada, 1980, p. 4).

In 1984, Statistics Canada formed the National Task Force on Tourism Data. The mandate of the Task Force was to recommend improvements in the collection and analysis of tourism data for provincial and federal tourism policy, planning and marketing decisions. Among the issues considered by the Task Force was the magnitude of the distance threshold to define tourism. The Task Force heard that there was still disagreement about the use of 80 km. The province of Ontario, most notably, pressed for a return to 40 km. Ontario wanted this shorter distance to capture data on trips by residents of Toronto (the largest city in Canada) to nearby resorts and attractions. There was, however, little support from other provinces and federal agencies to move away from 80 km as a national standard.

(Continued)

Case Study 1.1. Continued.

At this time, the survey used to collect statistics on travel by Canadians was named the Canadian Travel Survey (CTS), and was paid for by the provinces. The CTS was operated as an add-on to a larger social survey, the Labour Force Survey (LFS), that collected monthly data on a wide variety of variables related to employment and households. The CTS was administered as a subset of the LFS – about 85,000 surveys per year.

As a compromise, the Task Force (Canadian National Task Force on Tourism Data, 1987) suggested that Statistics Canada collect data on all trips and report them using a standard range of distances. In 1988, Statistics Canada implemented a version of this recommendation: data on all overnight trips were collected regardless of distance; data on same-day trips of 40 km or more were also collected. However, only data for trips 80 km or longer (whether overnight or same-day) were used for official tabulations. In 1992, in a cost-saving move, Statistics Canada began collecting data only on same-day trips of 80 km or more, with the exception of same-day travel by Ontario residents. The additional cost of collecting data for 40–70 km same-day trips was paid for by the government of Ontario so that they could obtain these special tabulations.

The Task Force also recommended the development of a Tourism Satellite Account (TSA) (see Focus Box 1.3). The TSA was based on tourism statistics utilizing the 80 km threshold. The investment of substantial time and money into the TSA reinforced the desire of many statisticians to stay with 80 km as the standard. None the less, in 1999, the province of Ontario once again pressed for cutting the threshold to 40 km. This particular proposal was made to the Research Committee of the Canadian Tourism Commission (CTC). The Committee examined the implications and costs of such a change. The arguments for reducing the distance threshold were that: (i) the shorter distance would allow the collection of statistics on trips to events and attractions near major cities; and (ii) all provinces, including Ontario, and the federal government would use a common definition.

The arguments against the change included: (i) the loss of 15 years of time series data; (ii) the recognition that cutting the distance threshold would increase the number of trips and tourism revenues by such an amount that the change would look self-serving and thus undermine the credibility of tourism statistics; (iii) the belief that a high percentage of the 40–79 km trips would include routine visits that were not consistent with the spirit of the UNWTO definition of tourism; and (iv) the inclusion of these trips would introduce a large number of low-value, routine trips unaffected by domestic tourism marketing initiatives into the performance assessment of the CTC's domestic marketing programme.

After a year's debate during which no consensus emerged, the CTC Research Committee referred the question to the CTC Board of Directors for a decision. The referral was partly due to the inability to reach a consensus but even more so because it was recognized that the question of an operational definition of tourism was more a policy question than a research question. In other words, the Research Committee recognized that tourism is subject to different definitions depending on who is making the definition and the purposes to which they apply the definition. Any national definition to be used by the sector at large should be made by a national body representing the leaders of the sector. Furthermore, the Committee was aware of the importance that federal and provincial governments use the same definition to ensure comparability in reporting the performance of tourism. Achieving consistency requires agreement among the opinion makers and leading decision makers in the sector, not just researchers who hold relatively junior positions in provincial and federal tourism departments.

(Continued)

Case Study 1.1. Continued.

The CTC Board of Directors agreed that the question of a national tourism definition was fundamentally a policy one and consented to consider the matter. After a presentation of arguments pro and con, the Board affirmed the continued use of 80 km as the threshold for defining both same-day and overnight tourism trips.

Independent of the issue of definitions, though, complaints about the LFS as the platform for delivering the CTS had been long standing. For example, tourism research managers in Canada's northern territories (Yukon, Northwest Territories and Nunavut) continued to be frustrated by the fact that the LFS did not cover their territories. The reason for this is that the territories have very small populations spread over a very large area, and sampling would be very costly. Furthermore, the LFS is prohibited from surveying First Nations (aboriginal communities), and a substantial portion of territory residents are aboriginal peoples. Another chronic complaint by provincial tourism researchers was that the LFS was not a travel-specific survey – approximately 40% of the people in the LFS did not take any overnight pleasure trips longer than 80 km in any given year. However, during 2000, changes to the administration of the LFS escalated frustrations. Most critical was the move to computer-assisted telephone interviewing (CATI) for the administration of the LFS, combined with a shift from using a large number of locally based surveyors to a small number of surveyors in regional offices of Statistics Canada under the direct monitoring of their managers. Changes in the wording of questions in the telephone-based survey were also implemented.

These changes had little impact on the LFS data themselves, but they resulted in dramatic shifts in the data collected for the CTS. For example, some provinces noted a jump of up to 25% of total person-trips as a result of these changes. This was eventually traced to surveyors being more diligent about 'capturing' data on relatively short, routine trips, such as someone visiting a parent in a nearby city once a month – because their interviewing styles were now being closely monitored. Other forces resulting from other changes in the LFS created additional, unexpected shifts in the CTS data. As one analyst with Statistics Canada put it, 'when the LFS sneezes, the CTS catches pneumonia'. In other words, apparently minor changes in how the survey was administered undermined the provinces' confidence in the data they were receiving from the CTS.

This growing dissatisfaction eventually caused Statistics Canada to agree to explore alternative platforms for the CTS. The opening of this door then allowed requests for other changes to be introduced. Some of these were relatively minor, such as changing the minimum age of respondents from 15 in the LFS to 18 for the new travel survey and limiting questions to domestic trips only (some limited data on trips by Canadians to the USA were collected in the CTS). However, sensing an opportunity, Ontario (supported by some political allies) again pushed Statistics Canada to change the operational definition of tourism. Given the provinces' financial contributions to the CTS, it was difficult for Statistics Canada – as a client-oriented agency – to resist. Due to a change in the leadership of the CTC Research Committee, and having been frustrated by the rejection of the proposal for a change in the definition of tourism by the CTC Board of Directors, the provincial tourism research managers decided to circumvent the CTC Board of Directors and proceed without approval. The managers' argument was that the definition of tourism was only a technical matter, not a matter of policy.

A variety of potential definitions were explored, including the use of a 40 km threshold and subjective criteria such as trips taken 'out of town'. Sample surveys with alternative wordings were conducted, and respondents were debriefed afterwards by the consultant

(Continued)

Case Study 1.1. Continued.

hired to test alternative definitions asking, in effect, 'If I were to have asked you [for example], "how many trips did you take away from home last month", would your answer have been different than to the question [on the test survey] "how many trips did you take out of town last month?" If so, how and why?' The results revealed that the specific words used could elicit very different interpretations (or misinterpretations) from respondents. For example, some respondents noted that they lived in rural areas, so the phrase 'out of town' meant nothing to them. They did not live in a town so they couldn't 'leave town'.

After months of testing, revisions and negotiations among the provinces, the CTC and Statistics Canada, a compromise was reached. As of 2005, the new definition of a tourism trip in Canada became: any non-routine overnight trip out of town or any non-routine same-day trip that is 40 km or longer. This definition became the core of a new national travel survey: Travel Survey of Residents of Canada (TSRC).

The compromise means that all provinces now use the same definition Ontario wished to use. However, problems remain. Confusion about the meaning of 'out of town' continues, particularly (but not exclusively) among rural respondents. The new definition also means that a 15-year time series on tourism trips was broken, and a new series begun. In turn, this not only means one cannot compare travel volumes and expenditures between years before and after the new definition, but the Canadian TSA had to be recalibrated using the new definition, which again breaks comparability across years (not to mention consumption of substantial human resources for recalibration). The full implications of the change have yet to be realized (at the time of this writing), but are likely to be substantial. The transition from the CTS to the TSRC took longer and cost more than anticipated. Indeed, the first data from the TSRC were delayed for 4 years, during which time government and industry had no current national or provincial tourism statistics, and had depleted budgets so that testing of the most recent version of the TSRC could not be done.

Incidentally, the search for a new platform for the TSRC ultimately was unsuccessful. After 2 years of work and over CA$2 million in research and testing, no acceptable alternative could be found. The primary alternative, random-digit dialling (RDD), was found to have problems, including cost and the difficulty of developing demographic profiles of the households contacted via RDD, that were more substantial than the problems with the LFS.

Whether a change from an empirical and unambiguous but arbitrary definition (80 km threshold) that did not have universal support to a political compromise based on a hybrid definition involving distance and the subjective and confusing notion of 'out of town', and the resulting financial and human resource costs as well as the loss of years of time series data, was a wise decision will be a judgement future tourism researchers will make.

REFERENCES

Bogdan, R. and Biklen, S. (1982) *Qualitative Research for Education*. Allyn and Bacon, Boston, Massachusetts.

Bradley, B. (1998) Two ways to talk about change: 'The child' of the sublime versus radical pedagogy. In: Bayer, B. and Shotter, J. (eds) *Reconstructing the Psychological Subject*. Sage, London, pp. 68–93.

Brunt, P. (1997) *Market Research in Travel and Tourism*. Butterworth-Heinemann, Oxford, UK.

Butler, R.W. (1980) The concept of a tourist area cycle of evolution: implications for management of resources. *Canadian Geographer* 24(1), 5–12.

Canadian National Task Force on Tourism Data (1987) *A Proposed Integrated Framework for Demand-Side Tourism Data Collection in Canada*. Working Paper 4. Statistics Canada, Ottawa, Canada.

Canadian National Task Force on Tourism Data (1989) *Final Report of the Canadian National Task Force on Tourism Data*. Statistics Canada, Ottawa, Canada.

Derrida, J. (1974) *Of Grammatology*. Johns Hopkins University Press, Baltimore, Maryland.

Foucault, M. (1972) *The Archæology of Knowledge*. Tavistock, London.

Frechtling, D. (1996) *Practical Tourism Forecasting*. Butterworth-Heinemann, Oxford, UK.

Gambrill, E. (2003). Evidence-based practice: implications for knowledge development and use in social work. In: Rosen A. and Proctor. E. (eds) *Developing Practice Guidelines for Social Work Intervention*. Columbia University Press, New York, pp. 37–58.

Gelman, A. and Weakliem, D. (2009) Of beauty, sex, and power. *American Scientist* 97, 310–316.

Glaser, B. (2001) *The Grounded Theory Perspective: Conceptualization Contrasted with Description*. Sociology Press, Mill Valley, California.

Glaser, B. and Strauss, A. (1967) *The Discovery of Grounded Theory: Strategies for Qualitative Research*. Aldine, Chicago, Illinois.

Gunn, C. and Var, T. (2002) *Tourism Planning*, 4th edn. Routledge, New York.

Jafari, J. (1977) Editorial. *Annals of Tourism Research* 5, 6–11.

Jafari, J. (1992) The scientification of tourism. In: El-Wahab, S. and El-Roby, N. (eds) *Scientific Tourism*. Egyptian Society of Scientific Experts on Tourism, Cario, Egypt, pp. 43–75.

Leiper, N. (1979) The framework of tourism. *Annals of Tourism Research* 6, 390–407.

Leiper, N. (1990) *Tourism Systems*. Department of Management Systems, Massey University, Palmerston North, New Zealand.

McIntosh, R. and Goeldner, C. (1977) *Tourism*, 2nd edn. John Wiley and Sons, New York.

McIntosh, R. and Goeldner, C. (1990) *Tourism*, 6th edn. John Wiley and Sons, New York.

Nisbett, R. and Wilson, T. (1977) Telling more than we know: Verbal reports on mental processes. *Psychological Bulletin* 84(3), 231–259.

Sessa, A. (1971) Pour une nouvelle notion de tourisme. *Revue de Tourisme* 1, 5.

Statistics Canada (1977) *Travel to Work Survey: Background and User Guide*. Statistics Canada, Ottawa, Canada.

Statistics Canada (1980) *Survey of Tourism Trips by Canadians: Introduction*. Statistics Canada, Ottawa, Canada.

Statistics Canada (2007) *National Tourism Indicators: Quarterly Estimates, First Quarter 2007*. Statistics Canada, Ottawa, Canada.

Taleb, N.N. (2007) *The Black Swan: the Impact of the Highly Improbable*. Random House, New York.

World Tourism Organization (2007) *International Recommendations on Tourism Statistics: Provisional Draft, Revision 5*. World Tourism Organization, Madrid.

Xiao, H. (2007) The social structure of a scientific community: a case study of the Travel and Tourism Research Association. PhD dissertation, University of Waterloo, Waterloo, Ontario, Canada.

chapter 2

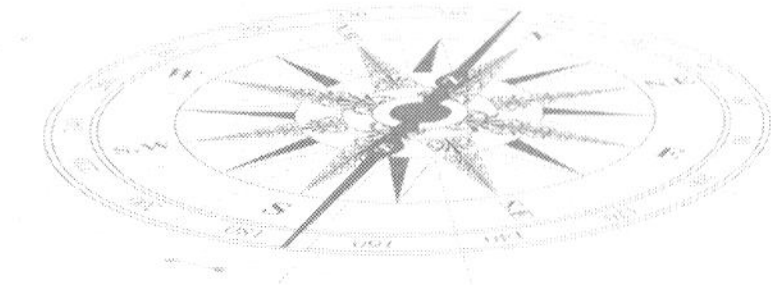

How to Plan a Research Project

WHY THIS IS IMPORTANT

Research projects involve multiple tasks, each of which must be done well if the project is to be successful. As noted in Chapter 1, research can be undertaken in a variety of contexts – from personal curiosity to consulting contracts.

The details of a research project will be different in different contexts, but there are some common elements. Each project begins with a goal in mind: that is, you need to decide what you want to do or be told what your research is expected to produce. This goal is then usually translated into a list of objectives and maybe further refined into a series of research questions. A review of what other work has been done on a topic is usually another important early task (some grounded theorists, though, believe literature reviews should not be conducted until after reviewers have collected their data so that the data collection will not be biased by preconceived notions of what they should look for).

Once the purposes of research have been articulated a work plan and, if relevant, a budget, schedule and inventory of needed resources are drawn up. Potential sources of data are then identified and, if necessary, approval from a university's ethics office or other oversight body is obtained. Only then can the process of data collection begin. After the data are collected, you begin your analysis. After the analysis, you interpret your results, articulate your conclusions and finally, prepare a report.

All this sounds like a fairly straightforward, linear process. In practice, because research is a creative act, you are likely to find yourself going back, changing your mind, redoing something and refining your ideas several times before you will complete your project. This chapter will give you practical advice on planning your research project, but remember there can always be surprises or complications in doing any research project. Flexibility and creativity can be very helpful in ensuring your research will ultimately be successful.

SETTING RESEARCH GOALS AND OBJECTIVES

As suggested above, the first task is to understand what you want to know, or why the research is to be done. Selecting a research topic for academic purposes, such as a thesis, can sometimes be the most difficult part of the research process. Students often begin with just a general sense of an area in which they are interested, but lack any specific questions, or they may have questions too broad to be practical. One way to either add depth to a general topical area or focus an overly broad interest is to read other research that has been conducted on the topic. In particular, journal articles, theses and dissertations often identify suggestions for additional research in their conclusions sections.

Alternatively, you might see assumptions or models made by other researchers that could be tested. You might find an interesting study that could be replicated or extended in a different area or to a different population. The choice of a topic for curiosity-driven (academic) research should normally meet the test of the '*three Fs*'. First, it should be **fun**. You should find a topic that gets you excited and that will continue to motivate you. If you are conducting research as a part of a degree requirement, or because you are a new professor who needs to publish to secure tenure in your job, it helps if the topic is intrinsically interesting and sustains your interest over the duration of the project so that you care enough to do a good job.

Next, the project should be **feasible**. The topic should be significant enough to make it worth doing. On the other hand, it should not be so big or complex that it becomes impractical to complete within a reasonable period of time. With experience, you develop a sense of whether a specific set of research questions can be answered within your time and budget constraints. Until then, discuss your research idea with a more experienced researcher who can suggest whether your problem is too complicated to be manageable or too trivial to be not worth the effort.

Third, the project should be **fundable**. Or, at least, it should be something you can afford if you do not have funding for it. Many student projects are self-funded, which means you pay for it out of your own pocket. This is not a desirable situation but sometimes it is unavoidable. In any event, when planning a research project, make certain that you have adequate resources to complete it.

Students preparing for an academic career as well as faculty-seeking tenure will usually consider a fourth test which, unfortunately for my little *F*-formula, does not begin with *F*: the project should lead to a publishable paper. The academic environment is sometimes described as 'publish or perish'. This refers to the fact that one of the primary criteria for advancing in an academic career in most universities is to publish in refereed journals. A refereed journal is a journal that uses anonymous reviewers (usually three) to evaluate submissions sent in for possible publication. Submissions normally are reviewed in a 'double-blind' process: the author does not know who the reviewers are and the reviewers do not know who the author is. This is to avoid allowing personal relationships – whether friends or foes – to influence a reviewer's judgement and to protect the reviewers from angry authors if their work is rejected. Incidentally, authors of academic journal articles usually are not paid for journal publishing or speaking at an academic conference: publishing and presenting are considered to be job requirements.

Academe is, of course, not the only context in which research is done. Much tourism research is conducted by an employee of a firm charged with doing research or by a consultant working under a contract. If you are the employee, you will have the opportunity to talk with your supervisor to clarify what information is needed from the research, but remember our discussion in Chapter 1 about the differences between management problems and research problems. You may find it necessary to help your supervisor refine his/her understanding of what sort of information is needed to solve a management problem *and* to articulate that need as a series of answerable research questions. The necessity of refining research questions is likely to be especially great when the request for research arises from a crisis in the organization. Research can help a manager make an informed decision, but it cannot replace management expertise or be, by itself, the basis for a business or policy decision.

In the case of consulting research, the contracting organization will have developed a request for proposals (RFP) (see Focus Box 2.1) that will specify the objectives to be fulfilled. Even here, though, there may be a need to get clarification about the scope of the project or about specific needs of the client. These questions can usually be asked while you work on a proposal for the contract. The contracting organization may share your questions and their responses with all potential bidders. After you have won the consulting contract, the client will usually request a meeting so that you and they can discuss in more detail what they expect from the project and how you and they will work together.

Focus Box 2.1. RFPs.

Requests for proposal (RFP), requests for quotation (RFQ) or invitations to bid (ITB) all mean the same thing and are fundamental to the process of contracting out research. If you work as a research manager, sooner or later you will need to develop an RFP (RFQ or ITB). If you work as a consultant, you will have to respond to an RFP when you bid on a contract. In either case, knowing how to write and read an RFP is an essential skill.

Decide what you need

This may sound obvious, but the key to developing a successful RFP is having a clear understanding of what you need. This needs to be more rigorous than just a wish list of 'things I'd like to know'. Research costs money and while you want to get the best value for your research budget, you need to understand – and your potential bidders have the right to expect – that your requests are appropriate and supported by a realistic budget. The development of an RFP often is a joint task, with co-workers and supervisors contributing to the final wording. Be clear about what you want, but do not ask for more than you are willing to pay for. This point is discussed further, below.

Complicated RFPs may require that you bring in outside expertise to assist in writing the proper specifications. You will also need, at the outset, to decide how the proposals are to be evaluated. You may choose among submissions yourself, get assistance from a colleague or create a selection committee.

Get the verbs right

This point is related to the first – knowing what you need – rather than being about grammar. Things you require from the contract should be articulated with words such as 'will' or 'must'. Features that you would like but that may be expendable depending on costs or delivery time should be introduced with verbs such as 'may' or 'could', or involve the adjective 'optional'.

Decide how you will choose the winner

Each consultant submitting a proposal will use his/her own format, unless you have specified an outline she/he must follow. Each proposal will reflect the consultant's emphasis, based on his/her understanding of your RFP. Some may emphasize research design, others will emphasize experience and still others cost-effectiveness. Again, you need to have a clear understanding what you are looking for so that you can objectively compare the strengths and weaknesses of each proposal. A common way of doing this is to set up

(Continued)

Focus Box 2.1. Continued.

a scoring system that specifies criteria to consider and the importance assigned to each. Common criteria may include:

- understanding of the need for the research;
- soundness of the data collection and analysis methods;
- previous experience;
- ability to meet deadlines;
- budget; and
- overall format and presentation of the proposal.

Draft the RFP

Once you know what you want and have decided on how to select the winning bidder, you are ready to draft the RFP. RFPs can vary substantially in their layout, from one page to more than 20, but most will touch on:

Introduction

Explain why you are issuing the RFP and what you expect the project to accomplish. The introduction may include a description of your organization and its mission. The due date and submission details might also be included in the introduction, as well as at the end of the RFP.

Technical requirements

This section provides potential bidders with information regarding what your project demands from them. It sets out research objectives or questions to be explored, the nature of the deliverables, the population to be surveyed (if relevant), sample size and/or statistical requirements (such as 'results must be accurate within ± 5%, i.e. 19 times out of 20'). This is the place to note if you expect interim reports to be produced or if the project is to be administered over a series of phases. This section is usually the most difficult to write and will often require input from colleagues or supervisors to ensure everyone agrees with the specifications. Getting specifications spelled out as clearly and as accurately as possible protects you from surprises when the final product is delivered and allows your potential bidders to understand more accurately what is being asked of them.

Selection process

It is customary to advise potential bidders how the selection process will be conducted. For example, if you will be using a weighting system (as described above) you could list the criteria as well as the relevant weights. Building on our previous example:

Criteria	Weight (%)
Understanding of the need for the research	20
Soundness of the data collection and analysis methods	30
Previous experience	10
Ability to meet deadlines	10
Budget	20
Overall format and presentation of the proposal	10

(Continued)

Focus Box 2.1. Continued.

Clients issuing RFPs may, if their regulatory environments permit, note that neither the lowest bid nor any bid may be accepted. This protects you from being put into a situation where you have to award a contract to someone you believe is not qualified to produce the kind of product you need, even though the submitter is the lowest bidder or has the highest score.

If you are preparing an RFP for a government agency, you will probably find that your agency has 'legalese' requirements in an RFP covering, but not limited to, liability for injury or loss, requirements for the contracting company to carry insurance, preferential treatment of certain groups and ownership of intellectual property resulting from the project.

This latter point deserves comment. Although some governments currently have little understanding of standards regarding intellectual property, you have an ethical responsibility – either as the contracting authority or as the bidder – to push for respect for the contents of submitted proposals. It is morally (and usually legally) wrong to take proposals submitted to you and either (i) use them for your own purposes or (ii) to share them with other parties, such as consulting companies with whom you have friendly relationships (perhaps the one who wins the contract) for their use.

Intellectual property is a personal issue with me because a friend who developed a proprietary business model that he incorporated into a proposal to a government agency discovered that his proprietary model had been given – after his bid was unsuccessful – to his competitor for 'information'. Sadly, this is not an isolated occurrence. Such actions can result in embarrassing and expensive lawsuits for the offenders, as well as serious damages to the firms whose intellectual property has been violated. Do not take the chance. When dealing with consultants, *guarantee* that all proposals will be treated in a confidential manner and that any unsuccessful proposal will be properly disposed of (or returned to the sender).

Other details

Complex RFPs might permit potential bidders to submit questions for clarification. These questions and your answers might then be made available on a website for all other potential bidders to consult. Some processes even feature information sessions where potential bidders can ask questions in a semi-public (i.e. in front of other bidders) meeting.

The RFP may explicitly state that costs associated with the development of any proposal will not be reimbursed – this is normally understood by bidders, but it can be a useful stipulation for cases where a proposal might involve an expensive development or design process.

Mentioning – or not – the budgets available for the project is an issue of debate. Some organizations prefer not to disclose their budgets because they presume bidders will increase their proposed costs to the maximum possible under the RFP. Not providing a budget 'ballpark' may also reflect the assumption that the bidder will come in as low as possible in order to maximize her or his chances for success.

These are legitimate perspectives. However, a potential problem with the lack of information on a project's budget is that the organization may receive a wide range of differently priced bids reflecting different assumptions on the part of a bidder about how big the project is expected to be. This can be a particular problem, for example, for open-ended projects involving the development of a marketing strategy or conducting of marketing research. Some market research projects, such as the one for Walkerton described later in this chapter, are highly scalable – in other words, the project could be scaled to cost CA$15,000 or CA$150,000. Withholding information about the order of magnitude, at least, of your budget potentially does a disservice to both you and your bidders.

(*Continued*)

Focus Box 2.1. Continued.

Submission details

The RFP should end with a clear statement about to whom (with address) to send the proposal, the format (e.g. original hard copy, fax, e-mail), time and date (it is common to specify a precise time, such as 6.00 p.m. on a given day). Ideally, you should also inform the bidders when you expect a decision to be made.

As a contractor, realize that deciding on a preferred vendor or consultant is only the first step. You may then need to negotiate details about timing, payments and other technical matters before a contract is finally signed.

Distribution process

Any agency who has previously issued RFPs will have a list of potential bidders. If your employer does, this is a good place to start. However, try not to limit yourself to the same vendors. You might find better ideas or better value from new (or, to you, unknown) vendors. Moreover, it behoves agencies to nurture a competitive pool of potential consultants. Again, with government agencies, they may have a formal mechanism for issuing RFPs, perhaps through posting on a government website. Your supervisor will be able to advise you on the proper procedures for your agency.

Once you have a list, or guidelines, about how RFPs are publicly announced, you are then ready to announce your contract opportunity to your potential suppliers.

The following is an example of how the objectives of a consulting project were refined through discussions between a client and a consultant. Walkerton, Ontario, Canada has a population of 1200 people. A few years ago, their water supply became contaminated by *Escherichia coli*, a bacterium that can cause serious illness or death. Seven people died while hundreds became ill. The tragedy made national headlines and the town's image as an attractive place to live and visit was virtually destroyed. A 'Walkerton Tourism Recovery Partnership' was created by local leaders and, with financial assistance from the provincial Ministry of Tourism, issued an RFP for a marketing strategy to address the negative images of Walkerton. The goal of the project was to develop a market image based on the strengths of existing products, customer perceptions and natural features to encourage potential visitors to view the Saugeen Watershed as an attractive destination. The RFP specified the following objectives:

1. To develop profiles of visitors who come to Walkerton.
2. To develop an inventory of existing tourism products and experiences.
3. To develop three themes for promoting Walkerton in the tourism market.
4. To develop a strategy for communicating each theme in new and traditional media.

I was part of the team that submitted the winning bid. After the contract was signed, the first thing we did was to meet with the steering committee that managed the contract to explore more fully what they expected. As we suspected, the steering committee wanted a number of things that were not clearly spelled out in the RFP. For example, in terms of profiling visitors, they did not expect original data collection; rather, they wanted us to use only secondary data sources to build these profiles. Instead of developing an inventory of existing products and experiences, they wanted us to review their list to get a better understanding of what they saw as their primary attractions and to identify potential opportunities for new products that would complement those that already existed. In terms of the development of 'themes' and the communications strategy, they wanted:

- a name that could be used to promote the area around the town of Walkerton but without using the name 'Walkerton';
- a graphic design to be used on tourism brochures, advertisements and other applications to support the new name;
- suggestions for several (not necessarily just three) new tourism products or packages that could be either sold by tour operators or promoted as independent itineraries; and
- an actionable market plan, including specific media, geographic markets, timing and budget estimates.

As you can see, these expectations are somewhat different from the expectations laid out in the RFP. It was only by face-to-face discussions and courteous, professional questioning along the lines of 'What do you mean by a 'theme?' that we were able to understand exactly what our client wanted. Clarifying the meanings of certain words or phrases, making implicit assumptions explicit and raising areas of uncertainty early in discussions are essential if contract research is to be completed to the satisfaction of both parties. Developing a clear understanding of what is wanted and establishing a pattern of open communication at the outset helps you avoid any awkward or embarrassing situations when you present your final report.

FORMULATING RESEARCH QUESTIONS AND HYPOTHESES

The first phase of research involves setting your goals and objectives. Once you have reached a decision about these, you need to translate them into practical questions. These questions focus your work and help you identify more precisely what information you need to collect. The answers to these questions will ultimately become the basis for your conclusions, so the questions need to be consistent with the overall goal of your research, but be precise enough that you can answer them. These questions may be expressed literally as questions or, more generally, as a list of specific issues to be looked at.

Continuing with our Walkerton example, our team, in consultation with the steering committee, identified a number of specific questions such as:

1. What are the most important origins of visitors to the region?
2. What are the dominant trip characteristics, such as length of stay, types of accommodation, most popular activities and spending levels by major categories of expenditures?
3. How is the region currently marketed by the existing destination-marketing organizations in the region?
4. What do local leaders – industry and government – see as the potential strengths and weaknesses of the region?
5. What are the current marketing priorities of the Ontario Tourism Marketing Partnership and what are the implications of these priorities for the region?

Additional tasks were also assigned, including working with a graphic designer to develop and test five designs and tag lines through focus groups. The development of a detailed market plan was also required. Eventually the project led to the selection of a single image and tag line (slogan) that was legally registered to protect its usage. A market plan was developed, including proposed media, budgets, timing and tourism experiences to be featured in press releases and fam (familiarization) tours. This project was a fairly typical marketing research project whose overall direction was known, but its implementation involved frequent review and refinement of the tasks being conducted.

The Walkerton example is a real-world research exercise. Very different types of research are done in academic settings. One of these types involves developing answers for specific questions; a second involves the formulation and testing of hypotheses. These two approaches are illustrated in the following examples.

The first approach, the use of research questions, involves posing a small number of relatively short questions that are used to guide analysis. For example, Nishimura *et al.* (2007) were interested in the use of guidebooks by Japanese tourists for international trips. They believed, on the basis of personal observation as well as from other research, that guidebooks are used for purposes other than just making decisions about what to see in a destination. For example, guidebooks might provide a framework for how visitors will experience a new place. In other words, the books may create a sense of place in the mind of the reader. After an extensive review of studies on the use of guidebooks, the authors proposed three questions (Nishimura *et al.*, 2007, p. 276):

1. 'Is the use of guidebooks restricted to pre-purchase search for travel decision-making? If not, what are their other uses?'
2. 'Are any different needs evident between guidebook users and nonusers in the sense of a particular trip?'
3. 'Are any different characteristics evident between travellers who use guidebooks and those who do not in a particular trip?'

A questionnaire was developed to provide data that could answer these questions. The questionnaire asked about trip type, length of trip, previous travel experience at the destination, general travel experience, fluency in English, age and sex. Questions about the respondent's information needs were also asked. Questionnaires were distributed to potential respondents through a technique called purposive sampling (described later in this book). Basically, the method involved finding ways to get the questionnaire into the hands of international Japanese visitors. The tactic used was to ask two Australian travel companies to distribute the questionnaires. After getting the questionnaires back, the researchers tabulated and analysed the data. They did that using a variety of techniques and explored different patterns that emerged as they conducted their statistical tests. They found, in brief, that guidebooks are indeed used for more purposes than just decision making, that there are substantial differences in perceptions of needs by different types of travellers, and that numerous other differences exist between those who use guidebooks and those who do not.

The use of hypotheses involves a different approach to presenting questions and analysing data. This approach is illustrated by Jun *et al.* (2007) who, like Nishimura and colleagues, were interested in better understanding the search for travel information. In this case, the authors looked at online and offline information searchers and associated purchase behaviours. Using models of trip planning developed by other researchers allowed them to articulate three hypotheses (Jun *et al.*, 2007, p. 268):

- H1: 'Travel information search behaviours will be more common than travel product purchase behaviours in the pre-trip stage.'
- H2: 'Travel information search and product purchase behaviours in the pre-trip group will differ by travel products.'
- H3: 'Travel information search and product purchase in the pre-trip group will differ by levels of past travel experience.'

The researchers used a secondary data set from a survey obtained from the Canadian Tourism Commission. The original survey focused on techniques used for collecting travel information for their most recent trip and the travel services purchased on the trip (accommodation, attractions, airline flights, car rentals, activities and events). Descriptive statistics were used to test each hypothesis. The results generally confirmed each hypothesis. In this study, the 'questions' asked were relationships that were tested to see whether they were true or false, rather than an open-ended question requiring more elaborate answers (it should be noted that the hypotheses were stated in a positive format rather than as null hypotheses, as described in Chapter 1). The researchers concluded that the generally positive results from the hypothesis testing offered support for the travel planning models on which the hypotheses were based. The results also suggested areas for future research.

LITERATURE REVIEWS

A literature review is an important task in most research projects. Looking at what other researchers have done on a topic related to yours is important for several reasons. Previous work can give you ideas about how to approach your study, including the collection of data, definition of terms and conceptualization of the problem. Literature reviews can also suggest specific research questions or hypotheses to be tested. They may give you an idea of the expected outcomes of your research, although it is very important not to let other authors' findings bias your views or cause you to prejudge your results.

There are many sources of information that can be consulted for literature reviews. Refereed journal articles are the most common source used by academic researchers. Books, trade magazines, government reports, reports by agencies such as the World Tourism Organization, and conference proceedings are also frequent sources of information. Academic journal articles are the most common literature used in research, and learning how to read them is a valuable skill. See Focus Box 2.2 for suggestions about how to approach these sometimes arcane sources.

Focus Box 2.2. Reading research articles.

Confronting an article in a refereed research journal for the first time can be a bit intimidating. Most articles have similar structures and features, although the vocabulary may sometimes be a bit arcane if you are not conversant with academic writing. There are variations among journals reflecting their different disciplinary foci, their readership (e.g. strictly academic versus a mix of academic and industry readers), their mission statements and the editorial practices of the publishers. However, the basic architecture of articles is similar in mainstream tourism journals.

Structure

The typical journal article has five components. The first is the title, which typically is the shortest. Academics often like titles with colons: a main title, followed by a colon and a subtitle. For example:

Reading Academic Articles:
Practical Advice on how to Read and Interpret the Musings of Tourism Researchers

The second component is author details, usually with contact information and perhaps a very brief description of the author's research interests. The author information may immediately follow the title or it may be placed at the bottom of the first page. The next component is an abstract, usually 50 to 150 words, describing the topic of the article in

(Continued)

Focus Box 2.2. Continued.

greater detail than the title alone permits (see Chapter 10 for suggestions about how to write an abstract). Several key words may also be provided as part of the abstract. These words are used in index searches (print or electronic) for articles. They typically refer to the main themes explored in the article, where the study was done and perhaps some aspect of the methodology.

The next component is the body of the article itself. This normally comprises 90–95% of the article. Different journals and different authors have their own styles of writing and presentation; however, the body of the article typically begins with a statement of the purpose of the research as well as a discussion of the background or significance of the topic. A literature review is provided, either as a separate section or integrated into the introduction and methodology. On occasion, the article will be a review article that summarizes research that has been done on a topic. In other words, the entire article is a literature review. Whether a review article or a research article, academic papers typically include numerous citations to the work of other authors. These citations can be a valuable resource for you if you wish to pursue a topic further. An important tradition in research is that you build on the work of others and that you give credit to those who have produced work you mention.

For articles presenting original research, the author should describe the conceptual foundation of his or her research. Research questions or hypotheses are spelled out, if used. Special attention is given to the methods used to collect and analyse data. Pay attention (as appropriate) to operational definitions, variables, scales, units of analysis, sample size, when and how the data were collected, assumptions and analytical tools.

Authors then normally present the results of their findings, often using tables and figures, although subjective research studies may use words only. After the findings are presented, a discussion of the implications typically is provided. Articles may conclude with a discussion of limitations in the research and/or suggestions for further studies.

The final component of an article is the reference list. References are conventionally put at the end of an article, by the alphabetical order of the authors' (of the references used) last name. Some journals present references as footnotes, but this is rare in tourism journals. There are a number of standard referencing systems such as 'Chicago School', MLA (Modern Language Association) and APA (American Psychological Association) – see Focus Box 10.2 for a brief description of key citation systems. Journals may also use their own referencing system.

Some journals permit authors to use footnotes or endnotes to provide supplementary information – comments that do not fit into the body of the text but are still pertinent. Finally, authors may provide acknowledgements to funding agencies or organizations that were especially helpful in providing access to information, sometimes in a footnote at the beginning or end of an article.

How to read an article

This topic may sound unnecessary but, in fact, there are a number of different ways to read an article. First, you need to know why you want to read the article. There are several reasons why you might voluntarily read a research article as opposed to reading it because it is a course assignment. The reason you are reading an article will shape how you approach it. You are not necessarily expected to read every word from beginning to end as you would with a novel. Your reading can be more selective:

(Continued)

Focus Box 2.2. Continued.

- **You are reading to get an overview of some topic**. In this case, you will scan titles and abstracts of multiple articles to look for articles that explicitly discuss a topic of interest to you or that provide an extensive literature review. If an analytical article provides an extensive literature review, you may chose to skip much of the methodological, results and discussion sections and focus on the literature only. Pay attention to how the literature is structured – are there special categories or sequences of presenting material?
- **You are reading to get an idea of how to design your own research**. Concentrate on the research design section. How are key terms defined? How were data collected and analysed? What problems does the author identify? What suggestions does the author have for further research?
- **You are reading to provide a conceptual foundation to your research**. Look at how the author positioned his/her study – what assumptions, models, perspectives, methods did the author use? Who are the other authors cited in the article? Are arguments or suggestions offered that will help you justify why your approach should be tried, or why the questions you want to explore should be asked? Look at the results: what do they tell you that might lend support to you for your proposed research? In the case of well-designed empirical studies, the results tables may tell you what you need to know. All the words just provide narrative that tells you what the author wants you to think. Do not hesitate to think critically about an author's interpretation of his/her research and perhaps come to different conclusions. Of course, with subjective approaches, usually all you have to work with are the author's own interpretations (perhaps supported by a careful selection of quotations from interviews). This is not a criticism; it is just a limitation in subjective research.

A few other points

- Be selective in what you choose to highlight or underline. Remember you are reading for a purpose. Choose only those passages that serve your purpose. Highlighting everything means nothing is important.
- Be disciplined. Record all bibliographical details as you read (ideally, in the format used by your intended publishing outlet or by your school). Having to go back to track down page numbers or year of publication of an important citation when you failed to record it the first time you read the article wastes your time and can even make you hate the research-writing exercise. Think about the level of detail you need in your notes. A few comments about key approaches, definitions or findings may be sufficient. At other times, you may want to write down specific quotations to cite in your own writing.
- Learn to write by learning to read. Pay attention to how authors structure their papers, how they express their ideas, how they build an argument and how they present conclusions. While you will want to develop your own 'voice' when you write, paying attention to how other authors use language and present their ideas can help you improve your own style. Authors really do have their own 'voice' that is readily apparent to experienced readers. As a result, plagiarism is sometimes caught when a student takes a paragraph or two from someone else's work and inserts them into his own work. The sudden shift in the style from the author's original writing to the plagiarized work can be immediately obvious to someone who reads and writes for a living (like a professor).

(*Continued*)

Focus Box 2.2. Continued.

A comment on style

You will find that most articles in tourism journals are written in the third person. This practice is not arbitrary or intended to make authors crazy. Avoiding writing in the first person is intended to remind authors that the focus of their article should be objective and on their data, their findings – not themselves or their opinions. The attention of the research should be on the research itself, not the researcher. However, researchers who work in the interpretist or constructivist traditions believe that a researcher cannot separate herself or himself from the research. Some comments on writing style are provided in Chapter 10.

Conducting a literature search on a topic that you've never explored before can seem intimidating. Most research libraries have electronic search indices that you can use by entering a key word or phrase. These search phrases or key words need to balance precision with breadth. If you enter 'tourism', you will likely be deluged with tens or hundreds of thousands of 'hits'. On the other hand, a phrase such as 'culinary tourism in central Chile' may be so narrow that you will find nothing. Practice with entering different variations on a phrase or key word will eventually yield a manageable return of references.

A tactic used by many researchers to identify potential references is to scan books, journals or research encyclopedias to identify a few 'seed' sources in their reference lists. These sources are then read and their reference lists are mined for additional sources. This 'literary chain reaction' can very quickly provide you with a large number of sources. It does not guarantee that you will not miss potentially important sources, but it is a practical way to get started.

The Internet has become a popular tool for tracking down publications. It is a wide-ranging resource, allowing you potentially to tap into sources virtually anywhere in the world. One engine that has been developed for academic researchers is Google Scholar (available at http://scholar.google.ca/). To use it, type in a topic or an author's name. The site then provides you with lists of publications (on the topic or by the author). The site can also provide estimates of the number of citations to works by different authors.

While free and with a wide scope of coverage, Google Scholar has limitations. The presentation of search results is not always logical or useful. Furthermore, as of the date of writing this chapter, some publishers do not allow their online journals to be searched by Google Scholar. As a result, the counts of citations of various authors, which are of interest to some scholars as well as to academic administrators and evaluators, are unreliable. The range of sources accessible to Google Scholar is confidential. Despite these concerns, it is one more tool that you can use to get started in doing a literature search.

Another popular source is the online encyclopedia, Wikipedia. Wikipedia is a free online source of information on a wide variety of topics, although some of its sites have content that carries an access fee. Wikipedia's content is contributed by users and reviewed by volunteer administrators who judge whether the new material or editorial changes should be posted. Some academics are uncomfortable using Wikipedia, or at least allowing students to cite Wikipedia as a source. (It should be noted that many academics assert that no encyclopedia should be used as a primary source in research because encyclopedia entries are, by their very nature, someone else's summary of other people's work.) Their discomfort comes from the potential that inaccurate or false information can be posted (there are anecdotal accounts that some postings have been deliberately falsified out of mischief or maliciousness).

Wikipedia entries vary greatly in terms of quality and can contain material that is inconsistent with other postings. However, other scholars, such as Rosenzweig (2006), have suggested the overall reliability of Wikipedia is comparable to other encyclopedias, although the writing style may be choppy. This is due to the fact that much of the content is like a quilt of many pieces sewn together by many different people.

The editorial approach of Wikipedia has been criticized for emphasizing consensus (opinions drawn from a variety of sources) over expertise (or, at least, the reputation of an author). This practice has been described as 'anti-elitist', and reflects a debate about what is the most reliable source of accuracy – commonly held beliefs by non-experts or assertions by experts. For example, what weight should we place on the finding by a survey conducted in 2007 by the Associated Press and Ipsos Reid that 34% of Americans believe in ghosts? Regardless of your position on ghosts, it is important to remember that neither consensus nor credentials are an infallible road to truth.

When using any web-based source, you need to be cautious about the reliability of content. Certainly this is to be expected in the case of controversial material. However, at least one scholar, Boyd (2005), admitted that she had posted some unintentionally inaccurate entries on minor topics in anthropology when she was a student, and that many of these have never been corrected (at the time of writing this chapter). She attributed this lack of correction to the fact that her topics were too obscure to have attracted any attention.

Anyone can create a website and post whatever he wishes. The same can be said, of course, of traditional printed books. While major commercial publishers will endeavour to ensure the veracity of material they publish, anyone with sufficient time, energy and money can self-publish and sell their books through the Internet or speciality bookstores. Judging whether content on a website or in a book is accurate brings us right back to the debate over whether information should be trusted because many people assert it is true or because a small number of experts who have deeply studied the topic assert it to be true.

In contrast to online sources, peer-reviewed journal articles are generally considered to be reliable. The reason for this is that such articles are critiqued by several reviewers in a double-blind process. This process is intended to filter out dubious or unreliable research. Given the nature of both empirical and subjective research, even refereed sources cannot be said to be guaranteed that they are either 100% valid or valid for an indefinite period of time into the future. However, these sources generally have been subjected to a more rigorous assessment of their credibility and validity than most other sources.

Another type of online source is a hybrid between printed journals and online sources. A growing number of publishers are making current as well as back issues of their journals available on the Internet. Access to these online journals, though, usually requires that you have borrowing privileges at a library that has paid for an online subscription. The articles are identical to those appearing in print – only the distribution vehicle (the Internet) is different.

Despite the popularity of the Internet as an information source, it still has many gaps. Anecdotally, some tourism researchers suggest that at least 90% of tourism research is still not accessible over the Internet. That figure cannot be proved, but the fact remains that much material you will probably need to read for any research project cannot be found on the Internet. Time spent in libraries and reference centres is still essential.

As noted, the purpose of a literature review is to learn about what others have written about your topic: definitions they used, models they developed or employed, how they collected and analysed their data or conclusions they reached. If you are doing research as a consultant or employee of a firm, you often will not be expected to write up a review of all the research you have read. However, if you are doing a research project in an academic context (such as a thesis), you will usually be expected to include a literature review as part of your report. The literature review may be presented as a separate section of your paper, perhaps even titled 'Literature Review'. Alternatively, you might integrate your literature review in other sections of your paper, such as the introduction or background to your topic, and in your discussion of your methods.

In either event, use your literature review to tell a story. It should not simply be a series of unconnected sentences or paragraphs summarizing different pieces of literature you have read. Your summaries and reviews of your sources need to be linked together. As you write about what others have done, you weave a story about what the literature teaches us. You might take a historical approach – how different authors at different times approached the topic. Or you might present highlights from your sources as a series of debates between competing schools of thoughts or different methodological approaches.

Your literature review should help provide a broader context of why your topic is significant, and why the approach you will be following is a logical one. You might also comment on some of the methodological issues you will need to address in the completion of your research. Your review should eventually lead to a series of conclusions that justify what you want to do and how you want to do it. Often, your review will reveal gaps in our knowledge, some of which you might fill; or your review will summarize the evolution of thinking on a particular topic and point the way for the next step forward.

One challenge you may encounter is a lack of literature on the topic. Not finding many references often is the result of your not having spent enough time searching. However, even if nothing really has been written on your precise topic, it is usually a mistake to write the equivalent of 'Nothing has been done on this topic' in an academic paper. This statement will often get a knee-jerk reaction from your professor who will suggest you have not looked hard enough. If, after assiduously searching the literature you still find no directly related publications, then look at your topic from a broader perspective. Look for broader trends or issues that relate to your topic, and support these observations with relevant citations. Then you can note there is a need to explore the specific topic you intend to research.

COLLECTING DATA

Once you have developed your research objectives and questions, you are ready to begin thinking about how to collect your data. Data can be obtained from many different sources. These are often categorized as either primary (original data you collect) or secondary (data collected by someone else that you are able to use for your own purposes). We will look at each of these types shortly. Many research projects use only one data source, but projects that look at complex problems or that are broad in scope may use multiple data sources. The use of multiple data sources can provide you with access to a richer and wider array of data with which to work, especially if you are using secondary sources. However, be alert to the fact that different secondary data sources might be of different ages, have used different samples, were based on different definitions or assumptions or approached a topic differently. As a result, the data from multiple secondary sources might not be directly comparable.

A term often used in connection with multiple data sources is **triangulation**. The concept of triangulation is an ancient one, dating from early work in trigonometry. In a general sense, triangulation refers to the measurement of three aspects of a triangle, such as two angles and the distance between their apices to calculate other distances and angles, perhaps to calculate the distance to some object, such as a ship at sea. In a modern context, triangulation is behind global positioning systems (GPS). GPS units receive signals from a number of geosynchronous satellites; integrating the time it takes to receive a signal from each given satellite and information about the location of each satellite allows the GPS unit to specify, with a high degree of accuracy, the user's location. Triangulation also refers to the use of three or more radio tracking devices at different locations to identify the location of a transmitter, such as wildlife scientists studying the movements of a grizzly bear that has been radio-tagged.

A defining characteristic of triangulation is the use of multiple sources of data from different perspectives to arrive at a desired new piece of information. In the social sciences, triangulation is used in a number of different ways, not all of which should properly be labelled as 'triangulation'. The intent of using multiple methods is laudable – to reduce bias or error in the observation of some variable. Single measurement tools can involve a methodological or measurement error, resulting in incorrect conclusions. The use of two or more methods to measure or observe the same phenomenon helps to reduce (or at least to identify the potential existence of) observational error. But not all use of multiple methods is triangulation. The following would be an example of the misuse of the term 'triangulation'.

Assume you are interested in travel trends to some destination over the next 6 months. You might use two different approaches. The first could be a market survey in the key origin markets for that destination to assess travel intentions. This could then be supplemented with checking reservation records with hotels and tour operators working in the same market. It should be noted that these two approaches will probably not yield the same numerical results, but can provide an indication of general trends.

This approach falls short of being true triangulation on several fronts. First, the ontology, methodology and even the epistemology behind market surveys, and behind surveys associated with talking with hoteliers and tour operators, are fundamentally different. These differences mean that you cannot reliably and meaningfully combine the findings into a single measure (Blakie, 1991). Moreover, triangulation connotes the use of at least three sources of information, not just two. The approach I have just described would be more accurately labelled 'multiple methods'.

A more correct use of 'triangulation' as a term can be seen in the following situation. Suppose you observe that changes in outbound travel from some country appear to be highly correlated with changes in that country's gross domestic product (GDP) and you'd like to argue that economic growth helps to drive tourism demand. You could verify the accuracy and generalizability of your observation by collecting outbound travel flows and GDP data from other countries to see whether the correlation holds true in those situations. This situation is more analogous to the original meaning of the term 'triangulation' in that the same methods and concepts are used to define and measure the same phenomenon.

Oppermann (2000) uses the term 'triangulation' in a different context. He notes that, for example, the gender of surveyors might influence the results obtained from the administration of in-person surveys. For example, female surveyors might elicit different responses from male tourists being surveyed than male surveyors would receive. The comparison of the results of surveys administered by female versus male surveyors to test for this potential bias is something Oppermann calls 'investigator triangulation'.

One should be cautious about using the term 'triangulation'. It does not mean simply the use of a combination of different methods. It is a matter of using three or more methods or data sources that share common epistemologies and ontologies to assess the reliability of findings or to identify potential biases in data or investigator characteristics. Moreover, while triangulation in the context of applications such as global positioning systems does denote a high level of technological sophistication, the term does not denote increased methodological sophistication. Don't be fooled into thinking that triangulation in the social sciences is somehow more sophisticated than 'ordinary', non-triangulation, techniques.

Secondary data sources

Secondary data sources are sources of data that someone else has collected for their own purposes. In tourism, one of the most common forms of secondary data is data sets collected by a government organization that have been made publicly available. These data sets may be sets of printed tables summarizing data from surveys. An example of this source would be an annual tabulation of the number of visitors arriving in a given country from different origins. Visitor counts by source nation, estimated spending levels, modes of transportation, month of entry and purpose of travel might all be presented in tables. These types of sources can be useful for certain projects, but they have a couple of disadvantages. The most immediate is that you have to input the data into a form that you can manipulate, such as by creating your own database. Second, such tables typically are summaries of individual data records to which you do not have access. Your analysis will be limited to working with the higher levels of aggregation, rather than allowing you to look at the details of individual data records.

Alternatively, some secondary data are available as micro-data files in which the original entries (or perhaps an edited version of those entries in which sensitive or personal data have been removed) are available for reanalysis. This allows you to do original analyses and data manipulations within the limits of the original data set. A limitation in secondary databases is that you have to accept the definitions, methodologies and questions set up by someone else. You have no opportunity to influence the content or scope of the data you are given. On the other hand, secondary data sets allow you to explore topics without having to spend time, effort and money collecting your own data. Secondary data sets created by government agencies often have much larger sample sizes and more sophisticated data collection strategies than you could ever achieve on your own. Using secondary data lets you focus on analysis and interpretation, and not have to worry about the technicalities, costs and headaches of collecting original data.

If you choose to use a secondary data set, you will need access to something called **metadata**. Metadata are data that describe other data. These include information about the structure and content of data sets as well as administrative details such as who created the data set and when, and how the data were collected and processed before they were stored and subsequently disseminated. Metadata typically are provided in two ways. Some are an integral part of the data tables disseminated, showing structural information such as variable names and values. Other data, particularly administrative details as well as information about data quality (such as confidence intervals), may be presented separately. Metadata are especially important if you wish to be able to compare how different data were produced, such as looking at tourism statistics produced by different national tourism or statistical agencies.

A potentially valuable source of data for management, marketing or operations research is **administrative data**. These include reservation and sales records for individual hotels, hotel and resort occupancy data, room rates, attendance data for parks and other attractions, airline bookings and flights for individual air carriers, purchase records for supplies by restaurants, enquiries made to destination-marketing organization (DMO) call centres and so on. Such information is, of course, proprietary and normally not made available to researchers. However, these data, when properly analysed, can provide very useful insights for business planning and decision making, by either an in-house research team or a consultant. One type of administrative data that may be less sensitive and thus available for use by a trusted researcher is a list of the postal codes of customers/guests of a business. This information can sometimes be paired with other demographic (usually from census) databases that provide geo-demographic profiles. For example, a list of the postal codes of campers at a park can be mined to provide demographic profiles of the park visitors, as well as mapped to indicate the most important origins of the campers. This type of geo-demographic mapping is sometimes provided by market research firms who specialize in such tabulations.

Tourism data can also be obtained from commercial sources. Market research firms sometimes conduct **syndicated surveys** – surveys operated on an ongoing basis, the data from which are then sold to clients on a subscription basis or as a one-time purchase. These surveys can sometimes be supplemented with additional customized questions for an additional fee. Syndicated data sources are most likely to be purchased by national and provincial/state tourism offices, large DMOs and large corporations with substantial research budgets. Data are typically obtained through the use of large-scale consumer panels recruited by the research firm. These panels receive regular surveys, often through the Internet, but mail-back is also used. The data are tabulated and standard format reports produced, or custom analyses done if requested by a client.

Another important source of secondary data for many tourism researchers is the official statistics collected by national statistical and tourism organizations. This information can be essential if you are describing the magnitude of and trends in a nation's tourism sector, or if you want to make comparisons between volumes and values of tourism in different nations. The United Nations Statistics Division has developed a set of general principles regarding the collection, use and dissemination of official statistics, including tourism statistics – see Focus Box 2.3.

Focus Box 2.3. Basic principles of official statistics.

Statistics on tourism are collected by national statistical and tourism agencies. These data are valuable sources of information for policy, planning and marketing. The United Nations Statistics Division has developed a set of ten principles regarding the collection of official statistics by government agencies:

Principle 1. Official statistics provide an indispensable element in the information system of a democratic society, serving the government, the economy, and the public with data about the economic, demographic, social, and environmental situation. To this end, official statistics that meet the test of practical utility are to be compiled and made available on an impartial basis by official statistical agencies to honour citizens' entitlement to public information.

Principle 2. To retain trust in official statistics, statistical agencies need to decide according to strictly professional considerations, including scientific principles and professional ethics, on the methods and procedures for the collection, processing, storage, and presentation of statistical data.

Principle 3. To facilitate a correct interpretation of the data, statistical agencies are to present information according to scientific standards on the sources, methods, and procedures of the statistics.

Principle 4. Statistical agencies are entitled to comment on erroneous interpretation and misuse of statistics.

Principle 5. Data for statistical purposes may be drawn from all types of sources, be they surveys or administrative records. Statistical agencies are to choose the source with regard to quality, timeliness, costs, and the burden on respondents.

Principle 6. Data on individual persons on individual firms collected by statistical agencies are to be strictly confidential and used exclusively for statistical purposes.

(Continued)

Focus Box 2.3. Continued.

Principle 7. The laws, regulations, and measures under which statistical systems operate are to be made public.

Principle 8. Co-ordination among statistical agencies within countries is essential to achieve consistency and efficiency in the statistical system.

Principle 9. The use by statistical agencies in each country of international concepts, classifications, and methods promotes the consistency and efficiency of statistical systems at all official levels.

Principle 10. Bilateral and multilateral co-operation in statistics contributes to the improvement of systems of official statistics in all countries.

Source: United Nations Statistics Division, 2006.

Primary data sources

This section provides a brief overview of major primary sources of data. More details of primary data collections are provided in the next few chapters. Primary data sources refer to data collected by the researcher for his or her own use. These sources can be roughly associated with either empirical or subjective paradigms. However, some sources have both empirical and subjective qualities. Moreover, a researcher may use two or more different types of sources in a single project.

Empirical sources

The most common primary tourism data source arguably is **surveys**. Surveys are a tool to solicit information from a group of people (such as visitors or managers) through the use of questionnaires (we will look at questionnaire design in Chapter 3). Surveys are usually administered to a relatively small portion – a sample – of a larger population (we will discuss the details of sampling in Chapter 4). Surveys can be administered in a number of ways, each with advantages and disadvantages. The most common techniques are personal contact with the potential respondent, distribution by postal mail, distribution by e-mail (either as an attachment or with direction to a web-based survey) or by telephone. Researchers may combine techniques, such as doing a short personal interview during which the researcher asks the respondent whether he or she would be willing to participate in a follow-up survey that would be mailed to him or her.

Travel diaries are a special version of surveys. In this case, the researcher prepares a standard format for the diary – usually in hard copy – that solicits specific information for each day of a visitor's trip, although text messages or e-mail can also be used. The information sought might include specific activities, sites visited, satisfaction levels with various aspects of the trip, or expenditures. Because diaries are (in principle) filled out every day, the data they collect should be reliable, accurate and detailed. However, they can place a heavy response burden on the subject. The diary needs to be as simple and as clear as possible to maintain the interest of the respondent. Respondents are usually provided with some sort of compensation upon completing the diary, such as a cash payment, to maintain their commitment to the project.

The term 'survey' is normally applied to the use of a structured questionnaire. Another form of data collection that resembles a survey in that it involves asking people questions is **personal** (or **in-depth) interviews**. In-depth interviews (discussed in Chapter 5) employ different tactics, but they generally involve posing questions and then probing the answers to obtain more detail and a better understanding of the respondent's answers. Interviews may be taped or the researcher may make written notes, depending on the comfort level of the subject with being taped, the need to have a verbatim transcript and other aspects of the interview context. The analysis of in-depth interviews may be done through a content analysis of a transcript of the interview, or it may involve tools of some of the subjective paradigms such as grounded theory, as discussed in Chapter 1.

Field research, another tactic for collecting primary data, may be either empirical or subjective (participant observation is a form of subjective field research and is discussed below). On an empirical level, field research means going to a location to make systematic observations of some phenomenon. The range of potential observations is quite broad. It can be as simple as observing the licence plates of cars at a destination to get a sense of the origins of visitors, or tabulating variations in the number of people arriving at an attraction, accommodation or restaurant over the course of a day. It can involve more sophisticated tasks such as mapping land uses, or the tracking of the patterns of movements of people (for example, in North America, field research has revealed that most people turn to the right, circulating counter-clockwise, when entering a theme park with a circular layout). Field study can be used to count the number of different types of services in a park, or to record the locations of different types of tourism businesses in a tourism district. It can be applied to an assessment of the condition of tourism infrastructure or the accessibility of tourism services to people with disabilities.

Field research can be a useful way to obtain information that would not be available from other sources (it can also be an occasion to spend time in a place you like to visit, but remember you are not there just to hang out!). There are several important considerations in doing field research (Zelditch, 1962). The spatial or temporal scope of your data collection needs to be appropriate to your project's objectives, as well as being feasible in terms of your time and budget. Observation of people's behaviours may involve ethical issues that you will need to clear through your institution's ethics office and/or the management of the site you visit. The use of a camera to record land uses or buildings may run the risk of violating privacy or security measures in some places. For example, the use of personal cameras is normally not allowed around customs counters in airports. Some countries prohibit the photographing of any security or police facility.

If your field research involves collecting data in a foreign country or in a remote area where there is a risk of injury or illness, you need to take precautions to ensure someone knows where you are, and that you have taken due care in terms of ensuring you have health insurance and the means to be evacuated if necessary. Educational institutions usually have formal policies and procedures regarding risks to students undertaking field study, including risk briefings of students by professors supervising their research.

Subjective sources

Focus groups (also discussed in Chapter 5) are sometimes described as a type of group interview. A focus group involves hosting a small number of people in a session to respond to a number of focused questions or issues. As in an interview, you probe participants' comments and ask supplemental questions to clarify the person's meaning. Unlike other interview settings, though, focus group participants respond to each other, supplementing or supporting a comment someone makes, or offering an alternative view. As with personal interviews, focus group sessions may be taped (either audio alone or video) or handwritten notes may be taken.

Researchers are sometimes interested in the content of tourism advertisements, tour books, newspaper articles or other published media. Research on such subjects involves **content analysis** (discussed in Chapter 9). For example, I had a student who looked at the appearances of people in promotional materials developed by DMOs. She examined the balance of females and males, different ethnic groups (based on visual appearance) and age (young versus old). She counted the number of appearances of each group in various types of photographs, such as active versus passive images, landscape theme, cultural themes or service environments such as restaurants. She also considered the size and placement of each advertisement in print material. She identified, through her analysis, broad patterns related to the frequency of different social groups in tourism advertisements, as well as the setting (e.g. active versus passive, visitor versus tourism employee) of the various images.

An unusual (but increasingly common) source of primary data is recyclable cameras. The researcher recruits a number of subjects and provides them with recyclable cameras and instructions to photograph some type of subject, such as the sights in a historic district of a city that catch the participant's eye. Once the film or digital memory has been used up, the subject returns the camera to the researcher who prints the photographs. One set is given to the participant as a 'thank you', and the second set is retained by the researcher for analysis. This method is sometimes called **visual analysis** as a variation of content analysis. This technique is explored in greater detail, too, in Chapter 9.

Participant observation (Bruyn, 1972) is a special form of field research in which you become involved in the organization or community being studied. The idea behind this method is that you can gather first-hand, personal knowledge of some situation, typically some form of interpersonal or inter-group interactions. This method of data collection may provide you with a deeper understanding of the dynamics and complexities of your study situation than the use of surveys or more casual observation. Not surprisingly, though, participant observation has a number of challenges you will want to understand before you try it.

Your presence can influence interactions in the group, unpredictably changing the social situation you are studying. Participant observation is especially vulnerable to both the narrative fallacy and confirmation bias. Any researcher using this method thus needs to be cognizant of the potential for error in interpretation of his or her observations. It should be emphasized that participant observation involves more than just observing a tourism attraction or attending a festival during which you make observations and collect data. Just as being present in the audience of a play does not make you a member of the cast of the play, being present at a festival (for example) does not make you a 'participant' in the sense of being a volunteer, organizer or performer at the event. Of course, if you were to take on one of those roles, you could be described as doing participant observation.

Ethnography is another form of field research. A researcher doing ethnography typically examines a community, which may be a geographic or other form of community such as an interest group or a profession, to develop a deeper understanding of some aspect of the community. Special attention is paid to the meaning of 'symbols'. Symbols are tangible artefacts of a culture, such as architecture, clothing or food. Symbols may also be intangible, such as songs or dances. An ethnographer may be interested in more fully describing and understanding the significance of some symbols, such as the cultural meanings of a particular food or social gathering. Alternatively, he may be interested in explaining some phenomenon, such as how the community responds to a sudden, substantial growth of the number of visitors to a small town. The search for understanding requires the ethnographer to recognize the broader social context of whatever he is studying, rather than looking at a phenomenon in isolation.

Ethnographers refer to two different perspectives in the search for understanding a culture. The first, and generally the goal of ethnography, is the **emic** perspective. This is the search for understanding how members of a group interpret their world. The second perspective is the **etic** perspective, which refers to how outsiders perceive another culture. A challenge for ethnographers is to move from the etic perspective in which she observes a community as a group of 'others' to the emic perspective, in which she is able to perceive the community through the eyes and values of the members of the community.

Ethnographic research generally begins with the researcher doing a literature review on the topic of interest and acquiring as much background information about the community as possible. Variables to be studied or questions to be explored are outlined at the outset, although these may be refined as the researcher gathers more information. Generally, ethnographers work to avoid having preconceptions of their findings, and strive to try to understand the experiences and perceptions of their subjects. Data are gathered in the field by identifying key informants who can offer insights and an overview of the situation. They are then asked for the names of other people who could provide additional information – this is sometimes referred to as chain sampling or snowball sampling. As a result, ethnographic research can require the researcher to be immersed in the community for months or even years.

A similar term, **ethnology**, sometimes leads to confusion or debate about the differences between ethnography and ethnology. Ethnology (also called cultural anthropology) connotes analysis, cumulative data collection and the explicit or implicit comparison of different cultures. As noted above, ethnography connotes a search for a more subjective and intuitive understanding of a single culture. However, the two terms are sometimes used interchangeably.

CHOOSING AN ANALYTICAL METHOD

Silverman (2000, p. 239) once opined, 'There are usually no Brownie points awarded for successfully gathering your data. In the final assessment, everything comes down to what you do with your data'. A similar view is expressed in an anonymous saying, 'Collecting data is a lot like collecting garbage. You better know what you are going to do with it before you start piling it up'. It can be annoying to discover, once you sit down to analyse your data, that you have far more data than you really need. And it can be very disheartening to discover, after all your hard work, that you have collected the wrong information or not enough information.

The choice of a method for analysing your data, and actually applying the method, also are essential components of the research process. Details about specific methods are covered elsewhere in this book. This section will provide you with a broad overview of some of the general types of methods that can be employed. Remember, though, that the range of analytical techniques is very broad, and your choice will be shaped by your data and research objectives. We will consider some of the broad types of methods from the standpoint of the three functional perspectives of research: description, explanation and prediction.

You should also note that while I have discussed sources of data before methods, the two topics normally are considered together, with each influencing the choice of the other.

Description

'If you are out to *describe* the truth, leave elegance to the tailor' (Einstein, undated) [emphasis added]. I have no idea what Einstein meant by that comment. The goal of most descriptive studies is to summarize, as clearly and succinctly as possible, observations you have made about the topic of your research. There are a wide variety of methods that can be used for descriptive research, but generally they are empirically based; that is, they are based on observation, not interpretation. Description means reporting what you have observed without interpreting the patterns; interpretation moves you into the realm of explanation or even action research. Description can be the sole purpose of a project, or it might be a part of a larger goal that includes the search for explanations or the development of strategies to address some problem. Descriptive research is an important type of research in that description can provide background on which other research may be based, or used to inform marketing or policy decisions.

Much description involves the use of statistics, or at least, numerical measures. Common measures include:

- frequencies (counts and percentages);
- measures of the 'average' value of numerical observations, such as mean, median and mode;
- measures of the spread of numerical observations, such as range, variance and standard deviation; and
- measures of skewness and kurtosis (the degree of asymmetry of the distribution of data and the 'peakedness' of the distribution of data, respectively).

More sophisticated statistical tools can also be used (see Appendix 1 for a description of the following terms as well as other statistical tools), such as **ANOVA**, non-parametric tests like **chi square**, scale reliability measures such as **Cronbach's alpha** and correlation measures such as **Pearson's correlation**.

Description can be non-numerical as well. You might describe the structure of an event-organizing body by developing a chart illustrating the various components and functions of the organization. You might collect historical information to describe the development of a destination. Maps can be prepared to describe land uses or transportation linkages between different places. Description is essential in developing an understanding of the physical, social or political environment of some tourism phenomenon you may study further or for which you wish to develop recommendations. If you are interested in examining the accessibility of resorts for people with disabilities, you will collect data on the layout and other physical characteristics of the resorts.

Case studies (see Chapter 8) are an important type of descriptive research, involving data sources that range from numerical administrative data through in-depth interviews to historical documents. It is worth noting that case studies illustrate the fuzziness of the boundaries of description and explanation, as we saw in Chapter 1. Descriptions presented in case studies are sometimes interpreted as providing explanations. For example, a detailed description of a management–labour dispute in a hotel, including the history of previous conflicts as well as the recent actions and perceptions of both parties surrounding the dispute, begins to suggest explanations for the conflict.

Explanation

Doing research to understand cause and effect is a familiar task; however, accurately identifying causal connections is challenging. Establishing causal links using empirical research is subject to the asymmetry limitations of empirical research – that is, you can determine whether your conclusions are wrong, but you can never confirm with 100% reliability that they are correct. The limitations associated with causal connections developed through the use of subjective paradigms are still applicable as well. Given these cautions, though, researchers employ a variety of strategies to explore possible explanations of tourism phenomena.

One of the most common empirical tactics is to look at correlations between a dependent variable and one or more independent variables using tools such as least squares regression or multiple regression. A truism drilled into the head of every social scientist is that correlation is not causation. However – and I hope this statement will not be misinterpreted – the finding of a statistically significant correlation between two variables can be tentative evidence of causation, although correlation is more reliably used for disconfirmation of – disproving – a hypothesized relationship. The failure to find a significant correlation strongly suggests that a proposed causal relationship is not valid.

The finding of a correlation may be only a spurious correlation, attributable to chance or, more insidiously, to the impact of a third variable that influences both your variables. For example, I once statically demonstrated that the volume of sunscreen sold in Canada (over the course of a year) is significantly related to the number of Americans entering Canada. However, this does not mean that most sunscreen is purchased by Americans while visiting Canada. Rather, the correlation reflects the fact that both phenomena peak in the summer and plummet in the winter.

A more subtle problem in the relationship between correlation and causation concerns being able to identify what is cause and what is effect. For example, drawing on a non-tourism example, some health activitists blame obesity in the USA on the increasingly large portion sizes of food from fast-food restaurants. This phenomenon gained substantial notoriety with the release of the film, *SuperSize Me*, in 2004. In this movie, the protagonist adopted a diet of large burgers, fries and soft drinks to 'prove' how unhealthy such a diet, when carried to an extreme, could be. However, as Landsburg (2007) notes, the rise of obesity began before the increase in portion sizes. Rather than certain restaurants' encouraging customers to eat more, it is more likely that they are simply responding to the demand for larger single sizes of food. In other words, while eating more (with no change in physical activity) may make you obese, being obese also makes you more likely to eat more. Obese people often eat more, and the growth of serving sizes is in response to demand for bigger portions by obese people. There are many hypotheses about what triggered the American epidemic of obesity, but changes in portion sizes are more likely an effect rather than a cause. Remember that not only does correlation not prove causation, but if there is a causal connection it may be more subtle than you think.

Another approach specifically designed to explore causal relationships is **means-end analysis** (Gutman, 1982). Means-end analysis is a tool that assists you in digging through a hierarchy of explanations for a person's choices or preferences to get at deeper causes. The results represent a hierarchy or 'ladder' of explanations from immediate explanations to deeper motivations.

This type of analysis is based on several assumptions about human values and behaviours. First, values (or desired end-states of existence) influence how consumers make decisions. For example, being perceived by your friends as being sophisticated might be a desired end state that could influence your choice of vacation destinations. Second, people cope with myriad options by grouping them into a smaller number of categories. Thus, activities such as drinking fine wine, going to art museums, attending concerts and taking out a season subscription to a repertory theatre company might be grouped together into a 'cultural recreation' category. This is a particularly important assumption because the number of means to any given end is very large, whereas the number of desirable ends is relatively small. Third, consumer choices have consequences. Your choice of a particular type of weekend getaway will influence the degree of satisfaction and pleasurable memories on Monday when you return to school or work. Closely related to this assumption, people tend to equate certain consequences with certain actions. For example, you may equate a sense of adventure with scuba-diving and skydiving.

Means-end analysis involves asking people about why they choose a particular option. You then listen to their responses and ask why they answered the way they did. When you hear that response, you probe again, until you reach what appears to be a desired end state. Judica and Perkins (1992) used the means-end ladder to explore why people chose to consume sparkling wines, such as champagne. The initial reasons included factors such as brand name, price, taste and carbonation. When pushed further, consumers explained they were interested in 'experience', 'quality' and 'alternatives to hard liquor'. Further rounds of probing led to explanations such as the desire to impress others, a reward for an accomplishment, to create and image of sophistication or to socialize. Finally, the authors identified four end states that they believed to be at the root of the decision to consume sparkling wine: self-esteem, belonging, accomplishment and family life.

There are many other tools, approaches and models that can be used to explore causal relationships in tourism phenomena. Time spent reviewing journal articles will help you identify these myriad other possibilities.

Prediction/forecasting

Charles Kettering, an important early 20th century entrepreneur and prolific inventor, once wrote, '[m]y interest is in the future because I am going to spend the rest of my life there' (Kettering, 1949). Being interested in the future is why people engage in forecasting. The specific motivations for being interested in the future may be related to the need to plan appropriate levels of tourism facility development; to estimate potential demand from different markets; to schedule workloads or human resource needs; to anticipate cash flow; to assist in the development of feasibility studies; to understand possible economic, environmental or social impacts; to conduct benefit–cost analyses; to undertake a feasibility study; to evaluate the potential effects of proposed governmental regulations; or to predict the trends or outcomes of many other situations or initiatives.

The forecasting of any social or economic phenomena is fraught with challenges, and tourism is no exception. Frechtling (1996) identified a number of special difficulties in tourism forecasting. The first of these is that historical data are often missing for tourism phenomena. This is a problem because many forecasting models require a time series of at least ten observations (such as data for each year for a 10-year period) collected with consistent definitions and procedures. Recall the example of Canada's change in its operational definition of tourism described in Chapter 1. Such changes destroy time series. In other circumstances, time series data are simply not possible. For example, attendance at a World's Fair or the Olympics is an idiosyncratic phenomenon because the occurrence of these events, at least in terms of location, is unique. In these situations, other modelling approaches are needed (see, for example, Xie and Smith, 2000).

Tourism demand can vary dramatically from season to season. Sometimes these patterns are fairly routine, which makes prediction easier. But if the fluctuations are volatile, prediction will be more difficult. Moreover, tourism is sensitive to other events such as economic recessions, natural disasters, crime, terrorism and epidemics. These events are fundamentally unpredictable in the long run, making accurate forecasting of tourism very challenging.

Tourism is motivated by many different forces – vacation or holiday entitlements, friends and relatives, business, religion, health, sports and so on, as well as the vagaries of fads and popular tastes. To complicate matters more, the same person may travel for leisure one month and then travel for business the next month – perhaps to the same locations. As we saw in Chapter 1, there is no single tourism commodity. Tourism demand consists of demand for many different products, and the demand for each is subject to different forces. Despite ongoing research, we still lack a thorough understanding of how tourism-related decisions are made, including budgets, timing and destinations. And, as Frechtling (1996) reminds us, most tourism sales do not occur where consumers live but can occur literally anywhere in the world. All these facts make tourism forecasting challenging.

Forecasting tools are often classified as either quantitative or qualitative (or we could use the distinction between empirical and subjective, as discussed in Chapter 1, as well). Quantitative tools can be further subdivided into extrapolation models, structural models and causal models. Extrapolation models make no assumptions about the forces driving change, other than the assumption that past rates of change will continue into the future. Put simplistically, an extrapolation model involves plotting the historical change of some phenomenon, such as the number of visitors to a destination coming from a given origin, over a period of time. Using either graphic tools such as drawing a line through a plot of the data or statistical tools such as least squares regression, the trend line is extrapolated to the target date. Despite its simplicity and lack of consideration of causal factors, extrapolation can produce reasonably reliable forecasts under stable market conditions in the short run (1–3 years). Extrapolation does not necessarily assume a linear trend. Other curve-fitting tools such as quadratic equations or logarithmic functions can also be employed.

Structural modelling is a more sophisticated approach that uses variables believed to influence the values of the target variable (say, visitor levels). This type of modelling usually involves the creation of some version of a general linear model, such as a multiple regression equation, relating two or more independent variables to a dependent variable. You might think the key difference between structural modelling and extrapolation is that structural modelling uses multiple independent variables. However, a more basic difference is that structural forecasting is based on explicit hypotheses about which variables shape changes in the phenomenon being studied. Structural modelling allows you to explore the nature of different relationships among variables in tourism behaviour, and to test the impact of different scenarios for market conditions. However, these models can be laborious and expensive to construct. You need to have a good understanding of the phenomenon you want to model in order to decide which variables to include.

Causal modelling (sometimes referred to as simulation modelling) builds on the notion of structural modelling. Whereas structural modelling describes a forecasting scenario in terms of dependent and independent variables, causal modelling allows for interactions and feedback among variables so that any given variable affects, and is affected by, other variables. For example, currency exchange rates, interest rates and GDP growth all interact with each other and influence volumes of travellers from other countries to a given destination country in complex ways. Thus, causal modelling more realistically reflects the relationships among variables in the real world. However, causal models are complex to construct and calibrate, and have substantial data requirements. They also require that you have a good understanding of all critical variables as well as accurate data for them. The omission of an important variable can greatly affect the accuracy of your forecast. Causal models can also amplify the impact of random error in your data.

There are two primary qualitative forecasting tools used in tourism – travel intentions surveys and Delphi methodology. Travel intentions surveys are discussed further in Chapter 3. Qualitative forecasting may be done when there are insufficient historical data with which to work, or the environment is subject to rapid and unpredictable change; for example, a quantitative model to accurately reflect the impact of a major terrorist attack in some country on travel to that country would be very difficult if not impossible to develop because of the largely unpredictable nature of terrorist attacks. Qualitative modelling may also be done for long-term forecasts and/or the emergence of new technologies; there is, as an illustration, no plausible way to quantitatively forecast when (or if) space travel will become available to the majority of travellers.

Travel intentions surveys are, as the name suggests, surveys of consumers that ask about the target population's intentions or expectations to take a trip in some specified period. The results of travel intentions surveys usually are presented as percentages of respondents reporting plans to take a trip in a given period, or to take a trip to a specific destination. These percentages have a more solid statistical basis if the sample on which they are made is reliable. However, the results still reflect expressed opinions only.

Delphi methodology involves the structured use of a panel of experts to generate a set of preliminary forecasts that are eventually refined (it is hoped) through multiple iterations of surveys of the experts' panel. The results of a Delphi forecast represent consensus of the experts, and may be expressed in probabilistic terms. However, these probabilities have no solid statistical basis and are fundamentally a matter of opinion.

CONCLUSIONS

The motivations for doing tourism research are diverse: academic requirements, job assignments, profit and intrinsic curiosity. Research, like the creation of art, mixes creativity and skill. The practice of either can be an intensely personal experience. The motivations for either may be intrinsic (driven by curiosity or the desire to create), mandatory (as an academic degree requirement or a job assignment) or commissioned (such as through a consulting contract. Your results are ultimately the product of your own intellect and intuition. If you don't enjoy the challenges of asking and answering questions using the best methods and data available, positioning your work in the large canon of work done by other researchers, and at least can tolerate the scrutiny of your work by others, choose another career path. Of course, students often find a research project imposed on them as part of their degree requirements. In which case, remember – the project, with the advice and support of your supervisor, can come to a successful conclusion. You may even learn some things or have some experiences that might be fun.

Tourism research is about asking and answering questions. As I argued in the Preface, the foundation of research is a good question – good in the sense that it: (i) is answerable; and (ii) leads to new knowledge. In tourism, as the title of this book suggests, that new knowledge often has practical applications. However, whether you, as the researcher, are in a position to apply the results or whether you share them with someone else who might apply them, depends on the topic, your position and the organizational, social or political environment in which you work. Thus, an important and humbling caution about doing research while a student: student research rarely has any significant effect in the real world. The reasons for this include: (i) the limited quality of the research (budget, time, data, analysis, interpretation); (ii) the fact that most student research papers will never be seen, regardless of their quality, by anyone other than the student and her/his family, friends and supervisor; and (iii) students lack the contacts and expertise to insert their work into the decision- or policy-making activities of organizations.

Do not let this discourage you. Your primary goal in doing student research is to learn (and, of course, to fulfil your degree requirements). You have your entire career to make a difference. Experience in doing research – and in learning how to think critically and express yourself logically – are valuable skills in any career, whether or not you become a researcher.

Regardless of your motivation, planning and conducting a tourism research project involves numerous tasks, from clarifying the purpose of the project, through review of related studies, specification of data sources and other resources, to the analysis of the data and reporting of results (techniques for reporting your results are covered in Chapter 10). Managing a research project is quite different from simply following a recipe or an instruction manual. It requires judgement, intuition and flexibility as well as technical knowledge.

Potential data sources include both sources that someone else has collected for other purposes but that are available for your use (secondary sources) and the collection of original data (primary sources). Data may also be empirically based or based on the use of subjective sources such as personal interviews or focus groups. The choice of a technique to analyse the data will be driven by both the nature of your research questions and the type of data collected. It is a wise practice to know how you will analyse your data before you begin to collect them. Otherwise you may have too much, too little or the wrong type of data for your problem.

The basic methods used in research can be classified as descriptive, explanatory or predictive. Other categories of methods sometimes mentioned by other researchers, such as action research or evaluation research, are actually combinations of these three basic types of methods. Description and explanation are fundamental tasks in much tourism research. Indeed, arguably the great majority of tourism research projects address what is (description), or how what is came to be (explanation). The distinction between these – describing 'what is' and 'why it is' – may seem clear in principle, but this distinction is often a matter of emphasis in a research project. Prediction is also an important objective of many tourism projects. However, forecasting tourism tends to be a challenging task because of the complex nature of tourism phenomena and the volatile forces that shape tourism demand, supply and impacts.

There are also different research designs that can be employed in tourism research. We looked at some of the major ones in Chapter 1. Some researchers select a particular design as a way of framing all their research, and largely limit themselves only to topics that are amenable to their particular philosophical orientation. However, the great majority of researchers – including me – take a more pragmatic approach. We identify and refine a question first, and then select a research design, data sources and methods that will help us search for the answer.

As noted before, tourism research is fundamentally about asking and answering questions. These activities should be intrinsically creative and rewarding. As you move forward in your own research, search first for the pleasure and satisfaction of creating new knowledge and of doing a good job, using the best standards of research. Worry about the degree, contract or employment requirements second.

REFERENCES

Blakie, N.W.H. (1991) A critique of the use of triangulation in social research. *Quality and Quantity* 25, 115–136.

Boyd, D. (2005) *Academia and Wikipedia: Many-to-Many*. http://many.corante.com/archives/2005/01/04/academia_and_wikipedia.php (accessed 15 November 2007).

Bruyn, S. (1972) *The Human Perspective in Sociology: the Methodology of Participant Observation*. Prentice-Hall, Englewood Cliffs, New Jersey.

Einstein, A. (undated) http://www.quotationspage.com/quote/3011.html (accessed 11 November 2007).

Frechtling, D. (1996) *Practical Tourism Forecasting*. Butterworth-Heinemann, Oxford, UK.

Gutman, J. (1982) A means-end chain model based on consumer categorization processes. *Journal of Marketing* 46, 60–72.

Judica, F. and Perkins, W. (1992) A means-end approach to the market for sparkling wine. *International Journal of Wine Marketing* 4(1),10–19.

Jun, S.H., Vogt, C. and Mackay, K. (2007) Relationships between travel information search and travel product purchase in pre-trip contexts. *Journal of Travel Research* 45, 266–274.

Kettering, C. (1949) http://thinkexist.com/quotes/charles_f._kettering/2.html (accessed 9 November 2007).

Landsburg, S. (2007) *More Sex is Safer Sex*. Free Press, New York.

Nishimura, S., Waryzak, R. and King, B. (2007) The use of guidebooks by Japanese overseas tourists: a quantitative approach. *Journal of Travel Research* 45, 275–284.

Oppermann, M. (2000) Triangulation – a methodological discussion. *International Journal of Tourism Research* 2, 141–146.

Rosenzweig, R. (2006) Can history be open source? Wikipedia and the future of the past. *The Journal of American History* 93, 117–146.

Silverman, D. (2000) *Doing Qualitative Research: a Practical Handbook*. Sage, London.

United Nations Statistics Division (2006) *Fundamental Principles of Official Statistics*. http://unstats.un.org/unsd/methods/statorg/FP-English.htm (accessed 5 November 2007).

Xie, P. and Smith, S.L.J. (2000) Towards improvements in World's Fair attendance forecasts. *Event Management* 6, 15–24.

Zelditch, M. (1962) Some methodological problems of field studies. *American Journal of Sociology* 67, 566–576.

chapter 3

How to Design a Questionnaire

WHY THIS IS IMPORTANT

Questionnaires arguably are the most important tool for gathering data for tourism research. Although questionnaires (sometimes called survey instruments) are familiar to most people, the design of an effective questionnaire can be surprisingly challenging. The wording and order of questions and the graphic design of the questionnaire may seem to be simple matters, but often are much more challenging than you might anticipate. Confusion about meaning, logic, content and the intent of questions frequently arises in questionnaires designed by someone who has not carefully considered their design. In the real world of professional research, it is not uncommon to take 6 months and a dozen drafts before finalizing a questionnaire's format.

Badly designed questionnaires annoy your respondents who may simply dispose of them rather than return them (when given a badly designed questionnaire, I sometimes make corrections on it and return it to the researcher/agency with my suggestions – but without the answers they were hoping to get). Your design must ensure that you get the necessary information in a form that allows you to code the responses easily, but still be respondent-friendly. The success of much empirical research depends on how well you design and administer your survey. Questionnaire design thus is one of the most important skills for a researcher to have. This chapter covers some of the basic skills associated with this task.

In addition to designing a questionnaire, you have to distribute it. There are numerous delivery vehicles, each with advantages and challenges. Which you choose requires an informed trade-off of their strengths and weaknesses in light of your research needs. We will thus consider some common delivery mechanisms. The choice of a delivery vehicle is influenced by the source of your sample. The topic of selecting a sample is sufficiently complex that we will look at it in the next chapter rather than in this one. This chapter will consider different types of questions and when you would use each. We will consider question format in some detail, as well as overall questionnaire structure. We will also look at tactics associated with coding the results from questionnaires for statistical analysis. Finally, we will examine the relative merits of different ways of administering surveys to help you make an informed choice when it becomes time for you to do a survey.

Surveys are encounters in which you ask people questions. This fact introduces issues of privacy and ethics. If you are doing a survey in the context of academic research, you will need to obtain ethics approval from your school. Ethics and/or political reviews of surveys may also be required for surveys done through governmental agencies; and typically, your supervisor will review any questionnaire being sent out by a private or not-for-profit organization. Be sure to start planning your survey sufficiently in advance so that you can obtain necessary approvals. A clear, well-designed survey that asks essential information only can help speed the ethics review process. Ethics requirements typically include how you will guarantee confidentiality of your respondents' answers, assurances that the potential respondent has the right not to answer any question or even to take part in the survey, as well as the disposition of the completed surveys (storage for a specified period of time or shredding upon completion of the study). Agencies will also want to ensure that the content of the questionnaire does not cast any negative light on the organization or could cause political embarrassment for them.

Before we begin, a few words about terminology may be helpful. 'Questionnaire' refers to the instrument you use to collect data. 'Survey' normally refers to the entire process of designing and administering a questionnaire to a sample of respondents. However, some researchers will use 'survey' to mean 'questionnaire'; the context of the word will usually make the intended meaning clear.

WHY DO SURVEYS?

Surveys are a common data collection tactic in tourism, but they are not the only way to collect data, as we saw in Chapter 2. Before doing a survey, be certain that a survey makes sense for your project. Instead of surveys, you may want to consider observation of crowd behaviour, participant observation, in-depth personal interviews or the use of secondary data (which may be based on surveys done by another organization).

Surveys are used when you need to collect original empirical information, such as opinions from a group of people. These groups may represent the general population in an area, or – more commonly in tourism – a subpopulation that shares some characteristic, such as being visitors to a destination or belonging to certain segments (backpackers or seniors, as two examples). Surveys may be administered to owners, managers or employees of individual businesses, or to representatives of organizations such as a local DMO or an industry association.

Surveys are useful for collecting information from a potentially large number of people. Tourism surveys may have sample sizes of tens of thousands and potentially from wide geographic areas. As a result, the types of questions that can be asked have to be relatively simple. Probing a respondent's answers or, conversely, answering a respondent's question about something on your questionnaire usually is not practical. In-depth information about meanings of an experience or explanations of answers usually is not possible through a survey. You would probably use another approach such as personal interviews (Chapter 5) to collect this type of information.

Questionnaires normally do not ask the respondent to provide extensive, detailed data. Instead, they pose questions the respondent can answer without having to consult personal records. Some surveys, though, such as business surveys conducted by national statistical organizations, may require the respondent to consult detailed business records. General population surveys, though, should be answerable just from the respondent's recall or opinions.

TYPES OF QUESTIONS

There are two basic formats of questions: closed-ended and open-ended. We will look at these in turn.

Closed-ended questions

Closed-ended questions present the respondent with a fixed set of options, perhaps as simple as 'yes' or 'no'. They are popular with researchers because they ensure a consistent set of answers from respondents. This makes the coding and inputting of data relatively simple. They are easy to administer, often providing respondents with an answer sheet on which they check off their responses. Alternatively, you might read the questions and the response categories to the respondent (for example, over the telephone) while you record their responses on a coding sheet. Sometimes you might ask your respondent to rank-order a number of options. However, ranking questions should not contain more than about five options. Too many items to rank can produce unreliable responses as well as annoy your respondent.

Closed-ended questions are popular with respondents because they are relatively easy to complete. No writing is required; the respondent needs only to mark the appropriate answer on the questionnaire. As a result, you can ask more closed-ended questions within a given period of time or budget than you can with open-ended questions.

Closed-ended questions take a variety of formats; Focus Box 3.1 illustrates some of the more common ones. The question may be formatted so that only a single response is possible,

Focus Box 3.1. Examples of closed-ended questions.

What is your approximate age?
[ ] Under 20
[ ] 20–35
[ ] 36–50
[ ] 51–65
[ ] Over 65

In which of the following activities did you participate on your most recent trip to Niagara? Please check all that apply.
[ ] Viewing Niagara Falls
[ ] Shopping
[ ] Dining out
[ ] Touring wineries
[ ] Attending a festival
[ ] Visiting with a relative or friend
[ ] Other (please specify) ______________________

Have you taken any of the following types of tours in the last year? Please fill in only one circle.
◯ An organized or guided tour involving overnight stays in more than one location
◯ An organized or guided tour involving one or more overnight stays at the same location

(Continued)

Focus Box 3.1. Continued.

◯ An organized or guided group tour excursion of less than one day's duration (a same-day tour) while on a trip of one or more nights
◯ A self-guided same-day tour excursion that was not part of an organized or group tour of one night or more
◯ None of the above

Please indicate the relative importance of each of the following tour guide features by ranking them from 1 (highest) to 5 (lowest).
Photographs _____
Restaurant recommendations _____
Accurate information _____
Maps _____
Glossary of foreign phrases _____

When choosing a destination for an overseas pleasure trip, different things are important to different people. Below are a number of items that might be important to you. Please check the appropriate box to indicate how important each item is to you when considering an overseas vacation destination.

	Very important	Somewhat important	Not very important	Not at all important
High-quality restaurants	[ ]	[ ]	[ ]	[ ]
Budget accommodation	[ ]	[ ]	[ ]	[ ]
And so on...	[ ]	[ ]	[ ]	[ ]

such as the respondent's age or sex. Closed-ended questions may also invite multiple responses, such as indicating which of a variety of activities the respondent did on a trip. Different formats can be used for the response 'box': boxes, circles, brackets, lines.

Closed-ended questions have a number of disadvantages. They require that you be able to anticipate all relevant answers your sample may offer. In some cases, this is not a problem; for example, there is a relatively limited number of age cohorts to which your respondent may belong. On the other hand, if you ask about things people consider in selecting an overseas vacation destination, you will not be able to anticipate all possible answers. The options you present (or do not present) may unintentionally bias your conclusions. The use of 'other' as an attempt to capture items you did not include is an option. However, many respondents will not bother to provide this additional information because of the effort needed to write out an answer. Moreover, responses to 'other' can greatly increase your work load by requiring you develop additional codes for each of the new responses.

Closed-ended questions do not allow you to develop a sense of rapport with your subjects; nor does the question format permit spontaneity and expressiveness in responses. The closed-ended format also makes it easier for the respondent to lie; simply checking off a box to provide a misleading answer involves less emotional effort than making up a written lie.

Open-ended questions

Open-ended questions invite respondents to compose their own answers to a question. In the face-to-face administration of questionnaires, open-ended questions allow respondents to elaborate or explain their answers, and you to probe answers or to clarify the intent of a

Focus Box 3.2. Examples of open-ended questions.

When you think of Australia as a destination, what three words first come to mind?

____

How much did you spend on this trip on the following items?:

_____ Local transportation (e.g. taxis)
_____ Petrol, oil purchased at the destination
_____ Accommodation
_____ Food and beverages purchase at restaurants
_____ Food and beverages purchase at retail stores (e.g. grocery stores)
_____ Admissions to attractions
_____ Gifts, souvenirs
_____ Other (please specify) _______________________________

____

Would you recommend this restaurant to a friend?
[ ] Yes
[ ] No
If 'no', why not?_______________________________

question for your respondents. Open-ended questions permit more spontaneous responses and promote a rapport between you and your subject.

This question format is also used in self-administered questionnaires. In such cases, however, personal interaction between you and your respondent does not occur, but the respondent is still free to provide his or her own answers to a question. Sometimes an open-ended question is combined with a closed-ended question, such as in the use of 'other' as a response category or as a request for an explanation of an answer. Focus Box 3.2 illustrates a few typical open-ended questions.

Open-ended questions also have a number of disadvantages. They impose a greater burden on the respondent than do closed-ended questions. This is due to the requirement for the respondent to reflect on their answer as well as the task of writing out a coherent response. The range of responses can be quite wide, which complicates coding if the results are going to be stored in a database. Open-ended responses can also be more difficult to analyse empirically. If the questionnaire is being administered in person or over the telephone, the respondent may choose to give a 'politically correct' answer rather than a truthful one.

DESIGNING QUESTIONNAIRES

There are several aspects to designing a questionnaire. These include the overall structure of the questionnaire, question sequence and flow, wording and the graphic layout of the questionnaire. The design of a questionnaire is more art than engineering. It is something that requires multiple drafts; even experienced researchers usually require multiple attempts to get the questionnaire right. So, once you have a complete draft of your questionnaire, test it with a few acquaintances, ideally people who belong to the same type of group you will be surveying.

Questionnaire structure

Questionnaires typically consist of five parts. The first part is an introduction that explains the purpose of the questionnaire and provides other information to help the respondent understand what he is being asked to do: a brief statement about the purpose of the questionnaire and why it is important, an expression of appreciation for the respondent's cooperation and perhaps some comment about how long it will take to complete the questionnaire. A brief descriptive title for your questionnaire helps position the focus of the questionnaire in the respondent's mind. A simple logo adds an aura of professionalism.

Most questionnaires then present some relatively simple questions designed to get the respondent in the mood to complete the balance of the questionnaire. These questions generally should not be complicated, controversial or too personal. Opening questions may also act as screeners, such as determining whether the respondent meets the criteria you have set for your sample. For example, if you are administering a survey orally to persons in a tourism destination community, you may first want to ask whether the respondent is a resident or a visitor. If a resident, you might then thank that person for their time and indicate that you have no further questions. If a visitor, you can then continue the questions.

After the initial questions, you can move into the core of the questionnaire – what Brunt calls 'crux questions' (Brunt, 1997, p. 87). These represent the essential issues you need to explore through the questionnaire. Finally, you can ask – if necessary – personal questions such as age, sex, education and income. Be certain, though, that any personal questions you ask are essential for your research. Demographic questions sometimes are asked just because they are common to ask even though the researcher has no real need for the information. Ask yourself, as you review the first draft of your questionnaire, whether each question is really needed. There is a tendency among researchers sometimes to add questions just because the answers might be interesting to know, but are not truly needed. Resist this temptation.

The questionnaire concludes with a brief thank-you and a reminder about what to do with the questionnaire, such as returning it to you in an enclosed self-addressed, stamped envelope. Some questionnaires also provide an optional box for contact details if you are offering a draw for a prize or the respondent a copy of the results (usually just a summary).

In addition to the overall structure of the questions, pay attention to their flow – the order in which you ask them. The questions should, to the extent possible, follow a logical order. Think about the order of questions as if the questionnaire were a script for a conversation. For example, begin with general questions that naturally lead to more detailed topics. Do not assume that the order in which you think of questions is the best order to present them. You might ask a colleague to look at a draft of your questionnaire to see if she thinks the order of questions makes sense.

Keep the questionnaire short. Longer questionnaires generally have lower response rates and poorer-quality data than questionnaires that are short and focused. Although there are exceptions, a rule of thumb is that a self-completion survey should not take more than 30 minutes to complete. Even at 30 minutes, you run the risk of significantly reducing your response rate.

Cautions about wording

The wording of questions is a critical element in the design of a successful survey. Finding the best way of expressing a question can be more difficult than you might first expect. Questions should be clear and concise, unambiguous and written using ordinary words. At the same time, they need to be as precise as possible. Wording questions requires a careful balancing of precision with simple language:

- Words that you might use in normal conversation, such as 'a lot', 'often' or 'frequently' can be too vague to permit the collection of reliable answers. If you are asking questions that involve some reference to frequency or quantity, consider creating quantifiable, closed-ended answer options.

- Jargon such as 'self-actualization' or 'commoditization' should be avoided unless your survey is being completed by people who use these terms in their work. Similarly, certain 'buzz' phrases such as 'responsible tourism' or 'pro-poor tourism' are likely to mean different things to different people, and should be used cautiously. Replacing or illustrating such terms with more specific expressions could better communicate your meanings to your respondents.
- Be as specific and clear as possible in your question wording. For example, 'Do you like to travel?' is too vague in terms of possible answers and explanations to elicit useful information.
- When possible, word questions in a simple, positive format rather than a negative format. Negative questions can cause confusion for your respondent and thus unreliable results for you. Consider the following example. Here, 'no' means 'yes', you are in favour of a ban.

	Yes	No
Are you against a ban on smoking in restaurants?	1	2

- Avoid questions that ask for unrealistic recall from respondents. Very few people could tell you how much they spent on various goods and services during a trip more than a month ago. Questions such as 'How many trips out of town did you make in the last 5 years?' are more likely to get you a rude comment than a valid answer.
- Questions that ask the respondent about future travel intentions may be important, but they can produce unreliable results if the forecast horizon is more than a few months away. Intervening situations easily can disrupt travel plans over a year or two.
- Resist the temptation to word questions as a way to elicit a particular type of answer. This is referred to as asking a 'leading question'. If you are interested in attitudes of your respondents towards policies designed to reduce greenhouse gas emissions, do not phrase the questions along the lines of 'The need to reduce greenhouse gas emissions is a global priority. How do you feel about each of the following policies designed to help save the earth?' Find a more neutral way of asking the question that does not give clues to the answer you want to hear.
- Ensure that closed-ended scales are properly balanced (we will consider scales in more detail in Chapter 6). For example, consider a closed-ended question asking students about the number of overnight pleasure trips they may have taken over the course of the academic year. Two alternative scales might be:

0 trips	0–5 trips
1 trip	6–10 trips
2 trips	11–15 trips
3 or more trips	More than 15 trips

Clearly, the left-hand column is a more appropriate scale to measure the number of trips students are likely to have taken during a school year, given that most students are not able to take frequent pleasure trips. Another example: a visitor satisfaction survey of various service aspects in a five-star resort might use the levels:

Excellent
Very good
Good
Fair

and *not* have 'poor' as a response category because one would not expect to observe poor quality service in a five-star resort.

- Make sure your questions present only one topic at a time. For example, the following question

> Do you think Lisbon is a romantic city and offers excellent dining opportunities?
> ◯ Yes
> ◯ No

is, of course, two questions. Each might elicit a different response.

- If you ask a question that presents a series of discrete numerical ranges, such as age or income, make certain the ranges do not overlap, as in this *bad* example:

> Please check the box that corresponds to your age group.
> ☐ Under 25
> ☐ 25–45
> ☐ 45–65
> ☐ 65 and over (note, here, that 'and over' is nonsensical – one cannot be both 65 and older than 65 at the same time)

- Researchers sometimes use an explicit 'don't know' (DK) category for closed-ended responses. For example:

> How long was your parents' honeymoon trip?
> ☐ 1–3 nights
> ☐ 4–7 nights
> ☐ Over 7 nights
> ☐ They did not take a honeymoon trip
> ☐ Don't know

The alternative is to not provide the explicit DK option and assume that respondents will skip the question if they do not know the answer. Studies such as those of Schuman and Presser (1980, 1981) suggest that the rate the DK option is chosen in comparable surveys is much higher than the 'skip' rate when the DK option is not offered. In other words, there is evidence that *not* having a DK option encourages respondents to guess or make up an answer.

- If you need to ask personal questions – age, education, income, sex and so on – you usually get a better response rate if you do two things. First, as noted above, place these questions at the end of your questionnaire. Your respondents may have become accustomed to answering your questions and will simply complete these as a matter of course. Or, if they do not wish to answer them, at least you have their responses to your other questions. Second, introduce the personal questions with a statement that acknowledges that the questions may seem personal but that they are important to the survey:

> Finally, we would like to ask you a few questions about yourself so we can put your other answers in context. Remember, all data are confidential and your name does not appear anywhere on this survey.

Graphic design

The graphic appearance of a questionnaire of a print- or web-based questionnaire deserves thought and, if you have a budget for it, professional design. However, you can develop an attractive and clear survey using just word processing software. The visual appearance of a questionnaire shapes your respondent's first impression of your questionnaire. This can determine whether she or he completes the questionnaire or pitches it into a recycling bin.

The paper should be an attractive colour: light blue, tan, beige or ivory are popular options. The ink should be dark and contrasting. The title of the questionnaire should be bold and in a larger point size, and perhaps a different colour, than the rest of the questionnaire. Point size should be easy to read, especially if your respondents include people who might have weaker eyesight. Vary the format of questions to prevent the respondent from falling into a 'response set' where he falls into a pattern of just checking off long lists of answers without really thinking about them. At the same time, remember that the flow of questions needs to make sense to the respondent.

A few simple visual embellishments such as a logo, arrows for complicated question structures, even a cartoon character in a general visitor survey can make the questionnaire more visually appealing. However, be careful not to overdue design work. Simple is better than cute, clever or elaborate.

Different cultures sometimes have different preferences or expectations for how closed-ended response sets are presented. Many Western respondents expect to see agreement scales start off with the positive categories on the left, moving to negative categories on the right, such as:

Strongly agree	Agree	Disagree	Strongly disagree
[ ]	[ ]	[ ]	[ ]

Many Asian respondents expect to see the reverse order:

Strongly disagree	Disagree	Agree	Strongly agree
[ ]	[ ]	[ ]	[ ]

However, scales that ask about the importance of something typically show importance increasing from left to right:

Not important	Somewhat important	Important	Very important
[ ]	[ ]	[ ]	[ ]

Columns normally are the same width. Interestingly, positioning the end points – especially if working with more than five categories – further away from the other responses (using slightly wider columns) can result in more respondents checking the end points than if the columns were the same width. Culture or personality can also come into play with respect to end point; some people tend to avoid checking the extremes, preferring more moderate responses.

Attitude or opinion scales that represent a spectrum such as those above should be presented as a horizontal sequence, ideally with a category label at the head of each column, as shown. Questions with dichotomous answers such as 'yes/no' or 'male/female', or quantitative variables such as party size, income, education or age can be formatted so that the closed-ended response options are arranged vertically. Note, though, that the top items in lists are often implicitly seen to be 'better' while the lower items are 'inferior'. Thus you may want to avoid giving offence by placing lower levels of education or incomes at the top of the list, with higher levels lower in the list. If you are presenting lists of options that do not have a logical order, such as activities, preferred destinations or sources of information, consider preparing several versions of the questionnaire with the lists rearranged randomly. This reduces the problem of people tending to check off items higher in the list than lower. Randomization of lists is a valuable feature available on some Internet-based survey platforms.

Respondents answer differently to lengthy lists of items when the items are grouped and presented in different formats. See the following examples of three different formats of an activities listing:

Single column, ungrouped list

Fishing – fresh water
Fishing – salt water
Kayaking or canoeing – fresh water
Kayaking or canoeing – salt water
Dog sledding
Ice skating
Skiing – cross-country
Snowshoeing

Single column, grouped list

Water-based activities

Fishing – fresh water
Fishing – salt water
Kayaking or canoeing – fresh water
Kayaking or canoeing – salt water

Winter activities

Dog sledding
Ice skating
Skiing – cross-country
Snowshoeing

Double column, grouped list

Water-based activities	Winter activities
Fishing – fresh water	Dog sledding
Fishing – salt water	Ice skating
Kayaking or canoeing – fresh water	Skiing – cross-country
Kayaking or canoeing – salt water	Snowshoeing

Respondents will typically provide a wider range of responses with the more compact double-column grouped format and least with the single-column, ungrouped format. The number of responses to a single-column-grouped format tends to fall in between. The more compact format makes the choices more readily visible and the use of groupings tends to communicate to respondents that they should consider a wider range of responses (Smyth et al., 2006).

Improving response rates

Self-completed, mail-back surveys traditionally have low response rates. My experience with surveys conducted by students is that response rates often run as low as 15% (even lower rates are not unknown). Response rates of surveys conducted of more targeted groups such as members of an association usually run higher, but rarely over 40%. Taking measures to increase response rates thus is a good idea, although these measures need to be carefully chosen because of the cost and effort associated with them.

The return envelope is an important determinant of the response rate of mail-back questionnaires. A self-addressed, postage-paid envelope should always be provided with your survey. Envelopes with postage stamps, as opposed to business reply envelopes, achieve higher rates of return. This tactic, though, is more expensive than the use of business reply envelopes because you pay for postage on envelopes that are never mailed back to you. As a rule of thumb, the use of postage stamps can increase your response rate by only 5%–10%, so the added expense may not be justified if you have a very large sample.

A pre-notification letter in which you advise your potential respondents that a questionnaire is coming can increase response rates by up to 15%. The letter adds credibility and a sense of importance to the questionnaire, and alerts your respondents to look for the questionnaire rather than to discard your mailing as junk mail. Pre-notification letters are rarely used for general population surveys because of the added expense for postage, printing, envelopes, etc., but they can be useful for small sample sizes and for questionnaires sent to members of an association or businesses. If possible, the letter should be printed on letterhead stationery and signed by someone of authority. For example, a survey of an association's membership might be signed by the President or Executive Director of the association.

If you use a pre-notification letter, some details to include are the following (these are in addition to any special requirements an ethics review office might have). However, keep the letter brief – no more than one page:

- The basic purpose of the study and, if relevant, the sponsor of the study.
- Why the potential respondent was selected for participation.
- A paragraph on the importance of the study and why the person's participation is important. Do not count on your respondent's sense of altruism. You might explain the social or professional significance of the study and the benefits of the study's results. You can also mention, if relevant, the availability of an incentive, such as a small gift or inclusion of the person's name or e-mail address in a chance for a prize.
- When the survey will be mailed to them.
- A closing expression of thanks and the hope your contact will be willing to participate.

A cover letter accompanying the survey that introduces it expresses your hope that the potential respondent will participate and explains the benefits of the survey (being consistent with your message in a pre-notification letter if you used one). Mention how long the questionnaire will take to complete, especially if it is only a few (less than 5) minutes. Write in a professional and friendly tone without being flattering, sounding insincere or demanding. Note the deadline for returning the questionnaire, and provide the return address.

Mention the incentive, if there is one. Emphasize that you have provided a self-addressed, stamped envelope for the recipient's convenience. Advise the potential respondent of your confidentiality or privacy policies (guidelines about this will often be provided by your ethics review office). Provide a contact name and details for the recipient to contact for any questions.

Again, print the letter on letterheaded paper if possible. Some researchers like to personalize the letter with the recipient's name, and to sign the letter personally. Personalization of the letter does not seem to affect response rates, although I prefer to sign letters, if practical.

Incentives tend to increase response rates if they are seen as of good value. These may include what some have sarcastically called 'trinkets and trash' such as pens, pencils, pocket calendars or relevant CDs (for example, a trip planner for a destination). An offer to enter the recipient's name in a draw for a prize can sometimes be effective if the prize is valuable, such as a weekend at a resort. If your sample consists of other researchers or professionals, offering a copy of your results can be effective. Cash is sometimes offered, usually in amounts ranging from a penny (as a token gesture) to the equivalent of five US dollars or Euros. Incentives, except for entry into a draw or a copy of your results, need to be mentioned in the cover letter to be effective.

The effectiveness of incentives varies substantially depending on the population being studied and the value of the incentive being offered (inexpensive prizes such as a chance in a draw for a T-shirt or poster are not effective). Increases in responses rates for incentives seen as valuable may range from 5 to 20%, so they can be a cost-effective tool for improving response rates.

Deadlines for return of the questionnaires usually do not improve response rates, but they can encourage respondents to return their questionnaires sooner than they might otherwise. They also provide you with a date to stop waiting for slow returns. The deadline may have the effect of reducing your potential response rate by causing laggard sample members to decide it is too late to return your questionnaire. On the other hand, most survey projects do have schedules for completion that will, in effect, impose a deadline on how long you can wait.

Follow-up with non-respondents can significantly increase response percentages, up to 60% in my experience. Set up a realistic schedule for anticipating returns, and then a date at which you will contact non-respondents. This might be 3 weeks after the initial distribution of the questionnaire. The follow-up can be in the form of a postcard with a brief message about the importance of submitting the questionnaire, although a letter with another copy of the questionnaire tends to be more effective. Potential respondents sometimes do not return questionnaires because the original copy was misplaced. A second reminder can be sent a couple of weeks later to encourage the slowest respondents. Subsequent reminders usually are ineffective and can annoy your contacts.

Telephone calls or e-mails to non-respondents can be especially effective if you have contact details and your sample is of a manageable size that permits personalized contact. Being able to contact non-respondents requires that you have some mechanism for determining who has replied and who has not. In some cases, the questionnaire will contain the name of the respondent (or the respondent's organization). If you will not have names on the returned questionnaires, you can place an identification code on each questionnaire. This can then be checked against a master list of codes and names to track returns. Researchers using online surveys (discussed below) may simply send out a mass e-mail reminder to everyone on their list asking that, if anyone has not responded to the online survey, to please do so by a given date. Expressing thanks to those who have already responded is a courteous addition to the reminder e-mail.

CODING

Coding refers to the process of assigning numerical values to each of your respondent's answers for inputting into a database such as an Excel spreadsheet or a statistical package data file (such as SPSS or SAS). In some cases you can simply enter the respondent's answer directly, such as the number of people in a travel party if you asked for the actual number, rather than asking the person to check off an answer reflecting a range of party sizes. However, most survey questions do not provide direct numerical values, so you have to convert the responses to numbers.

When setting up your coding scheme, it is useful to sketch out the types of tables you want to create for your report. Having an explicit understanding of the types of tables you need helps you plan your statistical analysis which, in turn, guides your coding scheme. And, of course, before anticipating what tables you will need, you should have a clear idea of what types of analyses you want to run, which – in turn – reflects your core questions and research objectives. Coding, therefore, is an important step in a long sequence of events in conducting empirical research.

Scales

Numerical codes can be categorized as four types of scales, each with a different range of analytical possibilities. The most basic scale is a **nominal** scale. The numbers on athletes' uniforms are a nominal scale – they are just identifiers, or labels. They convey no intrinsic numerical information. For example:

Are you:	Code
Male	1
Female	2

The values of 1 and 2 in the box above are simply labels; they have no quantitative meaning, and could easily be changed to 1 for females and 2 for males. The mathematical computations you can do with nominal scales are limited to counting and tabulating percentages.

An **ordinal** scale uses numbers to present as, the name implies, an order. The number tells us something about the sequence of what we are observing, but nothing about how far apart two adjacent observations are. For example, answers to a question about the respondent's educational level can be coded as an ordinal scale because the successive levels of education, each represented by a higher number, represent increasingly higher levels of educational attainment.

Level of education	Code
Did not complete high school	1
High school diploma	2
Trade school, technical certificate	3
Some college or university	4
College or university degree	5
Some graduate	6
Postgraduate (e.g. MA or PhD) degree	7

Note that having a high school diploma (2) does not mean that a high school graduate has twice the education of someone who did not graduate. Nor is the difference between 'some college or university' and 'trade school, technical certificate' (a scale difference of 1) the same as the difference between 'some graduate 'and 'postgraduate degree' (also a scale difference of 1). The scale is arbitrary as long as higher numbers represent higher levels of education. In other words, instead of 1, 2, 3, 4, 5, 6 and 7, you could use 9, 12, 13, 54, 66, 110 and 2027! The order of the numbers conveys information about order only, nothing else.

An **interval** scale is one in which the differences or intervals between numbers are consistent and meaningful. However, this scale does not have a fixed zero. Thus, it cannot be used to calculate ratios. A familiar example of an interval scale is the Celsius temperature scale. Zero degrees C is an arbitrary setting – it reflects the freezing point of water and the value of each degree set so that the boiling point of water is 100°C. The difference between 10°C and 20°C (ten Celsius degrees) is the same as the difference between 90°C and 100°C (also ten Celsius degrees). However, 20°C is not twice as hot as 10°C. This is because 0°C could have been used to designate any physical temperature changing the scale but not actually changing the heat level of, for example, a kettle of boiling water. Also, 0°C does not imply zero heat; water at the freezing point still contains heat energy. (The Kelvin temperature scale, which is based on 'absolute zero' – minus 273.15°C – is a ratio scale for temperature; however, tourism researchers usually don't use the Kelvin scale in their research.)

Interval scales are rare in tourism research; they most commonly appear as Likert or semantic differential scales (discussed further in Chapter 6). Many researchers assume these scales are interval scales, although this is not necessarily a valid assumption. The debate concerns whether the difference between 'strongly agree' and 'agree' is the same as the difference between 'agree' and 'weakly agree'.

The following table illustrates common ways of coding Likert scales. Note how any given response can have two different values, reflecting the fact that the scale values represent intervals only, but not absolute values.

	Strongly agree [ ]	Agree [ ]	Weakly agree [ ]	Weakly disagree [ ]	Disagree [ ]	Strongly disagree [ ]
Alternative codes:	1	2	3	4	5	6
	3	2	1	−1	−2	−3

Interval scales also have the powers of nominal and ordinal scales. The values can be used as labels and the order of the values is meaningful. Data from an interval scale can be summed and average scores tabulated.

Ratio scales are the most powerful. They have all the powers of the three previous scales but also have a fixed zero. This means that you can meaningfully perform arithmetic operations on the values from the scales. For example, visitor expenditures, when the actual value is reported (not expenditure categories), represent a ratio scale. A visitor who spent $2000 on a trip spent twice that of a visitor who spent $1000. Their expenditures can then be added for a total of $3000. Numbers of trips taken by a visitor in a year, lengths of stay in a destination, total room capacity in a destination, airline load factors, numbers of cruise ships calling at a port and many more variables on both the supply and demand side of tourism can be measured with ratio scales.

Missing values

Respondents sometime fail to provide an answer for one or more items on a questionnaire. If the number of missed items is too great, perhaps more than 10%, you may want to exclude the entire questionnaire from your sample. However, if only a few questions have been missed, you can keep the questionnaire but will have to deal with missing answers. A common tactic is to select a value that falls outside the range of possible answers. The value 9 is often used as a code for 'a missing' answer. If 9 were a code for a legitimate answer, you might use 99. This may be needless advice, but double-check that your missing data code is not also a legitimate value. I have seen examples where 9 was used as a missing value and also as a legitimate value. You can imagine the confusion that resulted in trying to interpret the results. Some software packages also allow you to use a period/decimal point (.) as a code for missing values. This allows you to avoid the risk of ambiguous numerical coding.

One special circumstance in which you will often find missing values is in the use of certain question sequences. Consider the following sequence:

B.1 Have you been involved in the planning of any out-of-town trips your family took in the last 2 years? (*Check one only*)
All of them [ ]
Most of them [ ]
Some of them [ ]
None of them [ ] Skip to Question B.5
B.2.... ⟶
B.3....
B.4....
B.5. Did you book or purchase any parts of any of these overnight trips over the Internet?
Yes [ ]
No [ ]
I don't know/can't recall [ ]

If the respondent answered 'none of them' in B1, they would skip questions B2, B3 and B4. You would then code these missing responses as a 'valid skip', meaning that the questions are not relevant to this respondent and that 'missing' values are appropriate responses. Use a different numerical code than the regular missing value code for valid skips. The use of a different code for valid skips allows you to know whether the respondent simply failed to answer or whether the question was appropriately left blank.

Multiple answers

Many questions permit respondents to check off all answers that apply, such as the lists of activities a respondent engaged in during a trip. However, other questions require a single response only. Still, you may find that respondents did not follow your instructions, and gave you a response such as the following:

What was the primary reason for your trip? *Please check one response only.*
[✓] Pleasure
[ ] Visit friends of relatives
[ ] Business
[✓] Non-business convention
[ ] Other personal

This may happen because the respondent did not carefully read the question, or because the respondent felt two reasons were equally important. You have at least two options for dealing with this situation. You can ignore the responses and code the question response as missing, or you can randomly select one of the answers as the primary reason and ignore the other(s). Decide which tactic to use on the basis of which is most acceptable and appropriate given your project objectives.

Open-ended responses

Coding open-ended responses in questionnaires can be a major task, and care should be taken not to ask more open-ended questions than necessary. There are four common types of responses obtained from tourism-related open-ended questions:

Numerical responses are the easiest to code. These are obtained when you ask a question about, for example, the amount spent in various categories of trip expenditures (the actual amount rather than using a series of specified expenditure ranges in a closed-ended format). In this case, you simply enter the amount as a ratio scale code in your data set.

Postal codes are sometimes collected as a way of recording origins of visitors. The postal codes can be stored in a separate database and then examined through geodemographic segmentation software to provide a demographic profile of the visitors, based on the profiles of residents of the geographic areas living in the area represented by the postal codes.

Single words or names may be collected in response to questions such as 'When you think of Finland as a tourism destination, which three words first come to mind?'. One low-tech way of working with this sort of response is to write each word on a separate piece of paper and then sort through the individual pieces, grouping them into broader themes. A good practice to improve the reliability of your results is to have a friend repeat the exercise, and then compare your groupings. Any differences in groupings are then discussed until you can resolve your divergent views. You can also type the words in word processing software and visually search for themes or logical groupings. Again, it is good research practice to have at least one other person repeat the exercise to improve the reliability of your groupings.

Short answers are obtained when you invite respondents to explain in their own words their viewpoint or reason for an opinion. For example, you might ask:

Do you think you will come back to Oktoberfest next year?
[ ] Yes
[ ] No
If 'no', why not? ____________________

The analysis of short answers is similar to that for single words except that, as you read the responses on the questionnaire, you categorize each answer as belonging to a response theme. You can retain the respondents' actual words to illustrate the themes you have identified for your report. Alternatively, you can assign each statement a nominal code reflecting the theme. For example, the themes you might find in going through the responses to the question about not coming back to Oktoberfest could be:

Response theme	Code
Too expensive	1
Too crowded	2
Too much public intoxication	3
Don't drink beer	4
Moving away from town	5
No explanation	9

Remember that the actual value of nominal codes, as used in this example, means nothing; they are simply convenient labels for answers.

DISTRIBUTING YOUR QUESTIONNAIRE

You have a number of options for distributing your questionnaire. Your decision will depend on the size and location of your intended respondents, your budget and any deadlines for completing your report. Some of these delivery mechanisms can be combined in a two-staged survey, such as collecting names and addresses through personal contacts, and then following up with a mail-back, self-completed questionnaire. As always, there are advantages and disadvantages to each method; certain methods work better in one circumstance than another. The methods involve a range of levels of personal contact between you and your respondent, from face-to-face conversation to long-distance and anonymous web-based survey platforms.

We look first at a general description of each vehicle. This is then followed by a summary listing of the key strengths and challenges or weaknesses of each.

Personal distribution

This delivery vehicle involves physically meeting potential respondents and either interviewing them in person or handing them your questionnaire for them to return to you, perhaps by depositing their completed questionnaire in a drop-box on site or via a self-addressed, postage-paid envelope. Personal distribution of questionnaires is often done in transient venues where there is a constant ebb and flow of people. These include theme parks, ski resorts, festivals, parks, scenic spots, parade routes or shopping districts. Personal distribution is also done for exit surveys at points such as ferry ports, airports or even highways that lead out of a destination. Exit surveys require approval and cooperation from authorities as well as special attention to the safety of both surveyors and respondents.

Personal distribution in most venues presents challenges in obtaining a reasonably representative sample. If you are surveying in an open area without gates or doors, you can position yourself at a location where there is a large volume of traffic flow, but where you will not interfere with the movement of people. You can then approach, depending on the number of people and your quota, every *n*th person to complete the questionnaire. If the flow of people is sparse, you can adopt the 'next past' approach, which simply means approaching the next person walking past you. After a predetermined period of time such as an hour, take a break, and then move to another location. Administer interviews in a diverse set of locations over the course of your sampling day. If you are interviewing at a location or event that is open for several days, or permanently, try to administer surveys on different days of the week, maybe even in different seasons of the year if your study can be extended over a long period.

Surveys conducted at gated venues (place where admission is controlled, such as through having to pay an admission fee) can be logistically simpler. Choose an appropriate sampling rate (again, say every *n*th person) and approach that person as he or she enters or exits the venue. Sampling of people as they exit a venue is usually more practical than as they enter. Persons leaving a venue tend to feel less pressed for time and will be able to respond to questions about their experiences at the site.

Most people in public places will be with one or more other people. You should ensure that you get a representative mix of females and males (unless you are studying just one sex) and age cohorts, as well as (if relevant) ethnic groups and persons with varying levels of physical ability (in other words, do not be shy approaching someone with a seeing-eye dog or in a wheelchair). Depending on your research purposes, you might specify one person in the group to speak for the group (although groups will often decide who will do the talking for them – you should generally respect the group's choice). You can also actively solicit answers from everyone in the group (or, at least, those above a certain age).

Researchers usually prefer to ask questions and record the answers themselves, not showing the questionnaire to respondents. However, some respondents may ask to see the questionnaire or even insist on completing it themselves. Unless there is a technical reason for resisting, it is prudent to comply. You are less likely to annoy the respondent, and are likely to get an improved response rate, than if you refuse to allow your potential respondent to see the questionnaire.

Personal distribution can be the most expensive form of survey distribution if you have a paid survey team and travel expenses. However, small scale surveys done locally can be accomplished with minimal expense, although the time required to complete your survey will still be significant. Face-to-face interviews, when done by a skilled interviewer, can keep the respondent's attention for up to an hour, or even longer. However, most personal surveying should be limited to no more than 30 minutes – less if possible.

Some practical matters associated with the personal distribution of questionnaires are discussed in Focus Box 3.3. The key strengths and challenges of personal contact with respondents are summarized in Table 3.1.

Focus Box 3.3. Survey survival.

Field surveys such as interviews done at a festival or an attraction are one of the more demanding experiences a tourism researcher endures. This focus box looks at a few practical issues that will help you have a successful series of field interviews.

Let's assume you have a research plan, a clear set of objectives and a survey instrument, and you know whom, where and when you need to interview. The following suggestions can help you survive hours or even days in the field:

- If you are going to be interviewing on private property or in a managed public place (such as a museum), make arrangements to meet with the responsible authority before you show up on site. This should be initiated with a telephone call rather than an e-mail. Set an appointment to meet personally. Introduce yourself at the meeting, explain the nature of your project and why your study is important. If relevant, highlight any potential benefits to your would-be host. Explain how long and when you want to be on site, and how long each interview is likely to take. Provide the management of the site with a copy of the questionnaire for review and approval. Sometimes you will be invited to do the surveys by the site management as part of a consulting project or action research project for them. Permission to be on the site is not then a problem, although you will still need to provide the management with a copy of the questionnaire for review and approval.
- If there are employees on site, be sure to visit the site and introduce yourself to them before you show up to start interviewing. Just because management has given you permission to be on site does not mean that the employees will necessarily know about your study or welcome your presence.
- Dress appropriately. This is impossible to define precisely, of course. Appropriate attire for doing interviews at a beach will be very different from doing interviews in the

(Continued)

Focus Box 3.3. Continued.

lobby of a five-star hotel. Comfortable clothing and shoes will help you get through long hours on your feet. If interviewing outdoors in the sun, wear a hat and be sure to have sunscreen and water. If possible, wear an ID name tag, shirt or hat with the company's/agency's logo that identifies you as someone who is entitled to be on site.

- Ideally, interview in a team. A team composed of a female and a male is often a good idea for several reasons. It provides you with company and someone to provide relief. A mixed couple is often perceived as less threatening than a single male (unless you are interviewing in a gay site). Single females are usually not perceived as threatening, but females should avoid being alone when approaching unknown men for interviews. You might also consider having a mix of ethnicities and/or ages on the team.
- Bring a folding chair if seating is not already available.
- Pace yourself. Approaching strangers with the request for an interview can be more draining than you might expect.
- Be respectful when approaching people. Be friendly and confident, but not aggressive. Be prepared for rejection. Don't argue or try to persuade a reluctant subject. When someone declines to answer your questions, say something like 'Thank you anyway. Enjoy your visit'.
- Be sensitive to any time pressures your subjects might be facing, such as rushing to tee-time at a golf course or the start of a concert. Learn to read body language that signals someone is in a rush, looking for someone or is otherwise having a bad day.
- If a subject asks to complete the questionnaire personally rather than by responding to your spoken questions, allow them to do so unless there is a very good reason not to let your subject see your questionnaire. You don't want to get involved in a contest of will or control for no good reason.
- If you are going to be in the field for an extended period of time, especially outdoors, think about bringing a cooler with bottles of water, snacks and perhaps a book or magazine to browse on breaks.
- Find a secure place to keep your completed questionnaires while you continue to interview.
- Upon completion of the interviews, personally thank the manager and anyone else who assisted during your stay.

Table 3.1. Opportunities and challenges in personal distribution of questionnaires.

Opportunities	Challenges
Provides access to populations that otherwise could be difficult to reach	Usually requires permission for you to distribute questionnaires in the location selected Random sampling can be a challenge
Relatively fast data collection	'Volunteers' may approach you seeking to complete the questionnaire if you are providing incentives, which could bias the representativeness of your sample

(Continued)

Table 3.1. Continued.

Opportunities	Challenges
Relatively high response rate if the questionnaire is completed in your presence	Often requires a team of surveyors who must be trained
Ability to explain personally the importance of the survey	
Ability to answer questions the respondent may have or to clarify the intent of your questions	Need to ensure diversity in people interviewed, which means approaching people with whom the surveyor might normally not interact; conversely, there is the risk of the surveyor approaching only interesting or attractive people
May provide you with an in-depth 'feel' of the environment of the venue in which you are sampling	
Data might be directly captured using palm-held digital devices that can facilitate analysis	Respondents may be unwilling to stop to answer questions, either out of suspicion about your motives or because they are in a rush
Can use prompt cards or other aids	Can be expensive if you have to hire professional surveyors

Telephone interviews

The telephone is a traditional tool for conducting surveys but is becoming less popular. Telephone interviews allow you to cover a wide geographical area with much less expense than physically travelling for face-to-face interviews. However, the rise of telemarketing, especially those abusive forms that disguise a sales pitch as 'market research' has caused many people to refuse to participate in legitimate telephone surveys. Further, call blocking and caller ID allow people to screen out calls from unfamiliar or toll-free numbers. The dramatic rise in mobile phone usage, as well as in unlisted numbers, has also reduced the sampling frame available through conventional telephone directories.

Researchers can use 'random digit dialling' (RDD) software to develop a list of valid telephone numbers. This software combines a random number generator with lists of legitimate residential and mobile phone numbers, allowing the researcher to obtain lists of mobile phone and unlisted numbers, as well as regular listed numbers. Smith *et al.* (2005), however, found that in a large health survey in Australia, RDD sampling did not produce results that were significantly different than numbers obtained through the use of telephone directories.

Telephone interviewing requires that you call back to numbers that do not answer. This can be quite time consuming. Professional survey firms may make up to ten callbacks before discarding the number. Telephone interviews must be shorter than personal interviews – 15 minutes is a practical maximum for a telephone interview. Telephone interviewers need to speak clearly, politely and succinctly. One of the biggest challenges in conducting a telephone interview is to keep the person on the line long enough to convince them your call is a legitimate survey and not a telemarketing or crank call. You will usually begin by saying something like 'Hello. My name is Stephen Smith with XYZ Market Research. We are conducting a survey on consumer travel habits and I am hoping you might have a few minutes to answer a few questions'. Be prepared for high levels of rejection – either direct refusals or people just hanging up on you.

While you can complete a telephone interview by hand-writing the respondent's answers on a printed form, professional telephone surveyors use software called computer-assisted telephone interviewing (CATI). CATI involves the surveyors (using a headset) reading questions from a computer screen while talking with the respondent and entering the answers directly into a pre-formatted data file. This can significantly save time and costs, and reduce coding errors.

As with personal interviewing, telephone interviews permit you to answer questions from your respondent regarding the intent of questions as well as allowing you to probe for more detail in answers. However, the use of visual aids is not feasible with telephone interviewing. The lack of face-to-face contact also means that the level of rapport between you and your respondent does not develop as fully as it can in personal interviews. Moreover, telephone interviews usually involve tightly scripted questions to ensure consistent questions and response, which can come across as an artificial exchange between interviewer and subject.

Respondent selection is a particular challenge with telephone surveys. Many households will have two or more adults, but they are not equally likely to answer telephone calls. Schedules may vary, as well as their roles within the household (my father refused to answer the telephone – that was my mother's 'job'). As a result, if you want to ensure a random sample of people you contact, you may need to utilize some tactic to choose potential respondents randomly within a household. Table 3.2 identifies some of the more common ones and briefly describes each.

These techniques typically require asking questions about the composition of the household before you can even begin to administer the survey, which can become a barrier to keeping

Table 3.2. Respondent selection techniques.

Kish Procedure	Lists household members by age and sex Uses matrices to determine the respondent in multi-adult households Difficult to administer, so it requires extensive interviewer training Intrusive, because the interviewer must inventory the household members before beginning the interview Takes time and is therefore costly
Troldahl–Carter Procedure	Interviewer asks informant the age and sex of adult household members Matrices are then used to select the respondent Also requires substantial interviewer training
Hagen–Collier Procedure	Uses a random procedure to determine which of four types of respondents are first asked for in the household – for example, asking (in random order as you move from call to call) – oldest female, youngest female, oldest male and youngest male Easy to administer, is not intrusive and requires little time While not fully random, does permit a representative distribution of sample persons Does not allow for middle person to be included in the sample when there are three or more adults of the same sex in the household

(*Continued*)

Table 3.2. Continued.

Last Birthday Procedure	Produces diversity among respondents Easy to administer, requires little time and is not intrusive Some researchers also report respondents find procedure not to be 'scientific', and thus interviewers had to work harder to maintain a professionally administered interview The procedure allows the informant to control choice of respondent by lying Birthdays are not randomly distributed throughout the year in many countries

potential respondents on the telephone. Further, the person you select using any one of these methods may not be available, requiring you to set up a time to call back.

An emerging form of questionnaire distribution by telephone is the use of cellphones and text messaging. This vehicle involves distributing a short series of questions through a cellphone provider to a sample of subscribers who have agreed to participate. The questions appear as a text message, requesting a brief reply. A common application of this methodology is the collection of expenditure information at the end of a day during a tourism trip. Cellphones also potentially allow the researcher to attach a location to the response through GPS features. Respondents are offered an incentive for participating such as free air time. This technology is more common in Europe than in other parts of the world, but it is likely to become more widely adapted in the future.

Table 3.3 provides a summary of the strengths and challenges in telephone interviewing.

Table 3.3. Opportunities and challenges in telephone interviews.

Opportunities	Challenges
Permits broad geographic sampling	Interviewer training is critical
Multiple attempts to reach the respondent are possible	Contact between interviewer and respondent is less personal than with face-to-face interviews
Questions can be clarified and responses probed	Increasing resistance by most consumers to answering telephone questionnaires
Answers can be directly entered into a database using computer-assisted telephone interviewing (CATI)	
Text messaging can be used to collect 'real time' data from persons during tourism trips, and to capture location of the respondent	Respondents usually not willing to spend much time-on the telephone Limited control over who responds to questionnaire; respondent selection techniques can be time-consuming and an impediment to recruiting respondents Random digit dialling (RDD) needed to deal with unlisted numbers and cellphones Multiple callbacks often needed Can be expensive

Self-completion (mail-back) questionnaires

Self-completion surveys refer to those instruments that typically are mailed to respondents with the request that they be completed and mailed back to the researcher. These surveys are sometimes distributed through personal contact, or by leaving stacks of questionnaires at a convenient location such as a counter in a visitor centre in the (usually vain) hope that a potential respondent will pick one up, complete it and mail it back or deposit it in a collection box. Much of the material in the first part of this chapter concerns the design and administration of self-completion surveys. Their primary opportunities and challenges are summarized in Table 3.4.

Web-based surveys

The Internet is increasingly used as a platform for distributing questionnaires. Initially, researchers had to design their own survey platforms (or attached questionnaires to e-mails, which did not exploit the utility of the Internet). However, services such as SurveyMonkey, WebslingerZ and Zoomerang (among many) now make it easy for you to create a web-based survey.

Respondents to web-based surveys for tourism research are reached generally through one of three delivery vehicles:

1. Website pop-up surveys.
2. E-mail lists.
3. Internet panels.

Pop-up surveys are administered through a destination or business website, with every *n*th visitor receiving a pop-up message inviting him or her to complete an online survey. If the

Table 3.4. Opportunities and challenges in self-completion questionnaires.

Opportunities	Challenges
Large sample sizes more easily achieved than by personal or telephone interviews	Response rates often are low As a result of low response rates, non-response bias can distort results
Training of interviewers not needed (or is minimized)	May take weeks for questionnaires to be returned
Respondents can complete the questionnaire on their own schedule	No opportunity to clarify respondent confusion or to probe answers
Little interviewer bias in delivery of questions	Questions have to be carefully and clearly worded
Wording of questions is fixed – no chance an interviewer will mis-state a question	Graphic design of questions and physical appearance of questionnaire can influence results
Content and format of questionnaire is easily reviewed by others	Pre-notification letters and follow-up mailings often needed
Can be translated into other languages as needed and accuracy of translation verified	

survey involves only a couple of questions, incentives usually are not offered. More lengthy questionnaires usually offer a chance for the respondent to have her or his e-mail address entered into a draw for a prize.

E-mail lists are probably the most common sampling frame for Internet surveys. The lists may be generated in a variety of ways. Two of the most common are the following. Association membership lists usually provide e-mail addresses of their members. With permission of the association, a researcher could use the list to conduct a survey of the membership. Alternatively, businesses or destinations may request e-mail address of those people who contact them for more information. These lists can then be used to compile a sampling frame. Again, potential respondents are offered an incentive such as a draw for a prize to encourage participation.

Internet panels are used by professional market research firms. The panels consist of people who have been recruited by the firm (perhaps through mass e-mailings) and who agree to respond to questionnaires on any or selected topics. Panel members often are asked for basic personal information when they join, such as general location of residence, age, sex and education. This information can then be used to custom-design panels that meet the user's criteria – such as females between the ages of 18 and 35. Panel members receive an e-mail inviting them to respond to a survey, and are provided with a personal identification number or code to access the survey. Incentives include draws or a contribution of a small number of points to the respondent's frequent flier programme if he is a member.

Internet survey sampling frames do not represent the general population. Obviously, anyone who is not an Internet user will be excluded from the survey. This often is not an issue. Virtually 100% of members of professional associations are likely to be frequent Internet users, so a web-based survey will potentially reach all of them. E-mail lists drawn from people who sent e-mails to destinations or businesses can also be assumed to contain regular computer users. Members of Internet panels typically have profiles that match those of potential visitors – well educated, reasonably affluent, comfortable with technology and interested in new experiences.

However, Internet panels may have another source of bias that could affect results. Web-based surveys of Internet panels can become quite time-consuming. I was on one such panel and began to receive up to three survey requests a week. As a result, I dropped off the panel. People who remain on panels are less likely to be employed full time, less likely to take business trips or attend conventions and may be more likely to have limited social networks. In other words, some respondents may use Internet surveys as a way of filling idle time.

As with printed questionnaires, the graphic design of web-based surveys can influence response rates and patterns. The availability of Internet services that provide web-based surveys does allow some customization of the appearance of questions, although the basic architecture is fixed. This architecture may have been influenced by research on web-survey design, but you should still look critically at question formats to ensure that the appearance matches your needs.

Bosnjak and Tuten (2001) found that some of the design problems that lowered response rates included the use of open-ended questions, especially early in the questionnaire. They also observed that questions arranged in visually complex, 'cute' formats or pull-down menus caused potential respondents to abandon surveys. Unclear instructions, a lack of navigation aids and overly complex or jargonistic wording also discouraged potential respondents.

Table 3.5 outlines the key opportunities and challenges of web-based surveys. Many of these are similar to those of mail-back questionnaires as both have visual formats. However, there are also key differences.

Table 3.5. Opportunities and challenges of web-based surveys.

Opportunities	Challenges
Large sample sizes more easily achieved than for personal, telephone or even mail-back interviews	Response rates may be low for general online population surveys
Training of interviewers not needed (or is minimized)	As a result of low response rates, non-response bias can bias results
Respondents may be able to complete the questionnaire on their own schedule, if the survey permits the respondent to leave and re-enter as desired	No opportunity to clarify respondent confusion or to probe answers Questions have to be carefully and clearly worded
Little interviewer bias	Graphic design of questions and physical appearance of questionnaire can influence results
Wording of questions is fixed – no chance an interviewer will mis-state a question	Randomized samples often are impossible to achieve
Content and format of questionnaire is easily reviewed by others	Some web-based survey software permits multiple responses from the same IP address, potentially biasing results
No mail delays in dissemination of questionnaires or return of replies	Web-based survey firms based in the USA are subject to the 'Patriot Act', which allows the US government to access their files. Thus the confidentiality of responses through services such as SurveyMonkey cannot be guaranteed
Data can be automatically tabulated into a database format	

CONCLUSIONS

Questionnaire design is an essential skill for many tourism researchers. It covers a variety of tasks, including the overall architecture of the questionnaire, question wording, question format, question flow and graphic design. In addition to the design of the questionnaire, you need to think about how you will code the answers provided by your respondents. These codes usually are in the form of a numeric scale, although some verbal coding may also be done for open-ended questions.

The distribution of the questionnaire is another critical task. The basic vehicles are personal (face-to-face) distribution, telephone, mail-back and Internet. Surveys can involve multiple distribution vehicles, such as having an initial short round of questions asked in face-to-face interviews followed by the use of a more detailed mail-back questionnaire to those respondents who agree to participate. Each distribution vehicle has distinctive advantages and disadvantages related to cost, time, ability to probe and clarify, reach, response rates and other characteristics. These strengths and weaknesses need to be weighed in the context of the purpose of your study, your sample, as well as practical matters such as time and budget restrictions.

A well-designed questionnaire that is effectively distributed and that permits efficient coding of the results is a powerful tool for answering many important tourism questions. However, the development of a questionnaire requires care to ensure that it achieves your objectives and is worded and designed in a way that your respondents can understand. This is a task that is often much more difficult than you might imagine. Be prepared to work through multiple drafts as you craft your tool, and be sure to test it with some volunteers before sending it out.

REFERENCES

Brunt, P. (1997) *Market Research in Travel and Tourism.* Butterworth-Heinemann, Jordan Hill, Oxford, UK.

Bosnjak, M. and Tuten, T. (2001) Classifying response behaviours in web-based surveys. *Journal of Computer-Mediated Communication* 6 (3) http://jcmc.indiana.edu/vol6/issue3/boznjak.html (accessed 23 November 2007).

Schuman, H. and Presser, S. (1980) Public opinion and public ignorance: The fine line between attitudes and nonattitudes. *The American Journal of Sociology* 85, 1214–1225.

Schuman, H. and Presser, S. (1981) *Questions and Answers in Attitude Surveys.* Academic Press, New York.

Smith, A., deVisser, R. and Rissel, C. (2005) Random digit dialling and directory-based samples in telephone surveys of HIV risk: a comparison from the Australian Study of Health and Relationships. *Annals of Epidemiology* 15, 232–235.

Smyth, J., Dillman, D., Christian, L. and Stern, M. (2006) Effects of using visual design principles to group response options in web surveys. *International Journal of Internet Science* 1(1), 6–16.

chapter 4

How to Select a Sample

WHY THIS IS IMPORTANT

Sample selection is an integral part of survey research. Once you have decided how to distribute your questionnaire (we looked at alternatives in Chapter 3), you need to decide whom to approach to deliver your questionnaire. Designing a questionnaire and selecting the distribution mechanism is a bit like planning a party. You carefully think about the reason, themes, design, presentation and so on to make sure the event will be a success.

The size and quality of your sample are key determinants of the accuracy and validity of your final results. A properly selected sample of an appropriate size and profile is essential if you are to be able to produce unbiased results that will be representative of your study population. A sample that is too small or improperly chosen will probably yield biased or otherwise unrepresentative results.

There are a number of core concepts related to sampling that we will explore in this chapter. These include the logic of sampling, as well as key tasks in selecting a sample, such as the choice of your sampling frame and developing a target for sample size. Practical guidelines for estimating confidence intervals for a given sample size, as well as for estimating whether differences in results between two survey percentages are statistically significant, will be presented at the end of the chapter. A short case study of the sampling of a community festival concludes the chapter. We begin the chapter by considering the logic of sampling.

THE LOGIC OF SAMPLING

Let's assume you want information on why people visit a particular theme park, how they got information about the park, their favourite rides in the park and their satisfaction levels with their visit to the park. You could, in principle, recruit several friends to stand by all the exits, all day, during the entire season the park is open to try to talk to everyone who visited the park. That is not a particularly good use of your time or of your friends' time. So, instead, you could be selective about dates, times and whom to interview. This process of choosing only certain times, locations and to whom to administer a questionnaire is known as sampling. It is usually a more efficient and less costly approach to interviewing people than a census (talking to everyone in some population).

The process of sampling begins with deciding what larger population you wish to study, and proceeds through selecting an increasingly targeted set of people whom you will eventually study, as shown in Fig. 4.1. We can call this larger population the **conceptual population**. Your access to the conceptual population will very often be highly restricted. For example, if you are interested in surveying culinary tourists (which we can define as all those people who are interested in sampling or learning more about local ingredients and foods characteristic of the destination visited), you will not be able to find a list of culinary tourists or all the locations where culinary tourists can be found. So, instead, you might decide to focus on visitors going to certain places where they are able to purchase, taste or learn about local foods. These might include a few wineries and restaurants that feature local ingredients on their menus in the region where you live. This is the **study population**.

Once you've decided on the study population, you need to figure out how to select specific individuals for your sample. In the case of wineries and restaurants, you might choose – with permission of the businesses – to interview people on certain days at certain times in the parking lot as they leave the premises. Alternatively, the wineries and restaurants might have a list of e-mail addresses of consumers they maintain for promotional purposes. If so, the businesses might give you access to those mailing lists for a web-based survey. The times, dates and location for face-to-face interviews or the e-mail lists define your **sampling frame**. A sampling frame may be either a list of potential people to interview or it can be a procedure for accessing a sample. The people you finally contact represent your **sample**. Note that your sample is not precisely the same thing as the people *in* your study. Some members of the sample may refuse to complete your questionnaire or might drop out of your study if it involves repeated questionnaires over a period of time. This phenomenon of people dropping out of your study is a potential source of non-response bias, and goes by the grim name of **sample mortality**. Let us now consider some different types of samples.

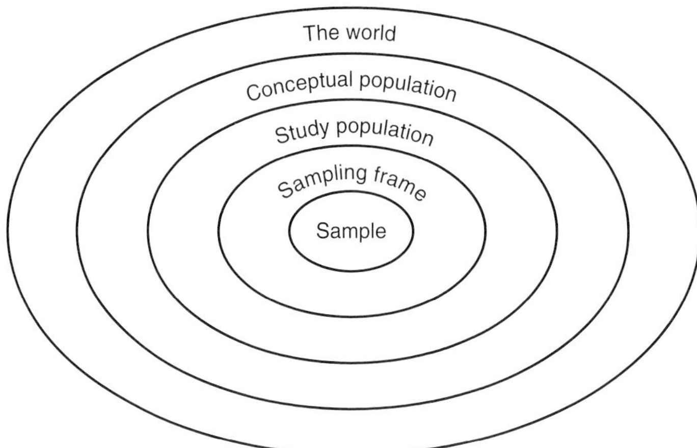

Fig. 4.1. Levels of population for sampling.

TYPES OF SAMPLES

Samples are classified as either probability or non-probability samples. The difference is whether the sample is intended to be representative of your sampling frame. As a result, probability sampling is sometimes referred to as representative sampling. Probability samples are the most useful for making valid generalizations about the population in your sampling frame, but there are times when a probability sample is not feasible. At these times, a non-probability sampling design must be used. We will look at several versions of each.

Probability sampling

Simple random sampling

Conceptually, the simplest random sampling design is called a simple random sample (what else would it be called!). In this context, random means that every member in your sampling frame has an equal chance of being selected. Actually drawing a simple random sample, though, is not always that simple. If your sampling frame consists of a list of names or addresses, you can select every *n*th entry, based on the sample size you require. An alternative method is to number all entries in the list and then use a random numbers table (or software that generates random numbers) to select your sample. The use of random numbers ensures a higher likelihood of your sample being truly random. The selection of every *n*th entry can be problematic if your list has regularities or cycles hidden in the order of the list. This is not usually a problem, but it can be in some cases. For example, if you have a list of street addresses and you select every, say, 15th address, it is conceivable that every 15th address tends to be a corner lot. People who live on corner lots often have larger homes and yards, and are more likely to have higher incomes, and thus have different characteristics to those who live mid-block.

If you have a list of names of people you want to sample, another trick is to copy the list into an Excel spreadsheet. Then, in the column to the right of the list of names, enter the function: =RAND(). This generates a random number between 0 and 1. You then sort both columns in ascending or descending order by the random number and simply select the number of names you need for your sample.

Much of the time, though, you will not have a list for your sampling frame. For example, if you want to sample visitors to an attraction, you won't have a list of all the visitors. Some other approach is needed. One common tactic is to position yourself (and, ideally, fellow surveyors) at each exit and then sample every *n*th as she or he leaves. This tactic is a practical tactic for drawing a more-or-less representative sample, although the degree of randomness you achieve will be shaped by the degree to which the times and dates you cover the exits provide a representative sample. There usually are substantial variations in the flow of visitors to and from venues by entrance/exit, day of the week and time of day. For example, families are more likely to attend a festival during the day, whereas singles and couples are more likely to visit in the evening. There may also be differences in the profiles of visitors depending on the exit they use when leaving a venue if there are multiple exits. For example, a large sports facility might have some exits that lead to public transportation stops (buses, subways) and others that lead to parking lots. As you might expect, people exiting near bus stops will be different on a number of measures to those who exit to parking lots. As a result, you need to sample at a variety of dates, times and locations to obtain the most representative sample possible.

Random sampling is not always an efficient way of ensuring a representative sample, especially if you are sampling from a large population that has a number of subgroups. Although a random design provides every person with an equal chance of being selected, the luck of the draw may result in some subpopulations being either under- or over-sampled. This is a special risk if your sample is only a small percentage of a very large population, as we shall examine in the next section.

Stratified random sampling

Imagine you want to administer an e-mail survey of members of an airline frequent flier programme. The programme has 100,000 members. You have decided you need to survey 1000 of them, or 1% of the population, to get results that are statistically valid at an acceptable level (we shall discuss sample sizes later in this chapter). Let's also assume that the frequent flier programme has four tiers of membership based on the number of kilometres the member flew in the previous year. Table 4.1 presents hypothetical data for this imaginary frequent flier programme: the percentage of the membership in each tier and the number of surveys (quota) to complete for a proportional sample of each cohort.

At 2% of the membership, there are 2000 Gold members. A 1% sample of them should net your quota of 20 subjects. However, random sampling could easily yield many fewer than that, causing you to miss important information from this group. One approach to avoid this problem is stratified random sampling. Stratified random sampling involves grouping your sampling frame into subgroups, such as different membership levels. You then draw a random sample from each tier equal to your quota. In the case of a sampling frame such as a frequent flier programme, identifying potential subjects by their membership level is fairly simple (as long as you have a good working relationship with the management of the programme).

If you are not able to identify, a priori, the subgroup to which someone belongs, you might try oversampling and the use of screener questions. In this tactic, you keep drawing potential subjects from your sampling frame and briefly ask them a question or two to determine whether they fit into a subgroup for which you need more subjects. This is a common tactic for Internet panel surveys. Potential subjects are contacted from the panel and asked (presuming the panel membership profiles do not already provide relevant demographic profiles for each member) questions about age, sex, education or other subgroup characteristics. If the quota for males aged 60 or over is not filled, and the potential subject fits that category, the survey continues. If the surveyor has filled his/her quota for a particular demographic cohort, then the potential respondent gets a brief message thanking her for responding and noting that, unfortunately, she does not qualify for the survey. Screener questions are also used in personal interviews and telephone interviews. Other tactics may be used to achieve your quota, such as snowball sampling or purposive sampling, but these are not representative sampling designs. We will look at them in the section on non-probability sampling.

Table 4.1. Hypothetical airline frequent flier programme survey.

Membership tier	Kilometres flown	Members (%)	Quota
Gold	≥150,000	2	20
Silver	75,000–149,999	10	100
Bronze	35,000–74,999	24	240
Regular	<35,000	64	640

Cluster sampling

Both simple random and stratified random sampling are useful in certain circumstances. However, a situation in which they are not useful or efficient is when you need to draw a sample from a wide geographic area, especially when you will be doing either telephone or personal interviews. A real-world example might be useful here. The Ontario Tourism Marketing Partnership (OTMP) is the provincial body responsible for promoting the Canadian province of Ontario. One of its key markets is a group of US border states: New York, Pennsylvania, Ohio and Michigan. OTMP periodically commissions a telephone survey of travel intentions of residents of these states. The sample size typically is about 1200 subjects. It is, in principle, possible to use RDD to draw a simple random sample of all telephone numbers in this broad geographic area. However, with such a relatively small sample size in a region with millions of residents, it is highly likely that some cities that are important markets for trips to Ontario could easily yield only two or three respondents or be missed entirely. So, OTMP uses a cluster sampling design. Key cities in the region that are the targets of print or television advertising – Syracuse, Rochester, Buffalo, Cleveland, Pittsburgh, Detroit, Lansing and Grand Rapids – have been identified as clusters for sampling. A quota of completed telephone interviews (using RDD) is then set for each cluster, based on a roughly proportional distribution of the sample of 1200 people.

Another version of cluster sampling is to choose, using a random numbers table, the geographical units in which to sample. For example, if you were doing a study of residents' attitudes towards visitors in a city, you could divide the city into neighbourhoods (or simply place a grid over a map of the city) and then randomly choose an appropriate number of neighbourhoods or grid cells. You then proceed by randomly sampling households in each area.

Non-probability sampling

The essential characteristic of non-probability sampling is that the sampling units are not chosen randomly. The selection of subjects is not done using the logic of probability selection, but through other tactics. This does not mean that your sample necessarily is not representative of your study population. It could be. The problem is that you do not know whether it is representative or not at the time you draw your sample. Once you have drawn a sample, you could include questions in your questionnaire that might allow you to develop a profile, perhaps some demographic variables such as age, sex, marital status and employment status that you compare to your study population. This would give you an indication of how similar your sample is to the larger population on the basis of the variables you use for the profile.

Researchers usually prefer a probability sample because they usually feel it is a more objective, empirically defensible way of drawing a sample. However, there are circumstances where probability sampling is not practical. Some examples of situations for which probability sampling may not be practical include:

- people at non-gated outdoor events;
- managers in tourism firms;
- backpackers during their trips;
- attendees at a travel trade show;
- passengers on a cruise ship; and
- passengers waiting in airport departure lounges.

Probability sampling may not be practical in these cases because of the challenge in: (i) accessing individuals generally; or (ii) selecting individuals on a truly random or representative basis. When needing to draw a sample from a group such as these, you can use one of the following approaches.

Convenience

Convenience sampling refers to choosing people to interview because you happen to have access to them. For example, my graduate students sometimes conduct surveys in my large undergraduate introductory tourism course. The topics of these questionnaires range from testing tourism decision-making models, through perceptions of ecotourism to developing attitude scales. The graduate students do not select this class because they believe my undergraduate students are representative of the general population or even of the undergraduate student body at my university (they most certainly are not). Instead, the graduate students use my class just because I give them permission to invite the students to participate in a survey.

Convenience samples can sometimes incorporate elements of randomness to increase the potential of the convenience sample to be more representative of the study population. For example, sampling at a non-gated event (such as a street festival) typically involves attempting to interview whomever you can get to stop to answer your questions. However, even here you can employ a sampling strategy that increases the likelihood that your sample is more random than just selecting attractive people at a time that is most convenient for you to be on site. See Case Study 4.1 to see how this was done at a 3-day street festival.

Case Study 4.1. Sampling at a non-gated event.

Sampling at a non-gated event such as a festival held in a city park presents more challenges than sampling at a venue where entrances and exits are controlled. The following describes some basic tactics you can use to draw a reasonably random sample at a non-gated event.

The specific details of sampling design at a non-gated event will depend on several factors:

- the estimated total attendance (if known);
- the length of the event;
- whether people will arrive over an extended period of time, such as going to an all-day art show in a city park, or whether they will tend to come at fairly specific times, such as just before an outdoor concert; and
- the number of interviewers available to conduct the survey.

Here's a brief practical illustration of how such sampling was done at a street festival in Waterloo, Ontario, Canada. The City of Waterloo puts on a Busker Festival (buskers are street performers such as musicians, jugglers and magicians) during the third weekend of each August. Approximately 60 buskers from North America and Europe show up and perform multiple shows from noon on Friday to 9.00 p.m. on Sunday. The performances last for 45 to 60 minutes and are staged at various locations along several blocks of the main street (King Street) in uptown Waterloo. The street is closed to traffic for the festival. Figure 4.2 shows a depiction of the venue.

(Continued)

Case Study 4.1. Continued.

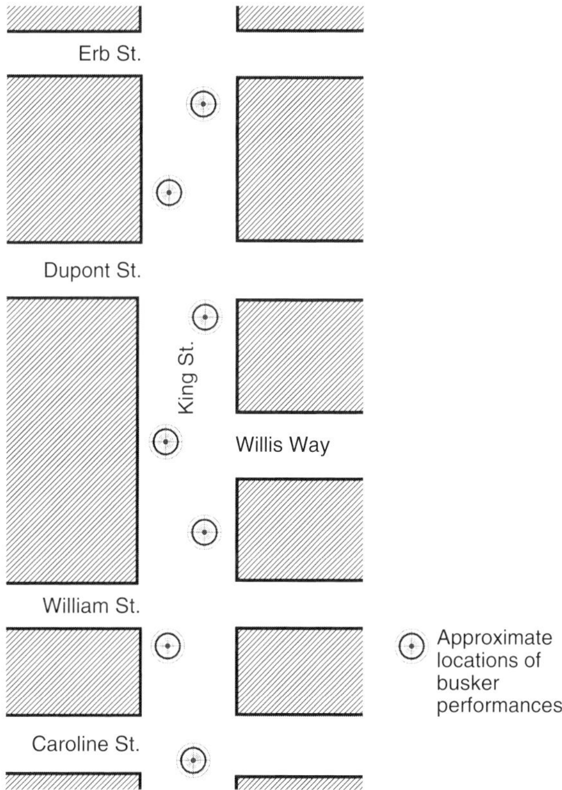

Fig. 4.2. Diagram of Waterloo Busker Festival venue.

The City wished to have a survey done of attendees to the festival to get more information on the origins of attendees, their demographics and satisfaction with the event. The survey was delivered in a face-to-face interview that took approximately 1 minute to complete. The design of a sampling framework presented a challenge for the following reasons:

- There are no reliable estimates of the number of people who attend the event.
- Access to streets where performances occur is completely unrestricted to pedestrians.
- Audience members are free to wander from one performing busker to another at any time.
- There is no information about the average length of stay by attendees at the festival, nor of the number of times they visit over the weekend.
- Performances overlap each other, and are scattered along King Street.
- The audience consists of individual adults, teenagers with friends, couples, groups of adults with friends and families with children.

A festival organizer provided the survey team with a copy of the schedule of performances and approximate locations for each busker's performance. The locations were not fixed,

(Continued)

Case Study 4.1. Continued.

but could be anywhere along the street within a half-block area. Three or four buskers would be performing at any given time, with the start of their shows occurring roughly every 30 minutes.

A 'stint sampling design' was developed. In this case, a stint refers to a sampling unit: a specific time frame and location for interviewing. We had five surveyors, each of whom would work one stint per day. A stint consisted of a 3-hour period and a specified zone, operationally defined as the stretch of King Street between side streets. A list of all combinations of zones and times during which buskers would be performing was constructed, and five stints per day were randomly chosen using a random numbers table. The assigned stints are shown in Table 4.2.

Table 4.2. Stint sampling schedule.

Time	Surveyor A	Surveyor B	Surveyor C	Surveyor D	Surveyor E
Friday					
12.00 p.m.–3.00 p.m.	Dupont to William				
3.00 p.m.–6.00 p.m.			Erb to Dupont		
6.00 p.m.–9.00 p.m.		William to Caroline		Erb to Dupont	Dupont to William
Saturday					
12.00 p.m.–3.00 p.m.		Dupont to William			
3.00 p.m.–6.00 p.m.			William to Caroline		William to Caroline
6.00 p.m.–9.00 p.m.	William to Caroline			Erb to Dupont	
Sunday					
12.00 p.m.–3.00 p.m.	Erb to Dupont				Dupont to William
3.00 p.m.–6.00 p.m.		Erb to Dupont	William to Caroline		
6.00 p.m.–9.00 p.m.				Dupont to William	

The surveyors were instructed to take a position somewhere in their assigned zone that gave them good access to the crowd but did not interfere with the buskers or pedestrian flow. They were asked to identify an imaginary square (2 × 2 m) on the ground near them,

(Continued)

Case Study 4.1. Continued.

wait for 3 minutes, and then approach the first adult (a person who appeared to be 18 or older) to invite them to respond to the questionnaire. The reason for waiting 3 minutes was to avoid the temptation to approach (or avoid) specific individuals for interviews. After completing the survey, they were to move to a different location within their zone, and repeat the same procedure. If the person approached declined to be interviewed, the surveyors were told to approach the next individual in the imaginary box. The surveyors were also instructed to let couples or groups themselves select which person would speak for the group. If the person approached noted that he had been interviewed previously, the surveyor was instructed to thank him for his cooperation and to select another person.

Each interviewer was given a minimum of 15 interviews to complete per stint. This would provide a total sample of 225 respondents. Although this was not a large quota, it was deemed adequate for the purposes of the study, which was exploratory in nature. This meant that each interviewer had 12 minutes per interview. The goal of 15 interviews per stint turned out to be unrealistic. The main problem was the time it took to recruit each respondent. In response to the greater time needed to complete a survey, the volunteer surveyors often extended the time they interviewed in order to approach their target of 15. A total of 213 interviews were attained. Although short of the 225 targeted, this was considered large enough to draw some tentative conclusions about the percentage of visitors coming from nearby municipalities, top-of-mind awareness of information sources about the festival and the percentage of respondents who said they would recommend the festival to family and friends, and hoped to attend the following year.

Internet survey panels

A special version of convenience sampling is the creation and use of Internet panels. Panels allow researchers easily to tap into a pool of potential respondents once the panel has been set up. The creation of the panel is a substantial task, requiring the compilation of e-mail addresses. Maintaining and managing a panel properly is even more difficult than creating one. Potential members are often recruited through the mining of existing e-mail lists by market research firms. Research organizations like the Council of American Survey Research Organizations (available at http://www.casro.org) and the European Society for Opinion and Marketing Research (available at http://www.esomar.org) have strict guidelines prohibiting research companies from blindly sending out e-mails to potential respondents. Instead, they have to be recruited through other methods such as online through banner ads, registration on websites and/or partnering with other organizations that send mailings to their customers.

Some panels have built-in profiles of their members so that a researcher using the panel can specify what sort of people he wishes to select from the panel. Other panels do not have member profiles, thus requiring the surveyor to use a series of screener questions at the start of the Internet survey to allow him to select only those people in which he is interested.

Panels can be particularly effective in tracking changes in, for example, travel intentions and behaviours over time. This may be done either by drawing independent samples in each wave or by interviewing the same panellists in each wave. Note, though, that some panels have an attrition rate as high as 50% in the first year, which makes returning to the original sample problematic. Panels can also be useful for studying the effects of experimental treatments, such as showing participants different advertisements or hypothetical tour package offerings. In fact, experiments such as these are the purpose of the bulk of online research.

Panels pose several problems. As you might expect, a key concern is the representativeness of the panel for the population you wish to study. Internet panels are, of course, limited to those that have access to the Internet and a comfort level in responding to web-based surveys. As noted in Chapter 3, panels tend to have a disproportionately high number of people who have the time to respond to surveys, which means they tend to have fewer people employed outside the home.

All panels lose members through drop-out, a phenomenon known as sample mortality. One of the major causes of sample mortality is 'burn-out' caused by fatigue with repeated surveys. Changes in personal situations including health or a new job will also cause people to quit panels.

Panel members may also become 'conditioned' with repeated surveys on the same topic. For example, if a panel is asked over a couple of years about their opinions on the design of tourism advertisements, they may become much more critical of advertisements than the general population. If panel members are asked to report spending on successive tourism trips, they are likely to begin keeping increasingly accurate records. While maintaining expense records for the purpose of responding more accurately to surveys may sound like a good thing, it means that results of successive surveys cannot be reliably compared because of variations in the level of accuracy among different respondents.

Internet panels are also vulnerable to a phenomenon known as 'professional survey takers' (PSTs) – people who make a hobby (or part-time job) out of completing surveys. This is a special problem with panels that offer tangible rewards for the completion of each survey rather than simply a chance to win a prize. Some PSTs use software to search out and sign up for panels, potentially dozens or even hundreds of panels. Companies who maintain panels are aware of this problem and work to put in countermeasures, but they must continue to be on their guard.

Another software threat is programs ('survey bots') that search out and complete online surveys automatically. This potential fraud can be caught if the company running the panels monitors completion times for surveys – survey bots complete surveys in a matter of seconds. Because the responses are essentially random, unusual or contradictory patterns of answers can also indicate the activity of a survey bot. Another trick is to ask a simple demographic question, such as age cohort or education level in two places in the survey. If different answers to the same question are provided, the questionnaire was probably completed by a survey bot. Delete the return.

Clients of Internet panels are increasingly demanding assurance about the quality of the panel, as well as protection against spurious survey completions or the unreliable results produced by PSTs and survey bots. If you are a considering hiring the services of an online survey panel, issues you should look at include:

- What steps is the provider taking to ensure the panel is free of serious distortions in its make-up?
- Does the online firm take active steps to catch and remove PSTs?
- How many clients does the firm currently have? Larger firms tend to provide better-quality service?
- How many surveys are administered per month? How many surveys is the average panel member asked to complete per month? What are turnover rates on the panel? How long does the average person stay on the panel?
- If the firm has difficulty filling its quota for a particular survey, does it draw from other panels (this is NOT a good practice)?

Internet survey panels can be effective, efficient and very useful, but they are subject to a variety of quality issues and questions about representativeness. As in so many areas of life, you should adopt a *caveat emptor* ('buyer beware') attitude in contracting the services of an Internet panel.

Internet panels are sometimes combined with other types of surveys to provide more balanced profiles of travel behaviours in a population. A good example of such an effective design can be read about in Focus Box 4.1.

Focus Box 4.1. Online survey panels: a US example.

Internet panels present researchers with an attractive proposition: faster data collection and lower costs. While speed and savings are desirable, statistical validity should be the primary consideration, especially when precision is required for estimating travel volumes and spending.

Online samples have rapidly gained acceptance in experimental designs where convenience samples are employed. However, in research requiring full population representation, acceptance of online samples has been much slower. Opinion research is an example where full representation is required, yet it represents only 2% of all online studies according to industry newsletter, *Inside Research*.

The biggest hurdle for online samples in the USA is being representative of the population. The PewResearchCenter[a] reports that three out of ten Americans do not have Internet access. In addition, panel member demographics such as age, geography, race, education and income usually are skewed. Despite these differences, research results can be representative depending on the subject being studied. The best way to know whether online samples can be a valid substitute for more rigorous and expensive samples is through comparability testing.

Since 2000, the research firm DK Shifflet & Associates has conducted side-by-side surveys using online samples and traditional probability samples. Their probability samples have been applied to more than 300 monthly surveys where more than 40,000 respondents are invited to report monthly travel behaviour, type of travel, destinations and the travel expenditures of US residents. Their historical results compare favourably to periodic, large-scale government studies and thus validate the traditional approach as accurate. Adding online samples and comparing results with the proven traditional methodology enables a comparison of the suitability of the alternative sampling method.

In comparing the demographic profiles of online respondents with mail respondents, online panel respondents were under-represented in the high school education category, the less than $25,000 per year household income category and the 65+ years cohort, while they were over-represented in the more than $75,000 per year income category as well as the 46–65 years cohort. While respondent weighting can address many of the demographic differences, the critical question remains: do online panel members have different attitudes or behave differently once demographic differences are balanced?

After weighting both samples to be comparable in terms of demographics, online sample travel behaviour differed significantly, reporting far fewer business trips, lower participation in business group meetings, more day trips and more stays with friends rather than in hotels; all of these result in underestimation of travel spending. This comparative analysis illustrates that travel studies using online samples alone do not provide accurate representation of the total US population's travel behaviour, even after weighting the data on the basis of known geographic and demographic characteristics.

(Continued)

Focus Box 4.1. Continued.

Despite these differences, the online interviews can be included in a mixed-mode sample if travel proportions are known from a probability sampling approach. Without the known proportions, it is impossible to balance online samples. This requires the availability of representative samples through traditional offline probability sample methodologies. Given the historical monthly and seasonal variations in travel, a large-scale representative sample is required each month. Online samples alone do not provide consistent and accurate measures of travel at this time. However, online samples can be used as a complementary supplement to recurring (monthly) representative samples that generate benchmarks for weighting the online responses. A mixed sampling approach, with controls for online results, prevents marketing and management decision makers from being misled by studies based solely on online samples.

[a]US Hitting a Ceiling of Internet Households. Parks Associates.

Courtesy of:
DK Shifflet & Associates Ltd.,
McLean, Virginia, USA
DIRECTIONS® Travel Intelligence System℠
2008

Data saturation sampling

The sample size in ordinary convenience sampling is usually set a priori (ahead of time) on the basis of ensuring that you have enough observations for an adequate profile of your study population. However, conventional statistical tests such as confidence levels and confidence intervals (sampling error) are not meaningful with non-probabilistic sampling. A different approach to determining the size of your sample, especially in the case of open-ended personal interviews, is to conduct interviews until you feel you are not hearing anything new from the interviews. Hearing the same set of responses over and over is referred to as 'data saturation'; when this occurs, you stop sampling. The problem here, of course, is that you do not know whether the next person you would have sampled, had you continued, would have provided dramatically different answers.

Quota sampling

While convenience sampling is almost certainly likely *not* to produce a representative sample, you can sometimes improve the representativeness by employing quotas for different types of potential respondents. For example, if you have reason to believe your study population has 55% females and 45% males, and you are aiming for a sample of 500 people, you continue to contact potential participants until you reach 275 females and 225 males. Once you've reached your quota for one sex, you draw a sample only from the other sex. This type of sampling is known as proportional quota sampling. Of course, an issue here upon which you have to reflect is on what will the quota be based: sex, age cohort, ethnicity, employment status, height or something else?

A variant on quota sampling is non-proportional sampling. In this case, you decide how many people in each category you need for your analysis. You continue to draw your sample until you have achieved the minimum number of people in each group. This approach works well when you have a relatively large number of different groups from whom you want to obtain data. Like stratified probability sampling, this approach helps ensure you have not inadvertently missed or under-sampled small but important groups.

Snowball sampling

This method is especially useful for drawing a sample from a population that can be hard to access. You begin by finding someone who meets the profile of the type of subjects you wish to survey. After you administer your questionnaire, you ask that person for the name of someone else you could contact. When you complete an interview with that person, you ask for another referral. The term 'snowball sampling' describes how this sort of sample begins small and grows over time.

Clearly, this does not yield a representative sample, but it can help you get in touch with people who otherwise would never be identified by you. For example, I used snowball sampling to survey students who worked in part-time jobs while backpacking in Europe. These students tended to know others like themselves, and could provide not only names but also an introduction for me. I have used the same approach to interview government officials with some form of involvement in tourism policy and programming in agencies that did not, on the basis of the agency's name, appear to have any programmes relevant to tourism but actually did.

Snowball sampling works well for a small number of potential respondents, say 25 or less. You can reasonably make personal contact for the interview or to deliver the questionnaire. However, as your potential sample grows, you will face logistical challenges. An example drawn from one of my students' experience will illustrate. She wanted to administer 100 self-completed mail-back surveys distributed through snowball sampling to parents with one or more children under the age of 13. Her plan was to provide the first set of five potential respondents with a supply of questionnaires and envelopes, with the instructions to: (i) complete a questionnaire and mail it back to her; and (ii) pass the package of remaining questionnaires and envelopes to another parent, with the same instructions. Her hope was that this would result in an efficient distribution to reach parents of young children.

However, she quickly discovered that her initial seed sample tended to move in the same social circles. Very quickly the same people were being approached by multiple respondents to complete the survey. She considered, at first, collecting the names of everyone who had been approached and sharing that growing list with those who had completed the questionnaire so they could avoid approaching the same people. This presented an ethical problem. It would have meant providing the names of respondents to all other respondents, which would be a violation of the condition of anonymity that was required by the university's ethics office. As a result, she was forced to switch from a snowball sampling tactic to personally handing out her surveys at recreation centres frequented by parents with children. This increased her time, effort and transportation costs for data collection, delayed her completion of her thesis and, ultimately, her graduation.

These problems could have been avoided to a degree through the use of an online survey. Time would still have been needed to identify the names of potential respondents (who, of course, have to have access to the Internet), but the online survey would avoid the hassles of distributing copies of the questionnaires via a snowball scheme.

PRACTICAL ADVICE ON SAMPLE SIZES

One of the questions most frequently asked by people interested in conducting or commissioning a survey is 'How many people should I survey?'. What they usually mean by that question is 'How few people can I get away with in my sample?'. Answering that question can range from the simple to the very complex and tedious, and as this is not a statistics textbook, we will go for simple.

Some issues influencing sample size

However, keeping it simple does not mean we can ignore some important questions and technical terminology. One of the most important questions to ask in determining sample size is 'What is the purpose of your study?' If you want to know whether visitors to a community festival had a good time, you can probably get away with asking a relatively few number of people. Your probably have an initial feeling of the general level of satisfaction by observing crowd behaviour and body language. You can test your intuition by speaking with perhaps a couple hundred people to rank their level of satisfaction on a scale such as:

[ ] Exceeded my expectations
[ ] Met my expectations
[ ] Fell short of my expectations

The consequences of having your survey results not exactly match those of the entire population of festival-goers are minimal. On the other hand, if you are studying levels of restaurateurs' support for proposed new health legislation regarding food storage, you will want to be certain your results are as accurate as possible because of the sensitivity of the issue. Other situations also influence the choice of sample size. A very limited budget for data collection will constrain how many people you are able to interview (the lack of a large budget for sample selection is also one reason why researchers choose convenience sampling). A tight time frame for data collection may also constrain your sample size. Ideally, of course, the budget and schedule should be commensurate with the scope of the project and data requirements – but money and time are often lacking for student-initiated surveys. Thus, constraints not only affect the potential for your sample size, they can also constrain the objectives of your research.

Another practical concern is the type of analysis you plan to do. At the risk of wandering too far into the jungle of statistics, consider a common test, X^2 (chi square). Chi square examines the relationship between two variables, such as whether a person's household income influences the number of trips he or she took during the past year. Data for chi square are usually presented in the form of a table such as Table 4.3. This statistic requires that the expected minimum number of observations in any cell of the table must be at least five. The six rows and five columns create 30 cells. If we assume an expected even distribution we would need a sample of

Table 4.3. Hypothetical table relating income and trips taken.

	Household income ($)				
Pleasure trips taken in previous year	**< 30,000**	**30,000–59,999**	**60,000–99,999**	**100,000–130,000**	**> 130,000**
0					
1					
2					
3					
4					
5 or more					

at least 150 (30 × 5). If the distribution of responses is highly skewed and too many cells end up having an expected frequency of less than five, you would have to have an even larger sample.

Selecting your sample size

Once you have reflected upon these issues as they relate to your study, you will need to set a target sample size more precisely. Before we turn to some pragmatic guidelines to determine sample size, a few terms need to be defined.

Confidence intervals and levels

You have probably heard news stories about the results of some opinion poll, perhaps in the context of what percentage of people intend to vote for a particular candidate. Such a news story might report something like 'The latest poll shows that 45% support the Purple Party where as 47% support the Orange Party, with 8% undecided. Results are accurate within ± 5%'. This indicates that the actual level of support for the Purples is probably somewhere between 40 and 50%, while the support for the Oranges is probably somewhere between 42 and 52%. In other words, the confidence interval reflects the width of probable range of an estimate of some variable you wish to measure. The confidence interval is sometimes (although imprecisely) called the sampling error.

The confidence level is a value chosen by the researcher to set the probability that the estimate derived from the sample will fall within that interval. In other words, the confidence level indicates how certain you are that the true value is within your confidence interval. Tourism researchers normally use a 95% confidence level. In other words, they typically want at least a 95% probability that the true value will be within the sampling error range (or two standard deviations). To put it differently again, most tourism researchers aim for a level of accuracy such that 95 out of 100 samples (if they were to draw 100 samples, which they wound not) would yield results within their confidence interval.

Sampling error reflects variability intrinsic in random samples and is fairly easy to estimate. Sampling error can be reduced by working with larger samples. There is another source of error – non-sampling error – that is much more difficult to estimate or correct if it does occur. Non-sampling error arises from things such as badly worded questions, interviewer bias, non-response bias, deliberately misleading answers by a respondent, miscoded data and so on. Such errors are often more of a threat than sampling error. The best strategy for minimizing non-sampling error is careful attention to all aspects of questionnaire design, the interview process, coding and data entry.

Here's another way to think about these two concepts. Let's conduct a thought experiment. Imagine that a researcher draws a sample and surveys the members of that sample once on the value of expenditures on their most recent trip. From that sample, she calculates the mean expenditure. Because this estimate is based on a sample, if she were to draw another, independent sample, she would probably find a different mean expenditure due to the vagaries of different samples. If the process is repeated numerous times, she could calculate the mean of the mean expenditures. In other words, if she observed a mean expenditure of €550 in her first sample, and €575 in a second sample, the mean of those two means is €562.50.

Continue the thought experiment to have the researcher draw an infinite number of samples and calculate a mean from the infinite numbers of means observed. A principle called the **Central Limit Theorem** states that the mean of their infinite number of means would equal the true mean of spending by the study population. We can never get to that conceptual perfection, of course, but the Central Limit Theorem provides another insight that does offer practical help to us.

The Central Limit Theorem states that the means obtained by all those samples are normally distributed around the true (but unknown) mean of the population's spending. The spread of the means the researcher has observed can be measured by the standard deviation of the observations (go back to your statistics text if you want to remind yourself of the definition of standard deviation). Approximately 68% of the observed values will be within one standard deviation, 95% will be within two standard deviations while 99% will be within three.

The notion of a confidence level implies, of course, that the true value of some variable can fall outside your confidence interval. It's not likely, but it could happen. A higher confidence level, such as 99%, provides a higher degree of certainty, whereas a lower confidence level, such as 90%, reduces your confidence about your results. There is a trade-off between the width of the confidence *interval* and the value of the confidence *level*. For any given sample size, a higher confidence level requires a wider confidence interval. Narrower confidence intervals result in lower confidence levels.

Here's a simple intuitive example of how that trade-off works. Return to our example of spending estimate on the most recent tourism trip. If our result was that the mean spending was €562.50, we could be very certain (perhaps 99.99%) that the true value would be plus or minus 50% – that is between €281.25 and €843.75. Such a broad interval is highly likely to include the true value because it is so wide. Of course, such a broad range is not very useful. Your high degree of confidence that your estimate is correct comes at the expense of precision. Alternatively, we could decide that we want a narrow interval, perhaps ± 1% (between €558.87 and €568.12). To achieve this, our confidence level would necessarily drop dramatically. For example, we might have a confidence level of only 65% that our true value is within ± 1% of our estimate.

A comment on study population size

As we will see in the following tables, the size of the study population has relatively little bearing on the sample size needed as long as the size of the study population is reasonably large. A sample of 500 will provide results that have confidence intervals and levels approximately the same for a municipality of 100,000 as for a country with 300,000,000.

The degree of variability in the attribute being studied in your study population is more important than population size when selecting an appropriate sample. At the extreme, if everyone in your study population had the same attitudes toward travel (measured, perhaps with a Likert scale (see Chapter 6)), you would need to sample only one person. Of course, you generally do not know the degree of variability in a population before you study it. The greater the variability in a population, the larger a sample you need to have to achieve a given confidence interval and level.

If you look at variability as the percentage of the population that has some attribute (such as scores on an attitude scale), the greatest variability is associated with a 50% incidence of some attribute. In other words, half the population has the attribute; the other half does not. If the percentage is 10 or 90%, the population is less heterogeneous (diverse) because a large majority has (or does not have) the attribute. Researchers normally want to be conservative in developing estimates of sample size, so they normally assume a 50/50 distribution. If your population is less diverse (more homogeneous) you have a larger sample than necessary, which gives you more accurate results than you would otherwise have with a 50/50 split.

Sample sizes

The question of sample size is a complex one. One of the rules-of-thumb that can be helpful is to note that there is a positive relationship between the number of items (questions in a questionnaire) and sample size. Your sample should allow for a ratio of at least 1:4 or 1:5, that is four or five respondents per question (Tinsley and Tinsley, 1987; Hinkin *et al.*, 1997). Ryan (1995), though, argues for a more conservative ratio of at least ten respondents per item. Thus, if your questionnaire has 20 questions, you should strive for a sample of at least 200 respondents.

Many statistical texts can provide you with equations for calculating sample size given population size, variability and desired confidence intervals and levels. Three classic texts are Mace (1964), Society and Community Planning Research (1972) and Barnett (1991). For many purposes, however, Table 4.4 can provide you with adequate guidelines for selecting sample size.

Note how the required sample size drops fairly rapidly as you accept a wider confidence interval (that is, you become more tolerant of committing a Type 1 error). For example, if you wanted a confidence interval of ± 1% for a survey of a study population of 10,000, you would need to interview nearly 4900 (almost half) the population; in contrast, if you were to accept a confidence level of ± 5%, you would need to sample only 370 people.

Note, too, how the sample size you require rises as the population rises, but at a decreasing rate. For a confidence level of ± 4% for a population of 1000 people, you would need a sample of 375 people. However, for a population of 1,000,000 (a thousand times larger), you need 600 respondents, only a 60% increase in sample size.

If you wish to present results related to particular subgroups within your sample population, such as comparing males and females in their answers to your survey, you would use Table 4.4 to set the sample size for each subpopulation. For example, if you were going to do a survey of attendees to a sports tournament that draws 4000 people, evenly divided between females and males, and you want to: (i) compare both females' and males' responses to your questions; and (ii) have a confidence interval of ± 4%, you might think you need a sample of 522. However, if you

Table 4.4. Sample sizes for various confidence intervals at a 95% confidence level.

Study population size	Desired confidence interval (%)				
	± 1	± 2	± 3	± 4	± 5
1,000	[a]	[a]	[a]	375	278
2,000	[a]	[a]	696	462	322
3,000	[a]	1,334	787	500	341
4,000	[a]	1,501	843	522	351
5,000	[a]	1,622	880	536	357
10,000	4,899	1,936	964	566	370
15,000	5,855	2,070	996	577	375
20,000	6,489	2,144	1,013	583	377
25,000	6,939	2,191	1,023	586	378
50,000	8,057	2,291	1,045	593	381
100,000	8,763	2,345	1,056	597	383
1,000,000	9,513	2,395	1,066	600	384

[a]At least 50% of the population must be sampled.

want that confidence interval to apply to the results of each sex, whose population is 2000 each, you would need to draw two samples: 462 men and 462 women, for a total of 924 interviews.

These sample sizes apply only to the number of completed valid questionnaires. As we saw in Chapter 2, questionnaires have varying levels of non-response rates. This means you normally need to sample many more people than the above table indicates in order to arrive at the required sample size.

Estimating confidence intervals

Tourism researchers often face a slightly different question than how many people to sample. Instead, they often interview as many people as possible (or are given secondary data drawn from interviews conducted by someone else), and they need to know that 'Given this sample size, what is the confidence interval of the results?'. Table 4.5 provides some guidelines for

Table 4.5. Approximate confidence intervals (±%) for different sample sizes and attribute incidence.

Sample size	10/90	20/80	30/70	40/60	50/50
50	8	11	13	14	14
100	6	8	9	10	10
150	5	6	7	8	8
200	4	6	6	7	7
250	4	5	6	6	6
300	3	5	5	6	6
350	3	4	5	5	5
400	3	4	4	5	5
450	3	4	4	5	5
500	3	4	4	4	4
600	2	3	4	4	4
700	2	3	3	4	4
800	2	3	3	3	3
900	2	3	3	3	3
1000	2	2	3	3	3
1500	2	2	2	2	3
2000	1	2	2	2	2
3000	1	1	2	2	2

common sample sizes. Note that the confidence interval differs depending on the heterogeneity of the sample. For samples that are relatively homogeneous (for example, 90% of the population share the same attribute), the confidence interval is narrower than for more diverse samples (such as where an attribute is split 50/50 in a sample).

To read Table 4.5, find the row closest to your sample size. Then read across to the column that most closely represents the incidence of some attribute in your sample. For example, if you have a sample of 527 people, and 38% of them reported swimming as an activity they engaged in on their vacation, you would go to the row for a sample of 500 and read across to the column for 40%. You find that the confidence interval for your estimate of 38% is ± 4%. In other words, the actual percentage of people who went swimming is likely (at a 95% confidence level) to be between 34 and 42%.

The values in Table 4.5 apply when the study population is relatively large (say, over 100,000). For smaller populations, the actual confidence intervals will be smaller, depending on how small the study population actually is.

Differences between results from two independent samples

Table 4.6 presents another set of pragmatic guidelines for interpreting survey results. This table allows you to estimate whether the differences between two survey percentages are

Table 4.6. Confidence intervals (±%) for comparing results from two samples.

Sample sizes	10/90	20/80	30/70	40/60	50/50
2000 and					
2000	2	2	3	3	3
1000	2	3	3	4	4
500	3	4	4	5	5
100	6	8	9	10	10
1500 and					
1500	2	3	3	4	4
750	3	4	4	4	4
500	3	4	5	5	5
100	6	8	9	10	10
1000 and					
1000	3	4	4	4	4
750	3	4	4	5	5
500	3	4	5	5	5
100	6	8	9	10	10

(Continued)

Table 4.6. Continued.

Sample sizes	10/90	20/80	30/70	40/60	50/50
750 and					
750	3	4	5	5	5
500	3	5	5	6	6
250	5	6	7	7	7
100	6	8	10	10	10
500 and					
500	4	5	6	6	6
250	5	7	8	7	8
100	6	9	10	11	11
250 and					
250	5	7	8	9	9
100	7	9	11	11	12
100 and					
100	8	11	13	14	14

probably real or just due to chance. To read Table 4.6, read down the 'sample sizes' column until you find the row closest to the two samples you are examining. Then read across to the column that most closely represents the incidence of some attribute in your two samples. If there is a wide difference in the incidence rate, say one sample has an incidence of some attribute of 10% and another has an incidence of 50%, use the column that reflects the greater heterogeneity (in this case, 50%).

Here's an example. A survey of travel habits of anglophone (English-speaking) Ontario (Canada) residents and francophone (French-speaking) Ontario residents sampled 497 anglophone and 116 francophones. The survey results indicated that, in the previous year, 17% of anglophones reported taking a trip to the USA whereas only 12% of francophones visited the USA. Is the difference of 5% points meaningful or just due to chance?

To answer that, go down to the rows for 500 and 100 (this is as close as Table 4.6 allows us to get to the actual sample sizes). Go across to the 20%/80% column (although the francophone percentage is closer to 10%, we want to be conservative in our test so we use the column associated with the higher percentage, 17%). We see that the approximate confidence interval for comparing these two samples is ± 9%. Given the relatively small sample sizes, we have to assume that the observed difference may well be due to chance, and not a real difference.

CONCLUSIONS

Administering a questionnaire to a sample rather than to everyone in a population is a very common practice in tourism research. Doing a census (interviewing everyone in a population) is usually impractical, if not impossible, and not worth the time, effort and money it would require. The choice of a sample thus becomes critical in shaping the accuracy, reliability and precision of your research findings.

There are two general types of sampling: probability and non-probability. The first is based on tactics designed to ensure randomness in the choice of potential respondents. Randomness, in this context, means that everyone has an equal chance of being selected for the survey. Representative sampling requires that you are able to identify an appropriate sampling frame and to develop tactics to choose potential respondents without bias – that is, without giving some potential respondents a greater likelihood of being sampled. There are a number of ways to do this, ranging from simple designs such as selecting every *n*th person from a list to complex designs involving geographical clustering and demographic (or other criteria) stratifying of respondents.

Non-proportional sampling is employed when proportional sampling is not feasible. Such situations occur when you are unable to identify a sampling frame that allows you to choose all respondents with equal probability. These can include trying to survey people who are difficult to physically contact and for whom you do not have a regular source of contact – such as backpackers, travellers with physical disabilities, CEOs or mid-level government officials. Alternatively, non-proportional sampling might be done when you have limited time and budget, are engaged in a pilot project or wish to test a model with a sample of respondents regardless of whether they represent a more general population. Numerous methods can be employed to develop non-proportional samples, ranging from interviewing students in large university courses ('convenience sampling'), through referrals from respondents you managed to survey to other people who might complete your questionnaire ('snowball sampling'), to recruiting participants in ongoing Internet panels.

The selection of the number of people to interview for a proportional sample can involve complex calculations. However, this chapter has presented some practical and relatively simple guidelines that obviate the need for detailed calculations. As such, these guidelines should be considered to be approximations only – but they are reasonable approximations. The sample size sought will depend on the size of the study population, the variability of that population in terms of the attributes in which you are interested and the level of precision and statistical confidence you need in your results.

Non-proportional sampling does not involve these sorts of considerations because the samples are not selected under the discipline imposed by proportional sampling. Instead, sample sizes for non-proportional sampling are based on subjective or practical measures such as: (i) a perception that you are not getting any further new information from each additional interview; or (ii) you are reaching the limit of your time or financial resources.

The distinction between proportional and non-proportional sampling can be blurry. This chapter provides an example of how a survey was administered at a non-gated, busker festival (see Focus Box 4.1). A sampling design involving a series of randomly selected stints over the 3-day event was described, as well as how specific individuals were approached for the survey. While the design was intended to ensure the sample was as representative as possible, the implementation of the sampling design still had the potential for personal 'interference' in the choice or avoidance of particular individuals to be interviewed (despite directions to the surveyors to avoid this temptation). Moreover, the selection of the stints was based only on general times and locations, and did not reflect (because it was not practical) variations in the numbers of festival attendees by stint. In other words, people who visited during a stint that had lower attendance were thus more likely to be sampled than those who visited during times with many more attendees. Furthermore, there could be variations in the responses of attendees in terms of whether they were on their way to watch a busker or were leaving a performance. People rushing to catch a show might be more rushed and feeling more annoyed about being interrupted for a survey than those who had just seen a performance and had some time to kill before the next show.

Thus, a degree of scepticism is always healthy when looking at the results of any survey. There are, as we noted in Chapter 1, potential sampling errors, even biases, based on how people interpret and respond to questions. There are also potential sources of bias arising from challenges associated with the researcher selecting potential respondents and then actually administering the survey.

REFERENCES

Barnett, V.D. (1991) *Sample Survey Principles and Methods*. E. Arnold, London.

Hinkin, T.R., Tracey, J.B. and Enz, C.A. (1997) Scale construction: developing reliable and valid measurement instruments. *Journal of Hospitality and Tourism Research* 21(1), 100–120.

Mace, A.E. (1964) *Sample Size Determination*. Reinhold, New York.

Ryan, C. (1995) *Researching Tourist Satisfaction: Issues, Concepts, Problems*. Routledge, London.

Society and Community Planning Research (1972) *Sample Design and Selection*. Society and Community Planning Research, London.

Tinsley, H.O. and Tinsley, D. (1987) Uses of factor analysis in counselling psychology research. *Journal of Counselling Psychology* 34, 414–424.

chapter 5

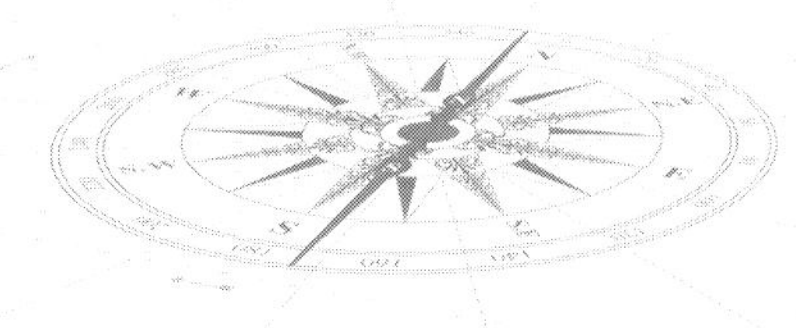

How to Conduct Personal Interviews and Focus Groups

WHY THIS IS IMPORTANT

Tourism researchers often are interested in issues that cannot be adequately explored through empirical methods. Questions about the meanings of experiences or personal travel histories generally cannot be answered through the use of structured questionnaires. Instead, they require asking carefully worded questions and listening to (and probing of) the answers. The intent of personal interviews is not to tabulate numbers, such as the number of people who hold certain views or engage in certain activities, but to understand how people think and feel about certain issues or experiences.

Personal interviews generally are not conducted on any sort of representative sample. Thus, the results cannot be generalized beyond the subjects interviewed. However, the findings from carefully conducted personal interviews can provide you with insights into some phenomena and richer data than are possible from questionnaires. Moreover, they can, if you wish, be used to develop more formal questionnaires that might be used in a proportional sampling design.

The term 'personal interview' as used here refers to in-depth, semi-structured interviews in which you have one or more topical areas to explore through a series of general questions to ask. The phrase 'semi-structured' means that you have a set of general questions that you will ask of every respondent but that you might probe answers or offer clarifications requested by the respondent. The intent is to ask a consistent set of questions but, at the same time, to tailor your interview to make it more personal and interactive. Thus, a semi-structured interview is more ordered than just an open-ended conversation but not as rigidly scripted as a questionnaire.

Perhaps more than with other forms of data collection, the quality of the data obtained from personal interviews reflects the skill of the researcher. Your ability to elicit information and to maintain the interest of the subject is very much determined by how effective you are as an interviewer. As we noted in Chapter 3, conventional print-based surveys give a relatively impersonal interaction between you and your subject. In-depth interviews are a more intimate form of human interaction. As Miller and Crabtree (2004, p. 187) put it, an in-depth interview 'is not political oratory, storytelling, rap, a lecture, a small group seminar, or a clinical encounter...it is a conversational research journey with its own rules of the road'. As a result, the quality and results of that interaction – or journey, as Miller and Crabtree put it – are shaped by the personalities of you and your subject, the level of rapport you establish with the subject as well as your interview skills.

Personal interviews are a key tool in most subjective research designs. To minimize the potential problems of subjective data collection, and particularly to minimize the risk of falling victim to the narrative fallacy or confirmation error, special attention needs to be given to how the interviews are conducted and the data coded and interpreted. This chapter will provide you with a useful introduction to some basic principles and techniques associated with doing personal interviews, as well as the basics of coding and analysing the transcripts of your interviews.

Researchers working in diverse paradigms use in-depth interviews. The two most common are grounded theory and symbolic interactionism. If you are interested in working in either of these paradigms, you should read more widely about either to appreciate more fully the specific methods, assumptions, nuances, debates and issues associated with each. A few sources for grounded theory include Glaser and Strauss (1967), Strauss and Corbin (1990), Glaser (1992, 1998) and Connell and Lowe (1997). Some references for symbolic interactionism are Blumer (1969), Neumann (1993) and Denzin (1994).

We will also look at a special form of interviewing: focus groups. Focus groups are a type of group interview in which you gain information by listening to how up to a dozen people in a room respond to your questions and to each other's answers. Focus groups are not used to probe into individual experiences, unlike personal interviews. Rather, they are used to identify issues, themes or concerns related to some topic through observing and listening to group interactions. We will look at the uses, limitations and techniques of focus groups in the second half of this chapter.

PERSONAL INTERVIEWING IN PRACTICE

Appropriate applications and limitations

Personal interviews typically are used when you want to explore issues in much more depth than is possible through structured questionnaires. Exploring the meaning of events in a person's life, personal histories, the dynamics of social interactions or obtaining a better understanding of personal experiences usually require personal interviews. Personal interviews can also be used to obtain insights into organizational issues or perspectives from people closely involved with those issues. Table 5.1 lists some of the types of topics that can be explored via personal interviews.

Ideally, a personal interview allows the subject's voice and thoughts to be heard, rather than yours. In practice, of course, you are the one who records, interprets and reports what is being said. However, researchers skilled in subjective or narrative approaches work to ensure that they are interpreting and reporting the words of the subject as accurately as possible. As a researcher using in-depth interviews, you will need to develop an intuitive understanding of what type of listening skills to use in any given situation. You might listen quietly as a disinterested (neutral but involved) party, asking occasional questions; you might get actively involved in eliciting and probing answers as might happen in an intense conversation; you might present your respondents with a mix of open-ended and forced-choice questions; or you might use a variety of other interview styles as appropriate to your research objectives.

Table 5.1. Examples of topics suitable for in-depth personal interviews.

General topic category	Potential interview subjects
Personal issues	
Meanings of a tourism experience	Individual visitors
Family dynamics and tourism decision-making processes	Adults in a household, interviewed separately or jointly
Personal barriers to travel and impacts of those barriers on life quality	Individuals who wish to travel but have been unable to do so for personal or family reasons
Perceptions/interpretations of various tourism advertising images	Potential consumers of tourism products
Public policy issues	
Policy-related impediments to the growth of the tourism sector	Mid-level managers in selected ministries/agencies involved with tourism
Perceptions of the importance of or key aspects of tourism as a policy area	Policy analysts and senior government officials
Emerging trends and issues facing the tourism sector	Mid- to senior-level officials; industry association representatives
Tourism as an election issue	Candidates
Industry issues	
Perceptions of tourism as a career	Students, new employees
Human resource issues affecting tourism firms	Human resource officers
Challenges to improving destination competitiveness	Industry leaders in a community
Perceptions of/openness to 'sustainable tourism'	Industry and government leaders, planners

Interviewing should normally be done in settings in which the subjects are comfortable responding in the same language as you require for your research. This means you should be sensitive to the level of education, maturity, social skills and vocabulary of your respondents. Thus, you will need to adjust your language and expectations for information depending on whether you are interviewing a CEO, a teenager or a person for whom English (assuming that is the language you use) is a second language. The focus of interviews is generally on the person you are interviewing, not on broader contextual or holistic matters such as might be sought by someone doing ethnographic research.

In-depth interviewing is a labour-intensive process. Not only do the interviews require time – sometimes as much as several hours over multiple sessions with a single person, but coding and interpretation are also time-consuming. As a result, personal interviewing is normally not practical for research designs in which you want information from a large sample of individuals. Rather than perhaps hundreds or thousands of surveys, personal interviews might be conducted with as few as 10 or 15 people. Thus, while the results of those few interviews can provide rich insights into some phenomena, such as the meanings of a tourism experience in the lives of your subjects, the findings cannot be generalized to a larger population.

Conducting the interview

Before you start

Before beginning interviewing, it is important that you have a thorough, explicit understanding of the objectives of your project. Because personal interviews are only semi-structured, you need to be familiar enough with the objectives of the project to be able to pursue new lines of relevant information that may emerge, and to allow the subject to expound on his or her answers without your losing sight of the ultimate objectives of the interview. Knowing what information is needed will help you ensure that you explore all essential topics while at the same time being open to unexpected but relevant new information. You may also be asked by your subject about the purpose of a given question. Knowing why you are asking each question and being able to explain the need for the information in a non-defensive manner is essential to a successful interview.

Developing and following an interview guide is key to ensuring that the information you collect from respondents is comparable. The guide is a list of questions to cover, often with some suggestions for how to probe responses. While not a script to be followed verbatim, the guide should provide you with consistent wording as you begin to introduce each new aspect of the interview.

Fitting in

Get a sense of: (i) the vocabulary used by your respondents; and (ii) how your subjects are likely to be dressed. Fit in as well as possible by using appropriate language and dress. Avoid academic jargon when interviewing non-academic subjects. If you are interviewing in a culture other than your own, be familiar with social customs, local names for locations, landscape features, units of measurement and so on. If interviewing government officials, be certain you know the proper name of the ministry or agency. Dress at a level of formality that approximates how your respondents will be dressed. Interviews in government or business environments will generally be 'business attire'; interviews with the general public should be more casual, but still tasteful.

Recruiting respondents

Recruiting participants can be a delicate matter. If you are interviewing people who might consider you to be a peer, such as government officials or industry leaders, you can probably contact them directly or through your network of people who can make introductions. Be aware, though, that in strongly hierarchical organizations, such as government agencies, the person whom you wish to interview may need to obtain permission from a superior before speaking with you. This means that you need to understand power relationships within the organization and approach a higher-ranking person to explain the nature of your study and to request permission to interview subordinates.

The need to obtain – and to be seen as having obtained – approval to speak with people is also critical in many small communities, such as an ethnic village. When working in such an environment, you may need an introduction through a local contact who can put you in touch with those in authority. Spending some time with local leaders or elders to let them get to know you, to understand the nature of your project and to develop a sense of comfort with your intentions, is essential. Many people are suspicious about speaking with strangers. You need to come across as open, approachable, interested, but not pushy or aggressive. Be sensitive to local calendars and the flow of time. Attempting to interview a resident of a fishing village during their fishing season may be a bad idea and will lead to repeated rejections. Timing is also an issue for interviewing executives and managers. Certain periods will be much more stressful or time-constrained than others. Periods leading up to finalizing next year's budget, for example, or the opening of the new season of an attraction can be times when your potential subjects will not be receptive to your approaches.

Give thought to the wording for your initial approach to potential subjects. You might even draft a script that you commit to memory. This will ensure that introduction of your project is consistent across all the people whom you approach. It also will help you avoid becoming tongue-tied or rambling as you speak with potential subjects. A good introduction of the purpose of your project can also reduce the time in the actual interview that you need to explain the purpose of the project. When interviewing residents of a community or visitors to a destination, you might be able to move directly into the interview if the subject agrees to speak with you. However, interviews with executives or public officials might require a two-stage approach. First, you introduce yourself and the project, soliciting their willingness to be interviewed. Then, if they agree, you schedule a time in the near future to conduct the interview.

The interview should normally be done in a locale in which the respondent is comfortable, such as home or office. While surveys might sometimes be conducted on site or in a laboratory setting, such 'cold' environments are usually not conducive to successful in-depth interviews. Privacy, good lighting, a comfortable temperature and some space – such as a table (the amount of personal space desired will vary depending on the respondent's culture) – between you and your subject will help set the stage for a good interview.

Commencing the interview

Once you are ready to begin the interview, thank the subject for participating and briefly review the nature of the project. Assure your respondents that their comments will be kept confidential. A bit of small talk at the outset can help to create a relaxed environment. This might include comments on weather, a sports event the previous night or some local bit of news in the community (especially if the news is good). The choice of topic should seem natural, and not be likely to create controversy at the outset or to seem as forced friendliness. However, again, be sensitive to any time pressures on your subject. This will be especially true if your subject is a government official or an executive in a firm. You don't want to be seen as wasting their time with idle chatter.

Try to keep the atmosphere relaxed, while remaining professional and respectful. Use the person's first name if your intuition is that she or he will accept this, and invite her or him to use your first name. When interviewing officials or executives, addressing them as 'Ms' or 'Mr' is probably a safer tactic than presuming you can use first names.

As you initiate the interview, offer the subject more insight into the reason for the project. This can give the subject of feeling of being taken into your confidence, making him/her more engaged and involved in the interview. If possible, identify potential benefits from the project that might be relevant to your subject. These benefits should be as specific as possible to the respondent, such as producing a report that can help shape a policy debate or provide industry with a better understanding of the importance of tourism to families, rather than vague benefits related to 'creation of knowledge'. People like to feel important, so – without being obvious – appeal to the person's sense of importance or the fact that you really need to learn from him/her.

Present your business card to officials or executives, and be familiar with the local customs for exchanging business cards. For example, in many Asian cultures a business card is offered and accepted with two hands and carefully studied upon receipt. The card is normally left on the table or desk top during the interview, and is treated with the same respect you show your respondent. In many European and North America contexts, on the other hand, business cards can be exchanged simultaneously with one hand. Still, it is a useful idea to keep the card out for consultation during the interview. The presentation of a business card may or may not be appropriate when speaking with the general public, and is normally too formal when interviewing, for example, rural villagers.

Provide an honest assessment of the time needed for the interview if you have not discussed this before, and confirm that the subject has adequate time for the interview. Reschedule if timing is going to be a problem.

During the interview

Without going overboard, display sincere interest and respect for your subject's comments. Avoid being seen to make judgements, whether positive or negative. Listen carefully, and try very hard not to forget your subject's answers to questions you've already asked. McCracken (1988) notes there are dual but paradoxical objectives for interviewers – to establish a rapport with the subject, yet to maintain a professional distance in order objectively to observe and listen to the subject's responses. Miller and Crabtree (2004, p. 196) describe the interaction as a dance in which interviewer and subject comfortably approach each other, but not too close, and in which any communication missteps are acknowledged and gently corrected.

Interviews in the context of tourism research usually do not evoke deeply sensitive emotions or tread into dangerous psychological waters, but you should still develop a sixth sense for observing your respondent and listening to the voice behind the spoken word. If you sense you've touched on a delicate or painful topic, back off or provide the subject with the opportunity to recover. Try to sense whether your subject shifts perspectives or roles, or disengages from the interview. You might ask whether the interviewee is feeling distracted or pressured for time, or whether they would rather not discuss the particular topic.

When the interview is concluded, try to spend a few minutes for each of you to disengage and emerge from the encounter. Expressions of appreciation plus a bit of small talk (as long as your respondent is not giving you signs that she wants to terminate the interview quickly) help to maintain goodwill and to leave your subject with good feelings about you and herself.

Recording the interview

You generally have two tactics for recording an interview. The first is to take thorough written notes – ideally, verbatim. Taking written notes while interviewing, however, can be a challenge if you are both asking questions and recording the answers. If at all possible, use a partner who will take notes for you. If you are forced to take your own notes, jot down key observations as quickly as possible during the actual interview and then supplement these with more detailed notes immediately after the interview. Even waiting 1 day before writing down additional notes will result in your losing potentially valuable information if the conversation touched on complex matters or covered a wide range of topics. The rate of decay of the memory of details of a conversation can be very fast, especially if you are engaging in a series of interviews over a short period of time.

Audio-recording of an interview can be more efficient, allowing you to concentrate on the interview. You can then go back and transcribe the conversation or make detailed notes, as appropriate. A recording also allows you to replay comments to reflect on them in the more leisurely and comfortable environment of your home or office. If you use a recording device, be certain you have fresh batteries (most interviewers use a small, battery-powered recorder, not one that must be powered from an AC outlet), and that the microphone is picking up your and your respondent's voices. This usually is not a problem if you are interviewing a person alone in a quiet environment. However, if there is a high level of background noise or you are interviewing several people simultaneously (as in the case of focus groups, described below), sound levels can be a problem.

Remember that not everyone will be comfortable being recorded, so be sure to ask permission first and to have a backup plan if the person does not wish to be recorded. Objections to recording are especially common with people in authoritative positions, such as government officials, who may not want their words captured and (in their minds) potentially used against them in the future. If you are interviewing officials and the first one says he does not wish to be recorded, you can safely assume that others will have the same objection, and you automatically switch to note-taking for all interviews.

It is worth noting that not all researchers take detailed notes or tape-record during interviews; Glaser (1998), for example, advises against detailed note-taking or recording. This perspective is based on the notion that you can develop a better rapport with your subject if you are not distracted by note-taking or thinking you don't have to listen carefully to your subject's responses because you can go back and listen to the recording. Moreover, listening to a recording at least doubles the time you spend listening to your subjects' answers, time that could have been spent doing more interviews. However, as noted above, relying on your memory alone or just brief notes is risky. Memory can be incomplete, and you could be challenged – especially if you are collecting your data in the context of a thesis that will have to be defended before your professors – about the accuracy of your recall. The lack of a transcript also means that you will not be able to provide direct quotations from interviews that could be useful for illustrating your findings, as well as for detailed coding, as described below.

Potential sources of error

Given the nature of personal interviews as an encounter between two people, many aspects of that encounter influence the quality of the information collected. These sources of error may come from either the interviewer or the subject. Understanding some of the more common potential problems can help you minimize the risk of biasing your results. We'll look first at potential problems created by the interviewer.

Having preconceived ideas of what you will hear. As we noted in Chapter 1, researchers may have ideas of what they expect to hear from their subjects and, as a result, tend to hear what they think they will hear. A scrupulous honesty in listening and the ability to suspend your preconceived assumptions, values and beliefs is essential to hearing what your subject really says.

Departing from your interview guide. You may be tempted, at times, to depart from your interview guide. This temptation can arise when you feel a particular connection with a subject and you want to make the interview a bit more interesting. Alternatively, you may become bored with using the same phrasing after repeated interviews, and try to find new ways of asking questions. This temptation needs to be resisted. Changing the wording of questions may elicit answers that are not comparable across subjects if the subjects hear different questions. This is also a problem if the subject indicates he doesn't understand a question and you want to find an alternative way of wording the question. Although you know what you mean, different words can prompt different subjects to hear and respond to what may turn out to be functionally different questions, with the result that your findings are not reliable across subjects. For example, you might use the term 'marketing' in a neutral context, but your subject may view 'marketing' as something manipulative or driven by greed.

Providing inappropriate feedback during the interview. Avoid expressing surprise, scepticism or agreement when responding to your subject's answers. Feedback to a subject can cause her to elaborate, even exaggerate, her responses to please you. Alternatively, if you display disbelief or scepticism, you may cause the subject either to shift her answers to match your cues of 'acceptable answers or, on the other hand, generate a hostile climate during the interview that will compromise the quality of information you gather. Maintain an air of respectful interest during the interview, perhaps nodding to acknowledge you are hearing the subject, but avoid making any comments that will inadvertently direct how she answers.

Getting emotionally involved. This doesn't refer to developing a romantic interest in your subject (which, of course, would be a violation of research ethics) but becoming sympathetic to or identifying with your respondent's answers. Getting too involved with the subject's answers introduces two risks. The first is that you unintentionally influence subsequent answers from your subject by indicating approval or active support of his/her views. The second is that you lose the ability to listen objectively to what is being said. Work to maintain a sense of disinterest (in the sense of objectivity or a lack of self-interest) in asking questions and recording responses.

Asking questions that are too difficult. These questions can take a variety of forms. For example, a question such as 'What was the experiential meaning of your family vacation trip to the Caribbean?' requires a level of self-reflection and insight that most people could not provide – even if they grasp the intent of the phrase 'experiential meaning'. Questions about traumatic experiences such as being present at a terrorist attack or surviving a plane crash may be too emotionally powerful for you to explore as a researcher. Such questions would be better left to counselling sessions between the subject and a therapist. Other challenging, albeit less emotional, questions might involve asking someone to recall details of a trip that occurred a long time before the interview. Asking someone 'What was your first impression of Hawaii when you visited there the first time 5 years ago' probably will not yield any reliable information.

Now, let's consider some potential sources of errors that subjects may introduce.

Misunderstanding the purpose of the interview. Just as the interviewer may have preconceived ideas of what he will hear, subjects may have a preconceived idea of the nature of the topic of the interview. They may view the interview as an opportunity to vent frustrations, resulting in exaggeration or going off on tangents rather than directly and honestly answering the question. Alternatively, the subject may be operating from a very different world view from that of the interviewer, with the result that although both are speaking the same language, their interpretation of words maybe quite different. For example, I interviewed a series of government officials related to tourism policy issues in Canada. Most of the officials understood the reason for my questions and willingly participated. However, an official from Transport Canada (the federal agency responsible for airport development and operations) noted at the outset of the interview, 'I'll try to answer your questions, but I don't see what I can really contribute. My job is concerned with air travel, not tourism'. Fortunately, this subject made it clear at the outset we had very different conceptions of what 'tourism' involved and we were able to find common ground for the balance of the interview.

Lack of interest. Your subjects may understand the purpose of the interview, but may not be sufficiently interested to provide the thought and level of detail you seek in their answers. Ideally, you will avoid recruiting people who will not be willing to participate fully in the interview, thus avoiding this situation during an interview. However, if you find yourself interviewing someone who is clearly giving incomplete or superficial answers and does not respond to probing, you might best thank the person for his participation, conclude the interview, and then not use those responses in your report.

Strategic answering. Strategic answering refers to your subject telling you something he thinks will either give him some advantage, raise his status in your eyes or will protect him from unwanted consequences of his answers. Strategic answering also refers to direct lies, such as answering 'no' to a question about the use of illegal drugs during the subject's most recent vacation trip. Be alert to the potential for misleading or manipulative answers when framing your questions. The risk of dishonest answers in connection with questions about illegal behaviour is probably easy to understand. However, other questions such as those about behaviours or attitudes that have politically correct answers may generate only politically correct answers rather than the truth. Such questions might be better asked with an indirect approach to avoid putting the respondent in a position where he feels uncomfortable articulating a truthful answer. A common indirect approach to asking sensitive questions is to ask the respondent to speculate on what 'other people' may think or do in certain situations. Often the respondent will project her own views on to these hypothetical 'other people', feeling that her answers do not betray her inner thoughts, even though they do. Be aware, of course, that your interpretation of your respondent's answers as 'projection' is highly hypothetical.

Coding and analysis

Once you've concluded interviewing, you are confronted by the task of coding the information you have collected. We will assume in the following that you have a transcript of the interviews, either from verbatim notes or a recording. You can begin coding as soon as you complete your first interview or you can wait until you have completed all your interviews. My preference is to code the results of each interview as soon as I've completed it. I feel 'closer' to the content of the interview if I code shortly after each interview. Furthermore, alternating between doing an interview and coding the transcript provides me with a welcome break so I don't feel overwhelmed by either a long stint of interviewing or working my way through reams of transcriptions. Of course, practical circumstance may cause you to complete all interviews before coding. For example, I had a graduate student who did a series of interviews in ethnic villages in rural Taiwan in a concentrated period of time. Her schedule for interviewing and the lack of a quiet, stable working environment meant she had to focus on interviewing while in the field, postponing transcribing and coding until she was back in her office in Canada.

The following discussion describes one common approach to methodically working through an interview transcript. The process begins with line-by-line coding that helps you read what was said with fresh eyes, and begin to identify themes or ideas that might not have occurred to you during the interview itself. I will use an example with quotations from a study by one of my former students who was interested in the meaning of cruising for seniors (Swain, 2008).

Read each line of the transcript with the intent of being able to generalize, from an analytical perspective, what was said. This involves looking at your respondent's words no longer as a transcript of a conversation or a story he might have been telling, but as a text rich with hidden themes. This search for themes can be facilitated if you have a series of questions in mind as you go through the transcript, such as:

1. What is the primary concern of the person?
2. What was happening in the situation he describes?
3. What themes are implicit in the phrases said?
4. How does the context of the event shape how the respondent responded to or reported the situation?
5. What motivated the respondent to feel the way he reported?

There are two different strategies for searching for themes. Some, such as Glaser's (Glaser, 1992), believe the researcher should not approach the transcripts with any preconceived ideas about what themes will emerge. Glaser pushed this point so far as to advise against any extensive reading on the phenomenon being studied in order to approach it with an open mind. The alternative approach, exemplified by Strauss and Corbin (1990), argues that the researcher should be well versed in the phenomenon being studied, searching the literature for sensitizing concepts or hypotheses that might suggest patterns and interpretations in the transcript. This debate can be an intense one among researchers using subjective approaches, and both perspectives have merits. However, from a personal perspective, I find it difficult to believe a researcher can approach the content of an interview without at least some preconceived ideas about themes that may emerge. However, caution must be exercised to avoid reading and interpreting the transcript in such a way that you see what you want to see. This challenge, as we noted in Chapter 1, is intrinsic in subjective research.

Preliminary and meta-coding

Coding the content of a transcript typically involves two general phases. The first involves identifying initial themes or ideas about what is being said. I call this preliminary coding. This phase is sometimes referred to as 'open coding' or 'line-by-line coding'. This is followed by a second phase in which you look at the themes identified in the initial phase and identify bigger or deeper themes that the preliminary codes reflect. This is 'meta-coding' (in this context, 'meta' refers to underlying principles, as in metaphysics or meta-ethics). This phase is also known as 'axial coding' or 'focused coding'.

The following example illustrates how both preliminary and meta-coding might be done. Preliminary coding is a tedious process. You need to consider every sentence, or even individual phrases, attempting to note meanings or themes in each. Table 5.2 contains a brief sample of a transcript from one of Swain's (2008, pp. 31, 33) interviews. The left-hand column in the table contains some lines from the interview; the right-hand column lists some themes that I inferred from the respondent's words. Note that I have worded the themes in a present, active voice. The reason for this is to give them 'life', to make them more personal and immediate. Using an active voice also helps illuminate processes that may underlie the themes. However, when writing your own codes, don't get too concerned at the initial stage about trying to word them in a concise or grammatically correct fashion at this time. The goal here is to create ideas. You can refine your codes as your work progresses.

This process is then repeated for the other respondents (Swain interviewed a total of ten cruise passengers). The process of preliminary coding helps you maintain some distance from your subjects' feelings and observations by causing you to look at their comments in more analytical terms. As you go through each transcript, look for common themes as well as begin to think about underlying patterns. This exercise normally is not linear. In other words, as you read and code more transcripts, you may go back and recode earlier transcripts in light of your evolving insights. This process of increasing insight can be facilitated by developing questions you ask yourself, such as:

1. Do any of the respondents' comments about their experiences reflect the various stages of the cruise (planning, on-board, post-trip)?
2. Are there common motivations for taking a cruise? Do these vary between people going on their first cruise versus those who have been on multiple cruises?
3. Are there common sources of satisfaction or dissatisfaction from cruising, and are there common patterns in the experiences or other personal characteristics of people who provide similar responses?
4. What, if any, are the effects of interactions with other people, including friends and family at home as well as people met on the cruise, on the cruise experience?

Table 5.2. Example of preliminary coding.

Transcribed comments (from cruise passengers after their trip)	Preliminary codes (or themes)
It was a feeling of satisfaction that I was in control of my life and could go wherever I wished	Feeling good about being at a stage of life where one has choices
I had the ability to have freedom of choice for a vacation	Feeling free to choose
I received the group itinerary of get-together plans and receptions	Doing research on activity options is important
Then the big decisions of what I really wanted to attend and where to make time to just sit and enjoy the weather and water	Understanding one's expectations, interests, emotions, resources
Checking out the number of days at sea, you think what your mood might be on that day and try to pick out what you would really like to do, what you can afford	Understanding one's expectations, interests, emotions, resources
Hoping there is sun and warmth every day	Desiring good weather
I think the excursions are the ice cream on top of the cruise	Taking excursions is enjoyable
How nice to be free to be able to make these pleasurable choices	Feeling free to choose
The planning of the cruise is an exciting time. Where to go, what ship to go on, and most important, what exciting excursions to take at the various destinations	Planning for a cruise is important and a source of pleasure
You find a list of them from the ships web page or other tours companies for each destination	Consulting different sources
Before the cruise, a common topic among people I socialize with was asking if one would be away during some part of the winter months. When I responded about my cruise, their eyes would light up and ask where, when and how long	Impressing peers is a benefit
They invariably wished me well and wished they could go on one also	Dreaming about a cruise is common
They implied my cruise was a great idea	Seeking validation from peers

The search for meta-codes involves more intuition and critical thinking than preliminary coding. As a result, meta-coding can be more enjoyable than preliminary coding because you have the chance to be more creative. On the other hand, it can be more difficult because the emergence of meta-codes requires insight, critical thinking, the ability to abstract, the necessity of going over the preliminary codes repeatedly and the ability to 'see' what is hidden. Your meta-codes need to be more general and encompassing, while at the same time still being rooted in your original data.

While different researchers will have their own ways of sorting and combining preliminary codes, I find that a simple and old-fashioned approach – writing each preliminary code on an index card or piece of paper – works well. I then sort these into a smaller number of increasingly more general themes (or meta-codes). As I begin the search for (or, more precisely, the creation of) meta-codes, I ask myself questions such as:

1. Do the themes reflect models or concepts expressed by other authors who have studied my topic?
2. Are there underlying processes reflected in certain themes?
3. Does the subject describe an evolution in her/his feelings or experiences as reflected in the themes implicit as the interview unfolds?
4. Are there some over-arching impacts reflected in some of the themes?

If you use this process, as you work through your preliminary themes place each card in a separate pile that represents a potential meta-theme. You may find that, as you do your initial grouping, your initial meta-code for some category of preliminary codes may need to be revised or redefined. Also, as you begin to develop meta-codes, you may note that some of your preliminary themes might reflect two or more meta-codes. This is quite acceptable, and reflects the richness and complexity of human experiences. Simply make two or more cards with the preliminary theme so that you can file it in the appropriate groupings.

Swain (2008, p. 75) followed a similar process of repeatedly examining, critiquing and generalizing his preliminary themes to arrive finally at a small number of meta-codes or final themes, as illustrated in Table 5.3. The left-hand column lists the 13 preliminary codes, in order, from Table 5.2. The right-hand column shows the three meta-codes proposed for each of the 13 preliminary codes.

While you are looking for meta-codes, you should also write notes to yourself – some researchers refer to this as 'memo-writing'. These notes (memos) to yourself reflect your observations and thoughts as you go through your preliminary codes. The memos might reflect your ideas about how different subjects express their views on common experiences, or what experiences tend to be associated more with certain phases of the cruise experience than with others. You might make also notes about the deeper meanings of aspects of the cruises to your subjects. For example, Swain recognized that talking about plans for a cruise with family and friends before departing, talking about cruise experiences with other passengers while on board and telling family and friends cruise stories after the cruise were significant sources of pleasure, and helped his subjects find meaning in their experiences.

An important part of writing memos is to look for similarities or differences among your subjects. Glaser and Strauss (1967) call this 'constant comparison', and note that it is an essential part of developing what they call 'grounded theory'. Swain (2008), for example, found that being able to talk with others who had gone cruising was a very importance source of information and reassurance among seniors who had never been on a cruise. The concerns of these subjects were frequently common, although they were sometimes expressed in different language. The concerns included the fear of being out of sight of land, a sense

Table 5.3. Example of meta-coding.

Preliminary codes	**Meta-codes**
Feeling good about being at a stage of life where one has choices	Seniors on cruises balance opportunities and constraints on the basis of personal goals
Feeling free to choose	Seniors on cruises balance opportunities and constraints on the basis of personal goals
Doing research on activity options is important	There are multiple sources of satisfaction in a cruise vacation
Understanding one's expectations, interests, emotions, resources	Seniors on cruises balance opportunities and constraints on the basis of personal goals
Desiring good weather	There are multiple sources of satisfaction in a cruise vacation
Taking excursions is enjoyable	There are multiple sources of satisfaction in a cruise vacation
Feeling free to choose	Seniors on cruises balance opportunities and constraints on the basis of personal goals
Planning for a cruise is important and a source of pleasure	There are multiple sources of satisfaction in a cruise vacation
Consulting different sources	There are multiple sources of satisfaction in a cruise vacation
Impressing peers is a benefit	Cruising is a social experience
Seeking to impress others	Cruising is a social experience
Dreaming about a cruise is common	Cruising is a social experience
Seeking validation from peers	Cruising is a social experience

of confinement in close quarters, long queues for meals, the costs for services not included in the cruise package, such as excursions, and not being able to escape potentially obnoxious fellow passengers.

Treat your memos as tentative findings, perhaps even as conjecture. They allow you to record ideas that might need to be reconsidered in light of your evidence as your analysis proceeds. Your memos are for only you to read, sort of like a research diary in which you can give voice to and experiment with thoughts. Some of your memos may become the basis for development and inclusion in your final paper, but many will never leave your desk or computer. The process of writing memos should eventually help you formulate your findings in a comprehensible and intelligible manner and communicate your findings in a coherent style.

Some researchers use software to assist them in finding themes and patterns in their transcripts. One common software package that supports this task is NVivo, by QSR International. Focus Box 5.1 provides a very brief overview of this software.

As you begin to move from coding and memo-writing, you will be able to present your findings in terms of the meta-themes you've identified, explaining the meaning and significance of each meta-theme and perhaps illustrating it with relevant, anonymous quotations from your interview transcripts. The use of quotations requires judgement. You will want to provide sufficient material to help illustrate your conclusions, but the bulk of your material should be your own thoughts and interpretations. Avoid providing just strings of quotations without commentary. Where possible, support your interpretations with reference to other

Focus Box 5.1. NVivo.

NVivo is the leading software for assisting researchers analyse subjective data obtained through interviews. Unlike statistical software that actually does the analysis for you, programs like NVivo assist you through storing and manipulating text, but the analysis is still in your hands (and head). NVivo can be used with a number of subjective research paradigms, but is most commonly used for grounded theory. It works not only with text files, but also with audio files, photographs, video files and spreadsheets. The software allows you to work with text as specific as a single paragraph up to very large documents and even multiple documents. However, the effort required to code large amounts of text can be onerous, so most researchers do not use NVivo for massive text files.

In NVivo, data (words, phrases) are categorized by 'nodes' that can represent concepts, people, places or other characteristics relevant to your topic. Nodes are a way of marking bits of text to highlight some important aspect of that bit of text. They are like using Post-It® notes as markers for significant passages of text. Each node has a name and a description that allows you to search through your document very easily. The description usually includes attributes such as location and time of interview, job title or sex of interviewee, and so on.

Three types of nodes are possible: (i) free-standing nodes that are not linked to each other; (ii) tree (or hierarchical) nodes that are linked to categories (such as market segment) and subcategories (mainstream youth, affluent seniors, middle income families, etc.); and (iii) case nodes that allow you to group cases (such as employees in an organization) and then create nodes for each individual.

With the creation of nodes, you can use NVivo to search your document to look for patterns. The simplest search is a single item search, in which you look for all instances of one item (text, node or attribute value) such as all the occurrences of the word 'souvenir' in your documents. You can also conduct a Boolean search using logic operators such as 'and', 'or', 'not' and so on. For example, you might search for 'souvenir' and 'authentic' and 'craft' but 'not' plastic. Finally, you can conduct a proximity search that shows you where items such as words or word patterns, attribute values or nodes that appear near each other in your text. By looking at the frequencies, locations and/or patterns of nodes and attributes in your text, you can then begin to identify themes and meanings within your text.

The software is designed to work with Microsoft operating systems and can be applied to virtually any language, not just English.

More information about Nvivo can be found on QSR International's website, at: http://www.qsrinternational.com /products_nvivo.aspx authors who have written on similar topics. This adds depth and credibility to your findings, and helps your reader appreciate the larger context of your research – where your findings fit in and what new discoveries you have made. The process of writing your report is covered more fully in Chapter 10. We will now look at another and very different type of interviewing widely used in tourism research: focus groups.

FOCUS GROUPS IN PRACTICE

Background

Focus groups are a type of group interview that is popular in market research but also is used in other research contexts (NB: the term 'focus group' is used for both the group itself and as the meeting of the group). The origin of focus groups usually is attributed to Merton and Kendall (1946) who wrote about 'focused interviews'. This then-new methodology was developed after World War II to elicit audience responses to alternative radio programmes (Stewart and Shamdasani, 1990). Over time, focus groups have been extended by researchers to explore a broad range of topics related to how people respond to different topics; however, the original emphasis on marketing rather than social enquiry still dominates.

Focus groups have a number of distinctive characteristics. They use groups to generate data on a specified topic by the researcher (often called a 'facilitator'). The facilitator (or an associate) is responsible for the creation of the group, which normally does not exist as a formal entity prior to the interview and ceases to exist after the interview. The data gathered during the focus group session are a function of the conversations and interactions among the members of the group, as facilitated and managed by the researcher. The researcher thus plays a key role in the creation of data derived from the focus group.

Focus groups may be conducted by a researcher for his/her own purposes, as described, below, or they may be conducted on behalf of a client. This latter situation is especially common in the context of marketing. When conducted for a client, the client may wish to be present in another room or behind a screen to observe the discussions. Alternatively, the focus group may be video-taped for detailed review by the client. When a researcher is facilitating a focus group for her/his own purposes, she has the same recording choices as for personal interviews: having an associate sit in and take detailed notes or recording the proceedings.

The following section describes the common applications and limitations in the use of focus groups. This is followed by some practical advice on how to run a focus group. Finally, some comments on analysis are presented.

Applications and limitations

Focus groups offer a number of advantages over other types of data collection. You can obtain information from people who may not be particularly literate and, with care, even from people for whom English (or whatever your working language) is a second language. Some groups, such as immigrants or other marginalized populations, may actually be eager to share their views on some topic when they find out that you are sincerely interested in listening to them. The focus group environment tends to be a pleasurable and social one in which people, given a good facilitator, quickly feel comfortable and enjoy interacting with each other. As a result, you can often develop a rapport with the participants and explore ideas comfortably and gain insights from interactions among all the participants.

As a form of group interview, you can explore shades of meanings, areas of debate and disagreement, nuances and issues that you could easily miss in a standard survey and might even miss in a personal interview. While they require effort to arrange and to conduct properly, focus groups are often easier to administer and usually quicker to complete than a formal survey or a series of in-depth interviews of an equal number of people. Indeed, you can listen to the opinions of many more people through a series of focus groups than you could normally personally interview. Finally, the results usually are expressible in terms a general audience can understand because they are based on the words of ordinary people. Arcane sociological jargon or sophisticated statistical techniques normally are not involved in presenting the results of focus groups.

On the other hand, focus groups do present some challenges. Recruiting an appropriate list of participants can be difficult. For example, I conducted a series of focus groups on a proposed brand image for a destination and worked through some local tourism contacts for contacts from the general population. A number of the people who showed up (motivated by the modest cash honorarium I was paying) appeared to be unemployed (and were not students, retired or homemakers), uninterested in the topic, and keen only to take the money and get to the local liquor store before it closed for the evening. For another, non-tourism, project I wanted to meet with refugees and recent immigrants. It took several weeks and working through 'someone who knew someone who knew someone' before I was able to recruit sufficient participants to fill four focus groups.

Group dynamics can be difficult to predict, and you may find it challenging to obtain the information you seek. Indeed, the results of some focus groups can be fundamentally chaotic and without apparent meaning or order. The small numbers of participants are not representative of any larger population, so the results cannot be reliably generalized to any larger group.

As noted, focus groups tend to be associated most closely with market research, and less with mainstream social science enquiry. However, social scientists do use focus groups, but usually in combination with other tools such as surveys. Morgan (1993) describes four different ways in which focus groups and surveys may be combined.

1. **As a preliminary step for a survey**. Because surveys require the researcher to specify topics to be explored and questions to be asked, researchers sometimes conduct focus groups with representatives of the study population to identify key topics to be examined in the survey.
2. **As the primary tool, building on initial survey findings**. Researchers sometimes use surveys to develop an initial profile of a study population, such as identifying different subpopulations within a larger population who are then used as the basis for a series of focus groups. In this context, surveys help the researcher focus the content or profile of focus groups.
3. **As a supplemental tool to help interpret survey findings**. In this combination, a survey is the primary source of data, but the researcher may turn to the more in-depth commentary possible in focus groups composed of members of the study population to help him/her understand the meanings of the survey results.
4. **As the primary tool with surveys supplementing findings**. This combination is, in effect, the reverse of the third combination. A focus group might identify a number of key topics that might need to be considered by a marketer. These topics would then be used to frame a survey that would identify the extent of concern or relevance among members of the study population.

Within the realm of tourism, focus groups still tend to be used most commonly in the context of market research. In this context, participants are selected from a population the marketer wishes better to understand. Examples of topics that can be explored via focus groups include the following:

1. Evaluating advertisement design or content. Individuals from a target market are presented with alternative designs or content of printed or electronic (radio, TV, Internet) ads and asked for their reactions. The graphic design of an ad, its specific content or the messaging or wording can be evaluated. Reasons for reactions may be explored as well as suggestions for alterations.
2. Evaluating potential new products or services. Participants are presented with descriptions or mock-ups of possible new products, such as tour packages or hotel room amenities. The level of interest in, or attractiveness of, each option is assessed and suggestions for possible changes may be solicited.
3. Designing advertising messages. Individuals from a market segment are presented with a marketing situation, such as what would attract their interest in visiting a particular type of destination or what messages that destination should present better to penetrate the market.
4. Soliciting opinions about a given topic. For example, an industry advocacy group might be interested in improving community understanding of, and support for, the local tourism sector. Members of the community would be asked about their perceptions of tourism in a variety of specific contexts such as economic, social and environmental impacts. By probing the reasons for opinions, researchers may be better able to help develop messages to increase support for tourism or, alternatively, to develop strategies to address problems within the community.

There are some important topics that do not lend themselves to focus groups. Because the method is based on group interactions, it cannot be used to collect information about individuals. Socially, politically or personally sensitive information cannot be reliably obtained through focus groups because of the potential for social pressure to shape each respondent's comments and because of the sensitivity of many people to revealing personal information or opinions to strangers. As noted, focus groups are idiosyncratic collections of people, so results cannot be reliably generalized to a larger population with any degree of empirical certainty.

One of the applications noted above was to evaluate the design or message of an advertisement. If the results of the focus group indicate that the ad needs to be revised, a marketing agency may do so. However, showing the revised ad to a follow-up focus group composed of different individuals does NOT allow you to conclude that the new ad is more or less effective. Any difference in group reaction may simply reflect differences in group membership, and not changes in the ad. Going back to the same group will not produce reliable results because the group will have been conditioned by their previous experience and may either be biased towards approving the changes, because their comments were accepted, or may have become sensitized to critiquing ads and will give even more critical thought to the new ad. In brief, focus groups *cannot* be used to assess pre-and post-designs.

Conducting a focus group

Conducting a focus group involves four general phases: (i) deciding that a focus group is needed and identifying its purpose; (ii) logistical arrangements including recruiting and arranging a venue; (iii) facilitating the focus group; and (iv) analysis and presentation of the results.

Deciding to do a focus group. Have a clear understanding of why you (or your client) want to do a focus group. Explicitly identify the information needed and why it is needed. This is fundamental to everything else, including recruiting participants, facilitating the session, analysing the results and preparing your final report.

In addition to understanding the objective of your focus group, give some thought to the number of groups to be formed. If time and budgets are adequate, at least two on any given subject are preferable to a single group. A second group can provide you with a degree of assurance that the results from your first group are valid; however, if you arrive at contradictory findings, you may need to consider a third or more focus groups to arrive at results in which you can have confidence. Needless to say, money and time may preclude multiple sessions.

Logistics. This phase is often the most complex and time-consuming phase. The tasks you will need to deal with include:

- Determine the budget and schedule for completing the project.
- Decide on the number of groups needed. This will be shaped by the objectives of your project as well as budget and schedule.
- Identify the types of participants. Generally, they will share certain characteristics, such as having visited a particular destination, having made travel bookings on the Internet or enjoying certain types of activities on vacation. Within this homogeneity, you will also want some degree of diversity such as a mix of males and females, ethnic groups or age groups. However, avoid having individuals from vastly different social backgrounds as this might lead to some participants feeling uncomfortable or intimidated.
- Recruit participants. This can be one of the most challenging tasks of a focus group. Some commercial market research firms have pools of potential focus group participants, and their services might be purchased. However, a more common practical approach is to work through your own contacts to search for people who match the profile of participants you need. Use the 'snowball' technique, whereby you ask people you know to recommend other potential participants, and then ask those individuals for further suggestions. I find it helps to explain to potential participants, at a general level, the topic of the focus group as well as the types of questions that you will be asking.
- Most focus groups have between eight and ten participants. I have run sessions with as many as 12 but, at that size, some people may tend to withdraw from the conversation rather than compete for time or attention.
- Select a location for the focus group. Choose a place that is easily accessible to participants and portrays an image of welcome and professionalism. Some market consultancies and research firms have special rooms available that provide for video-taping and discreet observation by the client behind a one-way mirror. However, many tourism research projects will not require (or be able to afford) such facilities. As an alternative, a hotel meeting room or a meeting room at a community facility such as a recreation centre or library can work well. Meeting rooms in government offices or university buildings normally should be avoided because many people find such environments uncomfortable. And for ordinary people, even trying to locate a meeting room in many university or government buildings can be frustrating.
- Select the time and date; evening meetings are often preferable for most participants.
- Remind each potential participant of the focus group time, date and location via e-mail or telephone a day or two before the session.
- Arrange meeting room amenities:
  - a flip chart may be useful (be sure to have markers, tape and other supplies as needed);
  - a choice of beverages such as water, juice, tea and coffee;
  - light snacks, such as cookies;
  - a table with sufficient chairs and space between the chairs; and
  - name tags (first names only are usually sufficient to help people communicate with each other but without revealing personal identities).
- Arrange for audio- or video-recording or enlist the services of someone to be a note-taker. Be certain he or she has a copy of your questions in advance and that he or she understands the objectives of the focus group.

- Compensation for participants is normally appropriate: it is a sign that you value their time and opinions and, if cash, can help offset any transportation costs in reaching your venue. Prepare receipts for each participant to sign if you are making cash payments. However, under some circumstances a cash payment would not be appropriate. For example, if your participants consist of government officials commenting on a policy topic, a cash payment would be inappropriate. If you were working with executives of medium to large firms, a token cash payment might come across as unnecessary or even silly. However, if you are working with owners of a small business, the offer of a cash payment – even if declined – shows respect for the value of their time.

Facilitating the focus group. The process of facilitating a focus group begins well before your participants arrive. You will, of course, need to finalize your list of questions before the session. They should flow in a logical sequence. Be specific enough to prompt the type of answers you seek but general enough to encourage discussion. If you are working for a client, you should share drafts of your questions with your client prior to the session.

Prepare an agenda for the session that you will share with the participants. This typically has the form of:

1. Welcome and introduction.
2. Overview of purpose of session.
3. Ground rules.
4. Questions and discussion.
5. Wrap-up.

The agenda should contain a descriptive title for the focus group and possibly a brief statement of the objectives of the focus group. Approximate times for each phase should be noted. The entire session should last between 1 and 1.5 hours. If the group is engaged and you are an experienced facilitator, 2-hour sessions are possible. Lengthier periods should be avoided. I prefer to avoid taking a break in the middle of the session because it disrupts the flow of the meeting, but sometimes a break may be appropriate.

You will find it helpful to have prepared a list of names and other pertinent information about participants for your use during the session. This should be provided to your note-taker, too. Even if your participants are wearing name tags, you and your note-taker may find it helpful to sketch out the table and write the names of the participants in their relative locations. Name tags can be difficult to read if people are seated around a table. Tent cards with first names placed in front of each person can be helpful.

Greet people as they arrive, introducing yourself and any associates with you. Encourage people to make themselves at home, helping themselves to any refreshments you have available. Once you get started, have everyone introduce him- or herself – again, usually first names only. If appropriate, you might have each person say a few words about him- or herself. Point out the location of washrooms at the beginning of the session. Confirm the expected length of the session.

Go over the ground rules of the session. These should emphasize that opinions are to be shared freely, but that no one should interrupt another while speaking. Participants should make their point clearly and briefly, and not monopolize the limited time of the session. Everyone's opinions are to be respected.

Begin with a question that is easy to answer and stimulates conversation. Wait a few seconds after a participant finishes his answer to allow another participant to comment. If no one volunteers another comment, invite further thought or clarification, as appropriate. You can probe or even pose a new, logical question that follows from the responses to your scripted question. When one question appears to have been thoroughly discussed and answered, introduce the next question.

Note whether anyone is not participating. Acknowledge the person by name and ask if he/she has any thoughts on the current question. Be prepared to manage any participant who attempts to dominate the conversation by noting that you would like to hear from others who have not yet answered. Be alert to the possibility of 'group-think'. It is common for several people to share similar views, but there is a danger that most (or everyone) in a session may begin to espouse the same opinions. If this begins to happen, challenge the group by asking if anyone has a different perspective. Other problems for which you should be prepared for include:

- **Late arrivals and no-shows**. I do not delay the start of a session waiting for late arrivals. The first few minutes are devoted to welcomes and administrative details, and most late arrivals come during that period so their late entrance is usually not a problem. Most focus group sessions I have facilitated will have one or two no-shows. Proceed without them. I often invite one more person to my focus group than I need in the expectation that one person will not show up.
- **Too much time spent on early questions**. Anticipate how much time you can afford to spend on each question. Do not hesitate to run a bit longer on important questions, but pay attention to the flow of time throughout the session.
- **Non-responsive group**. If the group does not quickly evolve into a lively interactive form, go around the room and ask each individual to respond to a specific question. After one pass around the table, try to open the discussion again.
- **Overly responsive group**. I have also had some groups who have been so enthusiastic about the session they did not want to quit. It helps to have a formal conclusion time that you can then use to gently terminate the formal session.
- **Inappropriate participant interaction**. On rare occasions, one of your participants will be interested in getting to know another participant on a personal basis after the session is over. Do not release any personal details or contact information about any participant to any other participant.
- **Bad weather**. If conditions are too dangerous, call everyone to cancel and advise them you will be rescheduling.
- **Unexpected volunteers**. I have had, on occasion, one of my participants bring along a friend who wanted to participate. If I have space, I welcome the individual. If I don't have space, I tactfully explain the situation and invite them to sit in – but I can usually accommodate the unexpected arrival. I make a point of having enough cash on hand (I put the specified amount of remuneration in individual envelopes) to be able to accommodate and compensate an unexpected participant if the person proves to be a productive member of the group.

If you are having a colleague take notes, be sure the notes are structured around the questions asked, with a clear division between questions. The note-taker should also provide a name or other identifier by each comment so that comparisons among participants can be made and themes raised by any one individual can be recognized.

As you prepare to close the session, comment that the time to wrap up has arrived, but you would like to give anyone a chance to make any brief final statements about the topic in case anything was missed. Then, thank the group for participating, and – if relevant – give the participants their compensation. Spend a few minutes socializing with the participants after the session has broken up, thanking them individually and listening to any personal comments they may make.

Once the group has dispersed, make notes about anything that may have affected the outcome of the session, including problems with the room, disruptive interactions among participants, problematic participants, the number of no-shows and so on. Comments about the level of interest and the general mood of the group may also be useful.

Analysis and presentation. The analysis of focus group comments is different to that of a personal interview. Focus group data include comments and observations from numerous people, sometimes generated through a disagreement or an intense exchange of ideas. Conflicting themes can thus be present that would not occur in an interview with a single individual. Alternatively, some participants may offer support for some comment and perhaps even elaborate on it. Ideally, you will have used two or more groups so comparisons among focus groups can be made.

Analysis normally begins by listening to the recording or reviewing session notes, from beginning to end, in one sitting. Go through the recording or notes a second time, making notes about key ideas or themes as well as about areas of consensus or disagreement. Listen to or look for words or phrases that appear to be meaningful, and note whether different people appear to have made the same point with different words. If differences of opinion are expressed, search for the potential reasons for the differences. For example, do the differences expressed reflect different experiences, different values or different backgrounds among the participants?

This task of interpretation is a difficult one, but it becomes easier with practice. You begin with raw text – individual phrases, disconnected comments from multiple sources responding to other participants – and ultimately look for themes and patterns. Not every comment should be given equal weight. For example, statements that are backed up by personal experiences probably are more important than those based on mere speculation or uninformed opinion. Statements made in the first person are probably more reliable and significant than those made in a more abstract context or hypothetical third person.

As you go through all the statements, keep working to find themes or ideas that answer your questions. Don't limit yourself simply to tabulating the whole range of answers; rather, strive to be able to provide a coherent interpretation of what was said, even if the session revealed some deep differences of opinion among participants. Illustrate your findings with direct quotations, and perhaps provide a brief statement about the background or position of the person providing the quotation if you have this information. And, as with any subjective methodology, reflect on any potential biases you may bring to the task that could affect your interpretation.

CONCLUSIONS

Personal interviews are an important data collection method in tourism research. They can provide rich, nuanced insights into personal experiences and the meanings of events to people. The quality of data from interviews is shaped not just by your subject's willingness to talk, but by your skills as an interviewer. Still, you need to ensure your analysis reflects the subject's words and experiences, and not your own biases or values.

Personal interviewing is a time-consuming task. Most research projects will involve not more than a couple of dozen interviews. The interview itself should follow an interview guide – essentially a script of broad questions that you ask your subject, and that allow you to probe or to ask additional questions for clarification as you listen to your subject's responses. An interview is more structured than a free-flowing conversation, but less structured than a conventional survey, even one using open-ended questions. Personal interviews can provide valuable insights but the findings, because the sample sizes tend to be very small (usually fewer than a couple dozen people), cannot normally be generalized to a larger population. In other words, the results of personal interviews reflect the views of those whom you interviewed, and no one else.

A successful interview requires attention to numerous practical matters. For example, the interview should be conducted in a setting in which the subject is comfortable and will not be distracted. You should work to 'fit in', dressing in a way appropriate for your subject and using appropriate language. Learn to read body language in order to sense when you may need to speed up, to try to re-engage your subject's interest or to avoid giving offence through insensitive or invasive questions.

Potential biases can arise from either the interviewer or the subject. For example, a good interviewer will suspend any preconceived ideas of what he will hear in the interview. He will avoid giving inappropriate feedback during the interview (such as expressing surprise at a subject's comments or affirming a subject's opinions). He will avoid asking questions that are too difficult or require unrealistic feats of memory.

A successful interviewer will also work to ensure that his subject understands the purpose of the interview and will avoid allowing the subject to use the interview to vent grievances or to express political views that are tangential to the purpose of the interview. He will work to avoid 'strategic answering' by framing questions in ways that minimize the temptation to offer politically correct answers or that could embarrass the subject.

Coding and analysing the words recorded (electronically or through note-taking) in an interview is a critical aspect of research using personal interviews. The chapter describes a two-stage approach in which a series of preliminary themes or codes are identified through a careful reading of the transcript and constant reflection on what is being said and why. These initial codes are then conceptualized into a smaller set of broader or abstract (but still grounded in the interviews) set of meta-codes. The meta-codes are developed by the continuing reflection on the content and possible meaning of words and phrases used by the subjects, as well as by comparisons among subjects. Finally, you present your findings from the interviews in a coherent fashion, supporting your conclusions with selected quotations that illustrate the point you wish to make based on what your subjects have revealed to you.

Focus groups are also a form of interviewing, but one in which the outcomes of the interview are based on interactions among a small number of participants in a formal setting facilitated by the researcher. Focus groups are useful for identifying potential issues to be explored in subsequent research, or problems associated with potential marketing messages or product designs. Just like personal interviews, the results of focus groups cannot be generalized to a larger population. Moreover, because of the social nature of focus groups, they are not an appropriate tool for collecting personal information.

The practical arrangements for conducting focus groups tend to be more complicated than for personal interviews, although you can collect information from a larger number of people than through personal interviews. The chapter provided advice on the various practical aspects of conducting this type of survey, ranging from recruiting participants to facilitating the session. As with personal interviews, the skill of the researcher is critical to success.

The analysis of results of focus groups is different to that of personal interviews. The outcome of focus groups is based on interactions among participants who may offer conflicting views, or alternatively, opinions that reinforce each other. The analytical process focuses (no pun intended) on a search for themes within the raw text. A skilled and experienced researcher will be able to intuitively identify which statements should be given more weight than others, based on how the statement is presented (for example, personal experiences normally are more important than uniformed opinions) and how the rest of the group responds to a particular statement.

Finally, for both personal interviews and focus groups, the researcher should be aware of potential personal biases or assumptions that can shape how he interprets the evidence he observes in the transcripts or notes from the interviews.

REFERENCES

Blumer, H. (1969) *Symbolic Interactionism: Perspective and Method.* Prentice-Hall, Englewood Cliffs, New Jersey.

Connell, J. and Lowe, A. (1997) Generating grounded theory from qualitative data: the application of inductive methods in tourism and hospitality management research. *Progress in Tourism and Hospitality Research* 3, 165–174.

Denzin, N.K. (1994) *Symbolic Interactionism and Cultural Studies.* Blackwell Press, Cambridge, Massachusetts.

Glaser, B.G. (1992) *Basics of Grounded Theory Analysis: Emergence Versus Forcing.* Sociology Press, Mill Valley, California.

Glaser, B.G. (1998) *Doing Grounded Theory: Issues and Discussions.* Sociology Press, Mill Valley, California.

Glaser, B.G. and Strauss, A.L. (1967) *The Discovery of Grounded Theory.* Aldine Press, Chicago, Illinois.

McCracken, G. (1988) *The Long Interview.* Sage, Newbury Park, California.

Merton, R. and Kendall, P. (1946) The focussed interview. *American Journal of Sociology* 51, 541–557.

Miller, W. and Crabtree, B.F. (2004) Depth interviewing. In: Hesse-Biber, S.N. and Leavy, P. (eds) *Approaches to Qualitative Research.* Oxford University Press, Oxford, UK, pp. 185–202.

Morgan, D.L. (2004) Focus groups. In: Hesse-Biber, S.N. and Leavy, P. (eds) *Approaches to Qualitative Research.* Oxford University Press, Oxford, UK, pp. 263 – 285.

Neumann, M. (1993) Living on tortoise time: Alternative travel as the pursuit of a lifestyle. *Symbolic Interactionism* 16, 201–235.

Stewart, D.W., and Shamdasani, P.N. (1990) *Focus Groups: Theory and Practice.* Sage Publications: Newbury Park, California.

Strauss, A. and Corbin, J. (1990) *Basics of Qualitative Research: Grounded Theory Procedures and Techniques.* Sage, Newbury Park, California.

Swain, R. (2008) Seniors and cruising: motivations and satisfaction. MA thesis, University of Waterloo, Waterloo, Ontario.

chapter 6

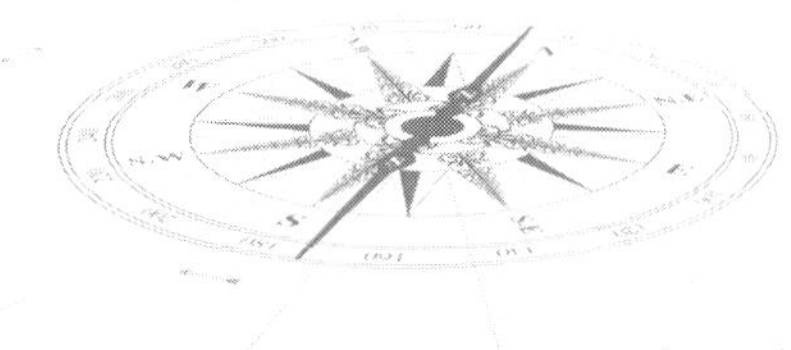

How to Construct and Use Indices and Scales

WHY THIS IS IMPORTANT

There are many analytical tools available for tourism research. Some of the more important ones are indices and scales. These terms refer to broad categories of tools used to describe, measure and track trends in some aspect of tourism. We will look at several and consider how to develop them and use them, as well as at limitations in their application. We will explore additional tools in Chapters 7, 8 and 9.

'Index', as a word, has multiple meanings, including the alphabetical listing of subjects at the end of this book. In this chapter, index refers to the combination of two or more variables into a single measure to provide a succinct indication of some phenomenon. Indices can be as simple as, for example, dividing the number of rooms in a hotel occupied during a given week by the number of rooms available. This is the 'occupancy rate', which is a simple index of business volume. Indices, as we will see, can be conceptually more complex than occupancy rates.

An early example of a tourism index is Defert's (1967) 'tourist function'. His goal in creating this function was to develop a single measure that reflects the relative magnitude of tourism in a local economy – a notion broader than simply calculating what percentage of hotel rooms in a destination are occupied. His approach to measuring economic importance was, however, still arithmetically simple. He divided the number of visitor beds in a destination by the resident population:

$$Tf = \frac{100(N)}{P} \tag{6.1}$$

Where: Tf = 'tourist function', N = number of beds or equivalent in visitor accommodation and P = resident population. The use of 100 as a multiplier in the numerator is arbitrary and has no significance other than to make the value of the ratio larger. The tourist function, as other indices, can be used as a new variable to study some larger tourism issue. It can also be tracked over time or across space to examine how the index varies in different situations.

In Defert's case, he examined the magnitude of the tourist function across cities in France to map the relative importance of tourism in each city.

Indices are descriptive variables, but they are frequently used as in explanation or prediction as well. A well-constructed index allows you to reduce a number of variables into a single, easily comprehended measure that supports further analysis. Indices can also provide you with a snapshot of current conditions and historical trends, such as changes in business efficiencies, price inflation, marketing effectiveness or tourism impacts. Focus Box 6.1 presents a light-hearted measure of the level of 'civilization' in different cities. We will look at three different indices that are particularly useful in more serious tourism research: the location quotient, the Gini coefficient and the nearest-neighbour ratio.

'Scale', like 'index', has numerous meanings. For example, it may mean a qualitative measure of data such as a nominal or ordinal scale, or it may refer to the magnitude of development,

Focus Box 6.1. Civilization index.

Shawn Blore (2002) proposed, as a humorous exercise, five indices to reflect the degree of 'civilization' in cities. He then used these to compare the level of 'civilization' among a number of world cities. His indices were:

1. **The soft drink/beer ratio**. In Blore's ideal city, beer would be as readily available as soft drinks. He proposes an index based on the price of a can of a soft drink divided by the price of a can of beer. He supplemented this with a 'paper bag factor', reflecting whether the beer can be bought at a street vendor for open consumption on the street, if it can be bought at a grocery for open consumption, if it can be bought at a grocery but has to be hidden in a paper bag, or if it can be purchased only at licensed outlets. He notes that cultures that place restrictions on the open and simple enjoyment of beer in public generally place restrictions on other innocent forms of pleasure, so he felt this index is a particularly good measure of the level of civilization.
2. **The signature carbohydrate comparison**. Most cities have some sort of carbohydrate favoured by their residents. In cities in southern Ontario, where I live, it is doughnuts; in New Orleans, it is beignets; in Brussels, it is French fries. Blore believes the ultimate carbohydrate food is a Parisian croissant, so this index reflects a subjective measure of the quality of the city's signature carbohydrate (such as doughnuts or bagels) compared with the quality of a Parisian croissant. Points are deducted for grams of fat per serving, but points are added for the number of different varieties of the signature carbohydrate.
3. **Babe and hunk index**. Other people are, for most of us, something we enjoy observing when we visit other cities. Blore proposed this index as a measure of the sense of style of residents of a city. He notes that the measure is not just based on the number of young and attractive people, but on their sense of style. The index reflects the percentage of well-dressed women and men out of a random sample of 100, selected at major intersections in the city, summed over four seasons with weights applied to reflect differences in seasonal attire.
4. **Street life index**. This index reflects the fact that commerce is a key determinant of the vitality of a city. Markets and retail districts provide much of the sense of liveliness in a city. This indicator reflects the degree to which food, drink, clothing and other necessities of life can be purchased on the street rather than inside shops.

(Continued)

Focus Box 6.1. Continued.

5. Public order index. Civilized cities manage to balance activity and vibrancy with a sense of orderly behaviour on the streets. In civilized cities, people tolerate minor infractions of trivial rules, such as jaywalking, as part of the sense of freedom and spontaneity of life. So, this index reflects the number of jaywalkers per 200 pedestrians at a given intersection. However, because jaywalking, if taken to an extreme, can snarl traffic, this index also includes a measure of the average taxi speed in minutes per kilometre.

Here's a summary of his application of these indices to New York and Paris, based on Blore's field observations in both cities (detailed calculations can be found in his original article):

Index	Soft drink/ beer ratio	Signature carbohydrate comparison	Babe and hunk index	Street life indicator	Public order indices	Total
New York	52	74	30	86	12	254
Paris	65	100	67	100	22	354

These indices are, of course, not meant to be taken too seriously. However, they do illustrate how imagination and creativity can be brought to bear on developing measures that can illuminate vary complex concepts such as a city's level of liveability. A more serious, but still fascinating, look at public life in cities can be found in William Whyte's *The Social Life of Small Urban Spaces* (1980).

such as a large-scale resort. However, in this chapter, scales are empirical tools used to measure some aspect of visitors' attitudes, opinions or values. Scales, in this sense, are also a measurement tool that is constructed by the researcher for the problem at hand. Two scales we will explore in this chapter are the semantic differential scale and the Likert scale. We will also look at a tool that combines two scales into a single tool: importance–performance analysis.

LOCATION QUOTIENT

What is it?

A location quotient (LQ) compares one measure of tourism between two or more locations, such as destinations or origins. LQs were originally developed in regional economics as a tool for examining regional variations in the distribution of basic (i.e. exporting) and non-basic industries. However, LQs can be applied to many other phenomena, ranging from the propensity of a population to travel to employment patterns. An extended discussion of LQs in the context of regional economic impacts can be found in Isserman (1977).

Location quotients are a ratio of ratios. Assume you are interested in regional variations of employment in various tourism industries. Let's use accommodation as an illustration. You begin by dividing the number of people employed in the accommodation industry in a county (or whatever) by the total number of people employed in accommodation in the entire province or state. That gives you the percentage of all accommodation workers in the province that work in your county. You then divide the total number of workers in all industries in your county by the total number of workers in your province. This gives you the percentage of the province's labour force in your county. You now compare your county's share of accommodation employment with its share of total employment by dividing the two percentages. This will indicate whether your county has an average, lower-than-expected or higher-than-expected concentration of accommodation employees. The following section provides a numerical illustration of this process.

How do I use it?

Let's continue with the accommodation employment example. Table 6.1 presents are some hypothetical data:

The equation for calculating an LQ is:

$$LQ = \frac{r/n}{R/N} \tag{6.2}$$

Where: r = county employment in accommodation industry, n = state employment in accommodation industry, R = total county employment and N = total provincial employment. Applying Eqn 6.2 produces the results shown in Table 6.2.

Counties A and B have a higher percentage of employees in the accommodation industry than the province as a whole. This is reflected by having LQs greater than 1.00 (1.00 indicates an average concentration of accommodation workers). County A has an LQ of 1.044, which means it has 4.4% more accommodation workers than would be expected from the provincial

Table 6.1. Hypothetical employment data for calculating location quotients in a province with three counties.

County	Workers in accommodation industry	Total workers in economy
A	12,947	197,860
B	6,881	96,334
C	10,313	185,634
Total (province)	30,141	479,828

Table 6.2. Location quotients for data in Table 6.1.

County	*r*/*n*	*R*/*N*	*LQ* = [*r*/*n*]/[*R*/*N*]
A	12,947/30,141 = 0.430	197,860/479,828 = 0.412	1.044
B	6,881/30,141 = 0.228	96,334/479,828 = 0.201	1.134
C	10,313/30,141 = 0.342	185,634/479,828 = 0.387	0.884

average. County B has 13.4% more accommodation employees. In contrast, County C has a smaller concentration, reflected by its LQ of 0.884. It has only 88.4% of its expected employment in accommodation, based on the provincial average.

What else do I need to know?

Location quotients are useful for making comparisons among subunits (such as counties) or between a subunit and an aggregate of subunits (such as a state). Although the technique is relatively straightforward and easy to understand, you should still think about several aspects of the LQ if you are going to use it. First, choose subunits as well as the aggregate (the larger unit) with care. Geographical subunits can consist of individual counties, or they could be some other unit such as metropolitan areas. Be aware that functional subunits may not always conform to political boundaries. For example, the metropolitan area of Niagara Falls in North America spills over into both Canada and the USA. Using economic or social data for only the US portion of Niagara Falls would yield misleading results.

An assumption of LQs is that all subunits are fundamentally comparable. That's usually not a problem, but circumstances can occur when one subunit can be quite different from other subunits, resulting in ratios that have to be interpreted with care. For example, let's assume you wanted to calculate county LQs for casino hotel employment in the US state of Nevada. One county, Clark County – the location of Las Vegas – has approximately 80% of all casino hotel employment in the state. As a result, Clark County would have a very high LQ and all other counties would have very low LQs. This reflects reality but, in fact, the low LQs are the norm for the state as a whole. The patterns would be distorted by Clark County's unusual economic profile. If you were to develop LQs for all counties in Nevada except for Clark County, you would find very different patterns.

There are a couple of other issues to think about. The choice of the denominator in calculating LQs is arbitrary. In our accommodation employment example, we used total employment. One could also use aggregate employment in the service sector or in just tourism industries. Finally, a location quotient is only a snapshot in time. It summarizes relative concentration at the time data were collected. It doesn't say anything about trends or about the forces that create differences in LQs over space or time. Questions about trends and forces shaping LQs require additional data and analysis.

GINI COEFFICIENT

What is it?

The Gini Coefficient is another way of looking at distributions. It was originally developed in the early 20th century by an Italian economist, Corrado Gini (1921), to analyse the distribution of incomes in a nation. However, the coefficient can be applied to other geographical entities such as metropolitan areas or non-geographical units such as occupational categories. The value of the Gini Coefficient ranges from 0, which indicates total concentration, to 1, which indicates an even distribution. In the case of the distribution of wealth in a nation, a value of 0 would mean one person has all the money where as a value of 1 would mean everyone has an equal share. A closely related measure, the Gini Index, is just the Gini Coefficient expressed on a 0–100 scale. In other words, the Gini Coefficient is the Gini Index expressed as a percentage. The coefficient is more commonly reported than the index.

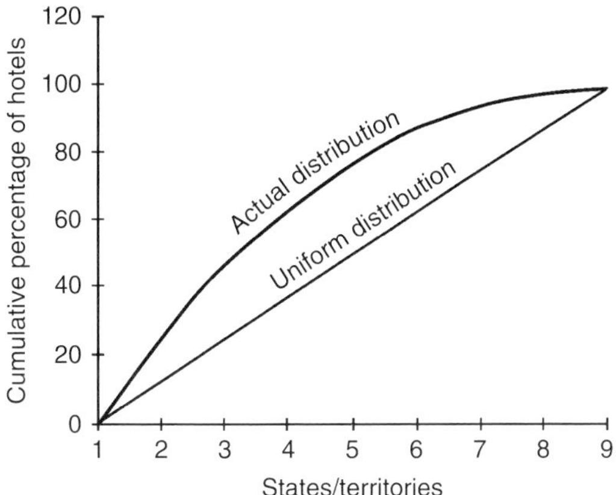

Fig. 6.1. Example of a Lorenz curve.

A graphic representation of the statistical dispersion of the variable under question is known as a Lorenz curve, named after its developer, Max Lorenz (1905). As we will see below (see Fig. 6.1), the Lorenz curve depicts the dispersion of values of some variable as a curve on a simple *X–Y* graph. The relative position of the curve vis-à-vis the diagonal on the graph reflects the degree of dispersion. The Gini Coefficient/Index is the ratio of the area underneath the curve to the area underneath the diagonal.

How do I use it?

The classic calculation of either the Gini Coefficient or the Gini Index involves integral calculus. However, an alternative approach utilizes basic arithmetic and can be done using a standard spreadsheet. That's the procedure we will look at here.

First, a few words about data requirements. The Gini Coefficient can be applied only to certain types of data. The data must be expressible as percentages and these percentages should be meaningful when they are summed. The data cannot include negative numbers. The data should also be associated with distinct entities such as geographical regions or social groups. Data related to tourist flows, numbers of businesses, incomes or employment can be analysed using a Gini Coefficient. In contrast, the coefficient cannot be used with nominal or ordinal data such as attitude scores or rates of change such as annual percentage changes in the number of visitors coming to a country.

Our example draws on the distribution of licensed hotels with 15 or more rooms in Australian states and territories. Data are from the Australian Bureau of Statistics (2007). Table 6.3 is an inventory of the number of hotels by state or territory. Column one lists states and territories by decreasing number of establishments. The next column lists the number of establishments. The middle column converts the number of hotels to a percentage of the total. The next column shows the cumulative percentage of the inventory. Finally, column five lists cumulative percentages assuming an even distribution of hotels across all eight regions: 100.00%/8 = 12.50% per state. The letters *A* and *B* have been arbitrarily assigned to the two cumulative totals.

$$G = \frac{(A-B)}{(C-B)} \tag{6.3}$$

Where: G = Gini Coefficient, A = cumulative percentage of individual state/territory establishments, B = cumulative percentage assuming an equal distribution of establishments across all eight regions and C = cumulative percentage assuming all establishments are located in one region (100 × number of regions or 100 × 8 = 800). Inserting the values from Table 6.3 into Eqn 6.3 gives us:

$$G = \frac{(593.09 - 450)}{(800 - 450)} = 0.41$$

Table 6.3. Number of licensed Australian hotels with 15 or more rooms (December 2007).

State/Territory	Hotels (*n*)	Percentage of total	Cumulative percentage	Cumulative diagonal percentage
New South Wales	202	24.08	24.08	12.50
Queensland	186	22.17	46.25	25.00
Victoria	147	17.52	63.77	37.50
Western Australia	125	14.90	78.67	50.00
Southern Australia	71	8.46	87.13	62.50
Tasmania	66	7.87	94.99	75.00
Northern Territory	27	3.22	98.21	87.50
Australia Capital Territory	15	1.79	100.00	100.00
Total	839	100.00	593.09 = *A*	450.00 = *B*

What else do I need to know?

As noted above, a Lorenz curve is a graphic representation of the Gini Coefficient (see Fig. 6.1). As such, it can effectively communicate not only the degree of dispersal but also the overall pattern of dispersal – whether hotels (in our case) are concentrated in a small number of states.

Lorenz curves always begin with a relatively steep upward slope, and then gradually level off. In our example, the curve is relatively smooth over its entire length, reflecting a fairly gradual decline in the percentage of rooms in successive states or territories after the initial concentration in New South Wales. If New South Wales had an even higher concentration – say 75% as opposed to its approximately 25% – the curve would have shot up very quickly at first and then been relatively level across the top of the diagram.

With respect to the value of the coefficient, the meaning of the value usually requires comparison with other coefficients measured over time or in other places. Our finding of 0.41 puts the degree of dispersal roughly in the middle of the possible range from 0 to 1. Whether that is high or low, good or bad requires other information or comparisons with other places or times. The value of the coefficient also is influenced by the number of units being reported – the 'granularity' of the data. If our data were reported for 18 regions instead of eight, we would usually find a lower coefficient reflecting a more even distribution of hotels.

NEAREST-NEIGHBOUR ANALYSIS

What is it?

If you've ever looked at a map of the distribution of some tourism facility such as restaurants in a city, you may note that they may tend to cluster in one or more areas of town. Other facilities might be evenly distributed or are just dispersed randomly. While the Gini Index can provide a measure of the degree of concentration in one or a small number of locations, it tells us nothing about the spatial pattern of distribution. You can visually look at a pattern and observe that it might be roughly uniform or tending to be clustered, but visual impressions can be unreliable, especially if the pattern is complex. Nearest-neighbour analysis is a tool you can use to empirically assess whether a pattern of points is clustered, random or uniform. It was developed in the 1950s by ecologists interested in understanding the locational patterns of plants in deserts (Grieg-Smith, 1952; Clark and Evans, 1955). As with the other tools in this chapter, it was quickly applied to a wide range of other problems, including tourism.

Nearest-neighbour analysis is based on comparing the mean distance between each point and its nearest neighbour (hence the name) to the mean distance you would expect if the pattern were random. An actual mean distance smaller than expected indicates that the points are clustered; a larger mean distance indicates that the points are more evenly dispersed. Thus, the nearest-neighbour statistic is defined as the ratio between the observed and a hypothetical (based on a random distribution) distance.

The technique is limited to data that can be spatially represented as points. Linear phenomena such as roads or areal data such as countries do not lend themselves to nearest-neighbour analysis. Furthermore, the phenomenon should be fixed, such as buildings or parks. The distribution of moving objects – cars or people – would normally not be studied using nearest-neighbour analysis, although a photograph showing the distribution of moving objects at one point in time could be studied with this technique.

Being able to determine the pattern of dispersal can help you explore the forces that gave rise to the pattern, thus giving you insights into processes that might otherwise not be obvious. For example, I studied the locational patterns of different types of restaurants (Smith, 1983) to develop hypotheses about the forces that shaped restaurant locations. I found that coffee and doughnut shops – a particularly common type of restaurant in Canada – tended to avoid locating close to each other. On the other hand, they tended to locate close to fast-food restaurants. This suggested to me that coffee shops do better when there is no direct competition nearby, but that they benefit from the visibility they get by locating close to fast-food outlets. Fast-food restaurants, on the other hand, were found to cluster close to each other. This suggests that spatial competition between them is not strong. Instead, the creation of fast-food clusters raises the profile of the entire group, thus attracting more potential customers so that all of the restaurants in the cluster benefit from higher customer traffic.

How do I use it?

Begin by plotting your data on a map using dots to represent the location of the phenomenon you are studying. Draw the smallest possible square around the pattern. You might have to experiment with different orientations of the square to achieve the smallest square. Getting the smallest square possible is important because the value of the nearest-neighbour ratio is a function of the size of the square drawn. The larger the square compared with the overall distribution of dots, the more likely you will conclude that the points are clustered. Figures 6.2a and 6.2b illustrate this. Both figures have the same pattern, but Fig. 6.2a uses a compact square where as Fig. 6.2b uses a larger square. A quick visual comparison of the two patterns suggests why a larger square biases your findings toward a conclusion of clustering.

Calculate the area of the square, and count the number of points within it. Calculate the expected nearest neighbour distance under the hypothesis of a random distribution:

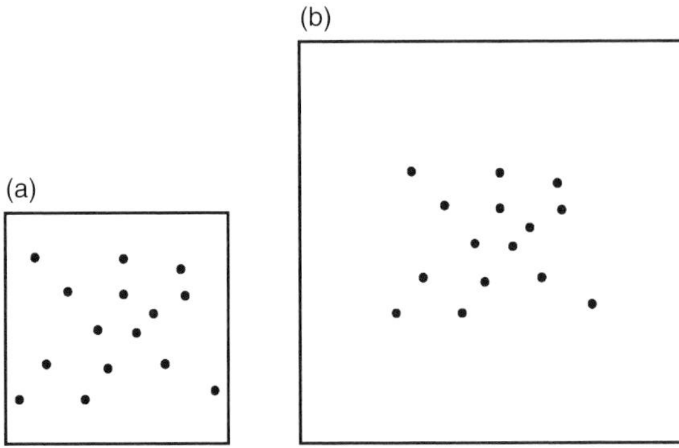

Fig. 6.2. Impact of study area size on perception of clustering.

$$d_r = C\left[\sqrt{a/n}\right] \qquad (6.4)$$

Where: d_r = hypothetical distance for a random distribution, C = 0.487 + 0.127[$\sqrt{(a/n)}$], a = area of the square and n = number of points. Next, measure the distance between each point and its nearest neighbour. Calculate the mean of these distances. Then calculate the nearest neighbour ratio:

$$R_n = {}^{d_0}\!/_{d_r} \qquad (6.5)$$

Where: R_n = nearest neighbour ratio, d_0 = mean observed nearest-neighbour distance and d_r is as calculated in Eqn 6.4. Finally, interpret the value of the ratio. As noted previously, values significantly smaller than 1.00 indicate clustering. The extreme would be where all points are located on top of each other, which would give a ratio of 0.00. Values larger than 1.00 indicate a more uniform pattern. The maximum degree of dispersal would be found in a hexagonal array, with a maximum of 2.15. A significance test for nearest-neighbour analysis is provided in Fig. 6.3.

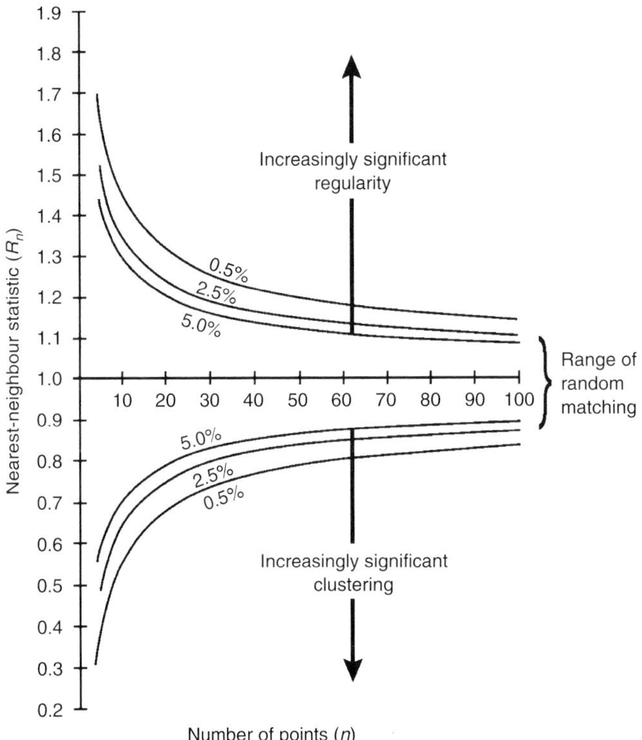

Fig. 6.3. Significance test for nearest-neighbour analysis (Pinder and Witherick, 1975).

Here's an example of nearest-neighbour analysis. Figure 6.4 is a map of China showing the location of 32 UNESCO World Heritage Sites (http://www.thesalmons.org/lynn/wh-china.html). The Great Wall, which is also a World Heritage Site, has been excluded because it is a linear feature, over 3200 km long. A square has been placed over the map encompassing the distribution of the sites. The distances from each site to its nearest neighbour were measured using a ruler, and are summarized in Table 6.4 (distance and area measurements are in arbitrary but consistent units).

The mean of these 32 distances (n) is 0.5875 units, and the area of the square (a) is 51.800 square units. With this information, we can perform the following tabulations:

$$\begin{aligned} C &= 0.487 + 0.127\,[\sqrt{(a/n)}] \\ &= 0.487 + 0.127\,[\sqrt{(51.800/32)}] \\ &= 0.6936 \\ d_r &= C[\sqrt{(a/n)}] \\ &= 0.6936[\sqrt{(51.800/32)}] \\ &= 1.121 \\ d_0 &= 0.588 \\ R_n &= d_0/d_r \\ &= 0.588/1.121 \\ &= 0.525 \end{aligned}$$

Consulting the appendix to this chapter, we see that the value of 0.525 is significantly less than 1.000, so we conclude that World Heritage Sites in China tend to be clustered at the national scale. This is not surprising, given the long and rich cultural heritage of certain regions

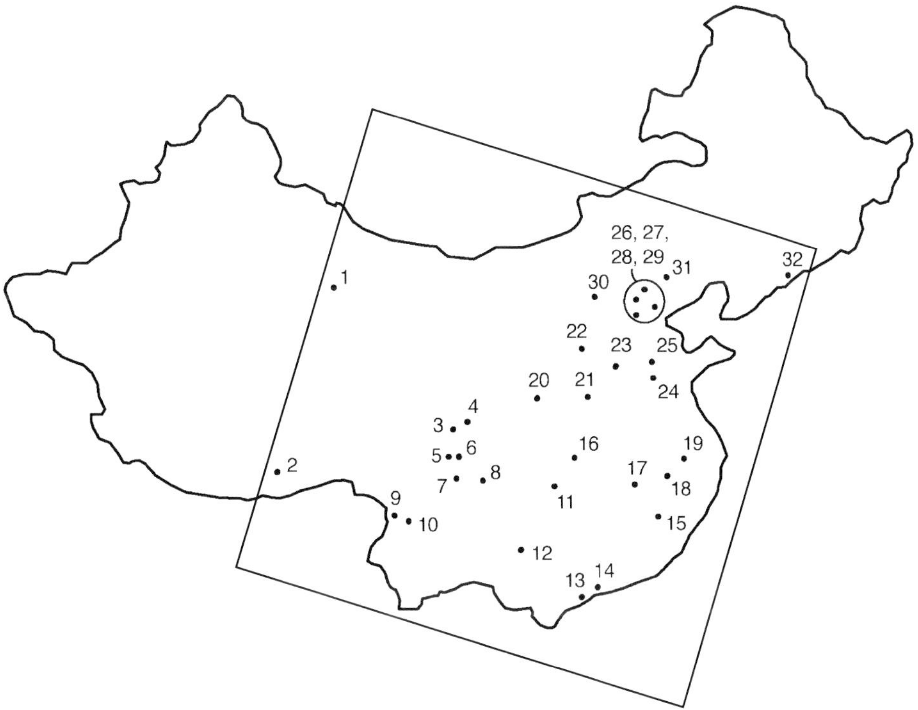

Fig. 6.4. Selected World Heritage Sites in China (see text for explanation).

Table 6.4. Nearest-neighbour distances for 32 Chinese World Heritage Sites.

Site	Distance to nearest neighbour	Site	Distance to nearest neighbour
1. Mogac	2.9	17. Lushart	0.6
2. Lhasa	2.0	18. Huangshan	0.4
3. Huanglong	0.2	19. Suzhou	0.4
4. Jiuzhaigou	0.2	20. Qin	0.8
5. Pandas	0.2	21. Longmen	0.6
6. Qincheng	0.2	22. Ping Yao	0.5
7. Mt Emei	0.4	23. Yin Xu	0.5
8. Dazu	0.5	24. Confucious	0.3
9. Yunnan	0.3	25. Taishan	0.3
10. Lijiang	0.3	26. Zhiukoudian	0.1
11. Wulingyuan	0.6	27. Summer Palace	0.1
12. Karst	1.3	28. Temple of Heaven	0.3
13. Kaiping	0.3	29. Ming Tombs	0.3
14. Macau	0.3	30. Yungang	0.4
15. Mt Wui	0.5	31. Changde	0.5
16. Wudang	0.6	32. Joguryo	1.9

of China, resulting in sites relatively close together at a national scale. For example, Beijing has (at the time of writing) four sites within a few kilometres of each other.

What else do I need to know?

Look again at the map of China. It illustrates a common problem with nearest-neighbour analysis. Many situations in which we might use the technique do not lend themselves to being mapped in a square. You can see that portions of our square include Mongolia as well as the South China Sea. As a result, the distribution of our points is functionally limited to only a portion of the square. This has the effect of biasing our results towards a conclusion of clustering. Some authors have used the actual shape of the region for analysis rather than overlaying a square. However, this can produce erroneously high values, biasing results towards a conclusion of a uniform distribution.

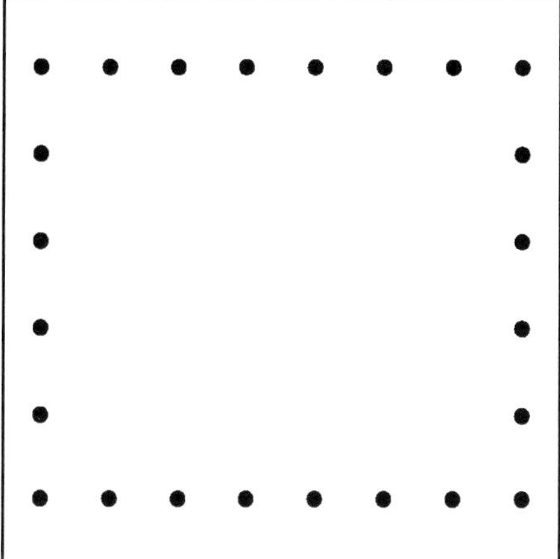

Fig. 6.5. A pattern yielding a small nearest-neighbour ratio.

A different problem is known as the boundary effect. This arises when the square covers only a subset of the distribution of points in a larger area. When only a subset of points is captured by the square, it is possible that the real nearest neighbour for a point near the edge of the square is outside the square. A solution to the problem was developed by Pinder (1978), who derived an alternative method for calculating the expected distance that avoids the boundary effect. His method has been incorporated into the procedure presented here.

As noted in Eqn 6.5, the nearest-neighbour ratio is based on the average distances between points. Relatively close spacing results in the conclusion of clustering, but certain patterns can yield low mean distances; these patterns, however, are not what most people would consider to be clusters. Figure 6.5 is one such example.

A version of nearest-neighbour analysis has been developed by Pinder and Witherick (1975) for use with points distributed along a linear feature, such as resorts along coastlines. The technique also is described in Smith (1995).

SEMANTIC DIFFERENTIAL SCALE

What is it?

The semantic differential scale is a tool that draws from both semantics and psychology to explore the connotative meaning of a concept. 'Connotative meaning' refers to the implicit, often emotional, qualities of a concept that are beyond its explicit definition. For example, 'car' refers to a mode of self-propelled wheeled transportation driven by one individual for the purposes of his or her own transportation. However, 'car' also connotes to some people freedom, power, affluence, sexual attraction, global warming or urban sprawl. The semantic differential scale is designed to explore these other meanings through the use of a series of bipolar word pairs.

The tool was developed by Osgood *et al.* (1957) to explore attitudes towards social entities – one phenomenon they examined was job occupations. The scale is very flexible, capable of being applied to many different concepts. It can also be used with even relatively young children and in different cultures.

Numerous empirical studies using a technique called factor analysis (not discussed in this book) have found that the results of most semantic differential scales reduce to three dimensions: evaluation (good–bad), potency (strong–weak) and activity (fast–slow). This structure is usually referred to as **EPA** dimensions (**e**valuation, **p**otency and **a**ctivity). Attitudes can, therefore, be thought of as existing in a three-dimensional space (see Fig. 6.6). For example, if the concept being assessed is 'art gallery', it might score near the 'good' end of the good–bad dimension, neutral on the strong–weak dimension and towards the 'slow' end of the fast–slow dimension.

How do I use it?

The core task in developing a semantic differential scale is the choice of the bipolar pairs. You will, of course, want to use pairs that make sense for the concept you are studying. If you are interested

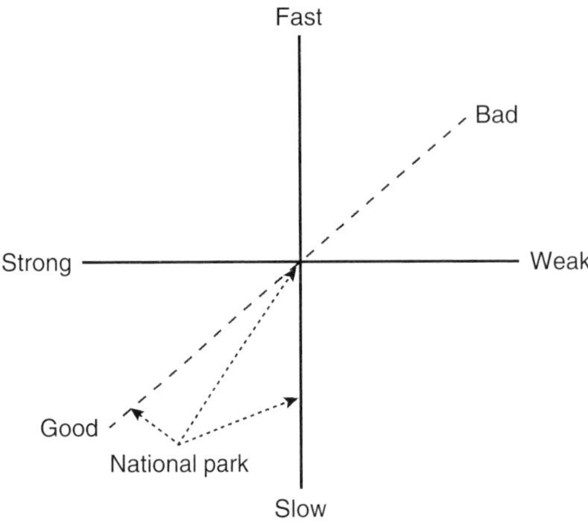

Fig. 6.6. The three dimensions of attitudes.

in attitudes towards commercial airline pilots, skilled–unskilled might make sense (presumably pilot would be placed at the 'skilled' end of the continuum) but sweet–sour would not. One technique for developing a set of bipolar pairs is to conduct an initial survey of a sample of your study population (this usually does not need to be a large sample) and present them with a list of possible word pairs and ask them to indicate the relevance of each pair (perhaps on a four- or five-point scale from 'very relevant' to 'not at all relevant'). You then select those pairs with the highest relevance scores. When you administer the final scales, avoid going back to the same people you used for this exercise.

The scales should also reflect the EPA structure that is believed to underpin the structure of all attitudes. Your goal should be to have a series of bipolar items that are as 'pure' as possible on each of the three dimensions – each pair should be associated with only one dimension. Some researchers will use intuition to develop these pairs and then conduct a factor analysis to confirm whether or not their scales match the EPA structure. However, this can be a time-consuming process and, unless you have a large number of pairs and a large sample, the results may not be reliable. A better approach is to identify published studies that can provide previously tested word pairs. These studies need not be tourism related – they can be drawn from any topic. Osgood *et al.* (1957) are a useful source for possible pairs. However, use judgement in selecting scales for your topic. The same pair of words can have very different connotations depending on the context of the study. For example, fast–slow may connote different qualities for restaurant meals than for modes of transportation.

The bipolar words are usually positioned at the end of a five- or seven-point scale with a neutral mid-point. Wells and Smith (1960) have found that the use of qualifiers to label each point (such as 'always', 'sometimes') results in better differentiation of responses (people are less likely to check just the mid-point or just the extremes). Qualifiers also help ensure that your respondents understand how to interpret the scale. When coding the responses, you can use either values such as 2, 1, 0, -1, -2 or 1, 2, 3, 4, 5. If your scales are good measures of each dimension, you can use as few as four or five pairs per dimension (Heise, 1970) for a total of 12–15 pairs. Some researchers use as many as ten per dimension, but this could be overkill if you chose your scales well.

There are several options for the graphic presentation of the scales. An approach that is easy to use and makes sense to respondents (Heise, 1970) is to put each concept to be evaluated at the top of a page, with the individual scales listed underneath. Thus, if you were exploring attitudes towards different countries as potential destinations, you might put 'Spain' at the top of a page, with scales such as warm–cold, friendly–unfriendly, strong–weak, safe–dangerous, inexpensive–expensive and so on, listed underneath. 'Australia' could be listed on the second page, UK on the third, until all your study countries were listed.

It's usually good practice to mix up the order of the scales on each page and to reverse the order of the ends of the scales (warm–cold and cold–warm) to minimize the chance that your respondents will fall into a habitual pattern of answering. If you reverse some word pairs, be sure you adjust your coding so that the coded scale is consistent between the original and the reversed scale. Give thought to the total number of evaluations you ask your respondents to make. Heise (1970) suggests that people used to completing surveys or multiple choice tests, such as students, might be able to handle up to 400 individual judgements. However, respondents not accustomed to scales or tests might be able to do no more than 50.

The analysis of the results of a semantic differential application can take a variety of forms. A good place to start is to calculate the mean scores and variances for the combined scales for each dimension. Thus, if you were studying attitudes towards different countries, you would calculate a mean score for the scales representing each of the three dimensions for each country. You could then compare the scores among the countries you studied, or among different types of respondents (perhaps those who had visited a country versus those who had not, or those who were residents and those who were not). Means can be compared using *t*-tests or other appropriate statistics.

You might also want to compare the relative positions of pairs of concepts in the EPA space. A formula you can use to do this is based on Pythagoras theorem:

$$D = \sqrt{[(e_1 - e_2)^2 + (p_1 - p_2) + (a_1 - a_2)^2]} \tag{6.6}$$

Where e_1, b_1, a_1 = mean scores for evaluation, potency and activity items for country 1 (etc.) and D is the D statistic (score of EPA dimensions). Assume you have calculated the following mean scores for Australia, New Zealand and Thailand using a five-point scale, coded 1 to 5.

	Evaluation	Potency	Activity
Australia	4.0	4.3	4.1
New Zealand	4.2	3.9	4.1
Thailand	3.9	3.5	3.9

Applying Eqn 6.6:

For Australia and New Zealand: $D = \sqrt{[(4.0 - 4.2)^2 + (4.3 - 3.9)^2 + (4.1 - 4.1)^2]} = 0.45$

For Australia and Thailand: $D = \sqrt{[(4.0 - 3.9)^2 + (4.3 - 3.5)^2 + (4.1 - 3.9)^2]} = 0.83$

For New Zealand and Thailand: $D = \sqrt{[(4.2 - 3.9)^2 + (3.9 - 3.5)^2 + (4.1 - 3.9)^2]} = 0.70$

The value of D reveals that Australia and New Zealand (in these hypothetical results) are more similar to each other than either is to Thailand.

What else do I need to know?

The semantic differential scale is adaptable to many different contexts. Once you have a set of bipolar scales that reflect the three EPA dimensions, you can usually apply the scales to different tourism concepts. The scales can also be translated into different languages and, after working with an experienced translator to ensure the competency of the translation, be applied in different cultures to permit cross-cultural comparisons.

However, the semantic differential scale presents a number of concerns. The first is whether your scales are truly valid. The semantic differential method has been extensively applied and there is consensus that, in principle, it produces valid results when applied properly. As noted, the individual bipolar scales need to reflect the three dimensions and be relevant to your problem. Performing a factor analysis on your data can indicate whether your scales do properly reflect the EPA dimensions. The use of a panel to select bipolar pairs relevant to your concept helps ensure your scales produce valid results.

Another concern is reliability. In other words, if you were to apply the same set of scales to your sample a second time, would you get the same results? The use of multiple scales for the three dimensions and a large sample size can improve reliability, but reliability is still open to question. If you have a sample of several hundred people, you can randomly divide your sample into two halves and then compare the results from the two halves. This is called a **split-half analysis**. If the results of your tests for the two halves are reasonably similar, you can assume reliability is probably not a problem; if they are different, you have a problem. In this latter case, you might either develop a larger sample or modify your scales to produce reliable results.

As with most surveys and interviews, there is also the risk that your respondents will give politically correct answers rather than honest opinions. It is important, therefore, in interpreting your results to understand whether you are probing for opinions on a topic that might be sensitive.

The D statistic, while a convenient summary of overall positions, has to be interpreted with caution. Because it combines three different measures into a single number, it does not reveal whether a large difference is due to a single, large difference on one dimension or to moderate differences on all three dimensions.

LIKERT SCALE

What is it?

Likert scales, named after their developer, Rensis Likert (1932), are arguably the most frequently used psychometric scale in tourism research. (Likert is usually mispronounced as 'lie-kurt'; the correct pronunciation of the family name is 'lick-urt'.) A Likert scale consists of a number of individual statements to which the respondent expresses her opinion on a scale, usually by checking a box associated with the appropriate level. Likert scales are unidimensional in that they measure responses along one dimension: that of the respondent's level of agreement.

Likert scales have several characteristics that distinguish them from other scales. First, they use multiple statements (referred to as items), often ten to 15 items, but sometimes as few as five or as many as 30. A single-item scale is not a Likert scale. The number of response categories is consistent across items, and the categories are presented horizontally. Respondents tend to comprehend a horizontal array more easily than a vertical array. These categories are identified by integers and consistent labels that denote the meaning of each category. The items and labels are bivalent: they have opposite values that are symmetrical. For example, a Likert item might resemble:

Strongly agree	Agree	Disagree	Strongly disagree
[ ]	[ ]	[ ]	[ ]

Here's a different type of item that is sometimes used in tourism questionnaires:

Not at all satisfied	Somewhat satisfied	Very satisfied
[ ]	[ ]	[ ]

This is not a Likert scale because the end positions are not bivalent. Rather, this is an ordered-category scale in that the scale describes a monotonically increasing level of agreement. Scales that use other categories – e.g. levels of perceived importance of attributes, self-assessment scales such as 'sounds very much like me', 'sounds a bit like me', 'does not sound like me', or frequency scales ('always', 'frequently', 'sometimes', 'never') – also are not Likert scales, even though some researchers incorrectly describe them as 'Likert-type scales').

How do I use it?

As with other scales, you begin by clearly identifying the objective for developing your scale. A Likert scale should focus on one issue at a time. You might have multiple scales addressing different issues, but each scale should consist of items related to only one topic.

Selecting the items is the next task. Researchers sometimes will use their intuition to develop an initial list of items. This can produce misleading, unreliable or invalid conclusions. A better process is to recruit some colleagues to suggest potential items for the scale, generating a list of perhaps 50 to 100 candidate statements relevant to your core concept. Avoid writing complex statements, statements with double negatives and vague or jargonistic language. The statements should represent a wide range of possible opinions, both positive and negative, on your core concept; statements that present both moderate and extreme but relevant positions are needed. You might want to review the comments on wording survey questions in Chapter 3.

Once you have the list, have a panel of judges assess the relevance of each item to the core concept. You can construct an ordered-category scale (note, this is not a Likert scale, because the extreme points reflect the end points of a gradation, not opposite attitudes) to do this, such as:

Highly relevant Somewhat relevant Not very relevant Not at all relevant

Note that you are not asking your judges about their level of agreement with individual items, but the degree to which they see the item relevant to the concept you are studying. Once your judges have completed their assessment, identify those statements ranked as 'highly relevant' and those deemed less relevant. You want items that are seen as highly relevant by most judges and not ones for which there was substantial disagreement across your panel. Assess the final pool of statements to ensure they represent a diversity of possible positions, both positive and negative. As suggested above, a final collection of ten to 15 items is usually a good number.

A topic often the subject of debate in designing a Likert scale is the number of response categories. I find that more than six or seven generally does not add additional useful information, and can involve spurious distinctions between individual scores. For example, I doubt that a respondent can make a meaningful distinction between 3 and 4 on a 10-point scale.

Another issue is whether the number of response categories should be even or odd. An odd number permits a subject to respond with a middle position variously positioned as 'neutral', 'don't know' or 'no opinion'. An even number forces a respondent to take a position. Most researchers automatically use an odd number of response categories without reflecting on whether this is a good choice. However, 'Likert did not believe that there were 'neutral' people walking around and that even if you were not passionate about an issue, you would at least feel a little something one way or the other' (Lodico *et al.*, 2006, p. 108). Beyond this philosophical question, there is the problem that the middle position often provides only ambiguous data. For example, does the middle response imply that the person is undecided between agreement and disagreement, has no opinion, doesn't know enough to decide or doesn't care? While there are situations where a middle category may be useful, I generally avoid middle-response categories. If someone is unable or unwilling for whatever reason to select one of the even numbers of responses, I find he/she usually just leaves the item blank. This is less of a problem than coding an ambiguous middle point as a 'neutral' response. A compromise position is to provide a 'don't know/no opinion' category to the far right of your scale. Any respondent checking this option can be noted as a non-response, and *not* coded as a 'neutral' mid-point. Generally, having a separate 'don't know/no opinion' category separate from the scale itself generally results in a larger number of respondents checking that option than leaving the option off and allowing people simply to skip the item.

Another important issue is whether the items can be assumed to have interval scale properties. The reason for hoping they have interval qualities is that you can then calculate means and perform other tests that require interval-level data. Technically, each item is only an ordinal scale; the magnitude of the differences between pairs of adjacent responses in an ordinal scale is not necessarily equal. However, if the labels are chosen carefully so that the differences between them can be assumed to be roughly equal, and if there are a reasonable number of items, many researchers assume that the results, when summed over all items, have interval scale properties.

If you are conservative and treat the data only as ordinal, you can use frequency tabulations, histograms (bar charts), modes and medians. You can also use non-parametric tests such as **chi square**, **Mann-Whitney**, **Wilcoxon signed-rank** and **Kruskal-Wallis** (Appendix A at the end of this book describes these tests). If you assume that the data are interval, you can use more powerful tests such as ***t*-tests** and **analysis of variance**, or even **regression analysis**.

What else do I need to know?

The Likert scale appears to be a simple tool but, as you have read above, the creation of useful scale items can be time consuming. The quality of your results strongly depends on the care with which you have chosen your statements. As with the semantic differential scale, one can question the reliability and stability (over time) of your results. The use of a split-half design (as described above) can help address any question about reliability. Validity – whether your scale is measuring what you think it is – is less of a concern if you used a panel to help select items; but, if the items are based on your intuition only, the validity of your scale can be questioned.

Because Likert scales are normally administered as part of a self-completion survey, you may find that some respondents tend to avoid the extreme response categories, especially if you are using six or seven categories. This central tendency bias can be reduced by using a lower number of categories and not providing a central category. Responding in ways that the respondent thinks will make him/her look more favourable in the eyes of the researcher rather than honestly is also a risk, of course. Finally, some respondents will tend to agree with every statement presented – this is called acquiescence bias. This can be avoided by having a mix of items that present statements that express both positive and negative views of the topic under study.

IMPORTANCE–PERFORMANCE ANALYSIS

What is it?

Importance–performance analysis (IPA) was developed by Martilla and James (1977) to assess quality in the automobile industry. Since then, it has been applied in a wide variety of contexts including the evaluation of tourism service quality, tourism product quality and destination competitiveness. The heart of the technique is a two-axis graph, with one axis representing the importance of an attribute and the other axis representing how well a destination or product provides or performs each attribute. Figure 6.7 illustrates the basic structure of an IPA chart. The vertical axis, 'importance', represents the relative importance of attributes; the horizontal axis, 'performance', represents the relative strength of a destination or business in terms of achievement (performance) on the same attributes.

The graph is usually divided into four quadrants (conventionally numbered left to right, first from the upper left-hand quadrant). Quadrant 1 represents those attributes deemed important by visitors but that destinations do not provide well. These are attributes that need to be improved for the destination to compete successfully. Quadrant 2 contains attributes that are important to visitors, and are well provided or met by destinations. This quadrant represents areas of success for a destination. Quadrant 3 contains attributes the destination does not possess to any significant degree, but are unimportant to visitors. These are attributes that the destination can ignore, or not worry about strengthening. Finally, Quadrant 4 represents attributes destinations possess to a significant degree but are unimportant to visitors. These are qualities destinations can afford to de-emphasize in development or marketing.

Importance–performance offers tourism marketers an easily understandable tool for grasping in which areas a destination or business excels and whether those areas are important to visitors. Such a tool helps marketers and product developers set priorities for areas of development or communication, thus making marketing more effective or providing strategic direction for development.

How do I use it?

Importance–performance can be used in two different contexts: (i) to compare different tourism destinations or businesses; or (ii) to evaluate a single destination or business on a number of attributes. We will use the latter context, evaluating Australia on a number of attributes.

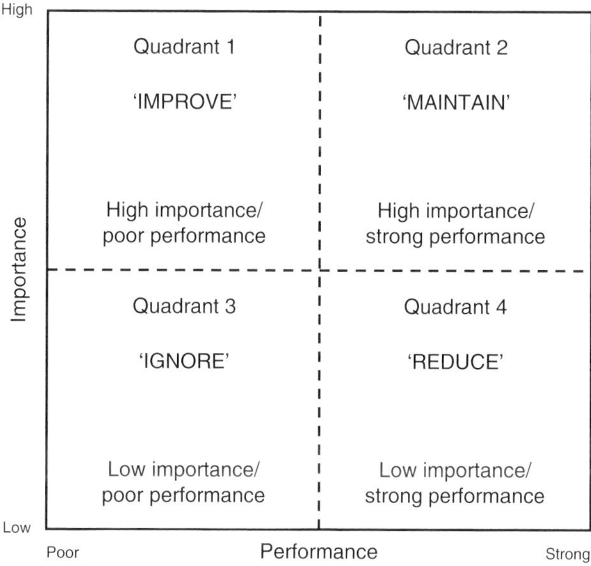

Fig. 6.7. Importance–Performance graph.

The data to conduct an IPA are collected through a survey in which you ask about the importance of specific attributes and the degree to which a destination (or business) provides or achieves those attributes. As you might expect, developing the list of attributes is a critical task in this method. Researchers who use IPA typically draw attributes from previous studies relevant to their particular task. This is a practical way to start, but you may also want to use a panel of experts to help identify the attributes to use. This typically is done by, first, clearly specifying the nature of your research problem and, second, proposing possible attributes to be considered. These are then presented to a panel in a simple questionnaire in which you ask each member to indicate how important the proposed attribute is. This process is parallel to that used for selecting items for a Likert scale. In fact, you can even use the same four-part 'relevance' scale described above for this task. However, you should also invite the experts to suggest additional attributes. This might involve a second survey if you receive numerous suggestions for attributes that should be assessed before you use them.

Once you have a finalized list of attributes, incorporate these into a survey in two questions. The first will be an ordered category scale, such as: 'When selecting a destination for an overseas trip, different things are important to different people. Here are some destination attributes that may be important to you. Please indicate how important each is to you by checking the appropriate box:'

	Very important	Somewhat important	Not very important	Not at all important
Good beaches	[ ]	[ ]	[ ]	[ ]
Lots of historical sites, etc.	[ ]	[ ]	[ ]	[ ]

This is followed by an ordered category scale along the lines of: 'You indicated how important a variety of attributes are to you in selecting a destination for an overseas trip. Please indicate the degree to which Australia possesses each by checking the appropriate box.'

	Possesses to a high degree	Possesses somewhat	Possesses to only a limited degree	Doesn't possess at all
Good beaches	[ ]	[ ]	[ ]	[ ]
Lots of historical sites, etc.	[ ]	[ ]	[ ]	[ ]

After you've completed your survey, compile mean scores over all your respondents for each attribute for both importance and performance. Then, plot the mean scores of attributes on a graph similar to that in Fig. 6.7. Finally, plot the grid lines to define the four quadrants.

The position of the gridlines can be selected using one of the following techniques. First, our two scales have four possible responses categories that would be coded 1 to 4. The grid lines can be positioned at the mid-point, 2.5. Thus any attribute whose mean importance score was below 2.5 would be plotted to the left of the grid line; those above 2.5 would be plotted to the right. This tactic assumes that the scale is an accurate representation of the variance in importance and performance of a destination on the attributes. However, an alternative and more relativistic approach can also be used. Once you have calculated the means for the importance of each attribute and the performance of Australia on each attribute, calculate the mean of the means. These means are then selected as the values by which to position the grid lines. The choice between the two methods is a matter of judgement. As a rule-of-thumb, choose the method that provides a reasonable distribution of points among the four quadrants. This advice, of course, is based on the assumption that performance and importance scores will be roughly normally distributed.

What else do I need to know?

The notion of attribute importance, a concept central to this method, is subject to confusion. Attribute importance is multidimensional. An attribute might have a high level of importance in a person's decision to select a destination, but might be of less importance in terms of the person's satisfaction with a visit. Or a person may feel socially obligated to assess an attribute such as 'sustainable tourism practices' as important but, in fact, not really care about it.

Responses provided by different subjects will be a function of previous experience, and may not be strictly comparable to each other because of differences in knowledge. Someone who has visited a destination will have a more informed opinion of that destination than someone who has never visited it. Indeed, in some cases, one might challenge whether a person is even able to make informed judgements about a destination he has never visited.

Different potential visitors can define attributes differently. For example, one person might interpret price in terms of the percentage of his budget that he has to spend for different services, such as accommodation. Another might define price in terms of the value received for a given level of expenditure. In other words, prices might be low but, if the quality of service is also low, he might conclude that the price was too high for the service received. Attributes such as weather or scenery that are, themselves, multidimensional can be especially tricky to evaluate as a single item.

Responses to both importance and performance of different attributes will vary, of course, among respondents. While IPA typically presents only the means on a graph, you might consider also presenting the standard deviations for each attribute. One method for doing this is to place bars above and below, and to the right and left of the dot representing the magnitude of the standard deviation of importance and performance (see Fig. 6.8). This graphic device can be especially useful in alerting you to ambiguities in interpreting your results when a point is located in one grid, but close to the grid line and its standard deviations extend into an adjacent grid.

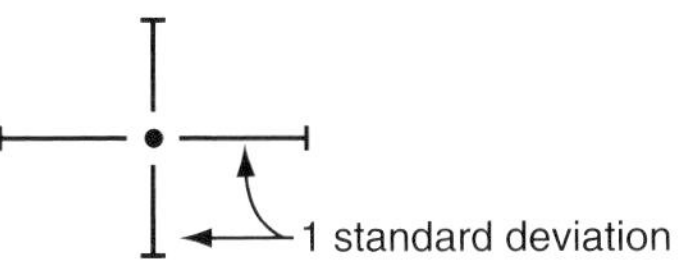

Fig. 6.8. Symbol for showing standard deviation.

CONCLUSIONS

Indices and scales are common tools for analysis of tourism phenomena. They provide a convenient and empirical way of summarizing distributions, trends, attitudes and other measures. In this chapter, we looked at indices that provide three different measures of dispersal and three tools based on scales.

The first measure of distribution, the locational quotient, provides a measure of the relative concentration of a wide variety of phenomena ranging from travel propensities, through employment to distribution of tourism enterprises on the basis of individual geographical units. The Gini Coefficient provides a measure of the concentration of some phenomenon over multiple units. This coefficient can be applied not only to geographical areas but also to social units such as industries or households. The nearest-neighbour ratio provides a different look at concentration. In this case, it provides you with a tool to make an objective judgement about whether a complex pattern of points is tending toward a uniform distribution, a clustered distribution or a random distribution. Knowing the nature of the distribution allows you to formulate or test hypotheses about the processes that give rise to patterns of distribution.

The semantic differential scale is a simple but flexible research method for uncovering the latent or connotative meaning people hold of a specific word or concept. Many words or phrases, such as honeymoon or national park, have explicit definitions, but they also carry substantial emotional meaning. The semantic differential helps reveal hidden attitudes and meanings held by persons in the context of specific words or concepts.

The Likert scale is one of the most common scales used in tourism research. It appears to be very simple to construct and use, although the creation of a valid and reliable Likert scale requires much more than just thinking up a series of statements to insert into a questionnaire. The development of a true Likert scale uses a multi-stage process involving a panel of experts to help develop and then select individual scale items for use in a research project.

Finally, we looked at a tool that combines two scales, importance–performance analysis. As with the Likert scale, the selection of specific scale items should be done with the assistance of a panel of experts, or the application of items that have been shown to be reliable and valid in other published studies. IPA produces graphic output that is easy to interpret but that does require some careful thought in terms of how the details of the graph are selected and how the scale items are operationally defined.

We will continue our look at indices in Chapter 7, in particular, the development of benchmarks for decision making in businesses and DMOs, and some other indices related to assessing market performance.

REFERENCES

Australian Bureau of Statistics (2007) *Tourist Accommodation, December 2007*, Cat. 8635.0. Available at: http://www.abs.gov.au/AUSSTATS/abs@.nsf/DetailsPage/8635.0Dec%202007?OpenDocument (accessed 14 May 2008).

Blore, S. (2002) High five: five indices of civilization in five countries worldwide. *EnRoute Magazine,* August. http://www.enroutemag.com/e/civ/index.html (accessed 20 May 2008).

Clark, P. and Evans, F. (1955) On some aspects of spatial patterns in biological populations. *Science* 121, 397–398.

Defert, P. (1967) Le taux de fonction touristique: mise au point et critique. *Les Cahiers du Tourisme* Serie C(5), 110–122.

Gini, C. (1921) Measurement of inequality and incomes. *The Economic Journal* 31, 124–126.

Grieg-Smith, P. (1952) The use of random and contiguous quadrats in the study of the structure of plant populations. *Annals of Biology* 16, 292–316.

Heise, D.R. (1970) The semantic differential and attitude research. In: Summers, G. (ed.) *Attitude Measurement.* Rand McNally, Chicago, Illinois, pp. 235–253.

Isserman, Andrew M. (1977) The location quotient approach for estimating regional economic impacts. *Journal of the American Institute of Planners* 4, 33–41.

Likert, R. (1932) A technique for the measurement of attitudes. *Archives of Psychology* 140, 1–55.

Lodico, M.G., Spaulding, D.T. and Voegtle, K.H (2006). *Methods in Educational Research: from Theory to Practice.* Jossey-Bass, San Francisco, California.

Lorenz, M. (1905) Methods of measuring the concentration of wealth. *Publications of the American Statistical Association* 9, 209–219.

Martilla, J. and James, J. (1977) Importance–performance analysis. *Journal of Marketing* 4, 77–79.

Osgood, C., Suci, G. and Tannenbaum, P. (1957) *The Measurement of Meaning*. University of Illinois Press, Urbana, Illinois.

Pinder, D. (1978) Correcting underestimation in nearest-neighbour analysis. *Area* 10, 379–385.

Pinder, D. and Witherick, M.E. (1975) A modification of the nearest-neighbour analysis for use in linear situations. *Geography* 60, *16–23*.

Smith, S. (1983) Restaurants and dining out: the geography of a tourism business. *Annals of Tourism Research* 10, 515–549.

Smith, S. (1995) *Tourism Analysis*, 2nd edn. Longman, Harlow, UK.

Wells, W. and Smith, G. (1960) Four semantic rating scales compared. *Journal of Applied Psychology* 44, 393–397.

Whyte, W. (1980) *The Social Life of Small Urban Places*. Project for Public Spaces, New York.

chapter 7

Metrics for Decision Making

WHY THIS IS IMPORTANT

A management aphorism posits 'What doesn't get measured, doesn't get managed'. Being a fairly independent (and some say, difficult) personality, I don't mind not being managed. However, when running a business, agency or a destination-marketing organization (DMO), not being able to measure and manage key activities would be a serious problem. This chapter continues our examination of selected measurement tools that we began in Chapter 6.

We will look, to be more precise, at some metrics (also known as indicators) for making decisions in a variety of tourism contexts, from DMOs, through regional planning and impact assessment, to the performance of tourism enterprises. It is important to understand that our focus is on the measurement tools themselves – not on their application in marketing, business development, planning, branding or myriad other contexts. Applications are important enough that they merit much more extensive coverage than we can provide in this text. Our concern is more modest – examining some basic tools that entrepreneurs, managers, planners and policy analysts may find helpful in their work.

Even though our objectives in this chapter are modest, the topic is still large and complex. The metrics you develop to support decision making should, of course, be relevant to the policy or business context of your research. In other words, the development and use of metrics is not an academic exercise. Metrics are meant to be used. This chapter is intended to provide you with an introduction to some of these tools – what they are and how they might be used. Our discussion will be only an introduction. Each of the metrics we will look at is the subject of multiple articles and books by other authors. Still, even an introduction can be very useful.

Good metrics have a number of characteristics. They should be based on a solid conceptual foundation, such as tested concepts and models from marketing, economics, business administration, community development or the natural sciences. They should convey information beyond just the raw data. For example, if I take my temperature and find that the thermometer reads

39.9°C, that is not only an empirical datum, but it also confirms that I am ill. Body temperature is an important indicator of health. However, not all indicators are as precise or reliable as body temperature. As we shall see later, some social indicators are based on perceptions or subjective feelings. Still, even these 'soft' indicators will be based on empirical sources, such as community surveys.

Indicators must also be feasible in the sense that the data on which they are based must be obtainable at an acceptable cost in terms of time and money. An indicator that cannot be supported by readily available and updatable data is of no value to decision makers. Indicators need, of course, to be relevant to the issue being studied as well as sensitive to changes in the phenomena being studied. For example, the number of ads by tourism businesses in a local newspaper is not particularly helpful in assessing the economic health of the local tourism sector. On the other hand, the number of jobs created the previous year in tourism businesses or hotel RevPAR (revenue per available room) could be. Ideally, the implications of changes in an indicator should be unambiguous. A reduction in the levels of *Escherichia coli* contamination in beach water is an unambiguous indicator of an improvement in water quality on at least one dimension. However, reductions in the number of visitors to a beach may signify either good news or bad news depending on the causes of the reduction.

We will begin by considering indicators relevant to assessing the performance of tourism destinations, particularly from a marketing perspective. We will then look at metrics relevant to the basic components of tourism sustainability: economic, environmental and social impacts. In practice, planners and managers often prefer an integrated set of measures for assessing the sustainability of tourism. A good example of how this can be done is shown in Tonge *et al.* (2005). But for our purposes, it is clearer to consider the various components separately. Finally, we will consider the concept of benchmarking.

A MARKETING STATISTICAL SYSTEM

Challenges in developing destination metrics

Measurement of the performance of a destination is important for effective evaluation, policy development, product development, planning and marketing. However, assessing the performance of destination marketing or, for that matter, a tourism business is difficult to do precisely and in a way that tracks cause-and-effect relationships. The difficulties arise from several characteristics of tourism:

- **Tourism is neither well defined nor understood.** Tourism is not, as we noted in Chapter 1, an industry. Rather, it is a collection of industries. Indeed, senior management of many tourism enterprises often do not consider themselves to be part of 'tourism'; they may view themselves, instead, as working in the accommodation industry, the airline industry or the food service industry. Moreover, tourism involves both supply and demand issues in the context of destinations, individual businesses, government activities, consumers, non-governmental organizations, environmental and social impacts and more. While 'tourism' is formally defined by the UNWTO, it has, to borrow a concept introduced in our discussion of semantic differential scales in Chapter 6, a rich and complex set of connotative meanings. These connotative meanings are not empirically based; instead, they can be highly subjective or even politically loaded. This is why empirical measurement of tourism phenomena is so important.

- **Tourism is subject to many external events outside the control of management and marketing**. External events include destructive forces such as hurricanes/cyclones, volcanoes, tsunamis, disease, civil or labour unrest and terrorist attacks. On the other hand, a destination can benefit from events outside the direct control of a DMO. A popular movie or television programme featuring a destination as the setting for the story can generate increased interest by viewers in visiting the setting. For example, New Zealand experienced a boom in international tourism demand for several years following the Lord of the Rings movie trilogy. Hallmark events, such as the 2010 World's Fair in Shanghai or the 2012 Summer Olympics in London, not only generate interest in the host city, but they can also generate international interest in the rest of the host country. Perversely, problems in one destination, such as a terrorist attack, can benefit other places as would-be visitors shift their choice of destination. For example, the terrorist bombing in Bali in 2002 created a spike in visits to Thailand for several months as visitors switched from Bali to Thailand.
- **DMOs are not the only source of information and promotion for a destination, especially at a municipal level**. Provincial/state or national tourism marketing efforts that feature the destination can supplement DMO efforts. This is, of course, desirable, but the relative impacts of various agencies' marketing efforts can be difficult to distinguish. In Canada, for example, Niagara Falls is a frequently used icon in both provincial and national tourism marketing aimed at the US market. The relative impacts of these senior governmental tourism activities versus the marketing by the local Niagara Falls Tourism DMO can be very difficult to separate. Marketing and development efforts of private sector enterprises also influence the overall performance of the destination in a way that can be difficult to separate from the results of public sector marketing. Thus, it is challenging to distinguish precisely between the number of visitors drawn to Orange County in Florida by the marketing efforts of the Orlando/Orange County Convention and Visitors Bureau and those drawn by the marketing efforts of Disney World and Universal Studios. Businesses that effectively market themselves can contribute to the overall image and brand of a destination, but calculating the relative contribution of DMO marketing versus the spin-off impacts of business marketing can be very difficult.
- **The impact of tourism marketing may extend well beyond the duration of a marketing campaign**. Although the effectiveness of marketing, as measured through indicators such as awareness levels or the intent to visit, fades over time, there are residual effects that can last for weeks, months or, in some cases, years. You may have seen tourism ads for a destination that planted the seed of desire for you to visit. However, your need to stay in school, limited money for travel or other commitments may preclude your realizing your dream for years. That doesn't mean the initial ad campaign was ineffective; rather, your ability to respond may require a much longer time period than the marketers anticipated.
- **There can be a spillover effect associated with tourism marketing efforts**. Marketing campaigns typically are targeted at specific geographic or demographic markets. However, potential visitors living in other origins or who are members of different market segments will still be exposed to the marketing campaign and may be prompted to visit the destination. Their visits and spending, however, are not likely to be attributed to the marketing campaign because they are not the target market. Such spillover benefits the destination but it complicates an accurate assessment of the return-on-investment (ROI – to be discussed later in this chapter). An example of the spillover effect can be seen in advertising conducted by the Atlantic Canada Tourism Marketing Partnership (ACTP – the topic of Focus Box 7.1). ACTP partners sometimes take out advertisements in the Boston Globe,

Focus Box 7.1. Examples of market performance metrics from Atlantic Canada.

The Atlantic Canada Tourism Partnership (ACTP) is an alliance among the four Canadian Atlantic provinces: Newfoundland and Labrador, New Brunswick, Nova Scotia and Prince Edward Island. It operates on a renewable, 3-year basis, with core funding provided by the federal government and the four provincial governments. Businesses provide additional project-by-project funding.

One of its goals is to market the region to US residents through an integrated campaign. Each province allocates a portion of its total marketing budget to the ACTP, while also maintaining its independent marketing activities. The integrated campaign involves print, provincial websites, participation in consumer shows and work with travel journalists. The federal and provincial governments require that the results of each year's campaign be measured to determine whether taxpayers' money is being effectively spent. A key measure is the ROI (return-on-investment). A target of 10.00:1.00 (ten dollars spent by visitors for every one dollar invested in marketing) has been set by the governments funding ACTP.

ACTP's partners use advertising to direct potential visitors to either a toll-free number operated by each province or to the province's website for more information. Each province then collects telephone numbers or e-mail addresses for people contacting the province's tourism office. At the end of the year, these contact details are combined from all provinces, and duplicate entries from people who contacted two or more of the provinces for information are culled. A survey is then conducted based on a random sample of unique telephone numbers or e-mail addresses.

The survey includes questions about whether the person made a trip to Atlantic Canada and, if so, how much she/he spent on her/his trip. Persons visiting Atlantic Canada were also asked whether the information they received influenced their decision to make the trip, or whether they had already decided to visit before receiving the information and were calling just for additional information.

Data are tabulated for each province as well as for the region as a whole. The following table summarizes the information collected in the survey (the results are for 2006).

Market performance metric	Description	Results
Media buy	Total investment (millions of Canadian dollars) by ACTP partners in joint annual marketing campaign	$3.65
Inquiries	Number of people calling a toll-free number or requesting information via a provincial tourism website; duplicate enquiries are deleted	222,379
Cost per enquiry	The marketing budget divided by the number of inquiries	$16
Conversion rate	Percentage of people making an enquiry who eventually visited Atlantic Canada and who indicated that the information they received influenced their decision to make the trip	29%
Converted party-visits	The number of enquiries multiplied by the conversion rate, assuming each converted enquiry represents one travel party	65,143

(Continued)

Focus Box 7.1. Continued.

Market performance metric	Description	Results
Cost per converted enquiry	The marketing budget divided by the number of converted party-visits	$56
Spending per visitor-party	Mean expenditures for trip on a party basis.	$1272
Total revenues	Total expenditures (millions of Canadian dollars), obtained by multiplying spending per party by number of converted party-visits	$82.89
ROI	Return-on-investment, obtained by dividing total revenues by media buy	$22.74: $1.00

The ROI of 22.74:1.00 is more than double the target of 10.00:1.00. Similar results were obtained for the two previous years. Thus the impact of the marketing campaign was judged to be a success and the partnership had its funding renewed for another 3-year contract period.

which is published in one of their key markets – Boston, Massachusetts. However, ACTP marketers have discovered that visitors from New York to Boston also see and respond to these ads, thus driving a small increase in travel from New York City, which is not one of their target markets. Of course, none of the businesses who were aiming at the Boston market has any objection to drawing visitors from New York City also, but it does complicate precise assessment of the effectiveness of the advertising.

- **Destination marketing typically employs multiple media**. Communication tools for tourism marketers include print and electronic advertisements; websites; familiarization (fam) tours for tour operators, travel agents and travel journalists; direct mail; brochures or travel guides sent out in response to telephone calls or e-mail queries; sales missions; and trade exhibitions and consumer shows. If properly integrated, they can have a synergistic effect that is greater than the sum of individual efforts. (Measuring the magnitude of these synergistic effects can be challenging.) On the other hand, if marketing efforts are not carefully integrated, different messages or campaigns by a destination can work against that destination's efforts to attract visitors. Despite these difficulties, efforts at measurement cannot be avoided. Measurement, ideally, should be approached through a destination-marketing statistical system. This is a set of integrated empirical measures intended to support decisions for the management and marketing of a destination. The information needed by a typical DMO can be grouped into two broad categories: marketing communications and visitor behaviours.

Marketing communications metrics

Tourism marketing is a form of communication. Thus, some metrics of particular use to tourism marketers are measures of the nature and consequences of communication activities. These can be categorized as **inputs**, **outputs** and **results**. Inputs are measures of internal activities related to marketing communications; outputs are performance measures arising from or associated with the input activity; results are the longer-term changes achieved in the external marketing environment as a result of marketing. Some metrics for marketing communication efforts include the following; many more are possible depending on the activities of the DMO. Inputs include:

- annual marketing budgets by geographic market, product line;
- mix of marketing media (budget allocated to Internet, TV, print, etc.);
- fam tours (travel agents, tour operators, media);
- participation in trade and consumer marketplaces;
- investment in market-related research;
- marketing staff wages and salaries; and
- number of partners for cooperative ad campaigns.

Outputs include:

- number of brochures distributed;
- number of participants – both suppliers and attendees – and their assessment of the tour;
- coverage in tour operator brochures (e.g. column-centimetres);
- number of stories resulting from media relations; and
- estimated advertising value-equivalence of media stories (How much would it have cost to purchase an ad equal to the media story in print or TV/radio time?).

Results include:

- changes in awareness levels before and after campaigns;
- recall or assessment of advertisements after campaigns;
- measures of intentions to travel by potential visitors to the destination;
- revenues spent by visitors attributable to marketing communications; and
- return-on-investment (ROI).

Ideally, you want to be able to demonstrate cause-and-effect relationships among inputs, outputs and results. However, it is difficult precisely to document these relationships for the reasons listed above. None the less, measures of communication activities still provide managers with useful information regarding the level of activity associated with various advertising and promotional campaigns.

Although causal linkages are often impossible to measure precisely, an assumption of tourism marketing is that visiting any destination is the result of a series of steps. The series begins with raising the awareness of potential visitors about the destination. Then there is the need to provide potential visitors with the information they require at various stages of the trip-planning process. Finally, there is facilitating the purchase by providing information to help the potential visitor make a reservation and the business to close the sale. Tracking the whole chain of communication activities to ensure your message is getting out and being well received is important.

Return-on-investment: first, I need to make a disclaimer. The notion of ROI in tourism marketing is different from how accountants or investors use the term. In accounting or investment, ROI reflects the rate of return an investor (person or business) receives as a result of money invested in some opportunity. In tourism, ROI refers to the level of expenditures made by visitors in the destination compared with expenditures made in a marketing campaign that presumably produced those expenditures. A key difference between the two concepts of ROI is that, in tourism, the investment was made by a government agency that does not receive the revenues generated by their advertising investment. Rather, individual businesses benefit. Of course, government will eventually recoup at least a portion of their expenditures through taxes and fees they collect from tourism enterprises and visitors. Equation 7.1 presents one equation for calculating ROI:

$$\mathrm{ROI} = \frac{\text{total revenues} - \text{total market campaign costs}}{\text{total market campaign costs}} \qquad (7.1)$$

Conceptually, the calculation in Eqn 7.1 is simple: determine total revenues generated by an advertising campaign and then subtract the costs of the campaign; next, divide the net revenue by the campaign costs. The challenge is in collecting the data needed in the equation. Besides the problems of collecting accurate expenditure data (which are assumed to represent revenues received by local businesses) that we will consider below, you should limit expenditures to only those that can be directly related to the advertising campaign being assessed. Getting this information requires several steps:

- Develop a sampling frame based on persons who visited the destination under study.
- Ask your respondents whether they recall seeing an advertisement for the destination during the time period over which the campaign ran.
- Then ask whether the ad caused them to make a trip that they were not previously planning or, at least, if the advertisement played a substantial role in their decision to make the trip.
- Finally, ask how much they spent on the trip in the destination (expenses made en route are not counted as local revenues).

Such surveys can be time-consuming and expensive if you are to collect data from a sufficient number of people to permit reasonably accurate ROI calculations. Also, one can question how accurately respondents will be able to recall whether an advertisement was a factor in their decision to make a trip to the destination.

Campaign costs are relatively simpler to obtain because this information will come from your operating budget. These costs are normally only those variable costs directly tied to a campaign. They do not include fixed or overhead costs such as salaries and wages, or office expenses. The costs, though, should include creative developmental or design costs for advertisements or other marketing communications during the campaign, as well as costs for media placement. An alternative ROI calculation is represented by Eqn 7.2:

$$\mathrm{ROI} = \frac{\text{total revenues}}{\text{total market campaign costs}} \qquad (7.2)$$

The difference between Eqns 7.1 and 7.2 is that 7.1 calculates ROI in terms of net revenues: revenues minus costs. As a result, the ROI obtained by using 7.1 will be lower than that from 7.2 because the value of the numerator – net revenues – will be smaller. Most market researchers prefer 7.1 because it focuses on 'profit' or, more precisely, net revenues in the destination rather than gross revenues. Thus it represents a more 'business-like' approach. However, many DMOs use 7.2 because the concept of 'profit' is not seen as relevant. Rather, they are interested in the efficiency of their investment in terms of the ratio of revenues generated for local businesses compared with the magnitude of marketing expenditures. In a sense, the difference between the two equations can be described in the following terms. Eqn 7.1 reflects a 'business investment' mentality in that it is structured around net returns. Eqn 7.2 is analogous to the benefit–cost ratio used for public investment decision making in that it compares all 'benefits' (in this case, revenues) with all costs to assess the efficiency of the marketing investment.

Focus Box 7.1 illustrates the use of ROI (as calculated by Eqn 7.2), as well as several other marketing metrics. This particular example is drawn from an annual marketing campaign in the USA conducted by a regional marketing partnership in Atlantic Canada. The example presents several metrics used by the partnership to track the performance of its annual campaigns, including the number of enquiries from US residents, conversion rates (the percentage of people who asked for information on visiting Atlantic Canada), costs for the campaign and the campaign's ROI. An alternative to looking at ROI only is the use of a 'marketing dashboard' – see Focus Box 7.2.

Focus Box 7.2. Marketing dashboards.

As you can see from Focus Box 7.1, a table showing different variables and associated values is a common format for presenting marketing performance indicators. However, a tabular presentation often is not the most effective way of presenting data. Many people comprehend pictures or graphics more quickly than just columns of numbers. This is why graphs such as pie charts are popular in reports.

Frustratingly, this focus box is in static black-and-white and does not provide the colourful, graphic and interactive functionality possible on a marketing dashboard. We are stuck here with a traditional medium of communication about an emerging form of communication.

Improvements in computer graphics technology now allow for the presentation of marketing data for decision making to move beyond just graphs on a printed page. By using visual metaphors that are intuitively easy to understand, such as bars of different sizes or different shades of colour, combined with the computer's power to store and manipulate information interactively, it is possible to present marketing data in a visual format that allows a decision maker to explore multiple levels of detail or content. Such a computer-based graphic tool is known as a dashboard. The analogy to a car's dashboard is based on the fact that a marketing dashboard presents a few key pieces of information to help you understand how well an organization's marketing efforts are performing, just as a car's dashboard provides you with a few key pieces of information about its performance.

A marketing dashboard typically provides multiple tabs so you can switch among topics and drill deeper into the information displayed, as well as providing the opportunity to 'slice and dice' your data by, for example, origins of Internet enquiries by the path they followed to get to your website, bounce rates and the length of time spent on a web page. Dashboards can provide a quick look at the potential impacts of marketing campaigns, show whether users tend to get distracted from certain pages of your website, and provide other insights into potential cause-and-effect relationships affecting marketing results.

The core task in designing a dashboard is to select the appropriate metrics as well as the level of detail you need to have. For example, if one of your metrics is the number of page-views of your DMO's websites, do you also want to be able to track trends in the number of views daily, weekly, monthly? Do you want to be able to track page hits by different sectors of members of the DMO such as attractions or restaurants?

Before selecting the specific metric to include on your dashboard, you need to understand the objectives of marketing in the organization. Is it to drive revenues, market share, ROI, total visitor numbers, or what? The answer to that question needs to be agreed upon not only by all those in marketing, but also by senior management and the Board of Directors (if relevant). They should be consulted from the start of a dashboard project

(Continued)

Focus Box 7.2. Continued.

to identify what measures they consider important to assessing the performance of marketing campaigns. Having great data on the wrong measures does nothing to help establish the importance of marketing and marketing research.

You should then work with a graphics specialist to ensure that the design of the various features on your site make intuitive and unambiguous sense, as well as developing a dashboard architecture that allows easy browsing.

Many private firms offer dashboard design services; a computer search of a term such as 'marketing dashboards' will lead you to numerous vendors, as well as to illustrations of the types of designs they offer. One service popular with DMOs is Google Analytics™: http://www.google.com/analytics/. It focuses on web usage analytics only, though, and does not support the addition of other metrics such as the numbers of visitors coming to a destination or aggregate hotel occupancy rates. At the time of writing (2009), the service was free to publishers, advertisers and owners.

Human resource and service quality metrics

A key factor influencing visitor satisfaction with a visit to a destination is the quality of service that visitors receive. Most visitors want not just competent service but a sincere welcome, personal attention and a caring attitude. Indeed, the word 'hospitality' is often used to describe many tourism services, especially accommodation and food services. It is also routinely linked with the word 'tourism' in courses, and book and journal titles, such as School of Hospitality and Tourism Management or *International Journal of Hospitality and Tourism Management*.

The roots of hospitality go back millennia. When people lived in isolated communities and travelled little, strangers to a settlement were both welcomed and feared. The stranger could bring news and opportunities for trade, or the threat of danger. People would offer hospitality to strangers – gifts, food, water and shelter – in the hope of receiving gifts in return. At a minimum, they offered gifts to ensure the strangers did not harm them. Over time, these pragmatic hospitality motivations became enshrined in the traditions of many religions and philosophies, including Bahá'í, Buddhism, Christianity, Confucianism, Hinduism, Islam, Judaism and Zoroastrianism.

After the Industrial Revolution, as people began to travel more and economies grew and became more complex, hospitality slowly became more a matter of contracts and law. In return for an agreed-upon payment, you could command food, drink or accommodation. However, people usually want more than just the technical fulfilment of a commercial exchange – they still want a sense of welcome and hospitality. Motivating employees to provide that level of service is a major challenge for employers, especially when hospitality positions are seen as short term, low pay, with long hours and lacking the promise of a career future.

Not surprisingly, then, human resource practices are critical to tourism businesses. A number of metrics offer information to managers to help them monitor employee performance and work quality. These metrics can be classified into four main human resource task areas: recruiting, retention, performance and development. Some examples of human resource metrics include the following:

Recruiting: ensuring that the right number of employees with the right skills are available when needed:

- retention rate of new employees after 3, 6 and 12 months;
- number of equity group members (women, visible minorities, persons with disabilities) hired;

- supervisor evaluation of new employees at 3 and 6 months, and annually; and
- employee performance appraisals.

Retention: keeping skilled employees committed to and involved with the organization:

- turnover rate;
- relationship between retention rate and performance ratings; and
- ratio of internal promotions to the hiring of external employees.

Performance: providing customer satisfaction and contributing to other organizational goals;

- supervisors' evaluations;
- performance of employees against workplace standards, e.g. length of time to serve a customer;
- customer satisfaction survey results; and
- performance awards and recognitions.

Development: helping staff to learn, improve skills and prepare for possible promotions:

- percentage of employees taking advantage of professional development opportunities;
- scores on performance evaluations; and
- training programme ROI.

The measurement of service quality is an area to which substantial research has been devoted, and one that continues to draw researchers' interests. There are several challenges in measuring service quality. A fundamental one is that the nature of service is much more complex than the nature of tangible goods. Goods typically are designed with empirical, verifiable specifications such as weight, length or colour. Services, on the other hand, are essentially intangible and often involve personal interaction between the consumer and the service provider.

Smith (1994) reviewed some of the different conceptualizations of tourism services and proposed his own model. His concept of tourism services is that they consist of multiple layers: (i) a physical core or foundation such as a restaurant or aircraft; (ii) the technical performance of a service function by a service provider; (iii) a sense of hospitality offered in conjunction with or in addition to the technical function; (iv) an element of choice; and (v) the psychological involvement of the visitor in a tourism experience. This is only one of numerous models, but all emphasize that tourism services are fundamentally complex, intangible and difficult to measure in terms of quality. Still, this does not mean that a manager can ignore measuring service quality. Moreover, assessing service quality should be done in the larger context of looking at human resource management in the organization (Schneider and Bowen, 1993; Morrison, 1996). Still, because this is a research methods text, we will not explore human resource management practices, but will focus only on general approaches for measuring service quality.

There are three fundamentally different ways a manager can assess service quality in a tourism operation: (i) manager's assessment of staff performance against standards; (ii) use of anonymous observers; and (iii) feedback/surveys from customers.

The first approach is based on the assumption that employee adherence to job performance standards is closely correlated with customer satisfaction – an assumption that most academic researchers are not willing to make. Still, this approach is useful in setting expectations for the technical performance of service jobs, and can often be a factor (although certainly not the only one) in a customer's satisfaction with a service encounter. An example of this can be seen in the many restaurants that set time goals for their wait staff. For example, restaurant management might set the specifications shown in Table 7.1 for breakfast service. As long as the staff meet these standards, supervisors will assume that the level of service is appropriate.

Such performance standards are based on what management sees as key indicators of service quality, in this case, time deadlines for various tasks. They provide staff with a sense of the expected pace of their work, but, in practice, supervisors often are too busy to monitor whether these standards are being met in day-to-day operations. They also focus on empirical measures of performance, not subjective measures such as the customer's satisfaction with the friendliness of the server or the perceptions of the quality of the food being served. Thus, they can be helpful to supervisors in communicating expectations to staff, although they do not address the softer aspects of service quality such as customer expectations and whether the service encounter is pleasurable for the customer.

A second approach is to use **mystery shoppers** (Wilson, 1988). This tactic involves hiring individuals or using staff from other properties to patronize a business to assess service quality. A hotel chain might ask some of its managers to check into properties where they are not known, or to observe staff performance on specified criteria such as timeliness of check-in, handling of questions, quality of bell service, cleanliness of the room and quality of interactions between staff and guest. This approach allows a firm's management to obtain a better assessment of the guest experience than simply comparing performance times against standards. However, the findings of mystery shoppers are idiosyncratic in that the performance observations are specific to a single observer and a single visit. The experiences of other guests or performance on days during which the mystery shopper did not visit are not known unless multiple mystery shopper and multiple consumer encounters are assessed.

Third, businesses may solicit feedback from guests. There are several ways to do this. The most common is the use of **guest comment cards**. These are the familiar cards found in many accommodation and food service establishments. Such cards typically are quite short, requiring less than a minute to complete. If properly designed with relevant questions, they can alert management to chronic problems. Moreover, they can be designed to invite guests to have their names and e-mail addresses provided for the business to develop a customer relations database for direct mail marketing. Some cards invite the guests to identify any staff person who provided exceptional performance. Guest comment cards can, however, provide only a biased picture of staff performance. Most guests will not bother to complete the cards unless they are frustrated with some aspect of their service. While it can be helpful for management to become aware of ongoing problems, the cards usually do not let management know what staff are doing right.

Table 7.1. Example of job performance specifications: breakfast service at a family-style restaurant.

Task	Performance standard
Customer greeted and seated	15 s after entering the restaurant
Menu provided and coffee/tea offered	60 s after being seated
Order taken	5 min after being seated
Order delivered	8 min after order is taken
Staff check on customer regarding meal quality	5 min after order is delivered

Focus Box 7.3 is an example of a comment card, in this case for the University of Waterloo (Ontario, Canada) Museum and Archive of Games. Note, in this case, that the card asks for information about how the person learned of the museum, the reason for his/her visit, a self-segmentation (type of visitor) as well as level of satisfaction with the visit. Sometimes cards also ask for the visitor's name and e-mail address for direct marketing.

Focus Box 7.3. Example of a guest comment card.

University of Waterloo Museum and Archive of Games
Visitor Comment Card

Date of your visit: ______________________

I heard about the Museum through:

[ ] Newspaper or magazine story
[ ] University website
[ ] Word of mouth
[ ] Class/school
[ ] Other: ______________________

I came to the Museum today:

[ ] To see the current special exhibit
[ ] Out of general interest
[ ] As part of a field trip or class visit
[ ] To do research
[ ] Other: ______________________

The category that best describes me is:

[ ] Student in the Department of Recreation and Leisure Studies
[ ] Student in another UW department
[ ] Student at another university or college
[ ] Teacher leading a school trip
[ ] UW faculty member
[ ] Faculty member at another university of college
[ ] Local resident
[ ] Out-of-town visitor

Please evaluate the following (1 = not satisfied; 4 = very satisfied)

	1	2	3	4
Courtesy of staff				
Overall appearance of museum				
Quality of exhibits				
Convenient hours				
Signage to find the museum				
Parking				

Please feel free to add any other comments on the reverse of this page.

Thank you for visiting! We hope to see you again!

A variation on guest comment cards is a formal survey of guests. Questionnaires designed for guest surveys tend to be more detailed, exploring specific aspects of the business's performance. Questionnaires may be distributed on site, such as on board a plane during a flight, or they might be administered after a trip is over via a mail-back questionnaire, online survey or telephone interview. However, survey distribution after a visitor has patronized a tourism business should be done only with the prior agreement of the visitor. Mailing someone a survey about the quality of his/her hotel stay to their home runs the risk of causing substantial embarrassment for your former guest depending on the nature of his/her trip away from home – and perhaps exposing you to a lawsuit.

Questionnaires can explore a wide range of aspects of the service interaction and also pose more general questions such as whether the respondent is likely to patronize the business again or if he would recommend the business to a friend. With respect to this latter question – the likelihood of recommending the business to a friend – a number of tourism managers have told me they believe asking a former customer about whether they would recommend the business is the single best measure of customer satisfaction. Indeed, it was included in the passenger survey summarized in Table 7.2.

Table 7.2 presents some of the types of questions that might be asked on a formal guest survey. This particular example is taken from a traveller survey on board a passenger rail service. Please note – only a few questions are shown here for illustration.

Another conception of service quality, also implemented through surveys, is **gap analysis.** This model views service quality in terms of whether the customer's expectations were not met, met or exceeded. This approach allows a firm to set priorities in terms of where to devote resources to improve service quality, as well as helping it understand what it is doing well. This logic may sound familiar – it is basically the same as that of the importance–performance analysis we looked at in Chapter 6.

The best known gap model is probably SERVQUAL (Parasuraman *et al.* 1988). The process involves the administration of a set of 22 statements about service quality, organized into five dimensions (with four or five statements per dimension). These statements, each coded on a seven-point Likert scale, were refined through empirical research by the authors, who believe the set of statements can be applied to any service organization. The five dimensions are:

- tangibles (related to appearance of equipment, and so on);
- reliability of performance;
- assurances to customers;
- empathy with customers; and
- responsiveness to customer needs.

Applying SERVQUAL involves asking respondents to: (i) assign weights to each dimension; (ii) rank each service need scale; (iii) rank each service experience scale; and (iv) apply weights and calculate averages to develop mean weighted scores for each dimension and a single SERVQUAL score for a business.

Although a widely cited approach, SERVQUAL has been criticized on several fronts. These include doubts about the authors' claim that service consists of only five dimensions. For example, Freeman and Dart (1993) suggested that service consists of seven dimensions, while Robinson and Pidd (1998) push it to 19 dimensions!

On another front of criticism, Stauss and Weinlich (1997) charged that SERVQUAL does not fully capture customers' service quality perceptions or experiences. In particular, the scales statements reduce complex experiences to a single score. For example, your stay at a

Table 7.2. Example of a questionnaire for train passengers.

	Poor									Excellent
How would you rate our performance on:	**1**	**2**	**3**	**4**	**5**	**6**	**7**	**8**	**9**	**10**
Overall train trip you are having now?										
When you called the reservation office, how was:	**( ) Did not call**									
The quality of information received?										
The quality of service received?										
. . .										
The overall condition and cleanliness of:										
Your car[a] washrooms										
Your car windows										
Your car seating area										
Your dining experience in the dining car?	**( ) Did not use**									
Quality of food?										
Quality of service/										
Atmosphere/ambience?										
Choice of meals?										
Price-value of meals?										
Overall?										
. . .										
	Definitely		**Probably**		**Maybe**		**Probably not**		**Definitely not**	
Based on your experiences today, would you recommend our train service to friends, relatives, and colleagues?										
In the next 3 months:										
How likely are you to make this same trip by any mode of transport?										
How likely is it to be VIA (Rail Canada)?										

[a]Car is used here in the North American sense of the word, i.e. railroad car, or carriage.

resort might have brought you into direct contact with 30 different staff, with some positive, some negative and some neutral interactions. Yet, you have to reduce all 30 interactions to a single score on a single statement. Furthermore, statements such as (using an example of one of the 22 SERVQUAL statements) 'customers at excellent resorts will feel safe in transactions' are so abstract that it is questionable whether they provide any practical insights into customer expectations and experiences at specific tourism businesses.

SERVQUAL is based on calculating differences – gaps – between service needs and experiences. While the individual scale items have been shown to be internally reliable (using Cronbach's alpha), this reliability does not extend to differences between statements (Peter *et al.*, 1993). There are numerous other critiques of limitations in SERVQUAL; Buttle (1996) provides a useful overview of some of these.

As a response to some of the perceived limitations in SERVQUAL, some researchers have proposed alternative models. SERVPERF, developed by Cronin and Taylor (1992), is a measure of quality based on the service performance component of SERVQUAL only. Fogarty *et al.* (2000) found support that SERVPERF's performance statements alone performed better than SERVQUAL's gap approach. They were also able to reduce the 22 performance statements to a 15-statement set that was easier to use. The authors also argued that the five original dimensions might represent stages of a service experience and are not separate dimensions of service quality.

Another approach, SERPVAL ('service personal values'), has been developed by Fernandes and Lages (2002). They related service quality decisions and experiences to higher orders of abstraction – namely, three dimensions: peaceful life, social recognition and social integration. As with the two previous approaches, this tool is based on a series of statements answered on a seven-point Likert scale. An example of a SERPVAL statement is: 'The use of X service allows me to achieve more tranquility' (where X is the particular service being examined).

In addition to being able to develop a reliable set of scales related to personal values as shaped through service consumption, Fernandes and Lages argued that their scale can help managers better understand what shapes consumers' values and perceptions of service. They also suggested their model could be used in benchmarking (see below) the performance of service companies.

Travel behaviour metrics

Travel behaviour metrics refer to variables that describe the number, characteristics and behaviours of visitors. Some of these variables, such as the number of visitors, are basic and most DMOs and some larger attractions collect these in some way. Other variables, such as levels of satisfaction with aspects of the visit, can be useful but are less frequently collected. The potential list of travel behaviour metrics is quite lengthy, but some common ones and typical tactics for collecting the data are shown in Table 7.3.

This type of information supports the development of marketing strategies, including a better understanding of the motivations and behaviours of key market segments. By collecting this information consistently over time, a destination can track trends in key markets, changing demands for various tourism products and experiences, and the performance of various marketing themes or campaigns in terms of visitor levels and spending. Data related to sources of information used by visitors to plan their trip can help the DMO or attraction assess the changing importance of various media and other sources actually used by visitors who have made the decision to visit.

Table 7.3. Common travel behaviour metrics.

Variable	Typical methods for collecting and frequency of collection
Numbers of visitors reported as person-trips, person-nights and/or party-nights	Surveys of registrations at commercial accommodations: continuous Use of secondary data sources collected by national tourism or statistical agency: annual Surveys of visitors to information centres: continuous Border-crossing counts: either original or secondary data sources – continuous Airport arrivals: either original or secondary data sources: continuous
Numbers of visitors by type of trip (same day, overnight, business, pleasure, etc.)	Surveys of registrations at commercial accommodations: continuous Secondary data from national tourism or statistical agency: annual Surveys of visitors to information centres: continuous
Type of accommodation used by visitors, both commercial (various types) as well as private homes and cottages	Surveys of registrations at commercial accommodations: continuous Secondary data from national tourism or statistical agency: annual Surveys of visitors to information centres: continuous Intercept surveys of visitors in destination: seasonal
Motivations or benefits sought by visitors	Secondary data from national tourism or statistical agency: annual Surveys of visitors to information centres: ongoing Intercept surveys of visitors in destination: seasonal
Visitor activities	Secondary data from national tourism or statistical agency: annual Surveys of visitors to information centres: continuous Intercept surveys of visitors in destination: seasonal
Sources of information used to plan trip	Secondary data from national tourism or statistical agency: annual Surveys of visitors to information centres: continuous Intercept surveys of visitors in destination: seasonal
Percentage of visitors making previous visits	Secondary data from national tourism or statistical agency: annual Surveys of visitors to information centres: ongoing Intercept surveys of visitors in destination: seasonal
Satisfaction levels with various aspects of the trip	Secondary data from national tourism or statistical agency: annual Surveys of visitors to information centres: continuous Intercept surveys of visitors in destination: seasonal

SUSTAINABILITY METRICS

The following subsections describe a variety of potential metrics that can be used to assess the sustainability of tourism in a destination. Sustainability is a comprehensive concept involving what is sometimes described as the 'triple bottom line': economic impacts, environmental impacts and social impacts. The development of sustainable tourism thus involves balancing all thee forms of impacts in a broader policy or planning context in which the objectives of tourism development are spelled out. For the sake of clarity, we will look at each component of tourism sustainability – economy, environment and society – separately. For further information on sustainability indicators, you can check out the work of two pioneering sources, the International Working Group on Indicators of Sustainable Tourism (1993) and McGillivray and Zadek (1995).

Economic impact metrics

Economic impacts are the *raison d'être* for government support of tourism and for entrepreneurs to start tourism businesses. The following briefly describes some basic metrics related to economic impacts.

A fundamental measure of economic impact is the value of **visitor spending**, usually reported on a quarterly or annual basis. Data on visitor spending are typically gathered through one of the following types of visitor surveys. As you will read, each has limitations. The validity of spending estimates can be somewhat improved by asking respondents, regardless of the type of survey you choose, to report their spending by specific categories such as accommodation, food from restaurants, food from grocery stores, recreation and entertainment, local transportation (such as taxis), gas and oil for a private car while in the destination, and gifts and souvenirs. The specific categories should, of course, reflect the nature of the destination and the activities in which visitors typically engage.

On-site surveys: visitors are contacted during their time on site and asked about their spending. This approach often is done when an exit survey (see below) or at-home survey (also below) would be difficult to implement. Response rates tend to be fairly good if the interviewer is properly trained, keeps the interview very short and selects people at times when they are not in a rush. However, on-site surveys require the respondent to estimate both past and future spending on the trip. Forecasts of spending are quite unreliable and thus this approach should be used only when spending patterns are simple and of low value, such as those associated with attendance at a parade.

Exit surveys: people leaving a destination are interviewed as they depart for home. Response rates are fairly good, although typically lower than for on-site interviews because people are more likely to be in a rush to go home. This approach requires that you be able to intercept visitors as they leave, which can easily be done for a gated attraction such as a theme park or museum. However, it is much more difficult to do for an entire city. Exit interviews are sometimes done in airport, bus or train lounges, but this gives you access only to people travelling by one of those modes of transportation. Exit interviews also depend on the person's memory. Spending on the last day of a trip might be fairly well recalled, but spending for earlier days becomes successively unreliable. Not only will visitors have imperfect memories, but many will not have paid much attention to how much they spent on individual items, especially for inexpensive items. More costly expenditures such as accommodation will probably be remembered better, but may still not be recalled precisely unless the person has to file a travel claim. In practice, exit expenditure surveys usually yield only rough estimates expressed only as rounded numbers.

Travel diaries: some researchers have experimented with travel diaries in which the respondent records spending as it occurs. This gives the most reliable estimates of spending. However, the diary method is onerous for the respondent. In particular, it is difficult to recruit participants without a substantial incentive. Even then, the drop-out rate from such a travel diary survey is high. Moreover, the process of having to record each expenditure may change the subject's spending habits.

At-home surveys: if you've been able to collect names and addresses of visitors, perhaps from brief on-site surveys or registration records, you might send them a mail-back survey or an online survey. This distribution tactic tends to generate a low response, only 15–20%. Moreover, because of the passage of time between the trip and when the respondent receives your questionnaire, the quality of recall will have deteriorated. As a rule-of-thumb, mail-back surveys should not be used more than 1 month after the completion of a trip.

There is a large literature on visitor expenditure surveys; just two of these are the following. Leeworthy *et al.* (2001) described some methods for correcting some of the response biases in visitor expenditure estimates. Pelaez *et al.* (2003) presented an innovative tool for estimating local visitor spending using data derived from visitors staying in commercial accommodation. Other economic impact metrics that often are of interest, especially to governments, are the following:

Government revenues attributable to tourism: governments get money from tourism through a variety of ways, such as taxes on incomes (both personal employment earnings and business profits), contributions to social insurance plans (health insurance, unemployment insurance, workers compensation funds), taxes on production and products (sales and property taxes), and from sales of government goods and services (development charges, admissions to government-run attractions). Direct calculation of government revenues attributable to tourism usually requires sophisticated accounting procedures and access to confidential information. An example of this approach can be found in Statistics Canada (2007), in which the calculations were conducted by staff with security clearances working in the Income and Accounts Division. Their method can be a model for other national statistical agencies, but is not practical for independent researchers.

Other estimates of government revenues have been developed through simulation models that can be used by other researchers. One example from Canada is the online economic impact model, Tourism Regional Economic Impact Model (TREIM), operated by the Ontario Ministry of Tourism (2008). This model is based on an input–output model of the provincial economy, and is available to anyone who wishes to use it. The Ministry particularly encourages its use by event organizers seeking government grants, because it provides a consistent and known methodology for estimating anticipated economic benefits of events. In addition to government revenues, TREIM also provides estimates of contributions to GDP (see next) and job creation. Government agencies in other jurisdictions have sometimes developed their own models, so you should make some enquiries about options.

Gross Domestic Product (GDP): GDP is a measure of the size of an entire economy (typically a national economy, although provincial or sub-provincial GDPs can also be calculated if data are available). The GDP generated by individual industries can also be calculated, such as for tourism industries. Tourism GDP is a measure of the net new wealth created by the range of private sector tourism services. Simplistically, it can be thought of as the difference between the total revenues from the sale of tourism services and the costs of producing those services. In other words, it represents the value-added figure of those services.

The calculation of GDP involves sophisticated analysis and extensive data sources. An example based on the accommodation industry will illustrate the types of data required. You begin by collecting data from a sample of firms on their expenditures for wages, salaries and benefits paid to employees. You also need to get an estimate of the costs of all the services and goods the hotel consumes in the course of its operations. These would run from the cost of utilities to insurance, from laundry and dish soap to bottled water to fine wines. Details of fees and royalties paid to investors and the government must be obtained too. Data related to the total revenues generated are also required.

The GDP is calculated basically by subtracting the costs of the various inputs, fees, taxes and other payments (except for wages and salaries) from total revenues to obtain GDP 'at factor cost' (roughly equivalent to the value-added figure). The actual calculations are detailed and will vary by the nature of the economy in which the accommodation industry operates. Thus GDP calculations are not normally undertaken by researchers working outside a provincial or national statistical agency, unless a simulation model, such as TREIM, is available.

Job creation: tourism spending provides revenues that support payrolls. Job creation is often a particularly important objective for governments to promote tourism, especially in areas where other industries are in decline or have never developed. Tourism-supported jobs are found not only in tourism industries (e.g. accommodation, transportation, food and beverage) but also in non-tourism industries such as the retail trade. These jobs cover a wide range of skills, from basic frontline positions such as ticket sellers and hotel housekeepers to professional positions such as airline pilots and hotel general managers. Tourism jobs are part-time as well as full-time, and seasonal as well as permanent positions.

Environmental impact metrics

Interest in the relationship between tourism and the biophysical environment dates from the 1960s. Over the years, a rich collection of environmental indicators has been developed reflecting the complexity of the natural environment. Literally thousands of indicators for various aspects of the natural environment are possible. Thus, one of the challenges in assessing tourism's environmental impact is to articulate clearly the scope of any study in order to choose the most relevant environmental indicators. Moreover, one also has to be cognizant of the budget and resources required to compile a set of indicators. You need to be able to collect data for your indicators on a continuing basis. One-off measures are of little value. Generally, a smaller number of indicators that can be monitored consistently over time are preferable to a large set of indicators that are measured only once.

There are even more fundamental issues that make the selection of environmental metrics challenging. Hughes (2002) reviews some of the key difficulties. The first is the question of scale, both temporal and spatial. Some environmental impacts may take years or decades to become apparent. Thus, a system of indicators needs to be capable of providing time-series data to reveal trends. Environmental impacts also can be widespread. Hughes gives the example of coral reefs far offshore that can be damaged by changes in mangrove cover along a coastline, and of the development of resorts on one island that result in the blasting of coral reefs for aggregate kilometres away. At an even larger scale, the effects of air pollution can spread for hundreds, even thousands, of kilometres. Developing an accurate profile of the causes and effects of environmental impacts can involve much more than a singular, site-specific study.

Some ecosystems are characterized by short-term natural perturbations. Wildlife populations, for example, can show dramatic fluctuations year to year due to both natural as well as anthropogenic (man-made) causes. While techniques for monitoring the size of wildlife populations are relatively well established, ascertaining the effects of tourism activity as a cause for those changes can be challenging.

The choice of indicators may reflect subjective values on the part of the researchers developing the indicators. Because, as we noted, thousands of indicators are possible, choices must be made. The choices typically reflect human values – especially those of the researchers. For example, impacts on air and water quality will probably receive high attention since people relate strongly to these issues because, in turn, they intuitively understand these conditions affect their quality of life. More obscure impacts, such as changes in biodiversity of insects in a remote biome, however, may be of less interest. Changes in the size of the population of large and cute mammals, such as pandas or seals, will also probably generate much more attention than changes in less photogenic species such as insects or arthropods, even though the latter might be a more useful indicator of ecosystem health.

Although most environmental indictors will be empirical in the sense that they are independently observable and verifiable, the interpretation of the meaning of changes is subject to legitimate differences in expert interpretation. These differences may reflect conclusions drawn from different sites, at different times or results obtained through the use of different techniques.

Environmental metrics may be developed at different scales, such as site-specific or at a national level depending on the scope of your interest. Table 7.4 provides a few examples of national-level environmental indicators. Note that most of these are not specific to tourism impacts. They include both empirical indicators related to environmental quality generally as well as the existence and practice of environmental planning and protection processes.

Table 7.5 suggests examples of site-specific indicators. Some of these are identical to the national indicators, except for the fact they are collected at a local level. Different types of sites would have more specific indicators, such as the percentage of a coral reef that has been bleached, or the extent of poaching in a wildlife preserve. One might also supplement these specific variables with inventories of local legislation or planning/design processes that promote environmentally friendly development.

A couple of examples of studies to help you get introduced to this large body of literature and that might be available in your college or university's library are Butler (1993) and Ding and Pigram (1995). Mason (2003) provides a good overview of both environmental and social impacts, and Wilson (2008) offers a combined look at social and economic impacts.

Table 7.4. Examples of national environmental indicators.

National environmental indicators	Percentage of national territory as protected land or water spaces Number of endangered species, and estimated population levels Consumption levels of water, energy resources Consumption of inorganic fertilizers Solid waste production Total CO, CO_2, O_3, NO_x, SO_2 emission levels (by sector if possible) Percentage of homes, hotels, businesses connected to sewage systems Existence and implementation of environmental review legislation Existence and implementation of environmental planning guidelines Existence and implementation of sustainable tourism policies

Table 7.5. Examples of site-specific environmental indicators.

Site-specific environmental indicators	Percentage of site that appears untouched by human activity Degree of fragmentation of natural areas Measures of visual alteration such as forest clear-cutting Number of wildfires Number of endangered species, and estimated population levels Consumption of inorganic fertilizers Energy consumption levels (electricity, petroleum products) Solid waste production Percentage of waterways (lake areas, river lengths) assessed as having 'good' water quality Water pollution levels by key locations (chemical waste, bacterial concentrations) Local air quality (e.g. percentage of days having pollutant levels above a specified threshold) Presence of invasive species Percentage of land area (or trails) having impacted soils Degree of soil erosion Vehicular traffic counts Pedestrian traffic counts Visitor satisfaction and crowding measures Visitor/community conflicts Problematic visitor/wildlife encounters Loss of outlook or viewpoints through development Sunlight restrictions

Social impact metrics

Interest in the social impacts of tourism emerged as a significant academic topic in the late 1970s, more recently than interest in environmental impacts. Smith's classic anthology, *Hosts and Guests* (Smith, 1977), is sometimes viewed as the seminal work for this line of research. However, scholars had written on the social impacts (as well as the sociology) of tourism since 1899 (Cohen, 1984). None the less, metrics for tracking social impacts are much less established and less systematized than those for economic or environmental indicators. This reflects the complexity and diversity of social impacts, as well as the fact that many social changes attributed to tourism may have more complex origins than just tourism. Tourism development often occurs simultaneously with modernization or broader development trends that have nothing to do with tourism. Thus, the impacts of tourism, per se, can be difficult, if not impossible, to measure precisely.

Social impacts can be classified as either macro – those that can be tracked through broad social statistics – or micro – those experienced or perceived directly by individual residents of a destination. Social impacts may also be either communal or personal. Communal impacts refer to those that reflect broad community patterns or conditions and that are usually empirically measured through official statistics. Traffic congestion or crime rates are a couple of examples of communal impacts. As with other indicators, while the magnitude of communal impacts can be measured, being able to prove a causal link with tourism may be difficult. Communal social impacts also may overlap with economic impacts. For example, the creation of jobs is usually considered to be an economic impact but job creation, especially for women, can be an indicator of empowerment for women who have never worked outside the home.

Personal impacts refer to the perceptions of individuals of some aspect of tourism development. These metrics are normally obtained through the use of methods such as surveys of community residents or content analyses of newspaper stories on tourism. Although these measures concern feelings and perceptions rather than some non-personal 'objective' social phenomena, these impacts should not be ignored or dismissed as unimportant or not real. They can result in powerful and empirically measurable reactions, such as protests against developers or voters ousting pro-tourism officials. A complicating factor with personal impact metrics, though, is that the perceptions of impacts can be contaminated by media or public discussions. There is always a chance that someone's reaction to tourism may not be a function of that person's own experiences, but shaped by what he or she hears or reads.

As with environmental impact metrics, a single, one-time measure, even if cross-sectional across a number of communities, is not likely to be very useful. It is important to be able to track changes over time, whether using a longitudinal research design or historical records.

Social impacts, as with environmental impacts, are not necessarily negative. For example, tourism can help stimulate revival of a local culture, contribute to the creation of new cultural institutions such as a museum or promote interest in education in order to take advantage of new employment or business opportunities generated by tourism.

The potential range of social impact metrics also is quite broad. Your choice of which to use will be a function of the specific situation you are monitoring, as well as available sources. Some of these data sources may be documents from governments or other organizations; others will require original data collection such as surveys of residents or content analyses of local media stories. Tables 7.6 and 7.7 suggest some metrics for social impact assessment. As noted

Table 7.6. Examples of communal social impact metrics.

General issue	Possible indicators
Congestion	Traffic volumes Travel times Parking tickets
Public safety	Level and changes in various categories of crimes (theft, violence, drug-related, prostitution, etc.) – ideally reported on the basis of whether the perpetrator is a local resident or a visitor, although this Information is rarely available Rise in 'neighbourhood watch' associations over time Trends in family abuse reports
Community evolution	Changes in numbers and types of community groups Level of volunteer participation, especially for festivals and events Shifts in demographic profiles Levels of in- and out-migration Changes in property values by neighbourhood
Education	School attendance levels Graduation rates Enrolment in language classes (especially if the visitors from the dominant origin market do not speak the local language)

(*Continued*)

Table 7.6. Continued.

General issue	Possible indicators
Cultural and heritage protection	Number and funding levels of cultural and heritage institutions Preservation and renovations of built heritage Participation in traditional art forms such as performing arts or crafts Emergence of new art forms Changes in culinary practices (styles of cooking, preferred foods)
Health	Incidence of sexually transmitted diseases Disease outbreaks attributable to visitors Changes in levels of obesity, especially among children Alcoholism and drug use Changes in quality of sanitation facilities (water, sewerage) Establishment of health-care facilities

Table 7.7. Examples of personal social impact metrics.

General issue	Possible Indicators based on resident surveys
Attitudes toward visitors	Recreation and cultural opportunities created by tourism Perception of economic impacts (e.g. job creation, pay levels in tourism businesses) due to tourism Crime rates attributable to the presence of visitors (either visitors as perpetrators or as attracting criminals to prey on visitors) Rowdy or disruptive behaviour, especially during festivals and events, or peak season Crowding of parks, beaches and other facilities due to visitor levels Perceptions of loss of privacy
Costs of tourism	Impacts of tourism development on local governmental budgets, e.g. whether too much money is spent on tourism development and not enough on needs of residents Impact of tourism on local prices
Community attitudes	Whether being a tourism destination instils a sense of pride in residents Whether being a tourism destination makes the community more attractive to new residents, business investment Level of voting support for candidates supporting/opposing tourism development Content analysis of letters to local newspapers or of calls to radio talk shows
Environment	Littering attributable to visitors Pollution attributable to tourism development Damage to natural areas attributable to tourism development or visitation levels

(Continued)

Table 7.7. Continued.

General issue	Possible Indicators based on resident surveys
Cultural and heritage protection	Impacts of tourism on protection of built heritage Impacts of tourism on local arts and crafts Whether tourism has changed the nature or cultural character of the community
Infrastructure	Improvements/changes in impacts of tourism on water, sanitation, transportation systems Changes in shopping, dining, cultural, recreational, sport opportunities attributable to tourism
Equity	Distribution of benefits, such as jobs, across the community (social groups, neighbourhoods) Distribution of costs imposed by tourism across the community (social groups, neighbourhoods)

before, though, caution must be exercised in attributing changes in any of these metrics to the presence of visitors in a community.

Even more so than for environmental impacts, social impact researchers do not agree on which indicators are the most important or on how data should be collected. Looking at the debates, Burdge (1999) argued that it is more important to be sensitive to social impacts than to worry about precisely identifying or measuring them. This observation has its merits, although as noted at the outset of this chapter, if one cannot measure something, it cannot be managed. While recognizing the limits and challenges in conducting social impact assessments is important, it is still important to make the effort to monitor relevant social changes as accurately as possible and to ensure that real problems are recognized and addressed by planners, developers and officials.

A couple of examples of social impact studies that might be available in your college or university library are Ap (1990) and Fan and Bao (1996). As noted above, Mason (2003) provides a good overview of both environmental and social impacts, and Wilson (2008) offers a combined look at social and economic impacts.

BENCHMARKING

Many of the metrics we have looked at in this chapter can be incorporated into a process known as benchmarking. Basically, benchmarking is a tool used by corporations and sometimes other organizations, such as DMOs, either to compare their operations to industry norms or, more generally, to identify best practices to improve the quality of their operations or products. The term 'benchmark' dates from 1842, when it denoted incised marks in rock that surveyors used to measure elevation. The term now is applied more widely to refer to a standard of performance or quality.

Benchmarking as a quality management process was first associated with Xerox in the 1980s. Xerox initiated what it called a 'competitive benchmarking process'. That corporation was losing market share to Japanese firms that were producing copiers of equal or superior quality at lower cost. Xerox engineers obtained competitors' machines and disassembled them to learn about their features and construction. They also studied Japanese manufacturing and business processes to identify how their competitors managed to keep costs low. This practice eventually became part of the corporate culture at Xerox, and was described in a landmark book by a Xerox engineer, Robert Camp (1989).

Benchmarking has now become well established in many industries. There are numerous types of benchmarking; we will look at two that are arguably the most common in tourism. Be aware, though, that this brief discussion is only a quick overview of this important topic.

Sectoral benchmarking is done by an industry association or government agency to produce industry averages (for example, for the accommodation, attractions, food services, transportation industries) of different business measures, particularly various financial ratios. It is essential, of course, that anyone developing sectoral benchmarks has a thorough understanding of what metrics are the most important for assessing business performance. Spending time and money to collect the wrong metrics is not only wasteful, but the wrong metrics can cause a business to overlook critical information that could warn the business if it is headed into bankruptcy. Some categories of sectoral benchmark metrics include:

- Operational efficiency: the percentage of operational budgets spent on marketing, wages and salaries, maintenance, insurance and so on.
- Industry-specific metrics: data specific to operations of businesses in different industries.

  A few examples include:
  - accommodations: occupancy rates and RevPAR;
  - airlines: load factors, revenue-passenger-miles, arrival or departure delays and number of lost bags;
  - restaurants: percentage of customers who are repeats, staff turnover, table-turn rates and average cheque size; and
  - attractions: attendance by paying customers on a daily or weekly basis, or percentage of seats occupied by paying audience members for shows and concerts.
- Liquidity performance: the degree to which a business has enough cash to pay day-to-day operating expenses and to retire debt on schedule.
- Debt coverage: measures that reflect the extent a business or industry may be overextended in debt, or the proportion of debt to equity.
- Asset management: metrics that reflect productivity, such as average collection period in days, accounts receivable turnover, inventory turnover and the ratio of daily sales to inventory.
- Profitability: measures reflecting efficiency and effectiveness of business practices, such as gross margins on sales, income after taxes, return on total assets and return on invested capital.

Sectoral benchmarking is particularly common in tourism because it provides information that is essential when analysing one's financial statements. It also provides data that you can use when applying for bank loans or approaching potential investors by showing how your firm's performance compares with that of your industry's averages.

Competitive or performance benchmarking involves comparing your business's products and services as well as performance against those of your competitors. This type of benchmarking usually begins with a review of publicly available information such as the range and price of various services (published hotel room rates, or the content and prices of tour packages). If a company issues public stockholder reports, these reports can also provide useful insights into its performance.

Business owners or managers may also visit their competitors' businesses to observe product ranges, layouts of public spaces, hotel room amenities, new rides being operated at amusement parks, items for sale and price points in gift shops, menu items and prices in restaurants, and service quality (perhaps by posing as a customer).

Firms may also hire strategic consultants who are well versed in the performance of other firms to provide insights into how your firm's performance compares with your competitors. There are anecdotal reports of tourism firms hiring private detectives to search through the dumpsters of rivals to look for copies of financial statements. This practice may or may not be illegal, depending on the location of the garbage. If it is still on private property, in most jurisdictions the search would be illegal. However, if the garbage is in a bin in an alley or left at the kerb, it may be legal – subject to the specific laws of the jurisdiction.

Beyond this, illegal industrial espionage for the purposes of benchmarking is not unknown in tourism. For example, in 2003–2004, an employee at one Canadian air carrier used a password he obtained while working at a rival carrier to tap into a website of the rival 243,630 times between May 2003 and March 2004. He downloaded confidential operational data to allow the competitor to anticipate its rival's moves in the market, such as planning new routes. The matter was eventually settled out of court when executives at the accused carrier admitted that the practice had occurred and negotiated a financial settlement.

The basic procedures in doing a competitive or performance benchmarking exercises are:

1. **Understand your objectives for doing benchmarking**. If you believe you have one or more areas of operational weakness, explicitly identify the aspects of your business that need attention. For example, are you concerned about losing market share, rising costs or high staff turnover? If you are starting a new business, you will want to look at the key strengths and weaknesses of potential competitors or other tourism businesses that might provide valuable lessons.
2. **Identify the key metrics or practices that will guide your evaluation**. This is a critical step. As we've noted, the choice of the wrong metrics or practices to examine can doom the whole benchmarking exercise to failure, as well as waste your time and money. Benchmarking is a time-consuming process and, initially, can be expensive (although costs tend to drop as the practice becomes more routine). The processes you will examine will, of course, be specific to your own circumstances, but they may include:

- research;
- product development;
- marketing;
- pricing;
- human resource management;
- reservation systems;
- operations; and
- applications.

3. **Identify other businesses that have similar processes**. Businesses in your industry would be logical choices, of course, but you should also consider examples from other industries. For example, if you are working with a passenger rail line and are trying to improve the efficiency of your cleaning crew, you might talk with some airlines about how they deploy their crews to clean passenger aircraft. If you have long lines for special exhibits at your museum, you may want to look at how theme parks deal with queuing.

4. Identify industry leaders, including potential competitors. You may have some ideas already, based on your own experience and reading of trade publications, of who the potential leaders with best practices in your industry might be. Also consult with executives from trade associations, financial analysts, suppliers and customers about whom they see to be leaders.

5. Collect data on best practices. Check out information on your selected businesses that is publicly available. Make on-site visits, where feasible, to observe practices. You might also contact executives of the companies you wish to study and ask to interview them. If they are direct competitors, they may not be very open to your questions. As a result, some firms hire an independent consultant or work with an industry association to collect data. The use of a neutral third-party consultant or industry association protects your identity and the third party can mask sensitive information or the name of the firms interviewed to ensure confidentiality of the data. Sometimes a group of companies can agree to share information in a benchmarking group, which is then shared among all members of the group for their mutual benefit.

6. Implement your findings. Use the best practices you have identified and incorporate the lessons you learned from these into your organization. This typically involves enlisting the support of other executives in your firm to support your proposed changes. Develop a realistic estimate of the costs of your changes and identify how your recommendations will add value to your firm's practices.

Pyo (2001) has compiled an edited volume of benchmarking studies in a variety of hospitality and tourism settings. Wöber (2002) has written a book on benchmarking in hospitality and tourism, as well. Wöber's book is a difficult read because of the density of information he provides. However, it does contain excellent advice on this complex topic and is a good source if you want to explore benchmarking in depth.

LEADING INDICATORS

All of the previous metrics and indicators share a common limitation: all are based on historical data. They reflect events that have already occurred. Such a focus, of course, is appropriate for monitoring how well your business or destination has performed in the past, but decision makers and planners also want information on the future. Some of these trends can be estimated through the use of forecasting models. A couple of useful sources on forecasting in tourism are Witt and Witt (1992), Frechtling (2001) and Wong and Song (2002). However, in most cases, forecasting models also are built on historical data, using statistical techniques to extrapolate historical patterns into the future.

Another approach to understanding emerging development is to use leading indicators. A leading indicator is an empirical measure that may presage a change in some phenomenon of interest because of a presumed causal connection. In practice, the term 'leading indicators' is used in two different ways. The first is in econometric modelling, in which a series of statistical measures, usually related to economic trends, are used to forecast some future level of tourism activity. An example of this approach in the hotel sector is that of Choi (2003). Choi examined 32 economic data series representing potential leading, concurrent and lagging indicators of turning points in the aggregate health of the hotel industry sector in the USA. The leading indicators included measures such as a US stock exchange index, a measure of US money supply and inflation rates for vehicle fuel. He developed an econometric model that produced reasonably reliable results in forecasting upturns and downturns in the health of the US hotel industry.

However, the concept of leading indicators is also applied to a simpler, non-econometric approach that can be more readily used by tourism managers and marketers. For example, the number of reservations for the following 3 months held by a sample of hotels in some destination at the start of summer, in comparison with the same time a year previously, may give an indication of whether overall levels of guest numbers – and, by extension, the total number of visitors to a destination – will be up, down or stable. This sort of comparison with previous seasons is a simple tool that a manager can employ in her/his own business. Alternatively, a DMO can collect such data, aggregate them to protect confidential information and then publish indices for the local tourism sector to use.

In the case of hotel reservations, the causal connection with actual room sales is direct and reliable, although some reservations may be cancelled and other people may just walk in without a reservation. Yet other indicators have a less direct connection with trends in tourism business levels, but still can be useful in judging whether the following season's tourism levels will be better or worse. Some examples of leading tourism indicators include:

- changes in seat capacity for airlines serving a destination;
- numbers of cruises scheduled for a given port;
- toll-free or e-mail enquiries to a destination regarding travel information;
- trends in visits to a destination's website;
- spending on tourism advertising;
- demand for fam tours by travel journalists or tour operators;
- stories published in newspapers and magazines about a specific destination;
- awareness levels of the destination in key markets; and
- travel intention surveys.

None of these provides precise forecasts of actual volumes of visitors or visitor spending but, when tracked over time, they can help alert destination managers and marketers to potential problems, or offer some tentative indication of how well their marketing efforts are succeeding. Moreover, such forward-looking information can be useful in terms of anticipating the need to change staffing levels at tourism facilities or making other adjustments to hours of operations.

The use of leading indicators is not without risks. The greatest one, of course, is that predictions based on them turn out to be false. To keep the use of indicators in a properly humble perspective, it is useful to recall a quotation by Paul Samuelson, a Noble laureate in economics. In looking at the history of the use of leading indicators, particularly trends in US stock markets to warn of an impending recession, Samuelson observed: '[t]o prove that Wall Street is an early omen of movements still to come in GNP, commentators quote economic studies alleging that market downturns predicted four out of the last five recessions. That is an understatement. Wall Street indexes predicted nine out of the last five recessions!' (Samuelson, 1966). In other words, in the cases Samuelson examined, the leading indicators based on the US stock market predicted four recessions that never happened.

CONCLUSIONS

This chapter has introduced a number of measurement tools that support policy, marketing or organizational decision making. The applications of these tools include planning – which is forward-looking – and monitoring or assessment – which are historical perspectives. Many of the tools can also assist with forecasting, setting management priorities and policy analysis.

The tools represent a broad spectrum of methodologies. At one end are direct numerical measures, such as the number of people visiting a destination through airport arrivals data, or budgets allocated to advertising in different media in different markets. Still numerical, but less direct, are visitor expenditure estimates and economic impact estimates such as contributions to GDP or jobs created. At the other end of the spectrum are subjective measures, such as supervisor evaluations of employees or the contents of guest evaluation cards and surveys.

Most of the metrics we considered have challenges or limitations. In some cases, such as estimating economic impacts, the primary challenge is obtaining reliable and valid data. In the case of service quality metrics, there is still substantial debate about what is actually being measured, as well as about the conceptual model on which the tool is based. There are also questions about the statistical reliability of some scales used to collect data. Environmental impact metrics constitute a set of literally thousands of variables, so choices need to be made about which are the most important for any given setting. Moreover, environmental impacts may occur over long periods of time or over substantial distances. This can greatly complicate the logistics of developing monitoring systems. Environmental impacts can be tracked at different scales, from site-specific to international.

Social impact metrics also comprise a large set of potential variables, including community-level empirical metrics as well as subjective, personal measures. In comparison with economic and environmental impact methods, social impact methodology is younger and enjoys less consensus among researchers. However, social impacts are arguably even more politically important in many communities than other impacts, especially in communities where the visitors come from very different social backgrounds to residents.

We also briefly looked at the concept of benchmarking, noting that this tool has a couple of connotations. The first is the comparison of a firm's performance (usually financial) with industry averages. The second is the examination of 'best practices' at other firms – possibly but not necessarily competitors – to help a firm improve its operations or services. Benchmarking is still a relatively new concept in tourism, although it is rapidly gaining attention as businesses realize its potential contribution to improve performance and competitiveness.

The indicators presented in this chapter can be very helpful in supporting planning, marketing, policy analysis and decision making in a business or DMO. However, it is important to choose the tools wisely and, especially, the specific variables to consider when taking decisions. It also is essential to understand the strengths and weaknesses of the tools you choose.

A tactic that can be helpful in presenting trends in indicators is to develop a 'dashboard' – an analogy to the dashboard of a car that presents the driver with a quick graphic synopsis of key performance measures of the car performance, such as speed, fuel and engine temperature. Check out Focus Box 7.2 for more information on the use of dashboards in tourism marketing.

In the final analysis, all these tools can offer valuable support to help you make a good decision, but they should not replace your own critical insights and reflections, especially as you gain deeper practical experience. Tools are to be used, but they cannot replace the intelligence, intuition and experience of a knowledgeable decision maker.

REFERENCES

Ap, J. (1990) Residents' perceptions research on the social impacts of tourism. *Annals of Tourism Research* 17, 610–616.

Burdge, R. (1999) *A Community Guide to Social Impact Assessment: Revised Edition*. Social Ecology Press, Middleton, Wisconsin.

Butler, R. (1993) Pre- and post-impact assessment of tourism development. In: Pearce, D. and Butler, R. (eds) *Tourism Research: Critiques and Challenges*. Routledge, London, pp. 135–155.

Buttle, F. (1996) SERVQUAL: review, critique, research agenda. *European Journal of Marketing* 30, 8–31.

Camp, R. (1989) Benchmarking: the search for industry best practices that lead to superior performance. ASQC Quality Resources, Milwaukee, Wisconsin.

Choi, J.G. (2003) Developing an economic indicator system (a forecasting technique) for the hotel industry. *International Journal of Hospitality Management* 22, 147–159.

Cohen, E. (1984) The sociology of tourism: approaches, issues, and findings. *Annual Review of Sociology* 10, 373–392.

Cronin, J. and Taylor, S. (1992) Measuring service quality: a re-examination and extension. *Journal of Marketing* 56, 55–68.

Ding, P. and Pigram, J. (1995) Environmental audits: an emerging concept in sustainable tourism development. *Journal of Tourism Studies* 6(2), 2–10.

Fan, D. and Bao, J. (1996) The social impacts of tourism – a case study in Dali, Yunnan Province, China. *Chinese Geographical Science* 6, 132–144.

Fernandes, J. and Lages, L. (2002) *The SERPVAL Scale: a Multi-item Scale for Measuring Service Personal Values*. Working Paper 423, Faculdade de Economia da Universidade Nova de Lisboa, Lisbon.

Fogarty, G. Catts, R. and Forlin, C. (2000). Identifying shortcomings in the measurement of service quality. *Journal of Outcome Measurement* 4, 425–447.

Frechtling, D. (2001) *Forecasting Tourism Demand, Methods, and Strategies*. Butterworth Heinemann, Oxford, UK.

Freeman, K. and Dart, J. (1993) Measuring the perceived quality of professional business services. *Journal of Professional Services Marketing* 9, 27–47.

Hughes, G. (2002) Environmental indictors. *Annals of Tourism Research* 29, 457–477.

International Working Group on Indictors of Sustainable Tourism (1993) *Indicators for the Sustainable Management of Tourism*. International Institute for Sustainable Development, Winnipeg, Manitoba.

Leeworthy, V., Wiley, C., English, D. and Kriesel, W. (2001) Correcting response bias in tourist spending surveys. *Annals of Tourism Research* 28, 83–97.

Mason, P. (2003) *Tourism Impacts, Planning, and Management*. Butterworth-Heinemann, Oxford, UK.

McGillivray, A. and Zadek, S. (1995) *Accounting for Change: Indicators for Sustainable Development*. New Economics Foundation, London.

Morrison, E. (1996) Organizational citizenship behavior as a critical link between HRM practices and service quality. *Human Resource Management* 35, 493–512.

Ontario Ministry of Tourism (2008) Tourism regional economic impact model. Available at: http://www.tourism.gov.on.ca/english/research/treim/index.html (accessed 27 May 2008).

Parasuraman, A., Berry, V. and Zeithaml, L. (1988) SERVQUAL: a multiple-item scale for measuring customer perceptions of service quality. *Journal of Retailing* 64, 12–40.

Pelaez, L.V., de la Ballina, J., Conejo, R.A., Fernandez, E.L., Manzaneda, E.T., Estébanez, J.M. *et al*. (2003) A methodology to measure tourism expenditure and total tourism production at the regional level. In: Lennon, J. (ed.) *Tourism Statistics*. Continuum, London, pp. 317–334.

Peter, J., Chruchill, G. and Brown, T. (1993) Caution in the use of difference scores in consumer research. *Journal of Consumer Research* 19, 655–662.

Pyo, S. (2001) (ed.) *Benchmarks in Hospitality and Tourism*. Haworth Press, New York. Also published as *Journal of Quality Assurance in Hospitality and Tourism* 2(3/4) (2001).

Robinson, S. and Pidd, M. (1998) Provider and customer expectations of successful simulation projects. *Journal of the Operational Research Society* 49, 200–209.

Samuelson, P. (1966) Science and stocks. *Newsweek* (12) September 1988, 20.

Schneider, B. and Bowen, D. (1993) The service organization: human resource management is crucial. *Organizational Dynamics* 21, 39–52.

Smith, S. (1994) The tourism product. *Annals of Tourism Research* 21, 582–595.

Smith, V. (1977) (ed.) *Hosts and Guests: the Anthropology of Tourism*. University of Pennsylvania Press, Philadelphia, Pennsylvania.

Statistics Canada (2007) *Government Revenue Attributable to Tourism, 2000 to 2006*, Cat 13-604-MIE. Statistics Canada, Ottawa, Ontario.

Stauss, B. and Weinlich, B. (1997) Process-oriented measurement of service quality applying the sequential incident technique. *European Journal of Marketing* 31(1), 33–55.

Tonge, J., Moore, S., Hockings, M., Worboys, G. and Bridle, K. (2005) *Developing Indicators for the Sustainable Management of Visitor Use of Protected Areas of Australia*. Sustainable Tourism Co-operative Research Centre, Griffith University, Queensland.

Wilson, A. (1988) The use of mystery shopping in the measurement of service delivery. *The Service Industries Journal* 18(3),148–163.

Wilson, T. (2008) Economic and social impacts of tourism in Mexico. *Latin American Perspectives* 35(3), 37–52.

Witt, S.F. and Witt, C.A. (1992) *Modeling and Forecasting Demand in Tourism*. Academic Press, London.

Wöber, K. (2002) *Benchmarking in Tourism and Hospitality Industries: the Selection of Benchmarking Partners*. CABI, Wallingford, UK.

Wong, K.F. and Song, H. (2002) *Tourism Forecasting and Marketing*. Haworth Press, New York.

chapter 8

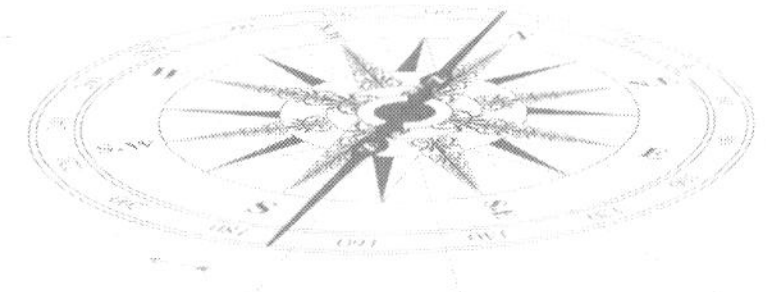

How to Do Case Studies

WHY THIS IS IMPORTANT

Case study is a well-established method in many disciplines and is increasingly popular in tourism studies. Despite – or perhaps because of its popularity and multiple applications – the term, 'case study' can be ambiguous. Part of the reason is that 'case study' is used in fundamentally different contexts. As just one immediate example, this book (and many others) presents brief illustrations of real-world situations as a 'case study' (see, for example, the case study in Chapter 1).

The more common applications of case studies are as either: (i) a pedagogical (teaching) tool; or (ii) a research tool. Case studies as teaching tools are perhaps most often used in medicine, law and business. Medical and law professors use case studies (sometimes calling them case histories or case books) to help their students learn how to solve problems. Through case studies, students learn what did or did not work in situations that they normally could never experience as students. Furthermore, case studies give students the opportunity to observe how practising professionals sort through complex evidence to define a problem and identify the central issue in a complex case. Students can also, through reading and discussion, learn how a diagnosis was made or how a legal strategy in a court case was developed, what information the professional identified as important and how that information was obtained and used.

In legal studies, cases help law students learn the logic and subtleties of the practice of law, how to interpret court rulings and how to create a persuasive case. Legal case studies, in effect, allow a student to observe how lawyers build and present cases and how judges make decisions. Legal case studies represent both successful prosecutions and successful defences, and the student can observe the logic and presentation of evidence and argument leading to a particular outcome. In medical school, case studies begin with details about a patient and his/her symptoms. The case study then describes tests done and other observations made by a physician and perhaps by nurses and technicians, and how a course of treatment was decided upon. Finally, the case usually presents the results of treatment and any changes in treatment that may have been needed. All this helps students learn how to gather evidence, sort through sometimes conflicting or misleading observations and prescribe a course of action such as medication or surgery.

In both medical and legal contexts, case studies usually are historical descriptions that present the story of how a problem was analysed and resolved (although not always positively if the patient died or the client was convicted). They tell you what was done, why and what the results were.

The use of case studies in business was pioneered at Harvard Business School in the 1950s (Bonoma, 1985). While some business case studies are similar to those in law or medicine in that they are histories of problems and their solutions, business cases in an academic setting more often present students only with a description of a real-world problem. The students are then challenged to develop and defend their interpretation of the key problems and strategies for solving them. This approach is sometimes called 'problem-based learning' (PBL). As a PBL tool, students are not given a completed history of a problem with the results of actions taken by someone to solve it. Rather, they are given a description of a situation that might not even present a clear statement of the problem but, instead, rich descriptive detail about an organization and its challenges. The students are then asked to articulate what they see as the core problem, identify any complicating factors and, eventually, to propose a solution.

Despite their differences, all these applications share the same goal of providing a summary of information about some event or entity. This commonality is reflected in the Oxford English Dictionary's (2006) definition of 'case study' as 'the attempt to understand a particular person, institution, society, etc. by assembling information about his, her or its development; the record of such an attempt'. The term 'case study' dates from at least 1933.

In a research context, 'case study' is best thought of as a research strategy or design rather than a distinct method. Case study design was first developed by anthropologists, ethnologists and sociologists in the 1920s. The pioneer behind the strategy is generally recognized as Park (see Park and Burgess, 1921), a newspaper reporter-turned-sociologist, who stressed the value and diversity of human experience. He argued that sociologists were essentially reporters who use 'scientific' tools to observe and report on the human experience. He was interested in generalizations about the human experience – generalizations that represented insights into phenomena or processes he labelled 'becoming', 'emergence' or 'experiences'. These insights are not fixed empirical laws of the sort that the natural sciences work to reveal. Rather, they are stories that provide insights into human nature and society.

Park's approach was highly influential among some early social scientists interested in documenting and understanding social behaviour. However, this approach was criticized by other scholars who were suspicious of any findings that were not replicable or falsifiable. In particular, some early case studies in sociology, anthropology and political science were criticized by empirical researchers as too often generating only 'common sense' conclusions that could not be independently verified (Campbell, 1961). Such studies were characterized as 'an intensive study of a single foreign setting by an outsider for whom this is the only intensively experienced foreign culture' and, furthermore, were seen as a method that often was based on idiosyncratic, anecdotal and naïve naturalistic observations (Campbell, 1975, pp. 178–179). Case study analyses were described as 'essentially intuitive, primitive, unmanageable, and less well formulated' (Miles, 1979, pp. 597–599).

In spite of these criticisms, as well as assertions that case studies should be used only in exploratory studies or as a method of last resort, the use of case studies has increased (Yin, 1981a, 2003a). Indeed, case studies are now an established research design in anthropology, business/marketing, community studies, education, ethnography, history, human resources, industrial relations, innovation and technological studies, law enforcement, organizational research, planning and development, political science, programme evaluation psychology, public health, sociology and social work (Yin, 1981b, 2003a,b; Gilgun, 1994; Ghauri and Grønhaug, 2002).

And, as noted in the first paragraph, case studies have become popular in tourism research. Xiao and Smith (2006) provide an overview of the uses, methods and topics of case study as a tourism research strategy. The reason for the growth in the popularity of case studies in many fields is that they can provide a richer understanding of interesting and important phenomena that could not be achieved through other methods, and in a way that provides a fuller description of the context of the phenomenon under study. Case studies are a tool to produce 'deep' insights into some phenomenon, including conclusions based on the context of the topic being studied, and involve the use of multiple methods and data sources.

The last sentence in the previous paragraph may sound like a definition of 'case study'. It's not. Another cause of the ambiguity of the term 'case study' is that the term is difficult to define succinctly. The meaning of 'case study' is more subtle than that of other research designs such as experiments, surveys or focus groups. For example, one of my students wrote a proposal for research on an educational tour by Canadian students in Peru, where they were to study Peruvian archaeology and culture. She described her approach as a case study. I asked her why she felt her approach constituted a 'case study', noting that I did not think it was a case study. She, in turn, naturally asked me to define what I meant by the term and why I didn't think her research was a case study. My immediate answer was the unhelpful 'I know a case study when I see one'.

I reflected on this interchange after it had occurred, and a brief explanation of my knee-jerk reaction might be informative; it was certainly helpful for me to force myself to articulate what drove my instinctive reaction. The tour involved about a dozen students visiting sites around Peru, such as Machu Pichu. My student's methods included administering surveys via Blackberries (a personal digital assistant) and the keeping of a travel diary. Another and unconventional data collection technique was her use of heart monitors to record students' heart rates at various stages in the trip. These data would then be downloaded into each student's Blackberry for analysing after the trip was over. Her focus was on trying to understand the emotional as well as the physiological (impact on heart rate) effects of the students' experiences in the places they visited.

Her research objectives were interesting and the methods innovative, and the project certainly worthwhile. However, they did not constitute a case study. My reason for this judgement is that a case study, as the term implies, involves a 'case' – typically a person, group or organization – facing some problem or situation. For this student, her topic was the experiences of a dozen students on a tour. The collective experiences to be reported by the students involved do not represent a 'case' in the sense connoted by 'case study'. If she had been studying the experiences of a single student – his personal history, especially the motivations for going on the tour, educational aspirations, how funding was arranged, the experiences of travelling with other students, the interactions between the student and others in the group, and the effects of the tour on the student's understanding of himself and his education – that would have been a 'case'.

Alternatively, if her focus had been on the organization and operation of the tour – why it was set up, how it fitted into the curriculum of the department offering it, the development of the itinerary, the negotiation with the various tourism service suppliers (airlines, accommodation, ground transportation, guides), pricing the tour, marketing the tour, selling the tour, evaluation of the financial and educational outcomes of the tour – that would have been a 'case'.

Just studying a group of students in some given context is not enough to qualify as a case. Even her use of multiple methods did not transform the research into a case study. A case study involves a 'case' that is more focused and deeper than simply conducting research on some phenomenon. It involves a situation with multiple aspects, including its history and context, links to other situations, entities, people, policies, preconditions, post-event impacts and the resolution of problems or the meeting of challenges. It examines the dynamics of a situation within the real-world context of the case, without necessarily attempting to generalize from observed cause-and-effect connections or to identify patterns that can be applied to other situations or a larger population.

Another example of the confusion surrounding 'case study' as a term can be found in the Wikipedia (undated) entry for 'case study' in 2008. An anonymous contributor refers to Galileo's famous test of Aristotle's view of gravity (whether larger or more massive objects fall faster than smaller or less massive objects, as Aristotle predicted) as a case study. In this particular instance, Galileo dropped two balls of greatly different sizes and masses from the leaning Tower of Pisa as an experiment. It was an experiment in that he used a narrow set of empirical conditions to test a prediction. His finding disproved Aristotle's notions of gravity. Galileo concluded that neither size nor mass had any impact on the acceleration of gravity and argued that his insights into gravity could be reliably applied to other objects on earth or even in the universe. A true case study presents a more rounded, comprehensive set of data to tell a complex story, often with historical development, that may or may not be generalizable. In other words, the story of Galileo and his testing of Aristotle's ideas might be presented as a case study, but the experiment itself was not a case study.

Yin, perhaps the leading thinker about case studies as a research approach, defines case study methodology as 'an empirical inquiry that investigates a contemporary phenomenon within its real-life context, especially when the boundaries between phenomenon and context are not clearly evident' (Yin, 2003a, p.13). He further states that such an inquiry:

> copes with the technically distinctive situation in which there are more variables of interest than data points (i.e. the number of cases), and as one result, [it] relies on multiple sources of evidence, with data needing to converge in a triangulation fashion, and as another result, [it] benefits from the prior development of theoretical propositions to guide data collection and analysis.
>
> (Yin, 2003a, pp.13–14)

In other words, the case study approach is an inclusive research paradigm covering the logic of research design, data collection and analysis. Hence, the case study approach is not merely a data collection tactic or a research design. It is a comprehensive research strategy.

Students sometime confuse case study and historiography (historical research). There are similarities in the overall logic and presentation of findings of case study and historiography, as well as the use of documents as secondary data sources in both approaches. However, historiography involves special ways of verifying documents and artefacts in dealing with non-contemporary events. Participant observations, direct measurements or interviews normally are not used in historiography for corroboratory evidence. Case studies tend to deal with contemporary events and use many more data sources than just documents.

In terms of situations and types of questions addressed, a case study strategy is used when 'how or why questions are being asked about a contemporary set of events over which the investigator has little or no control' (Yin, 2003a, p. 9). Hartley (1994, p. 212) notes that case study allows for 'processual, contextual, and generally longitudinal analysis of the various actions and meanings which take place and which are constructed within specific social or organizational contexts'. Focus Box 8.1 lists some criteria that characterize the case study approach. A case study will possess the majority of characteristics listed in this table.

Focus Box 8.1. Criteria characterizing case studies.

Your research design might be a case study if:

- Your study is intended to tell a story that provides in-depth insights in a specific case, and focuses on the history of some situation or organization, how a problem was solved, how some activity was initiated and managed or how an individual or group of individuals responded to some situation.
- The story is addressed to a clearly defined situation such as an organization, event or problem.
- The case is clearly and reasonably delimited in terms of geographic extent, time or organizational structure.
- Your story is based on developing an understanding of the dynamics and the larger context of the phenomenon you are exploring.
- Your story provides insights into the core issue of the story and illuminates how the issue fits into and is shaped by broader (possibly historical) forces and a larger context.
- You have developed a research protocol that anticipates and outlines the key tasks you will undertake in your research.
- You draw on multiple sources of information to develop the story and to understand the context You examine the evidence, making comparisons to support or contradict your initial interpretations. You use informed judgement and existing literature (including models, concepts) on which to develop your conclusions.
- Your research may involve some degree of participant observation, but you do not become too actively involved in your subject and do not conduct the project as a form of action research. The purpose of a case study is to understand a situation – not to change it.
- Your conclusions build on the evidence, leading to an articulation of new ideas. The findings provide original and deep insights into the central issue and are more than a summary of the empirical data you have collected.

We will, in this chapter, consider different types of case studies. We will then look at some of the basic methods used to conduct case studies, concluding with some comments about how to analyse your findings.

TYPES OF CASE STUDIES

Case studies can be classified in a variety of ways. For example, Wikipedia (undated) classifies them as: (i) extreme; (ii) critical; and (iii) paradigmatic. Tellis (1997) sees cases studies as being: (i) exploratory; (ii) explanatory; or (iii) descriptive. Becker et al. (2005) group case studies into: (i) illustrative studies; (ii) exploratory (or pilot) studies; (iii) cumulative studies; and (iv) critical instance studies. Table 8.1 provides a summary of each of these classifications. However, note that the differences among authors are more of vocabulary or emphasis than of differences in content.

A simpler classification system that I find useful is to describe case studies as either: (i) a single (unified) case; (ii) an embedded case; (iii) multiple cases; or (iv) a hierarchical case design. The **single case design** explores, as the name implies, one particular phenomenon,

Table 8.1. Examples of classifications of case studies.

Classification system	Function(s)
Wikipedia (undated)	
Extreme	Used to illustrate a dramatic case or situation
Critical	Used to study or test a strategic issue in a specific setting
Paradigmatic	Used to illustrate or reveal a prototypical situation or general paradigm for some situation
Tellis (1997)	
Exploratory	Used to identify questions and appropriate methods, or to test a research design prior to conducting a fuller study
Explanatory	Used to develop and/or test cause-and-effect models
Descriptive	Used to test or apply a descriptive framework or model to a real-world situation
Becker *et al.* (2005)	
Illustrative	Used to describe the nature of a particular situation or event
Exploratory (or pilot)	Used to identify questions and appropriate methods, or to test a research design prior to conducting a fuller study
Cumulative	Used to combine findings from a number of previous studies into a single, generalizable meta-study
Critical instance	Used to test assertions, beliefs, hypotheses or models

story or event. This may be a unique or extreme event, or it may be one that is believed by the researcher to reflect patterns or stories that might be found in comparable situations in other locations or times. An **embedded case design** is a special type of single case study. An embedded design still explores a single phenomenon, but one that involves two or more units of analysis, such as two different hotel properties within the same hotel chain.

A summary of a single case study is provided in Focus Box 8.2. This particular case study is of the Canadian regional marketing partnership ACTP (also discussed in Chapter 7) for the years 2000–2006.

A **hierarchical case design** is a special type of embedded case design. An example may make this clearer. Xiao (2007) used a case study of the Travel and Tourism Research Association (TTRA) as an example of a scholarly community. He had to decide whether to study the association as a whole or to look at differences among the several chapters that comprise TTRA. He chose to consider TTRA as a unified entity rather than as a composite comprised of individual chapters. There were two reasons for his choice. First, Xiao's focus was on the organization itself and not its subdivisions. Furthermore, because he was relying on a web-based survey as a key source of data, he felt he had insufficient numbers of responses from the membership of some of the smaller chapters to warrant treating them as separate units of analysis.

If Xiao had looked at one chapter of TTRA and then compared his findings with those from the entire organization, we would describe the approach as a hierarchical design. In other words, a hierarchical design compares a subset of a larger entity with the larger entity. You might use a hierarchical design if you wanted to look at management problems or strategies in one or more individual museums, for example, and then look at the all museums in a single metropolitan area. Both the embedded and hierarchical approaches are valid; your choice should depend on the goals of your study as well as the adequacy of data on which you will base your study.

Focus Box 8.2. Overview of a case study of the Atlantic Canada Tourism Partnership.

The original case study on which this summary is base was published is to be found in Reid *et al.* (2008). The Atlantic Canada Tourism Partnership (ACTP) is a marketing alliance among the tourism ministries of four Canadian provinces, four provincial industry associations and the federal government. The basic role of the partnership is, through the pooling of financial resources, to promote Atlantic Canada to the USA and selected overseas markets. This case study examined, for the period 2000–2006:

1. The motives for the creation of ACTP, as well as its structure.
2. The structure of ACTP and its evolution over the period of study.
3. Marketing strategies and tactics for the key international markets targeted by ACTP.
4. Management, governance and communication practices and challenges facing the funding partners.
5. The results of ACTP's activities within the context of its objectives, as well as that of the larger Canadian tourism market.

Before beginning the case study, the authors read extensively in the strategic tourism alliance literature, especially in the context of tourism marketing. They then developed a work plan identifying objectives and needed data sources, and decided which person was responsible for which part of the study. To conduct the case study, the authors drew on multiple sources:

1. Structured personal interviews with members of ACTP committees (marketing, executive and communications).
2. Internal documents such as project proposals, marketing plans, project assessment forms, communication strategies, reports on the results of tour wholesaler partnerships and written reports from ACTP delegates to various trade and consumer shows.
3. Quantitative secondary data sources, including Statistics Canada's International Travel Survey for 2001–2005 as well as original research studies commissioned by ACTP. Results of call centre surveys were accessed for numbers of enquiries, conversions, expenditures and return-on-investment data.
4. Review of the content of ACTP's websites, as well as usage levels and patterns (through web analytic reports).
5. Reports on media buys, and value added (such as enhanced distribution) negotiated by a media buying house under contract with ACTP.

The case study concluded with a dozen findings. These findings, although specific to ACTP, could be linked to existing literature and broader issues in tourism marketing. Among these were:

1. Effective tourism marketing partnerships require that partners negotiate their way through legitimate differences in objectives. The case study documented these differences and how they were resolved.
2. Partnerships require a sense of equitable participation and involvement. The case study documented how this was achieved among four provinces of greatly different sizes and the federal government.

(Continued)

Focus Box 8.2. Continued.

3. An efficient management structure is critical for a partnership to be sustainable. The case study tracked the evolution of structural and administrative changes in ACTP over the study period.
4. The effectiveness of an integrated, multimedia advertising strategy was documented, and its impacts were measured through conversion studies and other visitor statistics.
5. The importance of explicit a priori guidelines regarding spending allocations was identified.
6. Certain challenges in empirically measuring the effectiveness of specific programmes, such as motor coach partnerships and participation in trade shows, were identified and suggestions offered regarding the measurement of these programmes.

A **multiple case design** differs from an embedded case design in that each case is treated as a separate study rather than simply as another unit of analysis in an overall case study. A multiple case design treats each case as a separate study, and involves looking for common patterns, processes or results. In other words, as Tellis (1997, p. 7) puts it, a multiple case design uses the 'logic of replication'. The cases, while independent studies, may be read as a larger meta-study that provides you with insights possible only by examining a series of parallel, but independent, case studies.

Case study methodology

Whether your case study is a single (unified), embedded, multiple case or hierarchical design, the basic strategy for a case study follows a common pattern. Implementation of specific methods as well as the specific data sources will, of course, be specific to your project. The following describes a general design that can be used for many tourism case studies.

The first step is to establish a research protocol. A research protocol is, in effect, your work plan to achieve the objectives and goals of your research. Most research projects benefit from the development of a protocol, but it is especially important for case study research. This is because case studies involve multiple data sources, multiple methods and fairly subtle or subjective analytical techniques.

Your protocol should begin with a statement of objectives, the explicit identification of the case you will study and, if relevant, specific questions to ask of key informants or of secondary data sources. The protocol will explicitly describe the research design, such as single case or embedded case. It also describes the unit(s) of analysis, data sources and collection techniques (including persons to be interviewed, field studies, secondary data sources, participant observation and so on). Finally, the research protocol should provide guidelines about how the information collected will be analysed. The following sections describe in greater detail some of the key aspects of the protocol.

Specify objectives, issues and topics

As with any research project, you need to articulate explicitly what you want to explore in your case study. What questions, issues, topics and objectives will guide your research? Because case studies tend to be designed to explore issues in depth and with a broad look at the context of the case, using multiple sources of data, you will need to have, in effect, a mental map of the territory you want to explore. To express this point more pragmatically, you need to know when to keep collecting and analysing evidence and when you have completed your work and you can write up your results.

You might begin with a general issue you want to explore, such as sponsorship of a sport tourism event, and then look for a case you can use to explore the details, such as how sponsorships are negotiated and structured. Alternatively, you might begin with a specific case, such as a group tour operator, and then think about issues to explore, such as marketing, the creation of itineraries, relationships with suppliers or insurance and liability issues. This general topic could be expressed as an explicit goal, such as: 'The goal of this study will be to explore how a hotel addresses human resource issues such as recruiting, training, retention, employee evaluation and performance rewards or disciplinary issues'.

The goal would then be followed by a series of objectives (usually worded in the following action-oriented format) that outlines the broad steps to be undertaken, such as (NB, the following is totally fictional): 'This goal will be achieved through a single case study design aimed at fulfilling the following objectives:

- to establish a trusting, working relationship with key managers in the hotel;
- to collect administrative data on the number of employees, duration of service and job descriptions;
- to review training procedures and materials; and
- so on.'

These objectives might then lead to the identification of those research questions you wish to explore. Or the objectives may be precise enough that specific research questions may be redundant. A common experience of researchers doing case studies is that, as they begin to become more familiar with the case under study, the objectives evolve and new questions emerge that deserve to be explored. A case study project should, as I've suggested, have an explicit research protocol to guide your work, but don't treat the protocol as an iron-clad contract. Some flexibility and the opportunity for spontaneity or serendipity in collecting data and exploring sources and issues can be a good thing.

The choice of your case is not a random decision nor, of course, is it representative in the sense of drawing a representative sample for a survey. Often, the case will be based on your having access to key players and information. In other words, you may select a particular case for study simply because it is available to you. Other times, though, you may have a general question you wish to research and will need to consider alternative cases. In either case, certain criteria should be considered:

- Will the key players, information, locations and data you require be available to you on a timely and affordable basis? Are documents essential for your case study confidential and thus unavailable to you? Will key informants be willing to be interviewed?
- Is the case substantial enough to warrant study? The case you select to study should offer sufficient insights, lessons or illustrations to make your time on the case study justifiable. In other words, is there anything about the case that merits study?
- Does the case reflect a variety of phenomena, experiences or problems to allow you to explore your most important questions?
- Are there political or legal risks you might face if you pursue a particular case? Do not put yourself in any sort of jeopardy through your research.

Review relevant literature

A literature review will identify related studies that might give you some insights into issues to be explored by or approaches used by other authors. These can be helpful in developing your research protocol. Moreover, a literature review can help you place your study in the context of existing research. It may also provide you with concepts or models that could help you structure your questions or analysis. Of course, be cautious about the risk of confirmation error when interpreting your findings in light of an existing model. Be open to the possibility that your findings will contradict those of other researchers. You may want to review the section on literature reviews in Chapter 2.

Identify data/information sources

The objectives of your study shape the information sources you need to access. Case studies typically use a wide variety of sources – often many more than other types of research. These sources typically will be both empirical and subjective, as well as primary and secondary. Some of the more common sources of data and evidence useful in case studies are:

- administrative or organizational databases, such as customer surveys, occupancy or sales figures, budgets;
- documents (meeting minutes, internal memoranda, correspondence, reports, other studies on the organization or phenomenon being studied, process or operations manuals, etc.);
- maps;
- photographs, video/audio recordings;
- organizational websites;
- personal interviews with key informants, stakeholders;
- surveys of relevant individuals;
- field/personal observation;
- participant observation (such as participating on committees or as a volunteer); and
- physical artefacts.

You would normally not use all of these sources, although you will draw on as many of them as available and relevant. The sources need to be used with sensitivity and caution, and a degree of scepticism in some cases. Documents may not necessarily be accurate or might even be missing. Organizational websites can provide insights into how an organization wishes to be portrayed, but the content of websites can be inaccurate or highly biased. Photographs can be misinterpreted and, in the case of digital photographs, manipulated. Maps may be out of date or inaccurate.

Surveys and interviews are subject to the cautions we considered in Chapters 3, 4 and 5. Personal observation is necessarily selective and can result in misinterpretations or incomplete conclusions. Using one or more research colleagues or assistants can help improve the validity and comprehensiveness of your observation.

Participant observation allows you to gain 'insider' information about an organization or event, and thus can be a valuable source of evidence. A couple of risks with participant observation, though, are: (i) you may not be privy to sensitive information, especially if you are functioning as a volunteer in an organization; and (ii) your presence may influence the events or dynamics you want to observe. Artefacts can be useful, although the meaning of those artefacts may need to be determined in consultation with individuals closely associated with your case and thus possibly subject to their biases.

The use of multiple sources of information offers you several advantages. Multiple sources can provide you with a broader picture and richer insights into your topic. They not only add detail but also provide contextual or historical information that can be essential in producing a well-designed and informed case study. The use of multiple sources can also provide you with evidence supporting tentative conclusions or facts obtained from a given source, or alert you to the possibility of conflicting evidence/information. A careful examination of the sources, often supplemented with interviews with key informants, can sometimes resolve apparent contradictions.

However, not all contradictions can be resolved, and you may need to acknowledge that the available evidence sometimes does not present a single, conclusive picture of some issue.

The use of multiple sources is sometimes described as 'triangulation', as noted in Chapter 2. However, **triangulation** should be used to refer only to the use of multiple sources (typically at least three) that involve consistent assumptions, definitions and methods to confirm a piece of empirical evidence or to arrive at a single datum. If the sources employ different assumptions, definitions or methods, their use is more correctly described as 'multiple methods'. The distinction between multiple methods and triangulation is illustrated in Fig. 8.1.

The top part of the figure illustrates how different data sources, such as interviews, surveys and reviews of websites, can provide information to inform the development of your case study. The lower part of the figure illustrates the basic principle of triangulation – the use of a consistent method for several possible sources of information. In this case, the same questionnaire is administered to three different sub-samples. The purpose of such replication is to increase your confidence in the reliability of your findings, not to access multiple sources of different types of information.

Analysis

The analysis phase of doing a case study is the most difficult to describe clearly. Although some of the evidence you may use in a case study may be empirical, ultimately your analysis

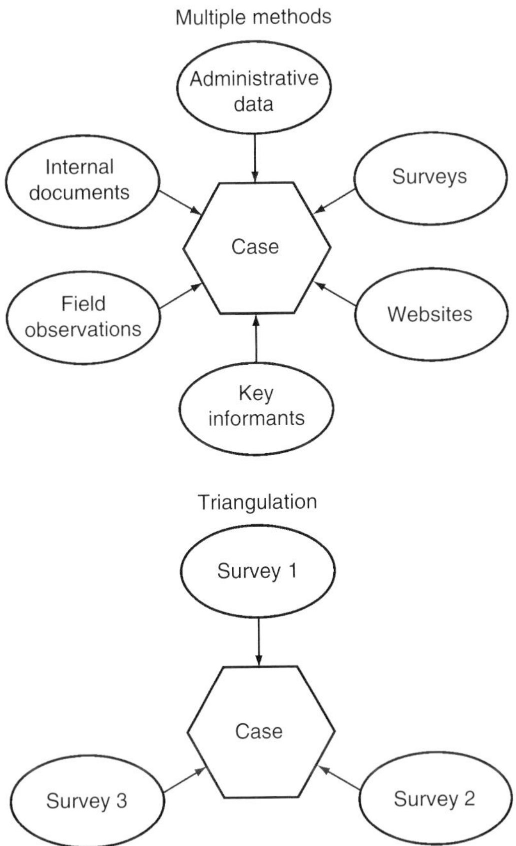

Fig. 8.1. Multiple methods versus triangulation.

will be largely subjective. The quality of your conclusions will be a function of your level of understanding, knowledge, preconceptions and intuition. It is important to remember that the analysis phase is designed to help you tell a story, so to speak, about the case you have studied. Case study results are not simply a description of what you did, observed and read.

Different researchers will employ different analytical strategies, reflecting both their topics and their own styles. One common strategy that can be useful is to start with a conceptual or hypothetical model (an a priori model) that you then round-out and test with your evidence. Beginning with a conceptual framework, you examine your evidence and then interpret it in light of your model – being prepared to adjust the model if the evidence becomes counter-indicative (i.e. your evidence suggests that the model is not complete or correct). This approach is sometimes described as pattern-matching. The logic of the approach is that you have a predicted pattern or set of relationships you expect to find. Through a critical review of your evidence, you attempt to determine whether the predicted pattern is confirmed or not. Patterns may refer to structures you expect to see in the phenomenon or entity you are studying, or cause-and-effect relationships.

As noted before, be alert to the risk of confirmation error (recall Focus Box 1.2) – in other words, consciously avoid interpreting your data in such a way as to justify foregone conclusions. Be open to unexpected findings. If you begin with a conceptual framework to guide your analysis, be prepared to examine rival explanations or conclusions to see whether one of them appears to be more valid than your initial model. It can be helpful explicitly to identify and consider alternative explanations and comment on why they might or might not be valid upon further reflection of all the evidence.

Another analytical approach is to employ coding, as described in Chapter 5. With this approach, you focus on examining evidence, especially documents and interviews, to identify initial categories or preliminary codes that illustrate tentative findings. These preliminary codes are then examined in greater depth to look for deeper levels of meaning, patterns or explanations (Eisenhardt, 1989). This approach is similar to that associated with so-called grounded theory (Glaser and Strauss, 1967). The logic of a coding design is quite different to that of pattern-matching or the use of an a priori model. In the case of coding, you begin with a blank slate, with no expectations of what you are going to find. Through coding, multiple and detailed readings, note-taking and reflection, conclusions begin to emerge.

This approach also carries a potential risk – the narrative fallacy. In other words, researchers using this design run the risk of creating and elaborating a story that sounds plausible but is incorrect. One strategy to reduce the risk of the narrative fallacy is consciously to avoid forming conclusions too quickly. Wait for a preponderance of evidence to point to defensible conclusions. You should also explicitly lay out a chain of evidence, explaining how various pieces of evidence build on each other and ultimately lead to a conclusion. Regardless of which approach you chose, Yin (2003a) suggests four principles on which you should base your analysis:

- Explicitly show how your conclusions are based on the evidence you have compiled, and that you have not ignored countervailing evidence.
- Identify rival explanations or interpretations of patterns you observe in your conclusions.
- Keep focused on the most significant aspects of the case study; avoid getting drawn off into less relevant tangents that detract from your main findings and discussion.
- Once you have developed more experience in doing case studies or other analyses of your topic, use this prior knowledge to inform your analysis.

Case studies, as we noted at the outset of the chapter, have historically been criticized on a variety of grounds. Although these studies are now more accepted by social scientists, some of the general concerns about case studies are still valid and need to be addressed in your research design. Yin (2003a) suggests that the four key challenges are:

- Construct validity: whether your logic and evidence are sound and lead to valid conclusions.
- Internal validity: whether your cause-and-effect conclusions make sense; in other words: (i) the cause precedes the effect; (ii) cause and effect are functionally related; and (iii) your evidence supports your hypothesized cause for an observed effect.
- External validity: how well your findings lead to deeper conceptual insights or support other models and concepts related to the topic of your case study.
- Reliability: the degree to which you (or someone else) would come to the same conclusions if you/the other person were to replicate the study.

Table 8.2 summarizes some of the tactics that can be employed to address each of these issues. While case studies are normally limited to describing insights gained from the specific case or cases under study, one of the temptations of case study research is to try to generalize from the findings to a broader conceptual set of principles. Most case study researchers are well aware that they cannot generalize to a larger population in the same way that someone doing an empirical survey based on a proportional sample could. Still, there is often a desire by researchers to report some general principles based on their findings that might have broader implications. This is not necessarily a bad thing. Good case study research can, just as can good historical research, tell stories that teach important lessons. However, one needs to avoid articulating overly idiosyncratic or complex concepts based on one's findings of a single case. Unwarranted elaboration can go against the principle of parsimony as articulated by 'Occam's razor' – the principle that a concept or model should be as simple as possible (but no simpler).

Table 8.2. Tactics for addressing key analytical issues in case studies (adapted from Yin, 2003a).

Issue	Tactic	Phase of research in which tactic is used
Construct validity	Use multiple sources of evidence	Data collection
	Document the sources of evidence used and how the evidence was interpreted	Data collection
	Ask your interviewees or key contacts to review your summary of their words and your conclusions	Report preparation
	Look for patterns and connections in your data	Data analysis
Internal validity	Create alternative explanations for your findings and the patterns you observe	Data analysis
	Assess the plausibility of alternative conclusions in light of evidence and logical explanations	Data analysis
	Use explicit models to represent logical relations	Data analysis

(Continued)

Table 8.2. Continued.

Issue	Tactic	Phase of research in which tactic is used
External validity	Develop conceptual models for use in single-case, embedded or hierarchical designs	Research design
	Compare evidence, specific findings and conclusions in multiple-case designs	Research design
Reliability	Develop and adhere to a case study protocol	Data collection
	Create a database for your study and review it periodically to search for ambiguities, contradictions or logical anomalies	Data collection
	Use multiple coders	Data collection
	Compare findings with those of previous studies you may have conducted or conduct multiple case studies	Report preparation

CONCLUSIONS

The term 'case study' is used in teaching, writing and research in numerous ways. It is a highly plastic term that can be bent and stretched to cover a range of techniques. However, as we noted earlier in this chapter, not just any research project can be labelled as a case study. Researchers have an ethical responsibility to be as precise as possible in their use of language; 'case study' does connote a certain research strategy and should not be causally used as a catch-all term. As a research strategy, the characteristics of a case study include:

- It is a legitimate and useful strategy to understand complex situations, such as those where the focus of the study cannot be easily separated from the larger context of the phenomenon or problem being studied.
- The history or background of the subject being examined often is an important part of a case study.
- Case study research requires a carefully developed protocol to guide the actual work. However, the method is highly flexible and can be applied to many different problems and situations.
- Multiple data or information sources, both empirical and subjective, are used to develop as full an understanding of the topic as possible. The information you collect is continuously examined to identify patterns, consistencies, contradictions and areas in which further data collection may be needed.
- Case studies emphasize context – what some researchers call 'deep data' or 'thick description'. A case study is not simply the use of multiple data sources whose content is then summarized in a final report. Case study work builds a nexus (a net of connections) among concepts, models, principles and human reality. Understanding, at as deep a level as possible, of an individual's or organization's experiences associated with the topic under study is a central theme of case study findings.

As with other forms of subjective research, case studies pose several challenges and risks. The intrinsic subjectivity of analysis and interpretation means that the researchers must actively guard against both confirmation and narrative errors. Personal interpretation is unavoidable, and can provide insights that go far beyond what simple empirical analysis can offer. However, the advantages of basing conclusions on informed and knowledgeable insights and the reflections of a skilled researcher come at the risk of the potential for misinterpretation or bias.

Case studies work with small samples, often a single organization. As a result, the temptation to generalize to a large population or context should be resisted. The story created by a case study can be informative and valuable, but the extent to which it applies to other contexts and circumstances is largely unknown.

Case studies can be time-consuming. Not only must multiple data sources be accessed, but substantial time and effort may be required to be able to get key informants to agree to interviews. Then, you need time to code and interpret the transcripts of the interviews. Finally, you should go back to your original subjects to show them your summary of those interviews to ensure that your interpretation is accurate.

Finally, case study researchers can become emotionally involved in their work and subjects. The development of personal relationships with your subjects and the opportunity to think deeply and critically about an issue can be a source of pleasure and satisfaction to researchers. However, a researcher doing a case study needs always to maintain a degree of separation from her or his topic to minimize the risk of bias or misinterpretation in her or his research.

REFERENCES

Becker, B., Dawson, P., Devine, K., Hannum, C., Hill, S., Leydens, J., Matsuskevich, D., Traver, C. and Palmquist, M. (2005) *Case Studies*. Writing@CSU. Colorado State University, Department of English. Available at: http://writing.colostate.edu/guides/research/casestudy/ (accessed 15 August 2008).

Bonoma, T. (1985) Case research in marketing: opportunities, problems, and a process. *Journal of Marketing Research* 22(2), 199–208.

Campbell, D. (1961) The mutual methodological relevance of anthropology and psychology. In: Hsu, F. (ed.) *Psychological Anthropology: Approaches to Culture and Personality*. Dorsey Press, Homewood, Illinois, pp. 333–352.

Campbell, D. (1975) Degree of freedom and the case study. *Comparative Political Studies* 8(2), 178–193.

Eisenhardt, K.M. (1989) Building theories from case study research. *Academy of Management Review* 14, 532–550.

Ghauri, P. and Grønhaug, K. (2002) *Research Methods in Business Studies: a Practical Guide*. Pearson Education, Harlow, UK.

Gilgun, J. (1994) A case for case studies in social work research. *Social Work* 39, 371–380.

Glaser, B.G. and Strauss, A.L. (1967) *The Discovery of Grounded Theory*. Aldine Press, Chicago, Illinois.

Hartley, J. (1994) Case studies in organizational research. In: Cassell, C. and Symon, G. (eds) *Qualitative Methods in Organizational Research: a Practical Guide*. Sage, London, pp 208–229.

Miles, M. (1979) Qualitative data as an attractive nuisance: the problem of analysis. *Administrative Science Quarterly* 24, 590–601.

Oxford English Dictionary (2006) Available at http://db.uwaterloo.ca/OED/search/oed-local/lookup.cgi (accessed 15 August 2008).

Park, R. and Burgess, E. (1921) *Introduction to the Science of Sociology*. University of Chicago Press, Chicago, Illinois.

Reid, L.J., Smith, S.L.J. and McCormick, R. (2008) The effectiveness of regional marketing alliances: a case study of the Atlantic Canada Tourism Partnership 2000–2006. *Tourism Management* 29, 581–593.

Tellis, W. (1997) Introduction to case study. *The Qualitative Report*. Available at http://www.nova.edu/ssss/QR/QR3-2/tellis1.html (accessed 15 August 2008).

Wikipedia (undated) Case study. Available at: http://en.wikipedia.org/wiki/Case_study (accessed 15 August 2008).

Xiao, H. (2007) The social structure of a scientific community: a case study of the Travel and Tourism Research Association. PhD thesis, The University of Waterloo, Waterloo, Ontario.

Xiao, H. and Smith, S. (2006) Case studies in tourism research: a state-of-the-art analysis. *Tourism Management* 27, 738–749.

Yin, R. (1981a) The case study as a serious research strategy. *Knowledge: Creation, Diffusion, Utilization* 3(1), 97–114.

Yin, R. (1981b) The case study crisis: some answers. *Administrative Science Quarterly* 26, 58–65.

Yin, R. (2003a) *Case Study Research: Design and Methods,* 3rd edn. Sage, Thousand Oaks, California.

Yin, R. (2003b) *Applications of Case Study Research*, 2nd edn. Sage, Thousand Oaks, California.

chapter 9

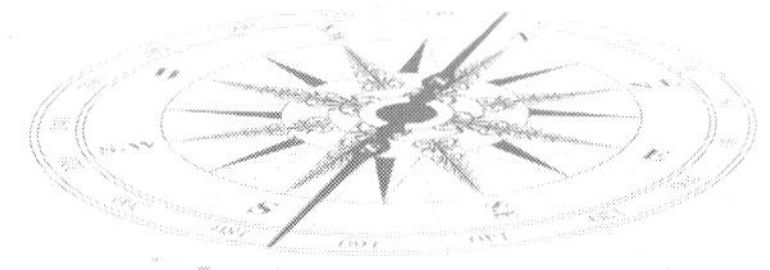

How to Do Content Analysis

WHY THIS IS IMPORTANT

Content analysis is a tool to examine print or graphic communications – what is said (written or visually presented), how it is said and by whom it is said. Communications are an inescapable aspect of the tourism experience. They occur in many forms, including conversations among family and friends about a recent trip, travel stories appearing in the popular press, guidebooks, destination websites, postcards or letters sent home during a trip, travel diaries, travel brochures and blogs. Tourism-related communications can also be found in non-tourism contexts, such as letters to a newspaper editor concerning some local tourism controversy, and in academic research papers.

The applications of content analysis are thus diverse and, as a result, the specific steps involved in doing a content analysis are numerous. However, Holsti (1969) offers a succinct and inclusive definition of content analysis that works for our purposes. He defines content analysis as 'any technique for making inferences by objectively and systematically identifying specified characteristics of messages'.

Methods used in content analysis are both empirical and subjective. As we noted in Chapter 2, empirical research involves analysis subject to independent verification and thus is potentially falsifiable. Empirical methods include counting words or phrases, measuring the space in a brochure or ad devoted to different topics, or the balance between photographs and text. Subjective research involves the researcher coding and grouping words, phrases or photographs (or elements of photographs – such as people) into researcher-defined categories. Such coding may be done by you alone or, better, with the assistance of one or more other coders who each code, and then identify and discuss any differences in their classifications. While the use of multiple coders does not constitute an empirical design because each person's coding is still subjective, it does increase the reliability of your results.

Content analysis can be used to answer different types of interesting questions. These include, for example, how different types of people – grouped, perhaps, by ethnicity, age or physical ability – are portrayed in photographs appearing in tourism websites. Content analysis can also be used to examine the themes that visitors emphasize in their personal travel blogs – what they liked, what they disliked, what they found worthy of comment. The method can also be used to examine how tourism service providers (resorts, airlines) position themselves in tourism advertisements or on their websites, or the themes that travel writers present in their stories about different destinations. If you are interested in a local political issue regarding tourism development, you might conduct a content analysis of letters written by residents to a local newspaper. The possibilities are numerous.

One of the distinctive features of content analysis, compared with other forms of data collection, is that it is unobtrusive. You don't need to convince someone to complete a questionnaire or to spend time with you in a personal interview. You don't have to spend time observing people, participating in committees or engaging in other forms of interaction with your subjects. Content analysis is based on the belief that we can learn important things about visitors, people in tourism organizations, residents of communities and so on by analysing text, photographs, recordings or other records people have produced. These records are, of course, not the people or organizations themselves, but artefacts people have produced that may provide insights into their views, values, experiences and perceptions. These records are analogous to artefacts that archaeologists excavate and then study to learn about another society – except, in the case of content analysis of tourism records: (i) the artefacts are communication media; and (ii) the society being studied is usually contemporary and may be one to which the researcher belongs.

Data collected through content analysis have several advantages. As noted, they are not influenced by interaction between the researcher and the subject. Although the producer of the text (broadly defined) can reflect on the content of what is being produced, it may more probably represent the author's/creator's true feelings than information collected in a face-to-face exchange. These types of data are sometimes called 'naturalistic' because they are not the 'artificial' product of a formal questionnaire or interview process that can sometimes generate information the subject has potentially modified for presentation to the researcher.

Also as noted, content analysis can be used to analyse diverse sources of text, including letters, diaries, photographs, sound recordings, television shows, brochures, websites, journal articles, advertisements and travel stories in books. The specific methods of measuring content and capturing data will vary by medium, but the basic logic and methods of content analysis are the same. It should be noted that content analysis can be applied to a single document, such as a newspaper story or blog, or to a collection of numerous documents. For example, the study described in Focus Box 9.1 examined several dozen websites in a single study.

The method can involve a blending of empirical and subjective research approaches. You might focus solely on counting specified words and phrases, which would be a strictly empirical approach. Alternatively, you might record meaningful passages/images/words in a communication and then work through a hierarchical coding system, as described in Chapter 5. The creation of themes or patterns by observing and interpreting the text is a form of subjective analysis, because your conclusions are the result of your own mental processes rather than an objective empirical process. However, you might then tabulate the number of times different themes appear in the text based on the words or phrases associated with them. This would be hybrid of an empirical and a subjective process.

The potential to do subjective hierarchical coding of observations taken from a text may remind you of the hierarchical coding process in grounded theory. The main difference is that, in content analysis, the emphasis is placed on who 'says' what to whom, for what purpose, in what context and using what arguments or logic. In principle, grounded theory should go beyond recording what was said and identify hypothetical relationships among various

Focus Box 9.1. A content analysis of website images.

Buzinde *et al.* (2006) conducted a content analysis of images of ethnic groups appearing in Canadian tourism brochures published by destination-marketing organizations (DMOs) to see the relative frequency of photographs of different ethnic groups in brochures and in what contexts these representations of individuals were made. Once the purpose of the study was identified, the methods involved these eight steps:

1. There is one national tourism marketing body in Canada and 13 provincial/territorial marketing organizations, so a census of their brochures was done. However, the number of municipal DMOs is quite large. To keep the number of brochures manageable, the researchers chose to review the brochures only from the largest city in each province or territory.
2. Coding was done by the senior author and a second coder. A coding scheme was developed for the project, and both coders practiced coding using non-sample images. Some refinement of the coding scheme was done to increase reliability and to refine the code categories.
3. Special attention had to be given to carefully defining and operationalizing three concepts: racial group, role and tourism themes. The meanings of these are described below.
4. Because the authors worked only with photographs, they operationally defined 'ethnic group' on the basis of the facial appearance of each individual in the photographs. Only broad racial groups were used because of the impossibility of identifying more precise ethnic or national origins of individuals. These groups were 'Blacks', 'First Nations' (aboriginal peoples), 'Other Minority' and 'Caucasians'. Photographs of individuals who could not be readily assigned to one of these categories were jointly reviewed and an assignment made on the basis of consensus.
5. Another question to be explored was the role in which each individual appeared. A review of relevant research led to the identification of three general roles: 'active', 'passive' or 'posing'. The coders discussed the meanings of these terms and, again, tested their categorizations using non-sample photographs. The authors developed a list of examples of the types of images that represented each role, to ensure inter-coder and intra-coder reliability.
6. Tourism themes, reflecting the dominant 'theme' of each photograph, were then defined. These included various landscapes (such as seashore, mountains or urban), 'culture' (such as history, art or entertainment) and 'service' (accommodation or food and beverage). Only the dominant theme in each of the three categories was recorded.
7. A journal was also kept during the coding process in which the senior author recorded her thoughts and observations.
8. The relative frequency with which the four ethnic groups appeared in the three roles and by theme were then tabulated and compared using chi square analysis (see Appendix A).

The results were then discussed – such as the fact that ethnic minorities tend to be featured more in the context of providing entertainment. For example, black men were often pictured as jazz musicians while First Nation men were pictured as drumming or dancing. Members of the dominant culture were more likely to be pictured in passive roles as consumers of tourism services. Implications of the findings for tourism marketing were also presented.

concepts or themes: what leads to what, how, with what effects. However, be aware that different authors may use the terms 'content analysis' and 'grounded theory' differently. The differences will reflect their own approaches to these methods, with the result that reading different authors who use these terms can become confusing.

In this chapter, we will first consider the types of questions content analysis can answer as well as the key elements of content analysis. We will then look at research designs and concepts you can use to undertake a content analysis. Finally, we will look at some special issues or problems associated with content analysis of photographs.

Focus Boxes 9.1, 9.2 and 9.3 provide an example of the use of content analysis to examine web-based tourism photographs, two different coding protocols and an example of the content of tourism blogs, respectively.

Focus Box 9.2. Two coding strategies for content analysis.

A priori codes

An a priori code refers to the specification of code categories to be used in your analysis prior to actually collecting data. For example, Alderman and Modlin (2008) were interested in the extent to which slavery was acknowledged and explicitly presented on the tourism websites of 20 historic plantations in North Carolina, USA. They specified the following categories before examining the websites:

- 'slave', 'slaves', 'enslaved' and slavery' were treated as synonyms -- the appearance of any one of these words was coded as representing the slavery theme;
- 'furnishings';
- 'crops';
- 'architecture';
- 'civil war'; and
- 'gardens'.

They then reviewed each website and tabulated the number of times each word appeared. This allowed the authors to draw inferences about the presumed emphasis on each theme in all websites as a whole and to make comparisons across the 20 websites. NB: the six categories were set up prior to data collection. They provided a framework for counting the number of appearances of each keyword.

Emergent codes

Emergent codes are those the author identifies during his/her review of selected text, as guided by a general research question. Nickerson (1995) was interested in the types of issues that appeared in three community newspapers in a region surrounding a small town (Deadwood, South Dakota, USA) after it legalized gambling. She began by identifying every article over a 5-year period that had 'gambling', 'tourism' or 'Deadwood' in the headline. A review of all articles that used at least one of these keywords was then conducted. Two hundred and twenty-six articles were identified.

Each article was reviewed to determine its primary issue. This resulted in 21 topics being identified, such as whether gambling was a good idea, concerns over impacts on parking, impacts on land values, the experiences of other towns that introduced gambling,

(Continued)

Focus Box 9.2. Continued.

sign ordinances, gambling near schools and the potential for increase in crime. In a subsequent, more detailed, review of each article, all these issues were grouped into one of five key themes:

- economics;
- negative impacts;
- logistics or planning;
- initial questions; and
- regulatory concerns.

Nickerson then discussed the relative frequency of appearances of each key issue, as well as the diversity and tenor of opinions expressed in the articles. NB: The author did not begin with any preconceived categories for themes. As she worked, she observed 21 different themes that were then grouped into five broader themes for further analysis and commentary.

Focus Box 9.3. Conducting a content analysis on blogs.

Choi *et al.* (2007) examined the representations ('images') of Macau on the Internet through a content analysis of the Macanese government's tourism website, tour operators' and travel agents' websites, online travel magazine and guidebook websites, and tourism blogs. The context of the study was to develop a baseline of representations of Macau so that future changes in its 'image' arising from governmental promotional efforts and other sources could be tracked.

A search of tourism websites, using Yahoo and Google during April, 2006, identified blogs on tourism visits to Macau. An initial sample consisting of the 'top 20' blogs (the criterion by which the top 20 were measured was not specified) was selected for analysis. Some of these were deemed to be redundant with other website sources such as online travel guides. These were deleted, leaving 14 blogs for analysis.

The text of each blog was saved as a Word file (.doc file). Certain grammatical and connective words were excluded, such as 'the', 'and' and 'I'. Plural nouns were changed to singular nouns, and all verb tenses were changed to the present. Attractions known by several names were changed to a single name, and names consisting of two or more words were concatenated. Thus, 'A-Ma Temple' was changed to 'AmaTemple'. Finally, words such as 'year' or 'afternoon' were deleted because it was felt they would not add to an understanding of 'image'. Visual images were classified into 11 categories such as historic buildings, cultural events and facilities, parks and gardens, and shopping.

The edited text files were then analysed using software known as CATPAC II, a text-mining software (Galileo Company, undated). The output provided the researchers with a list of the most frequent words appearing in the blogs. This initial output then permitted the researchers to tabulate the frequency with which specific attractions were mentioned, and types of 'images' that occurred. These listings were then compared with similar lists developed for the government's website, travel trade websites, travel guide websites and magazine websites.

The results were then analysed to assess differences among representations of Macau across different websites. For example, blogs included substantial detail on gambling and nightlife, whereas the official government website offered a more wholesome description. The authors concluded with implications for future marketing efforts and cautioned that the content of blogs could not be generalized to the fuller visitor population for Macau (or any other destination).

USES OF CONTENT ANALYSIS

The decision to use (or not use) content analysis should – as with the decision about using any other research design – be based on your research objectives and questions. Content analysis may be a logical choice as your research method if the questions you want to ask about a specific communication include two or more of the following:

- Who is initiating/articulating the communication?
- What is the content, meaning or form of communication?
- What may be the intent of the communication?
- Who is the intended audience of the communication?
- How are words, assumptions, definitions, concepts, arguments or images used or articulated to shape the communication?

These questions can be asked in two different contexts. First, you might have a hypothesis to test. For example, you might hypothesize that the relative percentage of images portraying seniors, visible minorities or persons with physical disabilities among all photographs of persons in travel magazines is no higher now than 10 years ago. You could use content analysis to test whether your hypothesis is true.

Alternatively, you might wish to explore, without any preconceived idea of what you might find, some general patterns or themes. For example, you might be interested in the types of wildlife featured on websites of ecotourism operators. What is the relative frequency of birds, amphibians, mammals and insects? What is the balance between flora and fauna, or close-ups of individual life forms versus panoramic landscape views? Or you might want to explore the content and structure of ecotourism websites in terms of patterns related to the coverage of activities, natural environment, services (guides, accommodation), prices, seasonal activities and so on – and whether there are systematic differences among countries, type of ecotourism operators or other aspect of the operators.

Possible elements to include in a content analysis

Your focus in a content analysis will reflect, of course, your specific interests. One useful distinction to bear in mind when doing a content analysis is that between manifest and latent content. **Manifest content** refers to the specific words or images that you can observe. For example, does a travel story focus on a destination's qualities, such as history, adventure, luxury or affordability? Does a letter to the editor emphasis job creation, impacts on taxes or traffic congestion? **Latent content** (also called **semantic analysis**), in contrast, refers to either what is implicitly meant by a communication, or inferences about the political/philosophical background of the writer. In other words, you attempt to infer why the communicator expressed what he did.

A caution about latent content analysis might be useful. As with other subjective approaches, this type of research is vulnerable to narrative fallacies and confirmation errors. For example, we will cite later a case study by Canton and Santos (2008) involving the use of photographs. They were interested in inferring the perspectives and values of students taking photographs on an international study course, with a particular focus on power relationships between locals and visitors. When they looked at the photographs, there was the risk they may have interpreted the images as showing an unequal power relationship regardless of the intent of the photographer, the meaning of the image to the person taking the photograph or the nature of the interactions from the perspectives of the people portrayed in the photograph. When doing a latent content analysis, try to consider whether alternative meanings might lie within the words or images and not just those that support a preconceived view of the world. Some of the elements or features of any particular communication piece that you will examine in a content analysis will usually include some (but not necessarily all) of the following:

Modes of communication. How does the author convey her or his messages, and to whom? To answer these questions, you might look at:

- medium used: newspaper or magazine articles, websites, blogs, radio or television ads;
- format of communications: text, photographs, sound recordings, scripted versus unscripted presentations;
- design/layout of communication content:
  - use of and relative frequency/spacing of text, graphic images, data tables (such as price lists), spoken words, music; and
  - column-inches/centimetres, page fractions (e.g. quarter-page versus half-page versus full-page advertisements), time duration for elements of recorded messages (e.g. television advertisements);
- counts of and percentage frequencies of keywords or phrases; and
- the intended audience of the communication.

Specific topics addressed in the communication. What are the content, focus and scope of the communication? What messages or themes are conveyed? How are they conveyed? These topics can be explored by looking at the following:

- the explicit topics, ideas or themes expressed in the communication;
- the author of the communication, his/her affiliation or role;
- definitions of core concepts or terms – whether implicit or explicit;
- implicit or explicit assumptions made by the author;
- the use and balance of empirical versus subjective information;
- the use and balance of text, graphic images and numerical data (such as prices, times, dates, capacity); and
- the presentation style adopted by the author:
  - 'narrative': the telling of a story in a way to convey context, findings, themes, important lessons;
  - 'objective': reporting focused on verifiable facts (as opposed to opinion or interpretation) such as locations, names, dates, prices, attendance numbers, revenues and sources of information;
  - 'evaluative': personal assessments of quality, experiences; evaluative content reflects the author's experiences, biases, values and interpretations; or
  - 'critical': similar to an evaluative style, but the orientation tends to be more 'political', reflecting the author's predetermined position or perspective in her or his interpretation and reporting of a story or observations.

Rhetoric

In the context of content analysis, rhetoric does not mean 'just words', as the term is sometimes loosely used. Rather, rhetoric reflects the intimate relationship between knowledge and language – the fact that our words and how we use them shape what we and others know, and how we communicate what we know to each other. Among the rhetorical elements you may want to examine are the following:

- the self-positioning of the author with respect to the topic, such as that of being an 'expert', an employer, an employee, a customer or a taxpayer;
- the position taken by the author on the issue – in favour versus being against some event or position;
- identification or clarification of key issues of debate;
- types of evidence presented such as: (i) anecdotal stories versus systematically gathered empirical data; (ii) numerical versus verbal evidence; and (iii) direct quotations versus summaries of documents;
- closely related to the type of evidence presented is the type of argument (in the sense of reasoning, not a quarrel) used by the author to present evidence. Borrowing terminology originally proposed by Aristotle, the more common types of argument are (NB: the brief examples below are fictional, but are based on real material):
    - logos:
        - **induction**: using specific examples, precedents or data to make a point, e.g. a television reporter commenting on attendance at a parade to honour a sporting team winning a national championships claims: '50,000 cheering fans turned out on a cold, snowy day to welcome home our victorious Fighting Fruit Flies';
        - **deduction**: using principles or propositions to make a case, e.g. a radio commentator looking at proposed changes to border-crossing formalities observes: 'As we all know, a healthy tourism sector depends on the friendly and efficient processing of visitors at our borders. However, the proposed tightening of visa regulations and border security measures will likely push the number of visitors coming to our country even lower'; and
        - **abduction**: suggesting the most likely explanation for something through inference (while recognizing that alternative explanations are possible), e.g. a newspaper editorial writer commenting on the drop in visitation to her local community opines: 'While the tourism sector is struggling these days as a result of many different forces, much of the dramatic drop in the number of visitors coming to our community has to be laid at the government's decision to dramatically slash its tourism marketing budget'.
    - ethos:
        - using one's reputation or position to add weight to an argument or assertion – such as a person being seen as credible because of his/her title or experience, e.g. a textbook author wishing to make a point about the importance of tourism, quotes a non-governmental organization: 'As the Global Tourism Association, the world's leading and most authoritative source of tourism statistics, notes, tourism is the world's fastest growing and largest industry'.
    - pathos:
        - using emotional statements to persuade one's audience of one's position, e.g. a presenter at a tourism research conference writes in his paper: 'The great majority of the world' population still live in abject poverty. While solutions to poverty, starvation and disease in the least developed economies require a multifaceted strategy, pro-poor tourism has a key role to play in helping the most fragile economies benefit from the growth in global tourism. Tourism businesses involved in unconstrained competitiveness can't help. What is needed is a fundamental restructuring of how tourism businesses are managed and how profits are shared among stakeholders in the communities that host visitors'; and

- a special form of pathos is **analogical argument** – the use of similarities or metaphors to draw comparisons between two different phenomena in order to push a position or conclusion, e.g. a tour operator promoting honeymoon tours to Italy writes in a brochure: 'Each of the beloved cities we will visit in Romantic Italy is fragrant with the rich aromas of luscious Italian cooking, colourful with cascades of flowers. Lovers holding hands, gazing into each other's eyes over a satisfying café latte – where better to celebrate your new marriage than Romantic Italy?'.

General procedures for undertaking a content analysis

The following is a step-by-step process that will apply to most content analyses. Some departures from this sequence may be appropriate depending on your specific project, but these steps will be relevant to most projects. Even though the steps are presented in a linear fashion for ease of reading, most researchers will move back and forth through the list during the course of a content analysis. For example, you might revise your objectives after you look at your sources and you think of other questions worth exploring. Or, the process of training your coders may cause you to go back to revise how you operationalize key concepts.

Formulate your objectives

Articulate what you want to accomplish through your research. For example, will you test a hypothesis or will you describe some general themes in the communication media that you will examine? If you don't have any hypotheses to test, then one or more specific research questions can be useful as a guide for your work.

Define and operationalize key concepts

Building on your objectives, hypotheses or research questions, identify the key concepts and terms with which you will work. Then, define them operationally. An operational definition explains how you will measure the terms. The definition should be as simple as possible but clear enough for someone else to understand how you are defining each term. This is especially important if you are using additional coders. For example, if you are going to do a content analysis on blogs written by heritage tourists, how will you operationally identify who is a heritage tourist? If you are going to do a content analysis on photographs, what explicit features of the photographs will you examine and how will you classify them?

Develop a sampling frame

Unless you are looking at the entire scope of some communication medium or campaign – such as all the articles written to a local newspaper on some tourism development controversy, you will need to develop a mechanism for choosing the items you will analyse. Often, you will want the method to provide a representative sample, as we discussed in Chapter 4. However, it is sometimes necessary to employ a purposive or convenience sample, especially if your intent is not to make generalizations but to focus on exploring analytical concepts or tentative themes. For example, I did a content analysis on the meaning of 'theory' in tourism journals. The potential number of articles to be reviewed in all tourism journals was overwhelming, and a representative sample was too difficult to develop. So, as a practical matter, I selected a convenience sample using the three leading English-language tourism journals and published in each of two lustra (5-year periods) 20 years apart to provide an indication of how the uses of the term 'theory' had changed over time in tourism research.

Develop a coding scheme

This step usually follows logically from the previous one. You begin with operational measures, and then develop a coding scheme that specifies what features, words, images or other phenomena you will observe in your selected media. The coding scheme should also spell out how you will measure whatever you are observing: word counts, numbers of people in a photograph, activities of people in the photographs, column-inches for specified topics or material in a brochure, and so on. Once you have developed a general scheme for coding, you can translate this into a coding sheet and, if you are working with other coders, the procedures for observing and coding that you wish them to follow.

Your coding scheme may specify precise categories such as specific words to be counted. Consider whether certain words can be treated as synonyms within the context of your analysis. For example, perhaps 'vacation' and 'trip' convey the same intent in the material you read. On the other hand, the connotation of some words might need to be understood in the context of the text around them. For example, 'beer' might connote: (i) a beverage available at a restaurant; (ii) the idea of a party; or (iii) disorderly behaviour. Alternatively, you can allow the codes to emerge from your reading. This tactic requires that you have a clear understanding of what questions you want to answer, even if you don't have the precise categories for word/phrase capture in mind at the start. You look for implicit themes and commonalities, slowly identifying a relatively limited number of categories into which you can categorize text. Examples of these two strategies are described in Focus Box 9.2.

Recruit and train coders

Ideally, use at least one other coder to ensure a higher degree of reliability than coding by yourself. The coder(s) should be briefed on the purpose of the study and then trained in the coding scheme and use of code sheets. The training session usually begins with a sample of the material to be analysed that is given to the coders for practice. They then code the same material independently. After the practice coding, compare the results by, for example, tabulating the percentage of agreement or using **Cohen's κ (kappa)** (see Appendix A). Some tools for comparing the results of two coders are discussed later in this chapter. Note any consistent areas of differences of coding. If necessary, adjust the coding scheme, or refine your instructions or operational definitions to improve reliability (the degree to which different reviewers code the same material the same way).

Do the coding

Once your coders are trained and your coding scheme has been tested and shown to be workable, begin reviewing your research materials and coding your observations. This can be a tedious process if you have a large amount of material or a complicated coding scheme. It is essential not to push too fast. Take your time and strive for consistency, reliability and quality. All coders should work independently when coding, although you can check for consistency after a block of material has been coded to ensure there are no misunderstandings about how to code. You might have your coders highlight or underline key words in the text being examined if you are working with paper copy. You may also find it helpful to make notes on page margins or on yellow post-it notes (although these can become detached and misplaced over time).

Alternatively, software is available to assist with word counts if you can create a text file of your material. A useful one is Worder (http://www.und.nodak.edu/instruct/kirilenko/worder/worder_kirilenko_org/ index.html). It was originally developed by Andrei Kirilenko to parse downloaded tourism destination websites. Worder allows you to define synonyms (such as singular and plural forms of the same word) or different spellings of the same word. Other software packages are also available through the Internet.

Coding involves two different styles, depending on your research objectives. First, if you are doing only word and phrase counts, or making similar empirical observations (such as the types or activities of persons appearing in photographs), you can probably make a direct, one-time-only pass through your material. This was essentially the approach used by Alderman and Modlin (2008) in Focus Box 9.2. Word-counting software can be especially helpful for this approach. This approach is sometimes called **quantitative content analysis**, because the emphasis is on counting. A variation on word counting is to categorize words or phrases into predetermined categories. For example, if you are reviewing the types of attractions featured in marketing materials put out by a DMO, you might set up a series of categories into which you would code the number of occurrences. Such a coding system might resemble:

Art galleries
Concert halls and theatres
Historic sites
Museums
Public sculpture
Restaurants
Walking tours
...and so on.

These categories need to be *exhaustive* and *exclusive*. 'Exhaustive' means that every attraction has a category into which it can be placed. Although it is often not difficult to develop a system that captures the great majority of observations, it is not unusual to find a few cases that don't easily fit your system. If there is a sufficient number of the same type of unexpected observations, you can simply create a new code for them. On the other hand, you might discover a few one-of-a-kind attractions. These can often be grouped together into an 'other' category. Depending on your observations, you might even have a couple of 'other' categories such as 'other – free' and 'other – paid admission'.

'Exclusive' means that the categories do not overlap and that any observation will be classified into only one category. This can be more challenging than developing an exhaustive list. For example, some museums might feature both collections of historical objects as well as paintings. How you decide into which category to place such an institution has to be made in a way that will allow for consistent coding – possibly by grouping 'museums' and 'galleries' into a single category. Clear, explicit operational guidelines for how to classify each observation need to be developed and your coders trained in how to interpret them. These guidelines may need to be refined once you have more experience with coding. If this happens, you will need to go back and apply the refined guidelines to your previous classifications to ensure consistency. This may be time-consuming, but it is essential to ensure your data are reliable, valid and accurate.

The creation of categories involves maintaining a balance between detail and simplicity. The more categories you have, the more precise your analysis can be. However, more categories require making more decisions and this, in turn, can reduce the overall reliability of your coding. There is no fixed answer about the number of categories to create – but more than about 15 is probably too many. A smaller number of categories simplifies your coding, but reduces the level of detail in your analysis. Fewer categories tend to result in less informed and less interesting findings.

An alternative to word counting is hierarchical coding, which offers a more subtle form of analysis. This alternative requires you to make several passes through your material, reviewing your codes several times, and regrouping them into more new or more general codes. Focus Box 9.2, which uses the Nickerson (1995) gambling study, illustrates this approach. Because of the need to look for implicit themes or linkages among terms or passages within text, word-counting software is usually of less – or no – help for hierarchical coding. The search for themes, commonalities and hierarchies of themes beyond word counts is sometimes called **qualitative content analysis**, because the development of categories is fundamentally an intuitive or subjective exercise.

Figure 9.1 illustrates a simple example of hierarchical coding. In this case, I have identified specific types of words connoting different trip experiences (activities). The initial coding involves noting specific activities as well as, perhaps, how many times each is mentioned. I then reviewed the codes and grouped them into more general categories, such as different mentions of walking in various environments become grouped into the general category of 'walking'. Another review of these more general codes might result in several other activities being grouped into a new category called 'outdoor activities'. The relative number of mentions of each activity, as well as the aggregated activities, can be tabulated to provide a measure of the incidence of the events. The frequency of incidents/events is not necessarily an indication of importance, although it may provide clues as to the relative psychological or emotive impact of each activity in the memory of the author of the original text.

In addition to developing themes, you may want to look for indications of the relative importance of certain concepts, entities or experiences as expressed by the author. The importance of certain concepts is not necessarily conveyed by a simple frequency of occurrence. Rather, look for meaning or indicators of importance within the context of the text itself.

Consider keeping a diary as you do your coding. You can record unexpected or significant patterns, incongruencies in the texts being examined, questions or other thoughts that occur to you as you work through the coding process. Your diary notes can then be helpful as you interpret your findings or discuss the implications of what you have found.

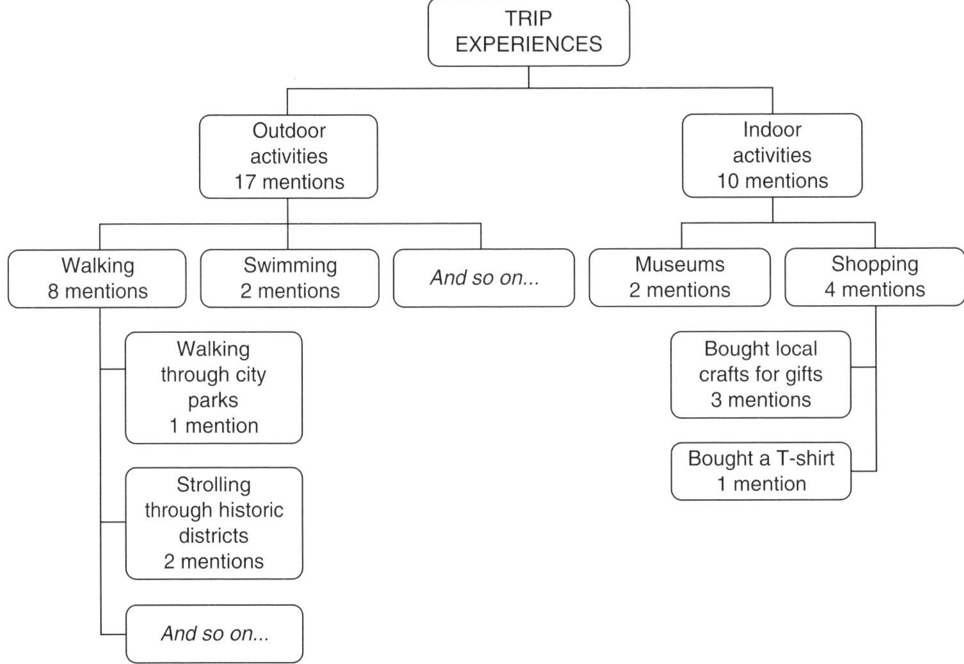

Fig. 9.1. Example of hierarchical coding.

Reliability testing

Unless you are only counting the occurrences of specific words in your content analysis, some subjective judgment will be required. For example, drawing from the image study in Focus Box 9.1, you have to decide to which ethnic group a person in a photograph belongs; whether they are being active, passive or posing; and the theme of the photograph. Sometimes the judgements are pretty obvious – anyone who sees a picture of me can reliably conclude that I am a male with European ancestry. However, other judgements about my political views or my tastes in music will be more difficult, if not impossible, to make.

A key aspect of the coding of your observations is its reliability. There are two forms of coding reliability, both of which are important. The first is **intra-coder reliability**. This refers to the degree to which you make consistent judgements about the classification of an observation. As you gain more experience in coding, you may find that you have changed how you categorize some specific observation. This can be especially true if what you are observing involves phrases or entire sentences and thus requires interpretation of similar but different expressions. Such shifts can arise from a growing sensitivity to subtle differences in wording, or it may reflect fatigue as you work your way through a substantial pile of material. It is difficult to test for intra-coder reliability (unlike for inter-coder reliability, discussed below). Your best assurances of intra-coder reliability are: (i) to code only when your mind is fresh and clear; and (ii) make explicit notes to yourself about how and why you categorize items. These notes might be part of your content analysis diary. If you find you are changing how you classify certain items that should be grouped together, you may have to go back and revise your earlier classification.

The second form of coding reliability is **inter-coder reliability**. This concerns whether two coders categorize the same observation in the same way. A comparison of the coding by two or more coders of their classification of objective nominal variables, such as the sex of a person appearing in a tourism advertisement, permits the most direct assessment of inter-coder comparisons. However, sometimes coding involves the use of scales, such as measuring the strength of an argument, on a six-point scale, for or against some aspect of tourism development. In this case, you need to decide whether you require your coders to assign exactly the same value or whether you can accept slight variation. In other words, if you code someone's position as a 5 ('agree') and your colleague codes the same person as a 4 ('somewhat agree') – do you count this as a match or not?

Measuring – and ultimately, ensuring – inter-coder reliability is an essential part of content analysis. While inter-coder reliability does not guarantee the validity of your concepts (that is, whether your measures are truly capturing what you think they are), reliability is a prerequisite for validity. Moreover, if you lack any test of inter-coder reliability, your results can easily be dismissed by a sceptical reviewer or reader.

The measurement of inter-coder reliability can involve any of several different tools or indices. None of these is universally accepted by methodologists as the single best measure. The intuitively most obvious and easiest to understand is the calculation of the percentage of agreement between coders' classifications. To do this, you either draw a sample of specific items that have been coded, or do a census of all codes if the number is not too large. As a simple illustration, consider the following example. We will use the case presented in Focus Box 9.1 again, but present only one of the qualities coded: ethnic background (see Table 9.1). In the real case, comparisons were also made between the various roles and tourism themes portrayed (see above).

Table 9.1. Calculating the percentage of agreement between two coders.

	Coder A	Coder B
Photograph	**Ethnic back ground of person**	**Ethnic background of person**
1	Caucasian	Caucasian
2	Caucasian	Caucasian
3	Other	Black
4	Black	Black
5	Other	Other
6	Indigenous	Indigenous
7	Caucasian	Caucasian
8	Black	Black
9	Black	Black
10	Other	Other
... and so on		

One method to calculate the percentage agreement is as follows:

$$\%\ \text{agreement} = \frac{(\#\ \text{of comparisons} - \#\ \text{of divergent codes})}{(\#\ \text{of comparisons})} \tag{9.1}$$

In our example, the two coders differed in their categorization of the person appearing in photograph 3: 'A' perceived the person to be 'Other'; 'B' perceived the person to be 'Black'. Ten pairs of rankings were compared. Thus:

$$\%\ \text{agreement} = \frac{(\#\ \text{of comparisons} - \#\ \text{of divergent codes})}{(\#\ \text{of comparisons})} = \frac{10-1}{10} = 90\% \tag{9.2}$$

In other words, there was 90% agreement between the coders. The level of acceptable agreement is a matter of judgement. Ninety per cent generally is considered to be quite good; 80% is usually acceptable for most purposes.

Neuendorf (2002a) provides several useful examples for calculating percentage agreement in different situations. Some authors argue that assessing the percentage of agreement is an inadequate measure of inter-coder reliability (for example, Lombard *et al.*, 2002). These authors object to measuring percentage of agreement on the grounds that the percentage of agreement inflates the estimate of reliability because the reviewers may agree 'by chance'. In my view, this argument would have merit if coding were a random or arbitrary process, but this should not be the case if you have carefully designed your coding scheme. While coders may still have differences of opinion, agreement in the assigning of a code is more likely to be due to substantive agreement, not random variation. Still, if you want to offer more rigorous evidence of inter-coder reliability, you can use statistics such as Cohen's κ or Fleiss' κ (see Appendix A). Popping (1988) provides a review of numerous inter-coder agreement metrics.

As you might anticipate, calculating inter-coder levels of agreement can quickly become overwhelmingly time-consuming. A number of authors have developed programmes to assist in comparing coders' ratings. One of the more popular at the time of this writing is Neuendorf's (2002b) *Program for Reliability Assessment with Multiple Coders* (PRAM), free on the Internet.

Clearly articulating the objectives of your study to your coders, discussing with them the concepts key to your research and developing an explicit operational definition of those concepts helps to facilitate the coding process. So, too, does having a clear and unambiguous coding form. Very importantly, having one or more practice coding sessions using material similar to that of your study, but which will not be used as data, allows you and your coder(s) to more clearly understand the task and how to make judgements. Assessing inter-coder reliability should be done near the start of your project to identify any potential problems, and then again at the conclusion.

Reporting results

The final step is to prepare a report describing the purpose of your study, the methods and sources of data you used and your findings. This would include presentation of the results of reliability testing as well as your substantive findings. For more guidelines about reporting results of your research, see Chapter 10.

CONTENT ANALYSIS OF PHOTOGRAPHS

Photographs can be viewed as a form of text that uses graphics rather than words to communicate. As a result, content analysis is also a relevant analytical approach to the examination of photographs. Much of the preceding section on the methods of content analysis applies to the analysis of photographs, but there are a few other important considerations.

Just as written text can be conceptualized in a variety of ways, such as writing done for potential visitors (e.g. brochures), writing by visitors (e.g. blogs) or writing about tourism services or destinations (e.g. reviews of hotels), photographs can be conceptualized in different ways. Hesse-Biber and Leavy (2006, p. 298) suggest two different perspectives: (i) photographs as a *visual record*; and (ii) photographs as a *visual diary*. The distinction is subtle but important, and has implications for how you collect and interpret photographs.

If you view photographs as a visual diary, you are treating them as an independent representation of some aspect of the world. Such photographs are typically made *by* tourists. With this perspective, you are considering photographs to be a type of artefact conveying information about some aspect of social reality.

Photographs studied as visual records usually comprise photographs made *for* tourists, such as in the context of advertising, postcards or souvenir books. Buzinde *et al.*'s (2006) analysis of website images as described in Focus Box 9.1 is an illustration of this conceptualization of photographs. Photographs as visual records are, in a sense, their own evidence – they are what they are.

Photographs as a form of visual diary, on the other hand, are a medium employed by the person taking the photographs, much as one might write about their experiences in a travel blog. In this case, you interpret the photograph as a 'lens' to understand the photographer's gaze – what she found interesting, what perspective she adopted, what story or memory she appears to be trying to capture. Thus, these types of photographs are usually associated with pictures visitors will take for their own pleasure and memories. Photography, from this perspective, often is an important part of the tourism experience. The stereotype of a visitor with a camera around his neck reflects this close relationship. Indeed Sontag (1978), Markwell (1997) and Larsen (2006) have suggested that, for many visitors, travel without a camera is virtually unthinkable and that the act of photography is integral to a visitor's experience.

When looking at photographs taken by visitors, researchers sometimes provide visitors, perhaps members of a group tour, with cameras they may keep in return for providing the researcher with a copy of the set of photographs. The visitors may be left free to take photographs of whatever interests them, or they may be given some general guidelines of things to photograph – such as aspects of a destination that mean the most to them or that best represent the experience of the destination.

Asking subjects to take photographs means that photography as a data collection tool is more intrusive than other types of content analysis, in that the subject knows the researcher will be viewing their images. This is a different situation from looking at photographs taken *for* visitors, such as in advertising or travel magazine articles. In this case, the author or editor who inserted the photograph intended the photograph to be viewed, but probably not in a research context. Whether you are looking at photographs taken by or for visitors, it is useful to remember Byers' (1964, p. 79) observation: 'Cameras don't take pictures, people do'. Obviously, the subject of a photograph is the result of a human decision about what to photograph. However, Byers' statement also implies that if the subject of a photograph is another human being and that person is aware of being photographed, the act of photography represents a form of interaction between people, which may or may not be unwelcome.

Your focus in doing a content analysis of photographs taken by visitors will be determined by the objectives of your research. Some of the types of content you may want to explore in photographs taken *for* visitors or potential visitors could include – but are not be limited to – the following. Whatever coding system you develop, remember that it should be exhaustive and exclusive:

General subjects of the photograph:

- people: e.g. locals, staff, other visitors, family, friends;
- buildings: e.g. historic, scenic, accommodations, attractions;
- landscape;
- vegetation; or
- animals.

Perspectives adopted:

- close-ups;
- mid-range;
- panoramic vistas;
- single subject (person) versus group (multiple people); or
- stereotypical images versus idiosyncratic images.

Framing:

- inclusion or exclusion of objects present at the site, such as public art, iconic features, power lines, signs of poverty, graffiti;
- inclusion or exclusion of other visitors;
- inclusion or exclusion of locals; or
- public spaces versus private spaces (such as outside a hotel versus inside a hotel room).

Other considerations:

- social context of photographs: parties, portraiture of a significant other, political demonstrations, staff persons (e.g. tour guide or driver); or
- time of day, such as being taken primarily early in the trip, evenly dispersed throughout the trip or concentrated near the end of the trip.

Coding of images in photographs could, of course, involve multiple categories such as noting, for example, that photographs taken early in the trip tended to emphasize famous sites whereas photographs taken later in the trip concentrated on travelling companions. Some of the types of content you may want to explore in photographs taken for visitors or potential visitors could include (but would not be limited to):

Types of person represented:

- sex, age, ethnicity;
- role: visitor, service staff, entertainer, 'locals' (as in sidewalk scenes); or
- active, passive, posing.

Theme of photograph:

- nature-based;
- exotic culture;
- sports;
- relaxation; or
- heritage/arts/'elite' culture.

Design aspects:

- colour versus black and white;
- size of photo (physical size or proportion of page, such as quarter-page, full-page);
- presence or absence of label/description with photograph; or
- location of photo (front cover of brochure, interior, rear cover).

The coding of the type of content listed above represents a systematic examination of manifest content – what is empirically observable. This is an important step in content analysis and can provide interesting findings in its own right. However, manifest content often does not provide the deeper insights you may be seeking. It can be a starting point, but may not be your ultimate goal. Deeper insights can be obtained through an examination of latent content – that is, attempting to infer the 'meaning' of the manifest content. It involves asking yourself why this particular image was made, usually in the context of looking at a larger collection of photographs by the same person or in the same publication.

Asking 'why' or 'what is the deeper meaning' behind photographs is sometimes referred to as **semiotic analysis**. Semiotics is the study of signs and symbols in terms of how they communicate messages and meanings (Van Leeuwen and Jewitt, 2001). As a subjective analytical design, visual content analysis requires a careful, methodical approach to coding and pattern interpretation, just as do other subjective approaches. Collier (2001) provides some practical guidelines for doing a visual latent content analysis. These are summarized here.

He suggests the first step is to look carefully at all the images you have available. Spend time looking at and comparing the photographs you have collected for analysis. Your goal is to achieve an overall impression of the photographs and their content: patterns, themes or perspectives, subtleties, and variations or consistencies in the images. Plan on spending a fair bit of time doing this. You need to develop an intuitive feeling for the photographs that will, eventually, help you develop a framework to shape your further analysis.

Once you have become thoroughly acquainted with your collection of images, your second step is to undertake a manifest content analysis. One goal of this stage is to develop an inventory of observations related to the goals of your research. These observations can then provide the basis for developing themes or general patterns you explore in the third step.

In the third step, you methodically look for themes, patterns and consistencies or variations across images. Develop a codebook to guide your recording and coding of patterns, and to ensure consistency in how you interpret the images you are studying. This codebook becomes a key tool for the fourth step of analysis.

In the fourth step, working with your codebook, return to the photographs and systematically examine them – tabulating images – noting not only frequency, but also patterns across the photographs, as well as any latent messages the images may be conveying. Your ability to recognize latent messages will be based on how well you have developed an intuitive understanding of your collection of photographs, as well as on the background reading you have done in preparation for your research. This reading should sensitize you to evidence of themes and meanings implicit in the photographs. These might – depending on your focus – relate to family relations, social group dynamics, environmental impacts or how visitors from one culture view people and destinations in another culture.

A tactic that some authors (for example, Canton and Santos, 2008) find useful for coding photographs is to describe images in photographs in terms of a bipolar scale. In other words, after coding images in terms of specific features (such as age, sex and ethnicity of subjects, or the types of landscapes/buildings appearing in the photographs), the images (either specific elements of photographs or each photograph as a whole) might be classified as being at either end of the following bipolar pairs. Not all pairs will be relevant for all photographs. However, you should have sufficient pairs to capture the themes in which you are interested. An example of such bipolar pairs (formulated in this case in the context of post-colonial theory) can be seen in those used by Canton and Santos in their study of photographs taken by students on an international study tour. Of course, different bipolar scales would be used for different types of studies:

- traditional/modern displays;
- subject/object role in interaction;
- master/servant relations;
- centre/periphery composition; and
- devious–lazy/moral–industrious portrayals of locals.

Whether doing content analysis of written text or graphic text, once you have completed the actual analysis you then need to write up your results – relating or interpreting your findings to your original research objectives or questions. Your findings may: (i) confirm your initial hypotheses; or (ii) offer mixed results or disconfirm your hypotheses. Or, if you posed more open-ended questions, your results will offer answers – even if only tentative – to those questions and may suggest areas for further research.

CONCLUSIONS

Content analysis is a research design in which you collect and interpret textual or graphic information that can provide insights into the perceptions, experiences and values of people involved in tourism, whether visitors, DMO marketers, service suppliers, travel writers or even the residents of destination communities. Moreover, this information usually is obtained though unobtrusive methods, potentially allowing you to capture opinions that have not been 'edited' by the subject in response to being interviewed by you.

Two general types of questions asked by researchers using content analysis include: (i) what is the content, meaning or form of the communication piece under study; and (ii) how words, assumptions, definitions, arguments or images are used to shape the communication.

Content analysis can be used either to test a hypothesis, or to explore patterns and themes without you having a preconceived notion of what you will find.

There are also two fundamentally different approaches to the interpretation of content. Manifest content analysis focuses on word counts or tabulations of specific, observable features in photographs without any deeper interpretation of the meaning of that content. This type of analysis can be useful in some contexts, such as seeking for an understanding of terminology or components of messages. Latent content analysis goes further than this. It involves the search for a deeper meaning behind the content of a communication. This search can offer greater insights than manifest content analysis, although it also carries a greater risk. As with other forms of subjective analysis, latent content analysis is subject to narrative fallacies and confirmation error.

Whichever type of content analysis you undertake, an important strategy is to approach the communication medium you are studying systematically. This process begins, as always, with a statement of your objectives and the articulation of key concepts to guide your analysis. You then develop a sampling frame (if you are not looking at every piece of communication associated with your topic). You next develop a coding scheme and, ideally, work with at least one other coder to share the workload and to provide a higher degree of reliability than coding by yourself. This assistant coder must be trained to ensure that the two of you have a common understanding of the goal of the research, as well as the specific procedures and criteria for coding.

Once you get to this point, you conduct the coding, occasionally checking for intra-coder and inter-coder reliability. Intra-coder reliability refers to you consistently coding the same content in the same way. Inter-coder reliability refers to two or more coders coding the same content in the same way. This consistency can be measured using a number of different statistical tools, as described earlier in this chapter.

Photographs are often used in content analysis. These may be either those taken by private individuals for their own use (and shared with you) or they may be those taken by tourism destinations or agencies for promotional or informational purposes. The basic steps of content analysis of photographs are similar to those associated with the analysis of text.

REFERENCES

Alderman, D.H. and Modlin, E.A. (2008) (In)visibility of the enslaved within on-line plantation tourism marketing: a textual analysis of North Carolina websites. *Journal of Travel and Tourism Marketing* 25, 265–281.

Buzinde, C.N., Santos, C.A. and Smith, S.L.J. (2006) Ethnic representations: destination imagery. *Annals of Tourism Research* 33, 707–728.

Byers, P. (1964) Still photography in the systematic recording and analysis of behaviour data. *Human Organization* 23, 78–84.

Canton, K. and Santos, C.A. (2008) Closing the hermeneutic circle? Photographic encounters with the other. *Annals of Tourism Research* 35, 7–26.

Choi, S., Lehto, X. and Morrison, A. (2007) Destination image representation on the web: content analysis of Macau travel-related websites. *Tourism Management* 28, 118–129.

Collier, M. (2001) *Handbook of Visual Analysis*. Sage, London.

Galileo Company (undated) CATPAC II. Available at: http://www.galileoco.com/N_catpac.asp (accessed 13 March 2009).

Hesse-Biber, S. and Leavy, P. (2006) *The Practice of Qualitative Research*. Sage, Thousand Oaks, California.

Holsti, O. (1969) *Content Analysis for the Social Sciences and Humanities*. Addison-Wesley, Reading, Massachusetts.

Larsen, S. (2006) Picturing Bornholm: producing and consuming a tourist place through picturing practices. *Scandinavian Journal of Hospitality and Tourism* 6(2), 75–94.

Lombard, M., Snyder-Duch, J. and Bracken, C.C. (2002) Content analysis in mass communication: assessment and reporting of inter-coder reliability. *Human Communication Research* 28, 587–604.

Markwell, K. (1997) Dimensions of photography in a nature-based tour. *Annals of Tourism Research* 24, 131–155.

Neuendorf, K.A. (2002a) *The Content Analysis Guidebook*. Sage, Thousand Oaks, California.

Neuendorf, K.A. (2002b) PRAM: a Program for Reliability Assessment with Multiple Coders. Available at: http://www.geocities.com/skymegsoftware/pram.html (accessed 2 February 2009).

Nickerson, N. (1995) Tourism and gambling content analysis. *Annals of Tourism Research* 22, 53–66.

Popping, R. (1988) On agreement indices for nominal data. In: Saris, W. and Gallhofer, I. (eds) *Sociometric Research: Vol. 1, Data Collection and Scaling*. St. Martin's Press, New York, pp. 90–105.

Sontag, S. (1978) *On Photography*, 3rd edn. McGraw-Hill Ryerson, Toronto, Ontario.

Van Leeuwen, T. and Jewitt, C. (2001) *Handbook of Visual Analysis*. Sage, London.

chapter 10

How to Prepare a Research Report or Presentation

WHY THIS IS IMPORTANT

The final step in any research project is to prepare a written report or make a presentation on your findings. For some, presenting results is one of the most enjoyable and creative aspects of research. For others, it is the most tedious or even the most intimidating. Regardless of your opinion, reporting your results is an integral part of your research. Doing research is usually intrinsically rewarding; communicating or sharing your findings is unavoidable, sometimes scary but always essential.

Learning how to write a report or to make a presentation is a skill that will serve you well in many aspects of your life. Many people who are more eloquent than I have provided excellent insights into writing and other forms of presentation, so I find writing this last chapter – giving you advice on how to present your own findings – a bit intimidating. I love writing, but I know that writing and presenting are skills that come with practice, not from just reading someone else writing about them. This is especially true when it comes to making an oral presentation. Still, this book would not be complete without my admittedly inadequate attempt to proffer you some suggestions for presenting your work (by the way, 'proffer' connotes something you may or may not accept whereas 'offer' connotes something I expect you to accept).

I like the following quotation by Ernest Hemingway on writing: 'There is no rule on how to write. Sometimes it comes easily and perfectly, sometimes it's like drilling rock and then blasting it out with charges'. Of course, if I believed that quotation literally, I would not be writing this chapter. Hemingway was writing about creative writing – short stories, novels and plays – not research. But I believe the experience of being an effective, persuasive and clear communicator of research can be as creative and difficult as writing fiction.

Hemingway's distinctive, lean and muscular writing style, combined with his creative talent, won him a Nobel Prize for Literature. He attributed his style to his time as an 18-year-old cub reporter for the *Kansas City Star* from 1917 to 1918. *Star* staff were given a copy of a style sheet consisting of 110 rules for writing. Years later, in a 1940 interview, Hemingway claimed that '[t]hose were the best rules I ever learned for the business of writing … I've never forgotten them. No man with any talent, who feels and writes truly about the thing he is trying to say, can fail to write well if he abides with them' (Fisher, 2007). The heart of the rules usually is now labelled as 'Hemingway's four rules of writing':

1. Use short sentences.
2. Use short first paragraphs.
3. Use vigorous English.
4. Be positive, not negative.

A few supplemental comments on each of these may be useful. Avoid the temptation to cram too many thoughts or words into a single sentence. Strive to keep a single thought per sentence. Keep your expression of that thought as concise as possible. Some scholars appear to believe writing 30 words to express a thought they could write in ten words as being more 'scholarly'. They appear to not understand that overly long or complex sentences obscure their message. Do not allow yourself to be intimidated by authors who ignore this rule. The fact that their writing is hard to follow doesn't mean they are smarter than authors who write simple, short and clear sentences.

Short first paragraphs invite the reader to get into an article or book. Just as each sentence should express one idea, each paragraph should represent one complete message or a series of closely related thoughts. As a rule of thumb, strive to keep your paragraphs to a maximum of 15 lines of 12-point text. Conversely, avoid single-sentence paragraphs. Each paragraph should stand alone, with enough material to communicate your thought, but without so much content that the reader will lose track of what he or she is supposed to understand.

The phrase 'vigorous English' may read like a concept more related to action stories or advertising copy, as in, 'NOW! NEW AND IMPROVED! GET YOURS TODAY! DON'T WAIT! BE THE FIRST TO OWN…' than to scholarly writing. However, as a researcher, you are still selling (in a generic sense) your ideas – not with hyperbole, but with style and clarity that will encourage your reader to follow your thinking and remain interested in your paper.

The fourth rule, being positive, applies to many forms of communications. However, it can be challenging. Look at the first paragraph in this chapter. I violated this rule in that paragraph. It is intentionally negatively worded, with words like 'unavoidable', 'tedious' and 'intimidating'. I wrote that way to acknowledge that many people don't like writing. But I also tried to get across the idea that writing can be creative and enjoyable. Academics who write up their research results should strive for honesty, and that may involve acknowledging gaps in the literature on some topic or limitations in their research design. However, even here you might be able to find a positive way of expressing yourself. For example, instead of writing 'There has been no research on X', you might write 'X represents a subject for further research'. Instead of describing your sample of respondents as all the friends, fellow students, co-workers and acquaintances you could persuade into completing a questionnaire, consider describing it as a 'convenience sample'.

This chapter is about sharing your ideas through some medium – not just writing, although that is the dominant mode of communication in our field – in a style that is fair and accurate and, at the same time, interesting for your audience. We will consider three forms of presenting research results: written reports, oral presentations and poster presentations. I will also include some advice on the use of PowerPoint slides as part of an oral presentation.

WRITING A RESEARCH REPORT

Some general guidelines

There are numerous forms of written reports. These include term papers, theses or dissertations, technical reports and papers submitted to a journal. The specific format of each varies and reflects the audience for whom you are writing. Your college or advisor may have specific guidelines for the format of an academic submission. Journal editors have different criteria for research papers submitted for review. The style of presentation for a technical report to an agency will be different from either of these. As a result, I cannot give you precise guidelines that will cover every circumstance in which you might be writing a research report. However, some general suggestions are possible. Adapt or ignore the following in specific situations if there is a good reason to do so.

Most academic research papers and reports have what might be called an 'hourglass' structure. You begin your paper broadly with a description of the background and significance of your topic, and then narrow your focus as you discuss the objectives of your research. You then focus more tightly on methods and results. Finally, in the conclusion, you broaden your paper's scope again by discussing the larger meaning of your results. You might conclude by presenting the limitations of your research design and making suggestions for further research.

Clarity in your writing is essential throughout the paper. Be conscious of proper grammar, spelling and word usage. Some specific suggestions are provided in Focus Box 10.1 that draw guidelines that I give my students. Misused words, improper grammar and careless punctuation are not pedantic cavils. These can be serious impediments to your effective communication with your reader.

Focus Box 10.1. Style guidelines for academic writing.

These guidelines are from a style sheet I provide my students for use in preparing term papers. These are not the only grammatical rules with which you should be familiar, but they address some of the most common errors I have observed in my students' papers. Your professor/editor will probably have other expectations or guidelines about how to present or format your papers. If there is a divergence between your professor/editor's and my views – remember, professors and editors rule.

- There is beauty and grace in simple language. Technical jargon is sometimes unavoidable; terms like 'heteroscedasticity' or 'Likert scale' are impossible to avoid in certain contexts. However, socio-babble is rarely justified. Here's a real example from an article in *Annals of Tourism Research* (I do not provide the author's name or citation to avoid causing embarrassment): *'To reduce the above grand-stage to symmetrical crystals of significance is to purify that demesne of its material complexity, to map out a bodiless landscape, and to pretend a science that does not exist and imagine a science that cannot be found'.* I suspect the motivations for this type of writing are either to impress (it doesn't) or to intimidate (it can, but why would one want to do this?).[a]
- Divide the paper, if appropriate, into headings and subheadings using a different format (such as bolded/not bolded and different point size) for different levels of headings.
- Indent paragraphs *except* the first paragraph of each new section or subsection.
- Avoid single-sentence and very long (more than 15 lines) paragraphs.
- Insert two spaces after the period (full stop) concluding each sentence.

(*Continued*)

Focus Box 10.1. Continued.

- Use left-justification only, not full justification. Left-justified with an uneven right edge is easier to read.
- Be sure nouns, pronouns, and verbs agree in number. For example, 'every 10th person through the gate will be interviewed to ask about how they learned of the festival' is incorrect. It should be, of course, 'every 10th person through the gate will be interviewed to ask about how she/he learned of the festival'. Mixing single and plural forms is common in English because of the desire to use gender-free pronouns. Some authors interpret the gender of 'he/him/his' in the traditional sense of being gender neutral, not just masculine. Others now use she/her/hers as a generic pronoun for both males and females. Still others use the combined form (he/she). As you will have noted, this book uses all three conventions.
- When reporting research papers, write in the third person only. The reason for this convention in most journals is to remind authors that the focus of their writing should be on research objectives, literature, data, analysis, and conclusions – not themselves. However, in some academic genres or venues, writing in the first person is considered acceptable. And, yes, I realize that I ignored this rule in this book in order to make my writing more personal.
- Minimize the use of the passive voice. For example, use 'The author focused on X' rather than 'The focus of the author was on X'. The passive voice is wordy and sometimes difficult or tiring to read. Which joke is likelier to get a laugh: 'Why did the chicken cross the road?' or 'Why was the road crossed by the chicken?'
- Insert a comma before the 'and' in a series of three or more terms, as in: 'The four Atlantic Canada provinces are Prnce Edward Island, New Brunswick, Nova Scotia, and Newfoundland and Labrador.' A comma used before the final 'and' in a series is known as a serial comma, Oxford comma, or Harvard comma. Be aware, though, that some authors, editors, and publishers do not use a serial comma. I feel the serial comma avoids ambiguity and awkward sentence constructions such as 'For breakfast, I had, juice, coffee, toast, and bacon and eggs' as opposed to 'juice, coffee, toast and bacon and eggs'. However, as an alert reader, you may have noticed CABI (the publisher of this volume) does not use a serial comma.
- On a related point, use a comma to clarify the structure of a sentence in which a series of compound names (or terms) are presented in a series. For example, 'my favourite Caribbean destinations are Trinidad and Tobago, and Turks and Caicos.' Imagine that sentence without the commas!
- Be conscious of your placement of 'only'. Adverbs normally modify the word or phrase immediately following them. Changes in placement can dramatically change the meaning of a sentence. Reflect on the differences among: 'Only she kissed him.' 'She only kissed him.' 'She kissed only him.'
- Italicize Latin abbreviations such as *e.g.* ('for example'), *i.e.* ('that is'), *cf.* ('compare to'), *etc.* ('and so forth'), *viz.* (namely), *NB* ('note especially') and follow each abbreviation with a commas, as in, 'The author provides numerous examples of strategic planning, *e.g.*, the planning of a new airport as part of a regional economic development strategy.' Do not use *etc* (*et* cetera) as the last item in a list of examples that begin with *e.g.*: (not: '*e.g.*, museums, galleries, historic homes, *etc*'). *Etc* means 'and so forth' or 'for example'; it is *not*, *per se*, an example. However, again, not all authors, editors, or publishers observe the practice of italicizing foreign words or abbreviations. You probably have noticed that CABI does not italicize all Latin abbreviations.

(Continued)

Focus Box 10.1. Continued.

- Use the subjunctive tense for verbs expressing hypothetical (or wishful) situations: 'If the author *were* to revise the book in a future edition…, *not* 'If the author *was* to revise the book in a future edition…'.
- Keep superlatives or extravagant adjectives, such as 'great', 'superb', or 'excellent' to a minimum. Scholarly writing is about credibility, not the fulsome praising of someone or something.
- Use 'between' when discussing or relating two entities, and 'among' when discussing or relating three or more, as in 'The exchange of policy documents between the two NGOs' and 'The exchange of policy documents among the ten NGOs'.
- A decade of years is expressed as 'the 1990s', not 'the 1990's'.
- 'Tourism' is not synonymous with 'travel'; the latter term is a more comprehensive noun or is used as a verb.
- Remember the words of Inigo Montoya. Montoya is a fictional character in William Goldman's novel, *The Princess Bride*. In the movie version (adapted by Rob Reiner from the novel), Montoya hears another character repeatedly misusing the word, 'inconceivable', whenever he encounters an unexpected situation. Montoya eventually says, 'You keep using that word. I do not think it means what you think it means' (Wikipedia, 2009). The point: be aware of the correct meaning of words. Some words often misused in scholarly writing include the following:
  - 'Unique' means one-of-a-kind. Few things are truly unique. The word does not mean distinctive or unusual. A student who correctly uses 'unique' is unusual and admirable, but not unique.
  - Observe the difference between 'which' and 'that'. 'That' is used to introduce a restrictive clause, while 'which' is used to introduce a non-restrictive clause. In other words, 'that', in effect, turns the clause that follows it into an adjective. For example, 'The nation that received the most international visitor arrivals in 2009 was…'. Here, 'that received the most international visitor arrivals' is part of the description of that nation. 'Which', or more accurately, ', which', because the preceding comma is an essential part of the construction, adds only an incidental descriptive phrase, *e.g.*, 'This nation, which receives many international visitors, also generates many outbound trips'.
  - Observe the difference between 'since' and 'because'. 'Since' connotes the passage of time, as in 'Since the 1950s when commercial jet aircraft were invented…'. 'Because' connotes cause-and-effect, as in 'Because of the invention of commercial jet aircraft in the 1950s…'.
  - 'Select' is a verb; the adjectival form is 'selected': 'Here are some selected examples', *not* 'Here are some select examples'.
  - 'Problem' and 'issue' are not synonyms. 'Problem' comes from the Greek, *pro'blhma*, meaning a thing thrown or put forward; hence, it is a task or situation presented for solution. Issue comes from the Old French, *eissue*, meaning to go out. It has several meanings, such as (i) the outcome of a course of action, (ii) the action of flowing out; (iii) child or children, (iv) topic, or (v) the entrails of a butchered animal. In brief: a problem is something to be solved; an issue is something to be discussed but not necessarily solved…unless you are trying to get rid of the entrails of a butchered animal. Then the issue really is a problem.

[a]Some academics remind me of Disraeli's gibe about Gladstone: he is 'inebriated with the exuberance of his own verbosity'.

Your logic – the structure of your paper and how you present your ideas – also is essential. I generally begin by developing an outline of the overall structure of a paper to assist me in ensuring that there is a logical flow to my paper. The outline also provides me with a road map so I don't go off on tangents when writing, or forget to cover important topics. A good outline can also help you avoid redundant sections in which authors sometimes present the same material two or three times in different parts of their paper.

Begin your paper with an introduction. Your introduction should not only identify your topic, it should also explain its significance and provide a context for your research so your reader can understand how your topic relates to other research. Use credible, authoritative sources for any quotations or numbers you provide. For example, if you want to cite trends in the increases of the numbers of international tourism trips globally, the World Tourism Organization is a credible source. Don't just pull a number out of a textbook. Go to an original, reliable source. Similarly, avoid sweeping, unsupported generalizations. Two examples that I see repeatedly in my students' papers are that: (i) 'tourism is the world's largest industry'; and (ii) 'leisure time is increasing' (in the context of North America). Both claims are widely made and both are false. These are not the only examples of incorrect platitudes that occur in research papers.

A clear argument for the importance of your research is important. That argument can be based on a gap in previous research; the use of untested assumptions in previous literature; topics that other authors have identified as requiring further research; or problems that exist, such as negative economic, social or environmental impacts that might benefit from research. Alternatively, you might have found a model that has produced mixed results or that you might be applying in a new context. Your problem might address an important policy, planning or marketing problem. There might be a new phenomenon that has been observed but that is not well understood. Managers might be struggling with some problem, perhaps related to human resources, innovation, finances or some other aspect of operations that needs solving. Whatever your justification, it should be based on careful reasoning and evidence, not on emotional appeal or hyperbole. I have seen too many student research proposals and papers that are essentially political rants rather than carefully reasoned, balanced and articulated arguments.

Once you have introduced your topic and explained its significance, present the objectives of your research. You may want to review Chapter 2's comments on this topic. One thing to watch out for is presenting inconsistent statements of the purpose of your paper. This is a surprisingly frequent problem when someone writes about the purpose of his or her research in several different places in the same paper over a period of weeks.

Carefully define or explain technical terms or concepts. To the degree possible, avoid using jargon to explain concepts. The use of simple examples often helps illustrate the meaning of a concept or bit of jargon. If you refer to some model or theory, briefly explain what it is used for or the types of questions it is designed to answer. Don't assume (unless you know otherwise for certain) that your reader will be familiar with the model or theory you cite. And be conservative in your use of the word 'theory', as we discussed in Chapter 1. Although there are exceptions, few models or concepts used in tourism research deserve to be called 'theory' in the sense of representing a coherent, consistent, broadly applicable, integrated, replicable and empirically supported view of the world.

Be cautious about claiming that your research – especially if it has been done for academic purposes – will be relevant to policy makers, marketers, planners or managers. Unless you have worked with such individuals and your research has been designed and conducted in cooperation with them, and you have some communication strategy to share your findings with potential users, your report will probably never to be seen, read or understood by them. The fact that many academic papers and books 'sit on the shelf' and are never read or applied by people who might otherwise use them is frustrating, but it is a fact of academic life. This is not intended to be a negative or cynical observation. If your work can be used to make a difference – wonderful. Just don't assume the world is waiting breathlessly for your results, or that busy managers or planners read academic papers.

Be cautious about using job titles such as 'tourism policy analyst', 'tourism planner' or 'tourism manager'. Very few government agencies actually have positions with these titles. They do exist, but they are rare. In Western countries, for example, one can find municipal planners, transportation planners, subdivision planners, event planners, but very rarely 'tourism planners'. 'Tourism manager' is also scarce as a job title. Most managers working in a tourism business will see themselves as being a manager in a restaurant, hotel, airline or some other specific business or industry. A researcher who casually refers to such job titles as a tactic to justify her or his research runs the risk of being seen as uninformed about the nature of our field.

On citations and quotations

The importance of citing sources that shape your ideas and from which you develop your thoughts is something you've probably heard from the beginning of your college or university education. Proper citation is a matter of fairness and ethics, and respecting and acknowledging the contributions made by others. (See Focus Box 10.2 for comments about different systems for including citations in your paper.) No researcher works in isolation of other people's ideas.

Focus Box 10.2. Reference systems.

There are a number of reference systems or style guidelines for citing the work of authors whom you use in your research. Citing your sources is, of course, important but so too is how you do this. Most tourism journals and book publishers use some version of '**parenthetical citation**', also known as the **author–date system**, or the '**Harvard system**' (note, the system has no connection with Harvard University – the name is just an historical curiosity).

As the name suggests, the author–date system involves placing the name of the author and the date of his or her publication in parentheses within your text immediately following the thought or fact you are citing in your paper. A common form would look like (Smith, 2010). The actual reference would be listed at the end of your paper as part of a list ordered alphabetically by the authors' last names.

The specific details of how the individual items in the reference list are to be formatted will vary by reference system. For example, some place the date of the publication in parentheses, others do not. These details and the inconsistencies among systems can be a source of annoyance for writers. However, careful attention to the details used by your intended publisher or your college is important.

There are, though, numerous systems, each favoured by different disciplines. Some of the more common reference systems in the humanities and social sciences are the following:

Chicago Manual of Style (CMS or 'Chicago'): http://www.chicagomanualofstyle.org/home.html

CMS is a flexible citation system that permits mixing of parenthetical citations with the use of footnotes or endnotes, as long as your use of these is clear and consistent. CMS is closely related to the Turabian system (named after Kate Turabian, the University of Chicago Graduate School Librarian, 1930–1958, who developed the system:

(Continued)

Focus Box 10.2. Continued.

http://www.press.uchicago.edu/books/turabian/ turabian_citationguide.html). CMS and Turabian are widely used by people working in history and some social sciences.

The Modern Language Association (MLA) System: http://www.mla.org/store/CID24/PID363

The MLA system is used especially by publications dealing with linguistic and language studies, cultural studies, media studies and related disciplines.

ISO 690

ISO 690 is an ISO standard for information to be included in citations, including electronic citations. It tends not to be in common use in tourism, but is the basis for citation guidelines used by many government and industrial organizations. I've not given a URL for ISO 690 here because: (i) it is lengthy; (ii) the guidelines must be purchased; and (iii) you can easily learn more about ISO 690 by doing your own Internet information search.

Modern Humanities Research Association (MHRA): http://www.mhra.org.uk/Publications/Books/StyleGuide/download.shtml

The MHRA style guide is a system widely used in the humanities, especially in the UK.

American Psychological Association (APA): http://apastyle.apa.org/

Although developed for use by the journals published by the APA, a number of journals, especially in North America, Australia, New Zealand and the UK, have adopted APA citation and referencing guidelines. The APA's 'style' covers many aspects of manuscript preparation, including treatment of tables, abbreviations and other aspects of writing style. Thus, if someone tells you to follow 'APA style' you should ask them to clarify exactly what aspects of that style they mean.

There are many other citation systems, including those used in the natural sciences and engineering. These probably won't be relevant to your work, but if you are doing work that might appear in a civil engineering journal, for example, you should be aware that the journal may have a citation and referencing system that differs from those listed above.

Individual tourism journals, book publishers or agencies may have their own variations on reference systems. Pay attention to the guidelines used by whatever agency or outlet you hope to use to publish your work. Editors are demanding – and editors rule when it comes to getting your work published.

All style systems are occasionally updated to reflect changes in custom as well as new forms of publications. For example, the emergence of online sources and publications has required that all the systems above be modified to accommodate these new publication and distribution media.

Proper acknowledgement of sources is a sign of professionalism, trustworthiness and scholarly maturity. Much of scholarly enterprise is fundamentally based on trust and an academic's sense of honour. Respect that tradition.

There are nuances in the use of citations in scholarly writing. Certain facts or ideas that you learn from others may not need to be cited if they are 'common knowledge'. This is a risky statement for me to make, but it is an important and valid one. My comment should never be used as a justification for failing to credit someone who has made a significant contribution to your thinking through his or her publications. But there are times when something you have learned from others will have come from so many different sources that citing a single (or a few) sources is simply impractical. For example, noting that certain countries are (or are not) democratic countries, or have (or do not have) a market-driven economy usually does not need a citation. (There can be debate about politics, of course, such as whether Iran's government can be considered to be truly democratically elected – but this is a tourism research book, not a political science text.) The suggestion that the development of commercial passenger jet aircraft permitted a significant increase in international tourism flows probably does not need a citation. Noting that AIEST, CAUTHE, APTA and TTRA are research associations (see Focus Box 1.3) does not need a citation, either. On the other hand, a statement about the number of people who voted in a recent election, the GDP of an economy, the magnitude of international passenger flows or the mission statement of specific tourism research associations would require citations. If you have doubts about whether a statement you are making requires a citation, check with your professor.

Any direct quotation will need a full citation, of course, including page number in the original source. However, be conservative in your use of quotations. As a rule of thumb:

Quote for colour; quote for evidence. Otherwise, don't quote.

Treat quotations as a type of verbal photograph or illustration. They can be very useful when used sparingly. Avoid stringing quotations together. I occasionally read term papers or research proposals in which the student has pulled dozens or scores of quotations from the literature on some topic and linked them together in the paper. They are all properly cited but the student has failed to understand that his or her paper should reflect some original thinking. A research paper should not be simply a 'cut-and-paste' job of quotations from other authors. Your thinking must be present; you must present some original thinking or, at a minimum, an original way of summarizing the literature. Your reader wants to know what *you* think, not what a bunch of other authors think.

When citing an author, whether or not it is in the form of a direct quotation, use the original source if at all possible. You may sometimes find an interesting idea in one article that is based on a previous paper by a different author. The usual form of this citation will be something like, 'Xiao (2008), cited in Smith (2009)'. The problem with this tactic is that you don't know whether Smith correctly interpreted Xiao. There may be times when this approach is unavoidable, but strive to consult the original source. Don't take the lazy way out by not searching for and checking the original source.

On abstracts and appendices

Abstracts and appendices are not found in every paper or report, but they are common in theses, dissertations and technical reports. They play very different roles, with the abstract presented at the beginning of the report and appendices at the very end.

The writing of a good **abstract** can be challenging. One reason is that the abstract is usually written after the rest of the report has been completed. You might be tired or bored with writing, and are ready to move on to something else. Moreover, the abstract requires substantial condensation of all your hard work. You may have written a 100-page report that now has to be condensed to 100 words. Although the abstract is the shortest part of any report, it can be the most important. In many cases, it is the only part someone will read. You'll want to ensure that the abstract presents your work in the best possible way.

Different publications or academic programmes will have different requirements for abstracts, but they generally share the following features. Abstracts are short. Many journal abstracts are limited to 100 or 150 words. Thesis and dissertation abstracts may be longer, up to perhaps 500 words – check your college's guidelines.

A useful way to write an abstract is to write two or three sentences on each of the major aspects of your research. The following describes the typical sections of an abstract. In this case, each section is illustrated with sentences (in italics) taken from an actual published abstract of a study by Xiao and Smith (2007). Note how, in only 98 words, the abstract covers all key information:

- **Introduction**. This briefly states the general topic, including something about the context of the study. Try to avoid starting your abstract with phrasing along the lines of 'This article is about…' Instead, tell the reader immediately what your topic is. The point of the abstract is very tightly to *summarize* your research, not to *describe* what you did for your research. The distinction is subtle but important.

  The use of knowledge has long been of interest to academics and practitioners, but research on it has been underdeveloped in tourism.

- **Statement of the research problem**. This statement will follow logically from your introduction. Your introduction positions your research in a larger context; the problem statement tells the reader what question(s) you are going to answer.

  This article offers a conceptual look at issues and perspectives related to how field practitioners apply knowledge to make decisions and solve problems.

- **Research design**. A succinct explanation about how your study was conducted should follow the statement of your research problem. This will include, as relevant, descriptions of your data sources, the conceptual foundation for your analysis and the methods or logic you used.

  The study draws from the utilization literature, and aims at locating this knowledge use in a conceptual framework.

- **Results**. A summary of your key findings is next. Avoid the temptation to provide numerical data – focus on a verbal summary of your key findings.

  Three sets of propositions are developed to address the related issues, factors or dimensions.

- **Conclusion**. This final section is a succinct statement about the implications of your results, perhaps in terms of confirmation of a model or hypothesis; management, policy or planning implications; or suggestions for further research.

  While the field-specific focus is deliberate and has its limitations, this research could potentially contribute to both tourism and utilization literature.

Appendices (sometimes called annexes) can be a useful part of a paper, especially in a lengthier thesis or technical report. An appendix is material added at the end of a document that is related to the content, but is of less importance. It can be used to provide detail in which the average reader may not be interested. Appendices might include copies of survey forms, lists of organizations contacted, useful websites and so on. For example, this book has one appendix on statistical tests, in which you may or may not be interested. Other books or reports will have numerous appendices. Some reports may have as many as 10 or 12 appendices. Each appendix is limited to one topic, and typically is no more than a few pages in length. Traditionally, each appendix is identified with a letter, as in Appendix A (if there is more than one appendix). A subtitle indicating the subject of the appendix is useful. The order of the appendices is determined either by the order in which the author mentions them in the text, or in order of decreasing importance if they are discussed in the text.

Dealing with writer's block

'Writer's block' is something every writer experiences sometime. Feeling 'blocked' may be a matter of not being motivated to write, not knowing what to write or not knowing how to write something. The frustration that people who must write for a living feel when experiencing writer's block was aptly described by novelist and dramatist, William Saroyan: 'Writing is the hardest way of earning a living with the possible exception of wrestling alligators'. One of the challenges of writing, especially for a student, is that writing is so easy to put off to another day. But eventually a deadline looms and you have to begin putting 'words on paper' (although for most of us now, it is a matter of inputting text into a computer). As I write this chapter, I am keenly aware that I have a deadline only 1 month away to submit the complete typescript for this book to CABI, my publisher.

Different people will have different strategies for dealing with writer's block that work for them; some of the ones I have found that work for me are the following:

- Honest self-reflection. I ask myself whether I actually have anything to communicate. Maybe my problem in starting to write is that I don't really have anything worth writing. In this case, I back off and spend some time reading, thinking or talking with my wife, friends or colleagues about what it is I want to do.
- Talking to myself...or others. This tactic usually follows directly from self-reflection. I will literally talk to myself (usually outdoors, far away from anyone) or with someone whom I trust and understands what I am experiencing. Forcing myself orally to articulate the thoughts with which I am struggling helps me actually create thoughts and to organize them. Sometimes I will combine this with writing notes to myself – scribbling out ideas or points to explore (often in the middle of the night, so I keep a pad of paper by my bed when I need to be creative – although my wife doesn't appreciate these midnight creative writing sessions). You can also try e-mailing a friend to describe what you are struggling with. Writing about what you want to write can be a surreptitious way to attack your topic.
- Go for a walk. A tactic closely related to talking to yourself is to go for a walk. Fresh air and mild physical activity can help release whatever block is in your brain or dilemma you are trying to resolve. There is a famous story in Canadian politics about former Prime Minister Pierre Trudeau, one of Canada's most charismatic Prime Ministers. After a long political career, he sensed it was time to retire. He was trying to decide when to retire as Prime Minister, but couldn't decide when. One day, Trudeau surprised the nation by his sudden decision to retire. He explained his decision with this story: 'I had a good day yesterday, worked on aboriginal rights, and it seemed like a good day to have a last day... I had a good day. It was a *great walk in the snow*' (*Globe and Mail*, 1984) [italics added]. A great walk – in Trudeau's case, a walk in a Canadian blizzard – can help you reach some place in your mind that has been out of reach. Personally, I prefer a walk on a beach to a walk in a blizzard.
- Rearrange the furniture. I am serious. When I was in graduate school, I was fortunate enough to have office space in the hayloft of a barn on the campus of Texas A&M University where graduate students were housed, which allowed me to reposition my desk and bookcase whenever I wished. I found that if I changed my physical position, I also changed my ability to write. A fresh physical perspective translated into a fresh mental perspective. If you don't have the luxury of rearranging your office furniture, try rearranging your desk top, your bookshelves or your files. This may sound silly, but it can help.
- Just do it. The Greek philosopher, Epictetus (1st century, Common Era), is credited with the dictum 'If you want to be a writer ... write'. The point here is that sometimes you just need to

start writing whatever comes into your mind related to your topic. When I was a student, we called this a 'memory dump' – one just dumped everything one was thinking about a topic on to paper. It is always easier to go back and then edit, refine or clarify something you've already written than it is to create. Don't worry about style, logic, grammar or any of the finer points of scholarly writing. Just get something written. You can polish and edit later.

MAKING AN ORAL PRESENTATION

It is ironic to offer advice on how to make an *oral* presentation by *writing* about it, but such are the limitations of a textbook. There are myriad different contexts in which one might make an oral presentation or speech – from giving an acceptance speech after being elected to political office, to offering a toast to a new couple at their wedding. Each has its own conventions and traditions. We will concentrate here on making a research presentation. Even these can have different styles and approaches, depending on whether you are presenting a thesis in a defence before your advisory committee, a PowerPoint file in a student seminar or a paper at an academic conference. However, the following advice generally applies to each of these settings.

There is standard advice that sounds somewhat 'cheeky', but is fundamentally sound:

Tell them what you are going to tell them; then tell them; then tell them what you told them.

However, there is much more to making a presentation than simply standing up and talking. First, it is useful to reflect explicitly on how an oral presentation is different to submitting a written report. Some of the key differences are:

- *You* are the medium of communication. Your style, personal appearance, comfort level and body language play a major role in how well your message is understood and received.
- A person reading a written report can put the report down if he/she gets bored or has something else to do, and pick it up later. He/she can make notes on the paper or flip back to reread a section. None of this, of course, is possible in an oral presentation. On the other hand, your audience can ask questions or probe for more information, which they cannot do with a written report.
- The physical environment in which you and the audience find yourselves can play a big role in the effectiveness of your presentation. Room temperature, lighting, sound systems, ambient noise, the audiovisual technology available to you, and the number of people in the room are factors that will influence your presentation. You may have some control over a few of these, but most will be beyond your control.
- You will usually be given a specified time period in which to speak. Fifteen to 20 minutes is common for a conference presentation, perhaps with time for questions afterwards. You may have less time or more. Whatever time you are assigned – *respect it.* Going over your time allotment shows disrespect to your hosts, the session organisers and the other speakers. It is not only a matter of being rude; running over time can cause problems for the rest of an event's schedule, such as causing other speakers to have to cut their time short or the audience getting out late for a coffee or meal break. You will *not* be liked if either of those things happens.

Preparing for your presentation

Before we look at how to deliver a presentation, let's note several things you will need to consider when preparing it:

- Who is your audience? Consider this book. My audience is you and other readers, who are unseen and largely unknown to me, except for those with whom I directly worked and shared this book. In the context of your research, your audience will probably be your professor, other students or researchers. In any event, think about whether your audience will be familiar with your general topic or whether they may be from difference backgrounds and might not have much understanding of your topic. Their level of familiarity with your topic should shape how you present your ideas.
- If possible, find out about the room, the expected size of the audience, the number of other speakers and their topics, and the format for presentations, including time restrictions for your presentation.
- Have a clear sense of the important messages in your presentation. What do you want your audience to learn? What was the overall purpose of your research? This is not always as obvious as you might think it is. I have seen numerous examples of a student writing one purpose for his study at the time of developing a proposal but then, in an oral presentation of his results (or, as mentioned earlier, in a written paper), describe a different purpose. The shift in the stated purpose comes as a result of the experience – the success, failures or complications – of actually doing the research. Sometimes the shift will be obvious to a reader who has seen both your proposal and final results, but not to you. Try to be very aware of both what you said you were going to do and what you actually did.
- What information, tables, graphics or other supporting information will you need to get your message across? Diagrams are often more effective in communicating numerical patterns than tables of numbers, but there are times when detailed tables are necessary. I touch on a few related suggestions about presenting data later in this chapter.
- What will be the most effective way of presenting your information? Will you need printed handouts? Is PowerPoint the best audiovisual tool? If so, see the following section on how to make effective use of PowerPoint. At other times different formats, such as flip charts or physical models or even an entertaining oral presentation free of audiovisual aids, may be most effective.
- If you are using PowerPoint, will someone be available to advance the slides or will you need to be at your computer each time you want to change a slide? Will you have a remote control unit to advance the slides?

Your presentation

Begin your preparation of your presentation with an outline of what you want to say, with estimates for how much time you can devote to each section. Most presentations will have three major parts: an introduction, the main body and a conclusion. The introduction is not only about explaining the topic of your presentation, it is your chance to connect with your audience. You want to convince them that your talk will interest them. Put yourself in their position and think of what would get their attention. Give them a sense of what you are going to say – the point of your talk and why it is important. This might be in the form of an agenda outlining your presentation, or it may be a more general description of what you are going to discuss. Help them to have a sense of direction about where you are taking them and what the ultimate destination will be.

The main body of your talk is where you present your key ideas and evidence. Your arguments or data need to be carefully developed and presented in a persuasive, logical way. What were the objectives of your research? How did you collect your data? What methods did you use for analysis? What are the key findings? Are there assumptions or limitations in your data or methods you should explain? Offer some clues or guideposts occasionally to your audience so they will have a sense of how you are progressing through your topic, such as saying 'Another key step in the research was to . . .'.

Handouts can help people follow your flow and can provide more detailed tables or graphs than you might be able to present through PowerPoint. However, be cautious about using handouts – your audience's focus should be on you, not some papers in their hands.

Signal when you are coming to your conclusion by saying something like 'In conclusion . . .' or 'So, what does all this tell us?' Use your concluding section to summarize the key points of your presentation and to suggest what might be future directions for research or the implications of your findings. Thank your audience for their attention and then, if appropriate, invite questions. If you are one of a series of presenters and there is a moderator, that person will probably be the one to invite questions, depending on the time available.

Some additional suggestions for your actual delivery are the following.

Let's begin with the jitters. Nerves. Butterflies in the stomach. Or whatever you call the fear of speaking in public. Nervousness before public speaking is normal. Anecdotal opinion is that public speaking is one of the most common phobias people face – worst than snakes, spiders, divorce or death. When I mentioned to my wife I was going to write some helpful pointers about dealing with presentation jitters, she laughed in a most unkind way. As she explained, 'All those helpful tips are worthless. I know myself – I'm going to be nervous and nothing anyone tells me is going to change that'.

Ultimately, you will need to find your own strategy for dealing with nervousness about public speaking, and the following comments may not be helpful to you. The suggestions I proffer to you are for tactics that are helpful for me. To me, the solution is *not* to try to not feel nervous, but to learn to control my nervousness (to get those butterflies in your stomach flying in formation). I try to convert my nervousness into energy to go out and really impress my audience. Some of the other tactics I have found useful include: (i) practising – repeatedly (I may rehearse a presentation as many as 20 times if it is particularly important or challenging); (ii) controlling my breathing – long, slow deep breaths before being introduced; (iii) spending some quiet time alone – not to think about my presentation, but to just be quiet; and (iv) bluff. If you can figure out a way to act as being confident, interesting and informed, odds are you'll actually come across that way.

Now, let's consider some additional ideas about actually making your presentation:

- Again, practice, practice, practice. Practice to ensure that you know your material, that you can present it smoothly and with style and that you are within time limits. *Don't* memorize your presentation but do *know* it. The distinction is important. If you try to memorize but you forget a portion, you are likely to panic. If you know your material without trying to follow a script, you will make a presentation that is informed, lively, engaging and sincere.
- Related to the preceding point, don't read your speech. Don't read your PowerPoint slides. It is insulting to your audience and a waste of their time, not to mention boring.
- Begin speaking in a comfortable, deeper pitch. People's voices tend to rise in pitch as they speak, especially if they become nervous. If you start with your voice pitched high, it has no place to go other than to begin sounding strangled.
- Speak slowly and clearly, but vary your tone and pace. Switching the speed of your delivery (but never too fast), volume and pitch can help you emphasize key points as well as retain the audience's interest.
- If you are going to be speaking at an event where there will be translation, adjust your presentation accordingly. There are two basic types of translation: concurrent and sequential.

Concurrent translation involves one or more translators (usually at the back of the room in a booth speaking to the delegates via FM or infrared transmission equipment and earpieces). If you are speaking in this environment, provide the translators with a copy of your speech. If you don't deliver it verbatim, stick as close to it as possible. If you cannot provide them with a script, speak slowly and very distinctly. Even the best translators need to time listen and convert your words of wisdom into another language. In the case of sequential translation, first you speak, and then you wait while the translator speaks. This is a challenging format within which to present, but sometimes it is unavoidable. Speak single, simple thoughts – usually no more than one or two sentences. Then wait for the translator to do her/his job. This makes for a very slow pace of presentation – requiring at least double the time you would normally need to give your presentation. As a result, you may have to limit substantially how much material you cover. For either concurrent or sequential translation, avoid jokes or puns. These normally do not translate well. I was at a conference in Japan when an English-language speaker made a pun that could not be translated into Japanese. I was told later that the interpreter said to the audience (via their earphones) 'The speaker has just made a joke. Please laugh'. Fortunately for the speaker, they did, even thought they never heard the joke.

- If you are using PowerPoint and are tied to your computer to advance the slides, you may need to stand pretty much in one place. But if you do not need to stand still and are comfortable moving around a bit, do so. However, avoid walking back and forth, repeatedly, as if you are pacing mindlessly. Relax and be natural – whatever your natural is.
- Figure out what to do with your hands. Gesture moderately to make key points, but keep them under control – out of your pockets, out of your hair, out of your underarms, out of your nose. Don't fuss with a paper copy of your speech. Don't jiggle coins or keys. Don't click ballpoint pens or play with the caps of pens. This may sound like needless advice, but I have seen nervous speakers do every one of these things.
- Maintain eye contact with the audience, but don't stare at just one friendly face.
- If you will be speaking for a relatively long period of time, such as an hour, you might ask for a glass or bottle of water before you go to the podium. Nervousness combined with talking will quickly give you a dry mouth.
- Finally, let's come back to presentation jitters. You don't want to embarrass yourself, of course, but what is the worst thing that can happen when you are presenting your research? At worst, you will come across as nervous – a feeling that everyone in your audience has experienced. Moreover, one of my professors claimed (without empirical proof, but I believe him) that, on average, 40% of the audience isn't listening to you anyway. They are nervous about their own presentation, thinking about where to go for dinner, how to introduce themselves to that attractive person across the room, why they haven't heard back from a job application they submitted last month, or any of 1001 more serious and personal problems. The odds are that you and your presentation are not that important to many of the people in the audience. So, relax and enjoy talking about your work.

PREPARING POWERPOINT SLIDES

PowerPoint has become a standard presentation tool in classes, conferences and meetings. It is not the only tool you can use in a presentation, and sometimes not the best one (Gurrie and Fair, 2008). However, PowerPoint has become so standard that it is hard to imagine a group of people coming together for a presentation without its use. In fact, PowerPoint was named in 2007 as one of the top 25 inventions that had changed Americans' lives in the 25 years between 1972 and 2007 (Pompa and Gainer, 2007).

We consider in this section both some guidelines about how to make more effective PowerPoint presentations, and some of the limitations with this medium. The following suggestions for preparing a PowerPoint presentation are some of the key ones that may be useful; you can find numerous others on the Internet by doing a search on 'PowerPoint presentations'.

Effective use of PowerPoint

- Most importantly, don't ignore your audience. Speak to *them*, not your screen. In the final analysis, *you* are the presentation, not your PowerPoint deck. Your audience's attention should be on you. PowerPoint is only a support; it should not be the focus of the audience's attention.
- Know your story. Tell it clearly, simply and in a logical order. This means you have to thoroughly know what you want to say, having such an intuitive understanding of your message that you don't need to read your slides.
- Be cautious about beginning with a slide of the outline of your presentation. This may be helpful, but often it is a waste of time. Your story should be organized clearly enough and with 'signposts' such as clear headings for each major section that your audience can easily follow you as your presentation unfolds.
- At the risk of being repetitious, PowerPoint is a visual aid, not a script. Use it to *support* your presentation – not *be* your presentation. Some presenters observe a 'six-by-six' rule (six bullets, with no more than six words per bullet); others advocate a 'seven-by-seven' rule. These rules are not always practical, but they remind us of the principle of keeping slides as simple as possible.
- You will find a lot of advice from different sources as to what font is 'best' or 'easiest to read'. Certainly some, such as Stataco220 are not good choices for most PowerPoint applications. However, with respect to the common serif versus sans serif fonts, such as Garamond versus Tahoma, there is no definitive research indicating that one is better than the other. *Italics* can be tiresome if overused but they do have value in making a point. Wharton Assitt, who describes himself as 'an ageing wastrel with a bulbous nose who lives in north-west England' (Assitt, undated) maintains a useful and witty website on the graphic impact of various aspects of fonts. He also offers some empirically based, common-sense advice about the use of capital letters and colours.
- Size does matter. Use at least 24-point size, with larger point sizes for major headings and smaller point sizes (but still 24-point or larger) for subheadings. If you can't get all your text on one slide using a point size this large – you have too much text. Make another slide.
- Use light backgrounds with dark lettering. Light lettering on dark backgrounds often is difficult to read.
- Check out the legibility of your presentation using a projector and screen before presenting. Don't trust how the image appears on your computer monitor.
- Use simple backgrounds. They should provide a pleasant context or 'frame' for your work and not overwhelm or distract from the content of your slides.
- Graphics should illustrate the central point of a slide. As the saying goes, 'a picture is worth a thousand words'. Make sure those words are related to what you are trying to communicate. Avoid using graphics just to make a slide look pretty.
- Minimize special effects such as sound and animation. They can be effective but quickly become distracting or even annoying.

- Ask a friend to review any charts to ensure they are easy to interpret. Edward Tufte's book, *The Visual Display of Quantitative Information* (Tufte, 2001), is an excellent source of insights into how effectively to use graphs and other graphic tools to present data.
- Check your text for spelling and grammar. This may sound obvious, but simple errors can easily slip through, especially if you are rushing to complete a presentation.

Cautions about PowerPoint

The graphic effects possible through PowerPoint can seduce users, especially new ones, into focusing on animation, fancy transitions, bright colours and complicated designs to the detriment of their message. All the 'bells and whistles' of PowerPoint will not compensate for weak content, poor logic or evidence, or a lack of thinking about your message.

In fact, because a PowerPoint deck can be so easy to construct, I've seen presenters who did not spent enough time thinking about the important things – the structure and content of their presentations. Instead, they seemed to focus on either showing off their PowerPoint skills or attempting to hide a lack of content behind special effects. PowerPoint is a useful tool to help you make effective presentations but it does not allow you to skip the process of crafting your thoughts, words and logic. And it certainly doesn't mean you can skip knowing your material by heart (which is not the same as memorizing a script) or skip rehearsing. Rehearsals – repeated rehearsals – are just as important when using PowerPoint as for any other oral presentation.

PowerPoint encourages very short phrasing. Complete sentences are discouraged (such as expressed by the 'six-by-six' rule – no more than six bullet points with no more than six words per bullet). All but the simplest grammar is largely ignored in PowerPoint presentations because of space limitations. Moreover, the space available on any individual slide prohibits large or complex tables, and the relatively low resolution of PowerPoint often constrains the creation of precise charts.

Another major problem is more subtle, and more profound. PowerPoint is a 'linear' tool in that it encourages you to present one idea after another in a step-by-step fashion. This is not necessarily a bad thing, but the format of PowerPoint does not lend itself to storytelling, poesy, oratory, ambiguity, paradox, surprise or complexity. A PowerPoint presentation encourages you to reduce your thoughts to a series of bullets. More complex messages, narrative styles, the potential for unexpected twists in how a story unfolds, allegory or imagery, or irony often are difficult to convey effectively through PowerPoint slides.

American readers of this book will be (or should be) familiar with Abraham Lincoln's Gettysburg Address – a speech delivered in 1863 at the dedication of a cemetery in connection with a pivotal and particularly bloody battle during the American Civil War. The speech is considered one of the greatest and shortest political speeches ever delivered by an American politician. Peter Norvig, Director of Research for Google (at the time of this writing) 'converted' the Gettysburg Address into a PowerPoint presentation to illustrate how much can be lost when someone reshapes and reduces their ideas into standard PowerPoint format. His 'translation' can be found at http://norvig.com/Gettysburg/. Even if you're not an American, you can still get the point (Norvig's site also provides the text of the speech – a mere 186 words). Moreover, his PowerPoint presentation is a rare example of satire and self-deprecating humour through the medium of PowerPoint.

PREPARING A POSTER PRESENTATION

Poster presentations are common in some disciplines such as planning and the natural sciences. They are less common at tourism conferences, although they are becoming more so. As a personal comment, I find poster presentations at tourism conferences to be often considered by the conference organizers as a second-rank medium of presentation. They appear to be used as a way of accommodating a large number of presentations that were not or could not be accepted (for whatever reason) for oral presentations. This view is reinforced by my own department. Poster presentations are not accorded the same weight in faculty or student evaluations as journal articles or even oral presentations. Your college may hold the same position or a different one. In any event, do not underestimate the effort required to produce a quality poster for a conference. They can take as much or more time than a speech, and can cost more in terms of financial outlay for preparation.

The techniques needed to communicate effectively through a poster are different from those of a paper or a speech. We will quickly consider these differences and then look at some specific suggestions for preparing effective posters.

Distinctive features of poster presentations

The focus of a poster presentation is, of course, your poster. Rather than a series of printed pages in a journal or you standing in front of an audience, a poster presentation involves: (i) having a graphic summary of your research on display; (ii) with you standing nearby to answer questions (often to the left of the poster from the perspective of someone viewing it); and (iii) in a room typically filled with numerous other posters and conference delegates wandering around (perhaps with a beverage in their hands), for a designated period of time, often an hour or two. The posters may be left on display after the formal poster session is concluded, or they may need to be removed. The decision will be based on the format and schedule of the event as decided by the conference organizers.

As with published reports and speeches, the goal is to communicate your findings to others. However, with posters, you can receive immediate feedback from people viewing your results, as well as networking with people. Questions following a speech can, of course, provide opportunities for feedback and networking, but the time for questions after an oral presentation tends to be very limited compared with a poster session. Furthermore, your poster conversations are literally face-to-face and personal, rather than at a distance and in front of a possibly large audience. You may also experience numerous people walking by your poster, casually glancing at it and then moving on without examining your work closely or speaking with you. Don't take this personally.

A poster presentation relies much more on graphic design than the two other forms of presentation. In fact, your poster should be capable of delivering your message even if you were not present. Graphic design is everything in a poster; by that I mean the quality of graphs, tables, maps or photographs; the amount and readability of your text; the overall layout of the poster; colour; and open space. All these are critical in determining the success of your poster. Unlike the papers or oral presentations, posters show, they don't tell. When you think about designing your poster, think 'FOG'. **F**ocus on one key message or finding. Ensure your content is well **o**rdered. The flow of your images and text boxes should be intuitively obvious to the viewer. The content of your presentation is fundamentally **g**raphic – you should use images more than words to communicate.

A general design principle to use is to have three to five columns of information, with the content organized so that the viewer can scan down the first left-hand column, then move to the next, scanning top to bottom, again. And so on, across the poster. This layout is the most intuitive for Anglophone viewers (see Fig. 10.1).

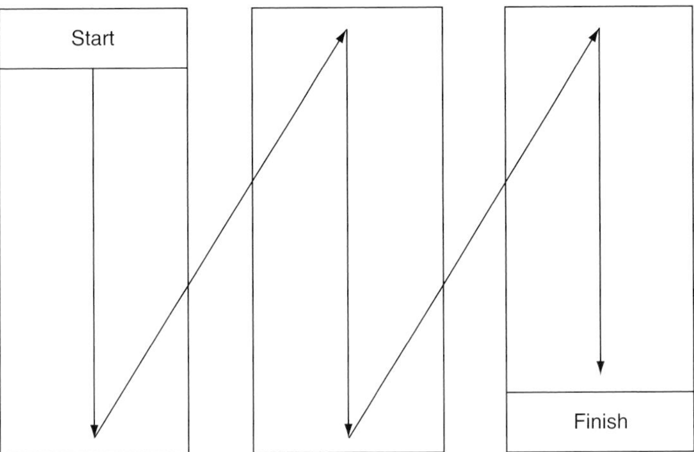

Fig. 10.1. Conventional flow of information for poster presentation.

Macro considerations

Macro considerations refer to the bigger issues of poster design, such as the size of your poster. The next section, on micro considerations, will look at the specific aspects of design. Give attention to both the big issues and to the details. One of the key principles in designing an effective poster – and the failure to respect this principle is an omission that poster presenters often commit – is using too much text. Posters are not about words, they are about images. This principle is addressed in more detail below:

- Decide how big your poster will be. Larger formats allow for more information and can make for a more visually appealing presentation, but (i) conference organizers may specific a maximum size; (ii) larger posters tend to cost more to produce than smaller posters; and (iii) they can be more cumbersome to bring with you. A common size for a large poster will be on the order of about 80–85 cm × 110–115 cm (32–34" × 44–46"). In contrast, presenters might use a series of individual 8.5" × 11" or A4 sheets of paper, possibly mounting them on poster board. Small formats are easier to carry and can be printed on your home or office printer, but you are severely constrained as to the amount of information that you can put on a single sheet.
- Consider using software specific to poster creation. It makes your life easier and the results more professional in appearance. There are numerous options, some more expensive than others. Microsoft's PowerPoint, Adobe's Illustrator, FrameMaker, LaTeX and OpenOffice are a few options. The creation of a large-format poster will require you go to a graphics shop that can print posters. Be sure to get a price estimate before signing a purchase order. Do *not* handwrite your poster.
- Decide on the overall design that gives the most pleasing appearance.. This is ultimately a matter of your judgement. You may want to look at examples of other posters or to talk with someone who has a good eye for design. For example, do you prefer 'landscape' or 'portrait' orientation. Most large posters are 'landscape' because this layout doesn't require the viewer to bend as much to look at the entire poster. A series of smaller posters, however, might work better in a 'portrait' orientation, especially if you can present them side by side.
- Posters normally contain a mix of text, images and open space. As noted in the introduction to this section, a common mistake in designing posters is to have too much text.

Another common and related mistake is to have too little open space. Posters are a way of rapidly communicating one main idea supported by a few details. Don't try to put too much content into a poster – it will just get lost. If you have too much text, you will be tempted to reduce your point size, which means a potential viewer will have to choose between coming up close and spending several minutes reading your poster or just pass by, ignoring your poster – and you. They will usually do the latter. Aim for the following proportions in your poster design:

 - 40–50% (by space) – graphics (figures, photographs);
 - 30–40% – open space; and
 - 15–20% text – title, your name block, bullet lists, paragraphs, tables.

- Sketch a map of the main elements of your poster before you actually begin to produce it. Where do you want the title? (Top centre is common.) Where do you want to put your name and affiliation? (Possibly with the title, but on either the left- or right-hand side of the top bar.) Where will you put acknowledgements or references, if you need to provide them? (The lower, right-hand corner is common.).
- Consider the overall symmetry of the poster. You have four basic options: (i) vertical symmetry (elements are mirrored left-to-right); (ii) horizontal (elements are mirrored top-to-bottom); (iii) vertical and horizontal symmetry (elements are mirrored left-to-right and top-to-bottom); and (iv) asymmetrical, in which the distribution of images and text is irregular, often with graphics dominating in one area of the poster and text dominating in another area. See Fig. 10.2 for examples.
- Creating a poster is time-consuming. Be certain to leave yourself plenty of time to refine content, as well as to experiment with different designs.

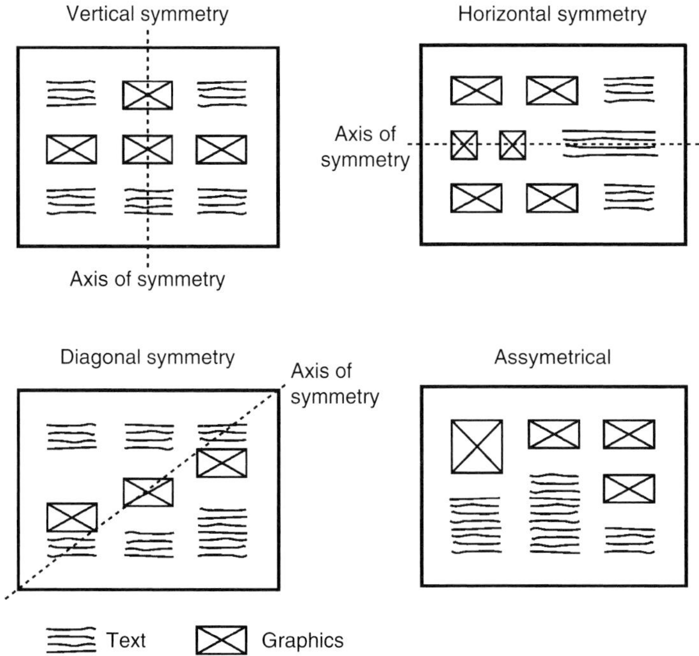

Fig. 10.2. Symmetry in poster presentations.

Micro considerations

These considerations refer to the details of layout and design.

- Use headings, numbers, bullets or other cues to divide your poster into smaller, discrete blocks of material to make viewing easier.
- Keep each block of text to a maximum of about 50 words. Bullet points are more viewer-friendly than paragraphs. Hemingway's four rules of writing are highly relevant for effective poster text.
- Use a consistent point size hierarchy for all text. The actual point sizes will depend on the amount of space you have (poster size as well as content), but use successively smaller sizes for the following elements:
  - title (should be large enough to be readable from at least 5 m away) – at least 5 cm tall;
  - author (omit initials unless essential; omit degrees, such as MSc, after your name);
  - affiliation (smaller point size than your name; limit to your department and college, but indicate your country if you are presenting at an international conference);
  - topic headings (may be the same size as your affiliation);
  - text and graphics (big enough to be understandable from 1 m away); and
  - references and acknowledgements (the smallest point) – no less than 18-point).
- Keep your title short (never more than two lines – preferably just one line) and, if you use verbs, write them in the active voice. For example, *Mines and Quarries: Industrial Heritage Tourism* (a title borrowed from Edwards and Llurdés, 1996) is a good, short and clear title. Compare it with my wordy version of the same paper I made up as a bad example: *Results from a Field Exploration and Development of a Typology of the Potential of Former and Current Mining Areas in Wales and Spain for Industrial Tourism Development*. Edwards and Llurdés' version is clearly superior.
- With respect to your title and text, don't pay much attention to advice about which fonts are 'best' – see Assitt's (undated) website for a breath of fresh air on this topic. Don't be 'cute' or crazy in choosing fonts, but don't obsess about serif versus sans serif. Point size and a bright, clear distinction between text and background are more important qualities. Some of the font principles we considered in the section on PowerPoint apply to posters.
- Colour is an integral part of a good poster; be careful how you use it:
  - A muted, consistent background colour enhances and unifies your poster. Strong colours – even black – could be effective, but you need to have a very good eye for design. Focus on what works best for presenting the actual content of your poster, not on how to make an eye-grabbing but unintelligible graphic statement.
  - Pay attention to hue (colour) combinations. For example, I once saw a presentation that used yellow print on a brown background. The effect was soothing, but nearly impossible to read.
  - Don't overuse colour. Too many colours are jarring for the viewer and may even come across as childish.
  - Be aware that some people are colour-blind (I have mild tritanopia, colour-blindness affecting blue–yellow hue discrimination). Use hue and brightness contrasts to facilitate the viewer's seeing distinctions but without creating harsh combinations such as red/green. By the way, red/green colour blindness – protanopia – is the most common form of colour blindness.
- Proofread before printing. Have someone else look at your poster before you print and discuss it candidly with them. Many poster software programs will allow you to print a

standard page-size version of your poster before you commit to the full-scale poster. This not only makes it easy to share your work with some colleagues, but it is also a test of readability. If you can't read everything on your page-size sheet, people will have a hard time reading your poster from a metre away.

Your presentation

Although your poster should 'speak for itself', you normally will be standing next to your creation to answer questions or to introduce your topic (and yourself). Here are some thoughts about what to do with yourself while you poster is on display.

- Stand *beside* your poster, not in front of it. In practice – in Western countries – this is usually to the left of the poster (from the perspective of a viewer). You want to be clearly visible, but not an impediment to someone coming up for a closer look or an intimidating social presence that may keep a mildly curious passer-by from taking a closer look.
- Make eye contact, smile and nod, but generally let the viewer determine the degree and timing of contact. You can make a few brief comments about the topic of your poster, but don't come on like a salesperson behind in their quota. A short and clear opening about the topic of your poster and a key finding can be very useful, but don't try to tell everything at once.
- Speak confidently, slowly and clearly. Avoid jargon ('eschew obfuscation' as the saying goes). Don't assume the viewer is an expert.
- Let the viewer initiate questions or comment. You are there in a supporting role to your poster, almost as if you are introducing two people to each other.
- Reflect on the most likely questions to be asked and have short and clear answers. If appropriate, repeat (or rephrase) the question to ensure you understood, but avoid sounding like a parrot.
- Have handouts available, if this is permitted by the event organizers. Also, have your business card available.

CONCLUSIONS

The presentation of your results is the culmination of your research project. Styles and formats of presentations are myriad, but the great majority can be grouped into three categories: written, oral and poster. Each has distinct advantages and disadvantages, and your choice will usually be a function of someone else's requirements (your college might require the submission of a thesis, for example) or an opportunity (you see a call for papers for a conference). Whatever format you use, the words of Joseph Priestley (one of the pioneers of chemistry and a political philosopher) are useful to remember: 'The more elaborate our means of communication, the less we communicate'.

Writing and speaking are basic skills that any manager, professional or researcher will need to develop. While your education and talents are essential in shaping your career development, how you present yourself to others is also important. Being able to put yourself into the position of your intended audience will help you understand how best to present your material in a way that will be fresh and interesting, and will convey the messages you want to get across to your audience.

Academic writing tends to be different to other styles of writing. The content usually is aimed at a specialist rather than the general public. Your vocabulary, content, structure and logic will be expected to adhere to academic standards. This requires practice. However, avoid overusing jargon. Hemingway's rules of writing apply to academic papers as much as they apply to novels. Find your own voice (that is, your own style of writing within the norms of academic publications) and develop it. Don't try to mimic someone else. Learning to write effectively for a professional or academic audience is a skill that requires effort. Ask a professor whose writing you admire to critique your work and to help you hone your style. Read widely and pay attention to how effective authors (you will intuitively recognize their work when you read it) convey their ideas. Remember that not all academic researchers are good writers. Avoid copying their styles but study them; bad examples can be useful, too.

Written presentations allow you to present your work in much greater detail than other formats. Even in the context of preparing a submission to a journal that has relatively tight word limits (5000–9000 words is a common limit), you have the opportunity to, in some detail, introduce your topic, why it is important, how it relates to the work of other researchers, what you did, what you learned and what it means.

Academic research builds on the work of others. Isaac Newton, the father of modern science, observed, 'If I have been able to see further than others, it is because I stood on the shoulders of giants'. Your work may not necessarily stand on the shoulders of giants, but it will build on the work of others. Learn the art of quoting effectively and how to attribute ideas to their sources where appropriate. Build on the work of others and then make your own original contribution. This, of course, is true for any form of presentation.

Oral presentations (NB: 'oral' refers to spoken words; 'verbal' refers simply to the use of words, and may be either spoken or written). The effectiveness of an oral presentation depends on how you present yourself and your ideas. In practice, your voice, mannerisms, body language and speaking style can be more important in the effectiveness of getting your ideas across to an audience than the quality of the ideas themselves.

Learn who and how many your audience will be and, if possible, find out about the environment in which you will be speaking. If you will be using PowerPoint, ask whether you need to bring a computer or projector. Prepare a clear, coherent story for your presentation and know your material so well that you can speak about it without reading a script. If all you do is read a script, there would no need for you to be present to speak – you could just send in your paper and let the audience read it at their convenience. A presentation is like one-half of a conversation: you are speaking to an audience, sharing ideas and something of yourself with them.

Use appropriate audiovisual aids. PowerPoint is a common one, but not the only one. You might also use a blackboard (or whiteboard), flip chart, overheads or handouts. I recall listening to one academic speaker who enlivened his speech with a couple of wardrobe props (donning a white lab coat at one point, and then later removing his coat, tie and shirt revealing an amusing t-shirt underneath). The tactic was appropriate for his topic and the audience loved it.

Perhaps the biggest challenge associated with oral presentations is nervousness. We considered a few tactics earlier in this chapter to try to deal with it, but the fact remains that most people, even veteran speakers, experience presentation jitters before speaking. Find your own strategies to deal with this, but try not to let your fear of public speaking consume you. Remember, a significant portion of your audience is thinking about something other than you, anyway – such as their own fears of presenting.

The third format, poster presentations, is used less frequently in tourism research than written or oral presentations. However, it is an increasingly common format at research conferences. The skills for preparing an effective poster presentation combine those of written and oral presentations, but in novel ways. Your poster will probably involve written text, but in a highly condensed format. Graphics will play a dominant role, much more than for other styles of presentations. A good mix of images, words and open space enhances the appeal of your poster, as does a sense of design. A poster should not simply be a collection of text-heavy PowerPoint slides that are reformatted on to a single, large sheet of paper. You may use PowerPoint, but your focus should be on the creation of a visually unified, graphically attractive presentation.

You will usually be present during a poster session, so speaking skills are important. However, rather than giving a speech, you will engage in personal conversations with people who stop to look at your poster. Poster sessions allow much more of an opportunity for networking than other styles of presentation.

I'll conclude with an insight from Edward R. Murrow, arguably the most distinguished American broadcast journalist of the 20th century. Although spoken in the 1960s, his words are still valid in many cultures and contexts: 'The newest computer can merely compound, at speed, the oldest problem in the relations between human beings, and in the end, the communicator will be confronted with the old problem of what to say and how to say it'.

Enough said.

REFERENCES

Assitt, W. (undated) http://www.hgrebdes.com/about.php (accessed 6 May 2009).

Edwards, J. and Llurdés, J. (1996) Mines and quarries: industrial heritage tourism. *Annals of Tourism Research* 23, 341–363.

Fisher, J. (2007) Of '*Star* Style' and a reporter named Hemingway. *Kansas City Star*. http://www.kansascity.com/hemingway/story/209954.html (accessed 20 April 2009).

Globe and Mail (1984) *Pierre Elliot Trudeau: 1919–2000*. http://www.theglobeandmail.com/series/trudeau/quit.html (accessed 22 April 2009).

Gurrie, C. and Fair, B. (2008) PowerPoint – from fabulous to boring: the misuse of PowerPoint in higher education classrooms. Paper presented at the *Annual Meeting of the National Communication Association 94th Annual Convention*, San Diego, California, http://www.allacademic.com/ meta/p257688_index.html (accessed 28 April 2009).

Pompa, F. and Gainer, D. (2007) Twenty-five years of Eureka moments. *USA Today*. http://www.usatoday.com/news/top25-inventions.htm (accessed 28 April 2009).

Tufte, E. (2001) *The Visual Display of Quantitative Data*. Graphics Press, Cheshire, Connecticut.

Wikipedia (2009) Inigo Montoya. http://en.wikipedia.org/wiki/Inigo_Montoya (accessed 23 April 2009).

Xiao, H. and Smith, S.L.J. (2007) The use of tourism knowledge: research propositions. *Annals of Tourism Research* 34, 310–331.

APPENDIX

A BRIEF OVERVIEW OF STATISTICAL TESTS

This appendix provides thumbnail descriptions of some of the more common statistical tests used in tourism research. There are scores of other statistical tests that are available, but these are the ones that appear most frequently in the tourism research literature.

The purpose of this appendix is to provide you with a quick reference to the intended application of the selected methods rather than to give you detailed instruction on how to use any given method. For information on applications, consult a statistics text, a user's manual for statistical software such as SAS or SPSS, or any of countless websites. This appendix, though, may help you decide which of the most common tests are best to use in a particular context.

All statistical tests are based on certain assumptions, such as the distribution of values (for example, a normal distribution) or a minimal sample size requirements. Become aware of these requirements before applying any statistical test.

It is prudent to remember that finding a statistically significant relationship does not necessarily mean you have found something of practical significance. Statistical tests are useful for disproving hypotheses (recall the discussion of Type 1 and Type 2 errors in Chapter 1), but they can't 'prove' anything with absolute certainty. At best – and this is an important benefit – they can alert you to incorrect hypotheses. Learning when we are wrong is an important step on the road to wisdom.

ANOVA

ANalysis **O**f **VA**riance refers to a powerful and large set of interrelated statistical tests. One of the most common uses of ANOVA is to look at how variation in some nominal variable (called the independent variable or 'factor') influences the value of some dependent variable (measured on an interval or ratio-level scale). For example, you might be interested in how visitor satisfaction varies across three different tour companies going to the same destination but with different styles of service. The factor or independent variable would be the identity of the tour company; the dependent variable would be customer satisfaction. The statistic calculated by ANOVA is called F.

The name of the test is a bit misleading. ANOVA does not compare variances – it compares means. The name of the statistic comes from how the means are compared – by comparing the variance *within* each group (the customers of each tour company) with the variance that would be expected *between* the groups (tour companies), taking into account the number of people in each group. If the differences are bigger than you expect, you have a statistically significant difference between the groups.

The ANOVA test is usually run when you have three or more groups. If you have only two groups and you compare the means, you are – in effect – running a *t*-test (see below). The examination of a single dependent variable using ANOVA is called a one-way ANOVA. The examination of the impacts of two independent variables is two-way ANOVA, and so on.

You can simultaneously consider two or more dependent variables – such as looking at levels of satisfaction with a tour across different tour companies and the season in which the tour was taken. This is referred to as **MANOVA** (multivariate ANOVA).

Factorial ANOVA refers to the situation in which you have two or more independent variables and you wish to look at their effect on two or more dependent variables. For example, you might be interested in comparing the reaction of females and males to five different styles of interpretive signs at a heritage site.

Bartlett's test of sphericity

This test is one of a couple of tests often used in factor analysis to determine whether a set of data is appropriate for factor analysis (KMO, below, is the other). Bartlett's is used to assess whether the correlation matrix on which a factor analysis is based is an 'identity matrix' – in other words, whether all the diagonal cells are 1s and all the off-diagonal cells are 0s. Factor analysis requires that the correlation *not* be an identity matrix. Bartlett's utilizes chi square (see below) to estimate the probability that the matrix is not an identity matrix.

Chi square (X^2)

Chi square (also chi-square, chi squared or chi-squared) is one of the more common tests for assessing whether two variables appear to be related. Chi square is known as a non-parametric test, which means it can be used to examine the relationship between nominal level variables, such as level of event management training (using a four-point scale for levels of training) in relation to perception of the probability of food services being the source of risk such as food poisoning (also on a four-point scale). In this example, chi square would indicate whether level of training had any influence on the perception of risk associated with food handling at events.

Chi square involves the use of a cross-tabulation (or contingency) table in which the rows represent one variable and the columns another variable. Actual counts – not percentages or means – must be used. Chi square compares the observed distribution of cell counts in the table with that expected if the two variables are not related.

The significance level of chi square tells you that the probability of any observed relationship between two variables is 'real' rather than due to chance. The significance does not tell you how strong the relationship is – only whether it is likely to be real. Nor does chi square, by itself, tell you whether two variables are directly or inversely associated. You have to examine your data in detail to assess the direction or nature of the relationship. Chi square is highly sensitive to sample size. The larger your sample, the more likely chi square will indicate a statistically significant association between two variables. Very small samples can also produce invalid or unreliable results. For some small samples, Yates correction (see below) can be used to calculate a modified form of chi square.

Cohen's κ (kappa)

Cohen's kappa (or coefficient) is a measure of the level of agreement between two coders, such as two people coding content from a travel writer's blog. Kappa is considered to be a more robust measure than simple percentage of agreement, because it adjusts for agreements hypothetically occurring by chance. **Fleiss' κ** is a similar measure but can be applied to three or more coders.

Cronbach's α (alpha)

This statistic measures the internal consistency of a series of statements used in a scale to measure a unidimensional concept, such as potential visitors' interest in risk-taking in tourism. Thus, it provides a measure of the internal consistency or reliability of a scale. Because it was designed to apply to statements measuring a single concept, it should not be applied in situations where a set of statements are intended to measure multiple concepts, such as personality measure or more complex attitude scales (reflecting the common belief among researchers that attitudes have three dimensions, as described in Chapter 6).

Kaiser–Meyer–Olkin (KMO) statistic

KMO is known as a measure of sampling adequacy in the sense that it provides an indication of the degree to which a set of variables share common variance – or, in other words, the degree to which variables are linked through their connection with some underlying factor. The KMO statistic is a useful test to perform on a set of data you are considering for factor analysis. If your results do not meet the recommended threshold for KMO, your data are not likely to produce a useable factor structure.

Kendall's τ (tau)

Kendall's tau is a measure of the degree of correspondence or association between two distributions. For example, you might be interested in looking at the density of restaurants in cities compared with the density of museums and art galleries to see whther there is a possible relationship. Kendall's tau can be used to compare the two lists over a number of cities to determine whether there appears to be any correlation. Kendall's tau provides similar information to Spearman's rank order correlation (see below), but the interpretation of Kendall's tau is more obvious (it reflects the number of matching ranks between two lists). It provides a measure of the probability of the difference between the probability that the order of two sets of observations are the same versus the probability that the order of observations is not the same. Kendall's tau also tends to produce more valid results with small samples than Spearman's. There are three versions of tau: (i) tau a, which does not correct for tied rankings; (ii) tau b adjusts for ties and is well suited to the analysis of square tables (the number of rows and columns is the same); and (iii) tau c, which is better suited for rectangular tables.

Mann–Whitney–U test (or Mann–Whitney–Wilcoxon test or Wilcoxon rank sum test)

This test is a non-parametric version of the *t*-test that can be applied to ordinal-level data. Like the *t*-test, it is used to compare means from two populations or samples. For example, the Chair of a school of tourism and hospitality management would like to know whether students who hold internships earn more than students who do not hold internships, after 10 years of experience. In this particular example, one would need to know only which students earned more than other students. Mann–Whitney can be used to answer this question. However, its underlying assumptions are not as stringent as those for the *t*-test. The **Kruskal–Wallis test** is a generalization of Mann–Whitney–U to more than two groups.

Pearson product-moment correlation (ρ)

This statistic is a popular tool for measuring the correlation between two variables that involve interval or ratio data. For example, you might correlate the marketing budget of several DMOs and the total expenditures by visitors to the destinations those organizations are marketing. It is often associated with a technique called least-squares estimation. Least-squares is a curve-fitting tool, but is frequently used in the calculation of regression statistics such as Pearson's ρ.

The correlation may be either positive (the values of both variables change in the same direction – e.g. expenditures on a vacation tend to be positively correlated with household income) or negative (the values of the variables change in opposite directions, such as the amount spent on a vacation trip tends to decrease as the number of small children in a family increases). The degree of correlation often is designated as r, the correlation coefficient. The squaring of the coefficient, r^2, represents the percentage of variance in one variable 'explained' by the other. 'Explain' is in quotation marks because correlation merely indicates an empirical relationship between two variables – not a causal relationship. Many correlations are simply coincidental.

Pearson correlation is based on a number of assumptions, including that the relationship between the two variables is linear – if you were to plot the values of the variables on a graph, the distribution would approximate a straight line. Other types of correlations are possible, such as logarithmic or quadratic relationships. Estimating the correlation coefficient for these requires other, specialized, techniques. Pearson product-moment correlation is also highly sensitive to 'outliers' – one or a few very large values in a data set – as well as to a variety of other data qualities such as non-normal distributions.

Phi square (ϕ) and Cramer's V

Phi square (also phi-square, phi squared or phi-squared) and Cramer's V are variants of chi square (see above) that are not sensitive to sample size (as is chi square). They are normally used as post-tests, after chi square had been calculated. Recall the food-handling risk perception from the description of chi square. If a chi square test indicates there is a significant relationship, phi square would provide a measure of the strength of the relationship between two variables – not just a measure of the probability that a relationship exists. Phi square is limited to 2 × 2 tables. For larger tables, use Cramer's V.

Spearman's ρ (rho) (or Spearman rank order correlation)

Rho is a measure of the correlation between two ordered lists of observations. It can be used in many of the same situations as Kendall's tau, although the interpretation is somewhat different and the underlying calculations are different. Whereas tau reflects the probability that values of two variables are in the same order, rho provides a measure of the strength of correlation between the two variables.

T-test (or Student's *t*-test)

The *t*-test is a common test of a null hypothesis about means and confidence intervals. It provides evidence about whether two means are significantly different or not. The test may be applied to a single sample, in which case the hypothesis concerns whether the observed mean differs from a hypothesized mean; or it may be applied to two samples to assess whether the means (and confidence intervals) are the same. Two-sample *t*-tests may be further classified as 'unpaired' or 'paired'. An unpaired example involves comparing two samples that have been independently drawn. For example, you might have a sample of 100 restaurant servers. You randomly divide the sample into two groups of 50; one group goes through a specialized training programme, the other does not. You then test some measure of performance, such as size of tips received from customers, between the two groups to determine whether the training has any effect on tip size.

Alternatively, you might have a 'paired' test such as a before-and-after (or 'repeated measure') test. In this case, you measure tip sizes before the training for each employee, and then compare them with tip sizes following training.

The test is based on a particular type of distribution known as the Student's *t*-distribution ('Student' was the pseudonym under which the developer, William Gosset, published his work because of intellectual property concerns of his employer, Guinness Brewery, who didn't want its competitors to know it was using statistics in its brewing quality control processes).

Wilcoxon signed-rank test

This is a version of the *t*-test that does not require the assumption that data be normally distributed, although the data still need to be at an interval level of measurement. Do not confuse this test with the similarly named Wilcoxon rank sum test (also known as the Mann–Whitney–U test), which is used with ordinal-level data. Referring to our example in the Mann–Whitney–U test, Wilcoxon signed-rank would be used if you knew the actual income levels of the various employees, not just who earned more than whom.

Yates correction (or Yates chi square)

Yates correction is a modification of the conventional chi square that may be used when an expected cell count in a contingency table is below 5. Thus, Yates can help avoid incorrectly concluding statistical significance for small data sets. However, it sometimes 'corrects' too far, leading a researcher to accept a false null hypothesis (i.e. concluding there is no relationship when, in fact, there is).

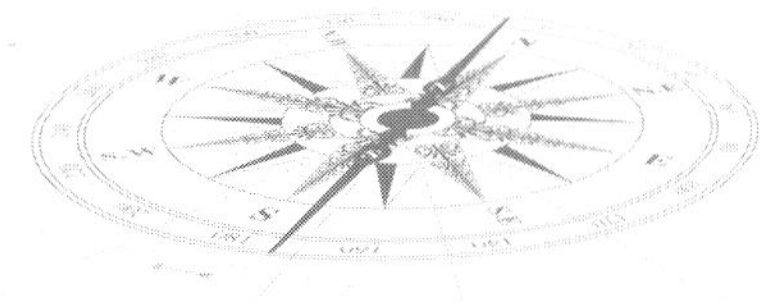

INDEX

Page numbers in **bold** type refer to figures, tables and Focus box text.